THE ARTFUL ALBANIAN

THE ARTFUL
ALBANIAN

Memoirs of
Enver Hoxha

EDITED BY

JON HALLIDAY

Chatto & Windus

LONDON

Published in 1986 by
Chatto & Windus Ltd
40 William IV Street
London WC2N 4DF

British Library Cataloguing in Publication Data
Halliday, Jon
The Artful Albanian: memoirs of Enver Hoxha.
1. Hoxha, Enver 2. Statesmen – Albania –
Biography
I. Title
949.6'503'0924   DR977.25.H67

ISBN 0-7011-2970-0 Pbk

Photoset by Rowland Phototypesetting Ltd
Bury St Edmunds, Suffolk
Printed in Great Britain by
Redwood Burn Ltd
Trowbridge, Wiltshire

For Francine
who put up not only with me,
but also with Enver

ACKNOWLEDGEMENTS

I would like to thank the following for their help:

Anthony Barnett and Peter Wollen for first alerting me to the rich vein of gold in Hoxha's memoirs.

James Fox for his warm encouragement at an early stage; and Susannah Clapp of the *London Review of Books* for running the original article which led to this book.

For the ideas which produced the title: Francine Winham ('Hoxha the Dodger') and Emma Tennant ('the Artful Hoxha'). They, together with Dominique Bourgois, Christian Bourgois, Jung Chang, Hans Magnus Enzensberger, Ronnie Fraser, Fred Halliday and Lynda Myles provided encouragement and help.

For accounts of their first-hand experiences visiting Albania: Laura Mulvey, Geoffrey Stern and Jane Thomas. I owe a special debt of gratitude to Berit Backer, a real Albania expert, who gave me the benefit of her vast knowledge of Albania over a few drinks the evening Enver Hoxha died.

I would also like to thank the following members of SOE, who agreed to talk to me. Several went over in detail Hoxha's version of his conversations with them. All, even where political differences were acute, were most courteous; several were most hospitable; some helped greatly with background information: Dr Jack Dumoulin; the Hon. Alan V. Hare; Sir Reginald Hibbert; J. M. Lyon; Lieutenant-Colonel Neil McLean; Colonel Dayrell Oakley Hill; Alan Palmer; Richard Riddell; Colonel David Smiley; Major General T. N. S. Wheeler (ranks only for those who use them). I would like to record here my special gratitude to the late Lord Glenconner for several memorable conversations. None is responsible for views or interpretations herein.

For help with texts and research: Berit Backer, Bernardo Bertolucci, Aidan Foster-Carter, John Gittings, Judith Herrin, Bradley Smith.

Lastly, my thanks to my editors, Jeremy Lewis and Ingrid von Essen, and to Carmen Callil for envisaging the idea.

J. H. September 1985

Contents

Acknowledgements *page* vi

Chronology ix

Abbreviations xii

Publisher's Note xiv

Map of Albania xvi

Editor's Introduction 1

1 World War II and its aftermath 19
2 From Liberation to the break with Yugoslavia 85
3 With Stalin 113
4 Battling Khrushchev 141
5 Decoding China 249
6 Mehmet Shehu and his strange end 325

Appendices
I The Kosovo question 341
II The Corfu Channel Incidents and Albania's gold 345

Notes 347

Biographical notes 379

Index 383

Chronology

15th century		Turks conquer Albania; fierce resistance headed by Skanderbeg
1878		League of Prizren (first modern nationalist movement)
1908	*16 October*	Enver Hoxha born, Gjirokastra
1912		Independence
1913–14		Foreign powers impose German Prince, Wilhelm of Wied, as ruler of Albania
1914–18		World War I. Albania invaded/occupied by armies of Serbia, Greece, Italy, Austria and France
1924		Bishop Fan Noli heads six-month progressive government
1924	*December*	Tribal leader, Ahmed Zog, seizes power (to 1939)
1928		Zog proclaims self King of Albania
1939	*7 April*	Italy invades Albania
1941	*8 November*	Albanian Communist Party founded; Hoxha elected leader
1942	*16 September*	National Liberation Front (LNC) founded, at Pezë
1943	*May*	First British SOE mission arrives
	July	National Liberation Army established, at Labinot
	1–2 August	Mukje Conference
	August	1st Brigade formed under Mehmet Shehu
	8 September	Italy surrenders; Germans occupy Albania with c. 70,000 troops
	October	Brig. Davies arrives to head British mission (captured January 1944)
	November	McLean and Smiley leave Partisans
	17 December	Davies recommends British recognition of Partisans: rejected
1944	*winter*	Partisans escape German encirclement
	April	McLean, Smiley, Amery to right-wing northern tribes

	May	Permët Conference
		OSS mission arrives
	June	Civil War begins; Partisans sweep north
	late July	LNC mission to Bari
	August	Yugoslav Military Mission arrives
		Soviet Military Mission arrives
	September	British landings in Albania
	October	Berat Conference establishes provisional government
	17 November	Tirana freed
	29 November	All Albania liberated
1945	*2 December*	National elections: Democratic Front (successor to LNC) wins 93% of votes
1946	*11 January*	New constitution; Constituent Assembly proclaims People's Republic
	June	Hoxha visits Yugoslavia (first official journey abroad)
	August	Hoxha attends Paris Peace Conference
	October	Corfu Channel Incidents
	November	Relations with Britain and USA break down
1947	*July*	Hoxha's first visit to the USSR
	November	Death of Nako Spiru
	c. December	Yugoslav Air Force units stationed in Albania
1948	*June*	Cominform denounces Yugoslavia; Albania breaks with Tito
		Purge of pro-Yugoslav Albanians; Koçi Xoxe arrested (executed June 1949)
	summer	Hoxha meets Vyshinsky in Bucharest
	November	1st Congress of CPA, Tirana
1949	*autumn*	British-backed landings by right-wing Albanian émigrés
		Greek civil war ends
1950–53		US-backed landings by right-wing émigrés
1953	*March*	Death of Stalin
1954		Shehu replaces Hoxha as premier (Hoxha remaining head of the Party)
1955		Soviet pressure on Hoxha for reconciliation with Tito
	end May	Khrushchev visits Belgrade
1956	*February*	20th Congress of CPSU; Khrushchev's 'secret speech' denounces Stalin's crimes

	April	Special Tirana Conference; purges
	September	Hoxha attends 8th Congress of Chinese Communist Party
	autumn	Hungarian uprising; disturbances in Poland
1959	*May*	Khrushchev visits Albania
1960	*June*	Bucharest Meeting; Sino-Soviet dispute erupts
	November	Moscow Conference; Hoxha denounces Khrushchev; rupture with CPSU; Albania leaves Warsaw Pact de facto; purges
1961	*February*	4th Congress of PLA; purges
	December	USSR breaks diplomatic relations with Albania
1967		Abolition of religion
1968		Invasion of Czechoslovakia; Albania leaves Warsaw Pact de jure; China pushes for Albanian alliance with Yugoslavia and Romania
1974	*July*	Defence Minister (Balluku) purged
1977	*August*	Tito visits China
		Albania breaks with China
1980		Death of Tito
1981		Riots in Kosovo
	December	Death of Mehmet Shehu
1982		Purges of real and alleged Shehu followers
		Ramiz Alia replaces Haxhi Lleshi as President
		Adil Çarçani succeeds Shehu as premier
	September	Landing in Albania by right-wing émigrés
1985		Settlement with Greece
	April	Death of Hoxha; Alia succeeds as First Secretary
		Cautious further opening to West; secret negotiations with Britain over blocked gold

Abbreviations

ACP	Albanian Communist Party
BLO	British Liaison Officer
CMEA	Council for Mutual Economic Assistance (Comecon)
CAP	Central Archives of the Party
CC	Central Committee
CIA	Central Intelligence Agency (USA)
CPA/ACP	Communist Party of Albania (later: Party of Labour of Albania)
CPSU	Communist Party of the Soviet Union
CPY	Communist Party of Yugoslavia (later: League of Communists)
FO	Foreign Office (UK)
GDA	Greek Democratic Army
KGB	State Security Committee (USSR)
LNC	National Liberation Front (Albanian: Levizje Nacional Çlirimtare)
LRDG	Long Range Desert Group
NLA	National Liberation Army (Albanian)
OSS	Office of Strategic Services (USA)
PLA	Party of Labour of Albania
PRO	Public Records Office (UK)
RAF	Royal Air Force
SAS	Special Air Service (UK)
SBS	Special Boat Service (UK)
SIM	Military Intelligence (Italian, fascist)
SIS	Secret Intelligence Service (UK)
SOE	Special Operations Executive (UK)
TASS	Soviet News Agency
UDB	Directorate of State Security (Yugoslavia)

Volumes of Hoxha's works (referred to by initials in the text)

AAT	*The Anglo-American Threat to Albania* (1982)
ACKR	*Albania Challenges Khrushchev Revisionism* (1976)
EIA	*Eurocommunism is Anti-communism* (1980)
I&R	*Imperialism and the Revolution* (1979; 2nd revised edn)

RC I   *Reflections on China*, vol. I (1979)
RC II   *Reflections on China*, vol. II (1979)
RME   *Reflections on the Middle East* (1984)
SW   *Selected Works* (4 volumes in English) (1974–82)
TK   *The Khrushchevites* (1980)
TT   *The Titoites* (1982)
WS   *With Stalin* (1979)

Publisher's Note

Albanian spelling is idiosyncratic, but it is precise and the number of differences from English is small:

c   is pronounced like ts
ç   is pronounced like ch (e.g. *çeta* as *cheta*)
dh   is a soft diphthong, like a soft th
ë   is as in English 'er'
j   is like English y
q   is close to k
x   is pronounced like dz (e.g. Xoxe as Dzodze)
xh   is pronounced like English j (dzh) (e.g. Hoxha as Hoja)

Among the more frequent words and names which are spelt differently in normal Albanian usage are:

Albanian	*Other*
Dibra	Dibar
Durrës	Durazzo (Italian; often used by English)
Kosova	Kosovo
Kupi, Abaz	Kupi, Abas
Ohri	Ohrid
Shkodër/Shkodra	Scutari (Italian)
Tiranë	Tirana
Vlorë	Valona (Italian)
Zogu, Ahmet	Zog, Ahmed

The spelling Hoxha uses in the original has been left (except where there were obvious errors in non-Albanian names); e.g. Hoxha's spelling 'Rumania' has been left, although the editor has used the now generally accepted 'Romania' in the commentary.

Hoxha changed his spelling of Chinese names in 1979–80 when China introduced *pinyin*. The same name can thus be found spelled in two different ways in his text, depending on the original date of publication. The editor has left Hoxha's spelling as is and has attempted to give both spellings for Chinese names where he uses them.

Hoxha's own footnotes have been incorporated within his text and printed inside square brackets. Very long Hoxha notes are asterisked to the end of this volume. Words inside square brackets in the text are either: (i) translations of foreign words supplied by Hoxha in his original; or (ii) explanations or linking words by the editor.

Albanian words, organisations, places

bajraktar	tribal chieftain
Balli Kombëtar	literally 'National Front'; right-wing movement, collaborated with Germans; hostile to LNC (q.v.); supported by right wing of SOE (q.v.); 'BALKOM' in SOE telegrams
Ballists	members/followers of Balli Kombëtar
çeta	armed group
Legaliteti	literally 'Legality'; conservative movement supporting ousted King Zog (q.v.); founded by Abas Kupi (q.v.), September 1943; supported by right wing of SOE
lek	the unit of currency
Mukje/Mukaj	Village in central Albania where LNC (q.v.) met in early August 1943 and signed agreement for united front with Balli Kombëtar (q.v.); Hoxha immediately denounced the agreement, probably under Yugoslav pressure: LNC delegates (including Abas Kupi, Mustafa Gjinishi) denounced
Shtab	Partisan headquarters

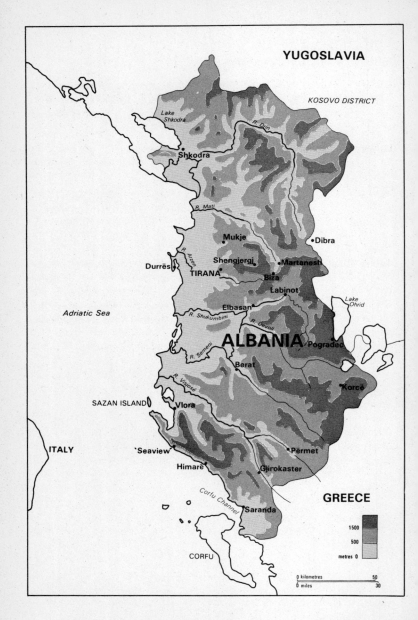

YUGOSLAVIA

KOSOVO DISTRICT

Lake Shkodra

R. Drin

● Shkodra

R. Mati

● Mukje   ● Dibra

R. Arzen

● Shengjergi   ● Martanesh

Durrës   TIRANA   Biza

● Labinot

● Elbasan

R. Shukumbini

R. Devoll

ALBANIA

Lake Ohrid

● Pogradec

Adriatic Sea

R. Semeni

● Berat

R. Vijosë

● Korcë

SAZAN ISLAND   ● Vlora

ITALY

●'Seaview'   ● Përmet

● Himarë   ● Gjirokaster

Corfu Channel

● Saranda

GREECE

	1500
	500
	metres 0

0 kilometres   50
0 miles   30

CORFU

Albania

Editor's Introduction

'The Albanian people have hacked their way through history, sword in hand.'

Enver Hoxha

'You spat on me; no one can talk to you.'

Nikita Khrushchev to Hoxha, November 1960

'We lost Albania, but we did not lose much; you won it, but you did not win much, either. The [Albanian] Party of Labour has always been a weak link in the international communist movement.'

Khrushchev to Liu Shaoqi, November 1960[1]

Communist Albania and its late leader, Enver Hoxha (pronounced Hoja), have hardly been prodigal with information and contacts with the outside world. Hoxha, who died in April 1985, had his last encounter with the Western media in August 1946, at the Paris Peace Conference.[2] For over a quarter of a century he did not set foot outside Albania, after visiting Moscow for the ill-starred Conference of Communist Parties in November 1960.[3] At that conference he broke with the Russians and appeared to enter into close alliance with China. He left Moscow in semi-flight with his then closest colleague, Mehmet Shehu, since denounced as a multiple foreign agent.

Suddenly, from the end of the 1970s Hoxha began to produce a series of memoirs covering the whole period from the beginning of the Second World War through his successive alliances with Yugoslavia, Russia and China and on to the demise of Shehu in December 1981.[4] Nothing like this flood of memory, suspicion, invective and self-righteousness has ever been published by the head of a Communist (or indeed any) regime. These memoirs constitute an absolutely unique set of documents. Dealing mainly with foreign relations, they vividly evoke the pressures put on Albania from 1941 onwards by a series of foreign countries, other than the Axis powers, starting with Yugoslavia; then Britain, the USA and their allies during the war; then by Yugoslavia, the British, Americans, Greeks, Italians and the Vatican after the war; Russia; and, finally, China.

The key issue is, of course, the reliability of Hoxha's account. In some cases, particularly for the earlier events, he manifestly relies too heavily on a faulty memory. In addition, he always wants to show that he was right. And, in everything which involves Stalin and his successors, the world is divided into black and white: Stalin was good; Khrushchev was bad.

On the other hand, Hoxha is extremely observant. He is also highly intelligent. He is suspicious, too – but this suspiciousness is often a plus, since there was plenty to be suspicious about. His general view that Albania was seen by larger powers as a piece of prey has a great deal of truth to it. Yugoslavia did want to annex Albania in the mid-1940s. Britain and the USA did try to invade Albania and overthrow Hoxha's regime in the years 1949–53 (as has recently been confirmed from Western sources). It seems most likely that Khrushchev did try to oust Hoxha in 1960–61, and perhaps in the mid-1950s, too.[5]

Hoxha, although self-righteous, also has some ability to be self-critical. He occasionally records incidents which are not to his credit (e.g. losing his temper, being rude to women).[6] And on the crucial break with Russia in 1960–61, the Albanians have published detailed information, including verbatim accounts of the final talks between Soviet and Albanian delegations, which have not been disowned by the Russians. Hoxha is *both* unusually frank and mendacious.

Hoxha grew up in a world of blood feuds and skulduggery. His country was still part of the Ottoman Empire when he was born. It was a world of Islam, male chauvinism and cultural and philosophical backwardness. He fought his way out of this. He played the major role in building a Communist movement in extremely harsh and adverse conditions and held power longer than any non-hereditary leader in the world – more than forty years. He saw it all. This alone entitles him to consideration, even if not respect.

Early life

Enver Hoxha was born on 18 October 1908 in the town of Gjirokastra, in Southern Albania. His family were landowners and, like some 70 per cent of the population of Albania, Muslims – though they belonged to the Bektashi, the most liberal form of Islam.

Enver was sent to the French lycée in the town of Korçë (this lycée had been set up by the French when they occupied the area in the latter part of World War I). He graduated from the lycée in 1930, 'reportedly with a brilliant record and a good foundation in the humanities'.[7] In 1931 he won an Albanian government scholarship and went to study law at the University of Montpellier in France, which, ironically, had originally been set up by Averroist refugees fleeing from the Almohades in Spain. While in France, Hoxha began to associate with radicals and wrote some articles for the French Communist Party newspaper, *L'Humanité*, under the pseudonym Lulo Malessori. In these he denounced the government of King Zog in Albania and as a result soon lost his scholarship. He moved to Paris, and apparently tried to go on studying. Later he went on to Brussels and took a job as private secretary to the Albanian consul there. He seems to have continued to study law in Brussels, but did not graduate. He continued his activities against Zog's regime, was discovered, and fired from his job.

He went back to Albania in 1936 and taught first in the capital, Tirana, and then at his old school in Korçë. On Good Friday 1939 the Italians invaded Albania. Soon after this Hoxha was dismissed by the new fascist authorities on the grounds that he had engaged in pro-Communist activities among his students. He moved to Tirana, where he ran a tobacco kiosk where he worked clandestinely as the leader of the Communist movement in the capital. He was sentenced to death *in absentia* in October 1941. On 8 November 1941 the Albanian Communist Party (ACP) was formally set up at a conference of about twenty people in Tirana. Hoxha was chosen as secretary of the Provisional Central Committee of seven members.

Hoxha and Albania's history

Enver Hoxha was at the head of his country's Communist movement for nearly half a century and at the time of his death the head of the regime for longer than anyone in the world, except one hereditary monarch, the Japanese emperor. This achievement is all the more remarkable since he held this position against three of the most redoubtable destabilising forces imaginable: Balkan tribal intrigue, Anglo-American subversion and invasion, and Kremlin plotting. Hoxha's path to power, and *in* power, was littered with the corpses of his old foes, and his old friends. No Communist regime has experienced such repeated purges and decimations as Albania's. But equally no Communist party has ever achieved such swift success as the ACP under Hoxha. Between its founding in November 1941 and November 1944, in exactly three years, the ACP led the Albanian people to total victory over both their many external enemies and their domestic right-wing enemies. Albanian forces even played a role in liberating another country, Yugoslavia.

After the Party was founded in November 1941, there was little violent action against the occupying Italians until early 1942. A fairly broad National Liberation Front (LNC) was set up in September 1942. And a National Liberation Army was formed in July 1943 out of the existing units; in August that year the First Shock Brigade was formed under the partisans' most able military commander, Mehmet Shehu. When Italy surrendered in September 1943 some 2000 Italian soldiers went over to the Partisans, who were also receiving some military aid from Britain. German occupation replaced Italian. By the middle of 1944 the Partisans had established considerable political control over large areas of southern and central Albania and routed their right-wing opponents, the Balli Kombëtar and Legaliteti, in a brief civil war (in which British officers were stationed on both sides). The partisans came to power in a liberated Tirana at the end of November 1944.

Between Liberation and June 1948 Albania was not only part of the Communist bloc, but in a very close alliance with Yugoslavia, which wanted (perhaps with Hoxha's connivance) to integrate Albania as a seventh province of Yugoslavia, or at any rate as part of a Balkan federation under Tito's leadership. This alliance with Yugoslavia, and the violent break at the end of the liaison, was the first of three such episodes which mark, and demarcate, Albania's history since 1944. Because of its size and position, Albania was virtually obliged to seek a larger and stronger partner-cum-protector within the world Communist camp. For the first years it was Belgrade. Between the break with Tito in 1948 and the end of 1960 it was the USSR. When Hoxha broke with Khrushchev in 1960, it became China. Then, when China made up with Tito, and even invited him to Beijing in 1977 (after Mao died), Hoxha broke with the Chinese. Hoxha presents each of these breaks as being based on high ideological principle and Marxist-Leninist purity (which he goes on about at some length). In fact, the break with Yugoslavia was more on grounds of nationalism than of ideology (Tito was then rather on the left wing of the world Communist movement). Since 1948 it is fair to say that Hoxha has been consistent – in his Stalinism. And the characterisation of Yugoslavia (as 'revisionist' or not) has been a constant criterion in Hoxha's policy towards other Communist parties.

Hoxha's vast experience at the head of a relatively weak and very poor Communist state within the bloc gives him an excellent vantage point from which to describe life at the top of the Communist camp, how relations really functioned within Comecon and the Warsaw Pact, and how the Communist leaders actually treat each other. It is a bleak and dismal picture which, discounting his ritual eulogies of the Stalinists, rings true. The other leaders were, on the whole, crashingly boring. The Russians seem to have been awash in a sea of booze. They were also boorish.

Nor were the Chinese much better. Hoxha's account of trying to deal with them through more than a dozen years of what seemed to the outside world like a close alliance makes them sound like phantoms. They refuse to answer letters. Chinese officials speak to him in slogans, or spout what he calls 'baloney'. Moreover, as Hoxha is quick to spot right from the beginning, behind the official politesse there lurked a strong streak of chauvinism, and considerable hypocrisy. In late 1969 (30 October) Hoxha confides to his diary: 'Their [the Chinese] words sound pretty hollow when they say, "criticise us", because, in fact, if you do so, they get angry.'[8]

Although Hoxha has no viable alternative model of socialism to offer, he nonetheless is extremely shrewd, and often frank, about 'actually existing socialism'. One thing he several times picks up on and sharply criticises is the way Communist leaders exaggerate their countries' economic performance: in the case of Khrushchev, Hoxha rightly points out that this undermines the ability of socialism to compete with capitalism by falsifying the terms of the debate. The Hungarian leader Rákosi is, Hoxha notes, completely out of touch with economic reality in 1956 (see p. 188). And the Chinese are producing fantasy statistics, which Hoxha rightly finds insulting, during the Cultural Revolution. Hoxha also seems to voice the unspeakable when he blames the Russians for abusing Czechoslovakia 'to the extent that they brought it to its present state' (see p. 170). Hoxha has an amusing account of how the Russians censored, in stages, a speech he made in Leningrad in 1957, even though Hoxha sent his aide (and successor) Ramiz Alia to the printers with the text to make sure nothing happened (a story which may strike a chord among many on the Left).[9]

Hoxha's character

'He is very handsome and leaves a good impression. He is quite cultured, but you sense Western influence on his upbringing.'

Molotov on Hoxha (to Stalin), 1947[10]

Molotov's thumbnail sketch, complete with its Kremlin 'but', is not a bad starting point to try to understand the complex and highly specific combination of elements in Hoxha's character.

First of all, unlike most of the East European leaders after the war, he was indeed very handsome, and very charming – to both women and men. He could turn his charm on and off. He was a good actor. He combined this ability to act with an unshakeable determination to prove that he was always right – and he had the doggedness to go on and on until he wore his opponents down. These are useful qualities in gaining and holding on to power. They are also qualities which can infuriate one's interlocutors.[11]

Molotov's second sentence both covers up a lot and reveals a lot. First of all, Molotov was putting in a good word *to Stalin*, who was both curious and suspicious, about the only leader of a Communist regime in the Soviet bloc who escaped from any historical ties or contact with the Soviet Union. And this was true not just of Hoxha as an individual, but of almost the entire leading group in Albania. Moreover, Albania was the only country in the bloc which had liberated itself without the Soviet Red Army setting foot on its territory.

Hoxha was not just 'quite' cultured, he was very cultured. In spite of coming from the most backward country in Europe, he was by far the best-read head of any Communist party in the bloc. On visits to other countries in Eastern Europe, he often comments on the philistinism of his bloc colleagues. Hoxha knew fluent French and had a working knowledge (either verbal or written) of Italian, Serbo-Croatian, Russian and English. The range of references in his memoirs is not what one would expect from a Balkan ex-Muslim Stalinist. Not only does he like Molière, Shakespeare, Goethe and Byron (who spent some time in Albania); he is an admirer of Jerome K. Jerome. Peter Prifti notes that 'Hoxha seems to be well informed about literature, the theater, and philosophy, particularly the philosophy of education ... He might well be pictured as holding the sword of the dictatorship of the proletariat in one hand and the Western "lamp of learning" in the other.'[12] He displays a lively interest in Egyptology.

Several things further are most unusual for someone in his position. First, he reads the Western press – and actually refers to *Le Monde* and the *International Herald Tribune*. Second, he has taken the trouble to read the memoirs of world statesmen – and not just the obvious ones like Churchill, but also less known figures like Harry Hopkins (Roosevelt's key aide). Third, he has read and refers to the memoirs of people who have crossed his path, like Julian Amery, Brigadier Davies (who headed the second S O E mission) and the Yugoslav wartime emissary, Svetozar Vukmanović Tempo. Hoxha only falters when he has to confront the many detailed memoirs written by Yugoslav leaders recounting conversations with Stalin in the early postwar years which reflect Stalin's unflattering views about Albania.

Here one runs into the apparent paradox signalled in Prifti's quote above: Hoxha is both unusually well read and intelligent, on the one hand, and an out-and-out Stalinist, on the other. These two sides of his character coexist without any resolution or synthesis. For Hoxha, Stalin can do no wrong. The world is divided into black and white: Stalin and those who agreed with him are good; those against Stalin are bad. In philosophical terms, Marxism-Leninism is good; 'revisionism' is bad. On these issues, Hoxha is entirely predictable and often boring. He manifestly distorts events and flatly refuses to confront the evidence, for example, on Stalin's purges and the show trials in Eastern Europe after the war. The conflict between Hoxha's shrewd observation and his purblind Stalinism is one of the oddest aspects of the memoirs. In effect, when in trouble, he wheels out Marxism-Leninism and deploys it like magic, in an incantatory, ritualistic way. But it is a magic straitjacket.

Thus, on modern philosophy and literature Hoxha is predictable. He castigates the whole tradition of 'revisionism' from Bernstein and Kautsky, via Lukács, on to the French writers Garaudy, Elleinstein and Althusser. He takes pot shots at Sartre and de Beauvoir, even Marguerite Duras. He dislikes Kafka; Tristan Tzara and the surrealists get short shrift.[13] Psychoanalysis, naturally, is anathema. In a curious passage in a 1967 speech (with the scintillating title, 'On Some Aspects of the Problem of the Albanian Woman'), Hoxha names five key sources for the oppression of women: Ecclesiastes, St John Chrysostom, St Thomas Aquinas, Nietzsche and Freud. Of the last two, he says: 'Bourgeois theoreticians like Nietzsche and Freud uphold the theory that the male is active while the female is passive. This reactionary, anti-biological theory leads – as it did – in politics, to Nazism, in sexology, to sadism.'[14]

The list of people Hoxha likes, or claims to have liked, seems to be determined by a priori, sometimes a posteriori, political considerations rather than personal qualities, although there are important exceptions to this generalisation. Apart from Stalin, Hoxha says he liked the Bulgarian leader Dimitrov (who probably was a decent man). But it is impossible to believe that people like the discredited Hungarian Stalinist Mátyás Rákosi or the head of the Chinese secret police, Kang Sheng, could be likeable characters. The only leading Communist towards whom Hoxha expressed ambivalent feelings and lets his ambivalence stand is the Korean Kim Il Sung (also Hoxha's only rival for political longevity in the Communist world). In 1956, when Kim is taking Hoxha round North Korea, Hoxha calls him 'kind and intimate'; later on he calls him a 'megalomaniac' and 'a pseudo-Marxist'. (Hoxha may well have been right to let all this stand, as Kim may indeed combine contradictory attributes.)[15]

The Memoirs

But what gives Hoxha's memoirs a considerable edge over any others, even those of Khrushchev, is that he combines his intelligence and powers of observation with brutal frankness as well as self-serving bombast and evasion. He really does spill the beans. And he thinks. Isolated in his tiny corner of the Balkans for twenty-five years, he had to think, to interpret signals, and to decode the acts, messages and evasions of friend and foe. The two volumes of *Reflections on China* are above all a fascinating exercise in decoding. Hoxha is alert to every nuance of protocol, every staged welcome and farewell, every ritualistic formulation and absence in the Chinese press.

Here, again, Hoxha presents a paradox. On the one hand, he is keenly alert to the role of ritual in the Communist world. He knows that ritual is the only method which Communist countries have to demonstrate support for their policies, or to greet foreign guests. Hoxha knows the ritual is hollow — 'a façade' and 'a masquerade', as he calls it. Yet he has no other way to demonstrate support for his own policies. He knows the truth, yet still applies blatant double standards. While denouncing the Chinese and North Koreans for bringing out the people 'like a mob of sheep which gambolled and bleated' for Tito in 1977, he can register his own delight at the Chinese trundling out 3000 people with banners and gongs to greet an Albanian delegation.

The role of ritual is in direct and converse relationship to the lack of democracy. Hoxha has his own concept of democracy, which he expounds to the Hungarian leaders in 1956 (see p. 189). In his memoirs Khrushchev says that 'The rift which developed between the Soviet Union and Albania stemmed mainly from the Albanians' fear of democratization.'[16] In Hoxha's account three issues stand out as central to his break with Khrushchev in 1960: the role of Stalin and the cult of the personality; rapprochement with Yugoslavia; and the rehabilitation of the victims of the postwar trials. The cult of personality and the issue of rehabilitations are at the core of the question of democracy.

Hoxha's remarks on the cult of personality, as on so many things, combine the illuminating with the obfuscating. Inevitably, he accuses his most disliked enemies, Tito and Khrushchev, of fostering their own cults on a major scale. Equally inevitably, he most unconvincingly denies that Stalin engaged in the practice. But Hoxha spends a lot of time analysing the cult of Mao, especially during the period of the Cultural Revolution, and his remarks on Mao's cult are extremely sharp. Among the points he makes are that the cult, far from enhancing Mao's standing, at least outside China, brought its practitioners – and, by extension, Mao, for tolerating it – into derision. And that the last person who really needs a cult is someone like Mao who was genuinely a towering figure in his own right. Hoxha reserves his harshest criticism on the issue of the cult for Kim Il Sung of Korea (see pp. 313–314). He is even prepared to discuss his own cult, in a way which is *partly* disingenuous, but also partly reflects the real situation (see p. 372).

Hoxha claims that a key factor in his worsening relations with Moscow from the mid-1950s was that the Russians, particularly Mikhail Suslov, were trying to get him to rehabilitate the Albanians who had been condemned after Tirana's break with Belgrade in 1948 – particularly the former Minister of the Interior and number two in the Party, Koçi Xoxe, who was executed in June 1949 (officially he was shot; in his memoirs Khrushchev says that Tito told him, Khrushchev, that Mehmet Shehu strangled Xoxe with his bare hands). Hoxha's reply to Suslov was clear: 'There is nothing for our Party to re-examine ... We have never permitted serious mistakes of principle in our line.'[17] Albania was the only country in Eastern Europe which carried out a major purge after the war which refused to rehabilitate the victims after Stalin's death.

Hoxha's handling of the rehabilitation issue is emblematic of his overall approach. He lumps together the Albanian trials (Xoxe and company) with those in Hungary (Rájk and others) and Bulgaria (Kostov and others). He purblindly refuses to accept the proof that Rájk and Kostov were framed. By so doing, he greatly weakens his own position vis-à-vis Xoxe. Suslov seems to have wanted Xoxe rehabilitated partly to smooth relations between Albania and Yugoslavia. But the fact is that Xoxe probably did conspire with Belgrade to oust Hoxha (and, perhaps, earlier with the Russians).

Although Hoxha's approach to democracy is woefully deficient, he is alert to, and loquacious on, the undemocratic methods widely used in the socialist bloc. One of the best things in his memoirs is his constant attention to surveillance and skulduggery. He can spot Chinese plain-clothesmen cramming the airport for Tito's arrival in China. He describes the Soviet and Chinese embassies in Tirana as centres for subversion and espionage. And on his last visit to Russia in 1960 his delegation brought special equipment to sweep their building for bugs, which they found in every room except the lavatory – whereupon a Soviet plumber turned up, but, of course, he was nabbed by a vigilant Albanian, as he should be. Hoxha seems to regard all this as par for the course in relations between Communist states. Indeed, he remarks, the socialist countries are 'more highly developed' in subversion methods than the capitalist countries.[18]

No one can doubt that Hoxha is extremely suspicious. Indeed, suspicion is almost the central motif of his memoirs. But where is the dividing line between vigilance and paranoia? The question is whether Hoxha is *too* suspicious. He certainly had plenty to be suspicious about. And even here, his account is unusual, since he describes at length the development of his own suspicions about colleagues and some of his methods for 'unmasking' traitors and spies. Even if these accounts are rewritten with hindsight, and some of them (especially the section on Shehu) are manifestly paranoid, they nonetheless constitute a unique genre from the leader of a Communist regime. What gives them added interest (and also contributes to the difficulty of separating out the real from the invented) is the vivid and often quite personal detail which Hoxha throws in. Hoxha is able to write about his enemies as real people, even when the framework is that of a fairy tale.

However, there is a curious proviso to Hoxha's suspiciousness. When senior figures, like Mao's secretary Chen Po-ta (Chen Boda), are purged in China and denounced as foreign agents, Hoxha explodes about the fact that they were allowed to remain so long in positions of authority. Yet, when writing about similar or even worse alleged lapses in Albania, Hoxha blatantly applies double standards. Hoxha even lists the fact that every single Minister of the Interior in Albania between Liberation and the end of 1981 was a foreign agent, allegedly.[19] Yet he refuses to reflect on this, except as a conspiracy. He refuses to confront either (if the allegations are true) his own responsibility in this state of affairs, or (even less) the possibility that the accusations were false.

The discovery and removal of enemies within the regime itself has been a central and defining practice of almost all post-revolutionary regimes. It is in connection with this unsavoury aspect that another side of Hoxha emerges, one that is brutal, almost delighting in his own brutality. Khrushchev called Hoxha and his then top colleagues, Shehu and Balluku, 'worse than beasts – they're monsters'.[20] And Hoxha was not alone in his brutality. Shehu is reported to have told the Fourth Party Congress, at a time when Soviet pressure was intense: 'For those who stand in the way of party unity: a spit in the face, a sock in the jaw, and, if necessary, a bullet in the head . . .'[21] Two of the most courageous leading women partisans, Liri Gega and Liri Belishova, were both executed in gruesome ways. Liri Gega was shot while pregnant in 1956 on charges of being a 'Titoist agent'; Liri Belishova, who had had an eye put out by the fascists during the war, was apparently strangled in 1960. Hoxha's brutality is manifest in his exchange with Khrushchev about Panajot Plaku (see p.

206), whom, Hoxha says quite brazenly, he want to hang from a lamppost in the middle of Tirana.

Hoxha's brutality is reflected in the curious combination in his invective. He enjoys invective – a dangerous and common trait among middle-class intellectual Marxists. Once again, he combines two disparate traditions: there is the rather colloquial and even lively invective of Albanian tradition, and grafted on to the top of this (like his Marxism-Leninism) the vicious but much stodgier tradition of Vyshinsky and the ritual Communist-type denunciation of enemies.

Absent themes

The extracts in this volume are taken from works by Hoxha dealing almost exclusively with external relations. A number of important themes and topics are thus inevitably left to one side, but deserve a brief mention.

The economy: Self-reliance in a small country

Albania's population in 1985 was estimated at 3 million. Due to poor statistics and secrecy, there is no agreed figure for per capita income; but probably Albania has the lowest standard of living in Europe.[22] This is a reflection more of its historical condition than of growth rates under the Hoxha regime, which have been creditable.

The experienced French agronomist René Dumont notes that prewar Albania was more 'under-developed' than 'ill-developed' (mal-développé), unlike most colonial economies, to which it approximated in standard of living.[23] Prior to Liberation in 1944, Albania suffered from a number of grave economic drawbacks. It had no rail links with the outside world (the only country on the European continent so isolated). Its internal communications systems – in a country with very high mountains – were abysmal. Much of the low-lying area was a malarial swamp. Almost 90 per cent of the population was engaged in agriculture. Industry was virtually nonexistent and there were very few skilled technicians. Emigration was high. At the time of Liberation, Albania was further hindered by the fact that it had no foreign currency reserves – the till having been looted first by King Zog, then by the fascist occupying powers (whose hoard was taken over by the British).

After Liberation Albania instituted a classic Stalinist 'people's democracy' type of economic regime, nationalising all major assets and collectivising agriculture. The domestic market was very restricted. On the other hand, the country had a number of very important assets, unusually abundant for such a small territory. It had large oil deposits (it is still the third largest oil producer in the European socialist world) – though it had no refineries. It had abundant gas and coal reserves. It had a very large hydroelectric potential. It also had several of the rarer and desirable minerals, including chrome (third or fourth in world output) and nickel. It was thus in the unusual situation of being able to aim for relative self-sufficiency (and certainly self-reliance) in industrial raw materials. However, it lacked entirely a machine-tool industry, which is still one of its weakest sectors.

The country was not self-sufficient in agriculture, though this goal was achieved by about 1976 – a considerable achievement, and one of great psychological significance, given the pressures exerted on Albania in the past.

Albania's two most signal successes have been to extract a very large amount of foreign aid from successive patrons – Yugoslavia, the USSR, and finally China. Secondly, to maintain an economy which has been relatively self-reliant and relatively insulated from external pressures and shocks: it is estimated that in the late 1970s, around the time of the break with China, foreign trade accounted for only 7 per cent of GNP – an astonishingly low figure for a very small economy. (There are, of course, heavy costs attached to this.)[24]

The story of Albania's economy since Liberation is partly the story of its three successive close alliances with Yugoslavia (to mid-1948), the USSR (to 1960–61) and finally China (to 1977–8), followed by its current phase of self-reliance combined with a cautious opening up to most of the outside world, especially the intermediate capitalist states (Japan, Italy, Canada, etc.). Hoxha's account consists largely of complaints about the pressures exerted on Albania by its allies. His version of events is probably not far off the mark on this side of things. But it fails to give due recognition to the sizeable sums of aid which these states doled out to Albania.

As of the early 1980s, Albania was not only self-sufficient in food, but exported some foodstuffs. It exports energy. And it has valuable raw materials which can easily find instant export markets for hard currency. It has had enormous problems in reconverting the direction of its foreign trade after its successive breaks. It also has trouble servicing and repairing the industrial equipment acquired from Russia and China. And it has had difficulty raising the capital to maintain the investments in major projects left high and dry when China cut off its aid in 1977–8.

One very important point about more recent Albanian development is that, whereas Soviet aid (as Hoxha complains) was limited to light industry, food and infrastructure, the Chinese gave Tirana aid to build up heavy industry – and thus a real base for long-term self-reliance. Financing for maintaining this sector is, however, made extremely difficult by the state's refusal, enshrined in the constitution, to borrow funds abroad or allow joint ventures.

Overall, Albanian economic policy has been a success, within rather rigid traditional Stalinist lines. Food self-sufficiency, in particular, has allowed the state considerable *political* leeway.

The position of women

The second absence is the relative emancipation and promotion of women, within the limits of socialist-style desubordination. This is all the more remarkable given that prior to Liberation Albania was an extremely poor, backward and mountainous country – and over 70 per cent Muslim.

The Communist movement in Albania has rarely received the recognition it deserves on this score, and the crucial historical experience of the wartime liberation struggle has been very neglected. In 1958 Hoxha told a delegation of Indonesian Communists that during the war the Party took an advanced line – and 'stern measures' so that 'such an attitude was created among the people that even the most fanatical old men allowed their daughters and daughters-in-law to go to war together with the partisans, or to help them'. According to Hoxha, 'nearly 6000 women took to the mountains. All peasant houses were open to the partisans . . .'[25] because the partisans established their credentials both as the liberators of women and as imposing very strict discipline on themselves. This was a key factor in winning the war and gave the partisans a qualitative edge over their conservative rivals, since the partisans could move and survive in the mountain areas, more than half the year in extreme cold, where houses were usually isolated and ideas very backward. It also meant the partisans could operate outside their home areas (unlike the right-wing tribal leaders). The ability of the partisans to achieve this enormous leap forward in three years, with very few means of communication at their disposal, was a signal success, and one which says a great deal about how they gained power so easily at the time of Liberation.

Although Islam was not nearly as deeply entrenched in Albania as in, say, most of the Arab world, the partisans linked the emancipation of women with a critique of Islam. One of the first things the partisans did when they first entered Muslim villages was to set up a school for women.

The veil had already been banned by Zog – although some women still wore it in remote areas.

One unusual element in Hoxha's approach to women is that, unlike most leaders of Communist regimes, he has actually talked about love. Although the regime is rather puritanical, it is also clear that Hoxha has thought about love and come up with formulations which differ from those trotted out by most post-revolutionary regimes. For example: 'It must be acknowledged that there exist erroneous and backward ideas about love among us. Love is considered as something shameful, impermissible and abnormal. Very often, even if not entirely, love is stigmatized as something immoral which leads women to prostitution and men to degeneracy. These are erroneous concepts. If there is something which has nothing to do with prostitution, that thing is genuine love.'[26]

Religion abolished?

The third absent theme is the elimination of religion, or at least the eradication of all institutions of religion. Since 1967 Albania has claimed to be 'the first atheist state in the world' – although it does not yet claim to have eradicated the legacy of all religious ideas.[27]

The claim to have wiped out all institutions and all teaching of religion is remarkable, if it is true. At Liberation in 1944 the country was 72.8 per cent Muslim, 17.1 per cent Greek Orthodox (mainly in the south) and 10.1 per cent Catholic (mainly in the north). As can be seen from their names, most of the main leaders of the regime, including Enver Hoxha, Mehmet Shehu, Haxhi Lleshi (long-time President) and Ramiz Alia (Hoxha's successor), all came from Muslim backgrounds.[28]

The partisan movement was much stronger in southern Albania than in the north, and most of its leaders came from the south (while Zog had come from the north). Islam had been unusually weak in Albania, but was nonetheless associated with the Ottoman occupation. Catholicism tended to be associated with Italy and the Vatican and much of the Catholic population collaborated (or 'accommodated') with the Italian occupation between 1939 and 1943, and with the Nazi occupation (1943–4). Hoxha, like some of the Yugoslav Communists, regarded the Vatican as a serious enemy.

Hoxha links the role of religion closely to the oppression of women. In 1955 he told the Fourth Congress of the Women's Union: 'The canons of the Sheriat [sharia] and of the Church, closely linked with the laws of the bourgeoisie, treated woman as a commodity, a thing to be bought and sold by the male . . . Just as the bourgeoisie had made the worker into its proletarian, so had the savage ancient canons of the Sheriat, the Church, feudalism and bourgeoisie, reduced woman to the proletariat of the man.'[29]

Hoxha makes a point of recording his conversations with Stalin about religion. Stalin urges a cautious line. Less than twenty years later, Hoxha had accelerated his atheism past any other Communist state, even North Korea. Hoxha continues to keep a beady eye out for religion and the reactions to it by other post-Revolutionary states. He castigates the Vatican's differential attitude towards Albania and China in the 1970s. He also derides China's soft approach to Islam, dictated by foreign policy considerations (or ideological capitulation). And Hoxha also scorns the conciliatory line of the then head of the Spanish Communist Party, Santiago Carrillo. Interestingly, Hoxha does not pull his punches on the role of Islam in 'third world socialist' countries. He condemns the Ben Bella regime for adopting what he calls 'Koranic eclecticism' in Algeria (in 1965), particularly because Ben Bella tried to slip this under the rubric of 'socialism'.[30]

Albania's decisive action against Islam, at least as an organised force, is a major achievement which deserves much closer study. Unfortunately, Tirana, and even Hoxha himself, usually so prolix on their successes, pay it little attention and give it little coverage in their propaganda.

Fear and loathing in Tirana

History repeats itself – and not always in ways which even Hoxha could predict. In his ruminations on China, Hoxha pours scorn on the authenticity of quotations by Mao produced only after his death. At the end of July 1985 the post-Hoxha regime announced posthumous pronouncements by the late leader, in effect urging further relinking with the outside world.[31] Authentic or fabricated? Who knows?

Hoxha's vision was guided by fierce nationalism. It turns out that he was one of the two contemporary statesmen most admired by de Gaulle.[32] In a way, even more than Stalin, Hoxha had a vision of 'socialism in one country' – not for geo-strategic reasons, but out of alleged ideological purity, which served as a convenient cloak for nationalism. This is different from isolationism, with which Albania is usually taxed. Rather, Tirana's policy has been one of *abstention* – refusing, for example, to participate in the European Security Conference (which Hoxha termed 'a conference of insecurity').[33]

Hoxha was often called a Stalinist. He was a Stalinist in two important ways. One was in his advocacy of a very rigid form of centralised planning (with, some observers claim, more flexibility in practice than

Stalin allowed). The other was in his use of brutal methods and often concocted evidence, compounded by his outspoken enthusiasm for harsh measures. But he was not 'Stalinist' in other important respects. He was a cultured and well-read man. He was also in much closer contact with the population of his country than Stalin, at least until his later years (this does not emerge from the memoirs extracted below). He was not only a good orator (which is quite compatible with having no contact with the masses), he was very good at folksy encounters, swopping anecdotes and quotes from local literature. In all this he was helped by his unusual combination of being both an intellectual and charming and good-looking. He shared Stalin's quality of brutality, but he was not brutish.

Although Hoxha cannot be compared in a linear way to most other Third World leaders (for one thing he is far too intelligent), nonetheless his memoirs are valuable in a paradigmatic way, especially since he stands in all 'three worlds' in a way no one else (except, possibly, Ho Chi Minh) has done. He knew the West from his five years in France and Belgium, during an exciting time, including the beginning of the Popular Front in France. He knew the Communist world and its leaders during the hardest period of postwar reconstruction and paranoia. He knew the Third World, because Albania, a poor, mainly Muslim nation, was itself in the condition of a Third World country, and had very recently been colonised.

Hoxha's memoirs show us how many Third World leaders must think. Nationalism is the predominant criterion. Security thus occupies a leading role, accompanied by genuine vigilance, but also obsessions and paranoia. In a sense, it is hardly surprising that all four postwar Ministers of the Interior have been condemned as traitors. How could it not be so?

As Hoxha's corpse was lowered into its grave, Albanian TV revealed a strange spectacle. One old woman was seen to cross herself right by the graveside (so, has religion really been wiped out?). And just as Hoxha was being laid to rest, his successor, Ramiz Alia, bent over and pinned one last medal to his chest. One more 'hero of socialist labour, first class'? Or a tangible token that 'the immortal Enver' will not be forgotten?

A note on the texts

The extracts in this volume are all taken from six volumes of memoirs by Hoxha: *The Anglo-American Threat to Albania*; *The Titoites*; *With Stalin*; *The Khrushchevites*; *Reflections on China*, I and II. These total some 3400 pages.

Not all these volumes are in the same form. The first four are written as memoirs; *Reflections on China* as a diary. There are therefore three basic issues: reliability of memory; form; and proportion.

Hoxha claims to have kept notes throughout his career, and, given his position from 1941, it is probably true that he or someone with him did. However, it is also hard to think that Hoxha was meticulous about this, particularly during the war, under very harsh conditions, often on the move and in danger. His reconstructions of conversations with British SOE officers in *The Anglo-American Threat* are particularly suspect. In addition, there is the perennial problem of selectivity. In *Reflections on China*, it is clear that Hoxha has left many things out, as there are gaps of up to nine months in the published diary. Hoxha also wants to show himself in a good light. *Reflections on China* are, I believe, mainly extracts from a genuine diary, but carefully edited, and from a text originally written with an eye to publication.

In the first four volumes, covering the years from the start of the war up to the break with Russia in 1961, Hoxha is almost all the time describing directly events and people when he himself was present. *Reflections on China*, totalling some 1600 pages, have a different form. During the period covered (1962–77) Hoxha not only did not go to China, he did not officially leave Albania (he 'compensates' for this by indicating where he was inside Albania). Some of the entries describe conversations with visiting Chinese officials, from Chou En-lai on down; others involve Hoxha talking to Albanian officials who visit China. But the bulk of the two volumes is an extended, sometimes meandering, often quasi-obsessive speculation on what on earth is going on in China, and what kind of ally Albania has found itself with in the fight against 'revisionism'.

Thus, the reduction in the material from *Reflections on China* inevitably, to some extent, modifies the pacing and rhythm of Hoxha's attempt to peer into the 'dark Chinese forest'.[34]

On the other hand, the different forms of the different volumes, reflecting as they do the different situations Hoxha was in, also produce a bonus. While the volumes up to 1961 describe Hoxha's first-hand experience as head of a regime in the socialist bloc, negotiating and arguing with the other bloc leaders, the diaries about China are a rich source in a different vein: how to decode and 'read' the mysterious signals of a remote and reluctant ally. One does not have to agree with Hoxha's Stalinist view of the world to see that in this work of decoding he can combine deployment of both facets of his character: his vigilant Balkan wiliness and his hard schooling in post-Leninist methodology and ritual.

I
WORLD WAR II AND ITS AFTERMATH

The invasion of Albania and Britain's role 1939–41

Hoxha's memoirs open just before the start of the Second World War. On Good Friday (7 April) 1939, Italy invaded Albania and annexed it. Hoxha largely blames Britain for allowing this to happen, and claims that 'Britain wanted Italy to occupy Albania'.

> Proof that this plan existed can be seen in the indifferent attitude of Chamberlain when Mussolini's Italy attacked our country on April 7, 1939. Chamberlain, who knew in advance what was going to occur, went fishing that day. This was the same Chamberlain who had approved the «Anschluss», who had signed the Munich Agreement selling out Czechoslovakia . . .
>
> The statement which the British prime minister made in the House of Commons on April 6, that Great Britain had «no direct interests» in Albania, gave Mussolini a free hand to carry out his plans towards our country. This stand by Britain was greatly in favour of Italy because it gave legal sanction to its special interests in Albania.[1]

Hoxha is quite correct to claim that Britain gave de facto recognition to Mussolini's seizure of Albania; and he is also correct to say that the seizure of Albania was allowed to pass with considerably less reaction from the main Western democracies than were Hitler's moves further north. Britain was, in addition, the main naval power in the Mediterranean at the time. Moreover, Britain had had a major presence in Albania prior to the Italian invasion. A British company, Anglo-Persian (later Anglo-Iranian) Oil, had a virtual monopoly on Albania's oil fields, the country's major asset. British officers staffed and ran the gendarmerie of Albania's King Zog from the late 1920s until 1938, when Zog terminated their employment under Italian pressure.[2] Britain was thus associated directly with the main instrument of repression in Albania.

In the early years of the Second World War Britain did not have the ability to do very much in Albania, but two factors came to play long-term roles. First, King Zog, who was ousted in 1939, eventually came to live in Britain. He resided in luxury at the Ritz, occupying an entire floor, which he paid for with gold bars looted from the national treasury. Second, British intelligence, the predecessor of Special Operations Executive (SOE), ran an Albanian operation from its Belgrade office in 1940 and early 1941 (until the German occupation of Belgrade). The two main agents involved were Captain (later Colonel) Dayrell Oakley Hill, who had been deputy head of Zog's gendarmerie for a decade; and Julian Amery. Both of these were subsequently involved in attempts to overthrow the Hoxha regime.

In early 1941 Oakley Hill accompanied an armed force of some 200–300 Albanians on a raid into northern Albania. The group encompassed men of very different political persuasions: it included a leading Communist, Mustafa Gjinishi; the chief ex-army supporter of Zog, Abas Kupi (later Britain's candidate for leader); and three members of the powerful Muslim tribal family, the Kryezius (whom Britain also later tried to manoeuvre into positions of power). The raid was a failure. Everyone associated with this enterprise became suspect to Hoxha.[3]

Albania during the Second World War

For Albania the Second World War started in effect with the Italian invasion in April 1939. Italy not merely invaded Albania, it annexed it. Albania was run as a colony. The struggle against Italy was not simply a 'resistance' movement, as in most of occupied Europe, but an *anticolonial* struggle, with many of the characteristics of a national liberation war. In addition, Italy used Albania as the base from which to attack Greece in 1940. During the occupation period, Italy combined the territory of what is now Albania together with the region known as the Kosovo (now in southern Yugoslavia, but with a majority of ethnic Albanians) and the area in the north of Greece called the Çamëria. This territorial agglomeration, sometimes referred to as 'Greater Albania', while it respected the boundaries of ethnic Albania, also caused major problems with Albania's two land neighbours.

The Albanian Communist Party (ACP) was founded clandestinely in Tirana, the capital, on 8 November 1941.[4] Enver Hoxha, then aged thirty-three, was named provisional head of the Party. The ACP was a highly specific formation, quite unlike most European Communist parties, and quite different from the Yugoslav CP. First of all, it was set up without any known direct contact with Moscow. It was not at all a 'Moscow creation'. Secondly, it was able to build on a strong radical tradition among the intelligentsia (unlike in most Balkan countries). Third, the bulk of the founding leadership were middle-class intellectuals on whom the strongest influences were *Western* intellectual traditions (the only 'proletarian' among the core group was a tinsmith from Korçë,

Koçi Xoxe). Hoxha brought French radicalism – both that of the enlightenment and the more modern Popular Front version. The main partisan military commander, Mehmet Shehu, brought the experience of the Spanish civil war and that of internment in a camp in France where he had joined the Italian Communist Party. Lastly, the Albanian Communist Party, like the Yugoslav, was strengthened in a very harsh war, during which it won over the mass of the population.[5] The Albanians waged a struggle which was both a national liberation fight and, as Tito acknowledged, a real revolution at the same time.[6]

During the winter of 1941–2 only small-scale individual actions were undertaken against the Italians. On the other hand, given the mountainous nature of the terrain and the nation's traditions of armed resistance, the Italians were never able to subdue much more than the main towns and the main communications routes.

By September 1942 the ACP felt strong enough to convene a congress in the town of Peza, only 18 kilometres from Tirana, to which it invited representatives of the other, more conservative political movements, with a view to setting up a broad united front. This was formed, with the name National Liberation Front, usually referred to by its Albanian initials, LNC (see Glossary). This front held for one year, during which the Communists did virtually all the fighting there was against the Italians and greatly increased their strength, especially in southern and central Albania.

In the northern half of the country the mainly Muslim tribal leaders continued to hold sway over their fiefs throughout the period of the Italian occupation. Some collaborated outright with the occupying power. Many coalesced (loosely) behind the Balli Kombëtar (National Front), a nonmonarchist grouping, which made little effort to engage the Italians and soon began to reach accommodations with them.

In July 1943 a National Liberation Army was formally established out of existing units. By this time tension between the Communists and the Balli was acute and a civil war seemed to be imminent. The Communists invited the Balli to a meeting at the village of Mukje (Mukaj), near Tirana, on 1 and 2 August 1943. An agreement was reached: (1) to form a united resistance front against the occupying power; (2) to set up an ethnic Albanian state, including the Kosovo and the Çamëria; (3) to hold free elections after the war.

However, within a week of the signing of the Mukje agreement, Hoxha denounced both it and the ACP delegates who had signed it. This murky episode is almost certainly connected to the complicated question of the relations between the Albanian and the Yugoslav Communists at the time. The Yugoslavs can reasonably be assumed to have objected strongly to the inclusion of the Kosovo in postwar Albania. They may well also have objected to the 'soft' line, apparently espoused by Hoxha, vis-à-vis the Balli Kombëtar (the then hard-line Yugoslavs seem to have suspected Hoxha of being a dangerous liberal).[7]

Immediately after the denunciation of the Mukje agreement three things happened. First, the Partisans set up the First Shock Brigade under their most able military commander, Mehmet Shehu. Second, within a few weeks of Hoxha denouncing the Mukje agreement, one of the three LNC delegates at it, the northern tribal leader, Abas Kupi, broke away and set up a pro-Zog movement, Legaliteti (the Legality movement). Third, in September Italy surrendered to the Allies. Some 15,000 Italian troops in Albania surrendered to the Partisans, while some 2000 Italian troops went over to the Partisans and constituted themselves into a brigade named after Antonio Gramsci, the leading Italian Marxist, who was of Albanian origin.

The Germans rapidly substituted for the Italians, ultimately placing some 70,000 troops in Albania (about half or more of them being defectors from the Red Army, many of them Muslims from Central Asia). During the winter of 1943–4 the Balli and the Germans took the offensive and attempted to exterminate the Partisans.[8] By the spring of 1944, however, the Partisans were able to strike back and by the early summer of 1944, when communications had improved after the spring floods, the Partisans were engaged in a full-scale civil war against the Balli Kombëtar and the Legaliteti. In the space of less than half a year the Partisans routed the two right-wing Albanian movements, swept through the north of the country, and got rid of the Germans. On 29 November 1944, the Communists proclaimed the total liberation of Albania.

Relations with Yugoslavia

According to Hoxha, his first problems came from the Yugoslavs.

There were two central issues in relations between Albania and Yugoslavia during the war: first, the future of the Kosovo; second, the role of the Yugoslavs in the establishment and guidance of the Albanian Communist Party (ACP) and the Albania partisans. On this, there are two starkly opposing theses.[9] The official Albanian line is that the Albanians founded their own Communist Party in November 1941 without any outside influence, whether Yugoslav or Russian. The Yugoslav version is that the ACP was founded on the initiative of the Yugoslavs, and that Yugoslav emissaries played a determining role in keeping the ACP, the

LNC and Hoxha on the right track politically. Both sides have published detailed and, to some extent, documented accounts of their respective versions. Since the Yugoslavs have a much better track record on truth, their version is inherently the more plausible. But this needs to be qualified by the fact that some of Yugoslavia's *worst* behaviour – and at a time when Tito was following a very left (even 'ultra-left') line – was towards Albania (as Djilas has acknowledged).[10]

What is beyond dispute is that there was a succession of Yugoslav envoys with the Albanian partisans right from the start, beginning with Miladin Popović, a Montenegrin who was freed from an internment camp in Albania by Albanian Communists, and Dušan Mugoša ('good' and 'bad', respectively, in Hoxha's account). The first official Yugoslav emissary to the ACP was Blažo Jovanović, who reached Hoxha's headquarters in December 1942.

In his version of events, Hoxha tries to show two things. First, that Yugoslavia meddled extensively in Albania's affairs during and after the war, with a view to establishing some form of Balkan federation with Belgrade at its head; second, that, although the Yugoslavs interfered, they did not, on the whole, substantially affect the political line of the Albanian Communist movement.

Whatever the specific Yugoslav input, it is just as impossible to recognise the vigorous independence of Albania in later years without giving due recognition to the long-term nationalist component in Hoxha's policies as it is to recognise Tito's independence from Stalin without giving due credit to Yugoslav nationalism. Hoxha was first and foremost an Albanian nationalist.

One item which is no longer in dispute and which deserves to be recorded is that Albanian partisans fought inside Yugoslavia in the period October 1944 to February 1945 and helped to liberate the Kosovo (including the capital Priština) and parts of Macedonia, Montenegro, Serbia and the southern part of Bosnia-Herzegovina. This important contribution, in which some 350 Albanian troops are reported to have lost their lives, was long ignored by Yugoslavia after 1948, but finally officially recognised in the mid-1970s, when the bodies of the dead Albanians were returned to Tirana.[11]

In this extract Hoxha describes the arrival of Tito's main envoy in charge of Balkan affairs, Svetozar Vukmanović Tempo, in March 1943.

Tito's «roving ambassador» spins the threads of the web over the Balkans

We had just successfully concluded . . . the 1st National Conference[12] . . . [when] suddenly and in totally unknown circumstances, a Yugoslav popped up in Labinot of Elbasan. I say «popped up», not so much for the fact that until that moment we did not know who this person was, where he came from, where he was going in those difficult times or why, but more especially because of the endless problems, the tangles, the accusations and traps which he created for us from the moment we met him and for years on end subsequently. An anti-Albanian and anti-Marxist of the first water, a frenzied Great-Serb chauvinist, brutal and a power-seeker, this is how he would seem to us when he turned up three or four months after our first meeting, again in the difficult autumn of that year, and again in 1945 and 1947. This political gangster (in calling him this I am not exaggerating at all), who in the spring and summer of 1943 was suddenly to push his way into the leadership of the Party and sow the seeds of disruption and diversion, just as «suddenly» after Liberation was to find the way to push himself into and dictate to the supreme organs of our army. Years were to go by, matters were to take the course they did and when we had completely forgotten him, just as unexpectedly as in March of 1943, he was to turn up again on another black night, this time thousands of kilometres from Albania, in Moscow. One night, well after midnight, the telephone was to ring insistently and the voice of Anastas Mikoyan informed me that Svetozar Vukmanović Tempo,[13] the man of March 1943, was seeking a meeting with me!

Very soon I was to be convinced that his frowning self-important attitude at the moment of introduction had not arisen from the fact that I kept him waiting for some time . . . this was his permanent nature.

«On my way back from Macedonia and the Greek zones en route for Montenegro and Kosova, I heard you were here. Let's see what these Albanians are doing, I thought, and decided to pay you a short visit,» he said solemnly and waited apparently for me to express my thanks. I merely remained silent in order to let him know that he ought to correct the expression . . . «these Albanians».

But this made no impression on him. He told us (in confidence!) that he was the main delegate of the CPY and the General Staff of the Yugoslav NLA for Macedonia and went on:[14]

«Since Macedonia, on account of its past and present history, is the key problem of the Balkans, I am more or less obliged to involve myself with all these territories where Bulgaria, Greece, Macedonia, Albania and Serbia converge . . .»

Tempo went off to Greece, taking with him one of the leaders of the ACP, Koçi Xoxe. Xoxe, who had been in prison at the time the ACP was founded, subsequently became Minister of the Interior in the postwar government and the second most powerful person in Albania. After the break with Tito in 1948, he was arrested and condemned to death as the number one Yugoslav agent.

In the extract here, Tempo has just returned with Xoxe from Greece (about the end of July 1943). According to Hoxha, the Yugoslavs, via Tempo, were attempting to seize the leadership of all the resistance movements in the Balkans via the creation of a 'Balkan staff' to be controlled by Tito. The question of a Balkan federation became a central issue in the 1948 break between Tito and the Soviet bloc.

I cannot say that at those early moments we understood that behind the idea of this «staff» lurked the megalomaniacal hegemonic ambitions of the leadership of the CPY to rule the Balkans. This we were to realise later. But right at those moments, apart from the grave doubts which arose in our minds about the character of the «staff», a number of Tempo's expressions also left a bad impression with us. He boasted about «the marvellous experience» of the General Staff of the Yugoslav NLA, about «its proven ability» to undertake and carry out large-scale battles successfully, the «readiness» of this staff «to make the necessary contribution to the realisation of the new idea», etc. He went so far as to call the experience of the Yugoslav NLA «unrivalled», «a model of mountain warfare», «the only successful form of the war in the conditions of the Balkans», etc., etc. All these things gave rise to our suspicions that behind the idea of the «joint staff» he saw the possibilities of making this «staff» subordinate to the

Yugoslav staff, and hence, putting the armies of the Balkan countries under the dependence of Yugoslavia.

However, we could not extend this suspicion any further than Tempo personally. At that period it could not even cross our minds that it was the leadership of a whole party which had chauvinist and hegemonic tendencies. What's more, Tempo declared and insisted that the idea was «his alone».

Precisely these doubts which arose in our minds were the main reason that we never gave the question of the Balkan staff serious consideration. Meanwhile we waited to see what stand the other sister parties would take on it and what the «opinion» of the CC of the CPY itself would be. However, in the autumn of 1943 Tempo disappeared and his abortive plan along with him. The idea of the «Balkan Staff» was never mentioned again and much later we were to learn that the other parties, too, had quite rightly rejected it.

So, that is how this history began and ended in the summer of 1943, and as I said, after it had been completely forgotten, all that remained of it in my mind was the arrogant figure of the man of the abortive «staff» — Tempo. When he spoke and dictated in cut-and-dried phrases about what «havoc» his «dream staff» would wreak in the Balkans, it seemed as if the god of war himself had come down and arrived as our guest at Kucaka, except that the «god» we had in front of us did not launch thunderbolts and flame from his mouth and knapsack, but only orders and directives.

The custom of keeping notes, as accurate as possible, about the problems that were worrying me, about different events, about talks and consultations I held, I have had since my youth, but I developed it further, especially during the years of the war, even though the conditions were difficult. In this meeting, too, I remember that I jotted down, there and then, the main ideas which were expressed, having in mind that we might need them if we ever had to analyse the problem in the leadership of the Party. However, when Tempo was making ready to set out again «through the Balkans», he approached me and said:

«Comrade Enver, I saw that during the talks you kept full notes.

Unfortunately, I did not do this, because mostly I was speaking. Now I have to talk with the Bulgarian and other comrades. Would you mind giving me your notes to use in the meetings which I am to hold?»

«I don't mind at all,» I said. «But, first, they are written in Albanian, and second, they are more a summary of the ideas which were expressed here rather than complete minutes.»

«So much the better, because they won't tire the translators,» he said, and I noticed that his face was beaming.

Later I thought that these notes of mine would have been forgotten like the idea of Tito and Tempo itself. But I was wrong. Tempo kept them in the archives, in order to bring them out one day to add to the Yugoslav book of a thousand and one slanders a new slander: Enver Hoxha allegedly agreed with Tempo's idea! «See, here is a document in his handwriting»!

However, from the Serbo-Jesuit Tempo nothing but accusations, slanders and a series of similar immoral actions could be expected. As I said earlier, from the first moment we met him, the impression we formed of this person was not good, and four or five months later, at the end of July and the beginning of August 1943, we were to quarrel very fiercely with him. He came back to Kucaka again, just as haughty and arrogant as before, but this time, he no longer threw the question of the «Balkan Staff» on the table. He came, all fury and indignation, on another mission — to launch a heavy attack on the line pursued by our Party. He was together with Koçi Xoxe in whom, on the two trips which they had made to Greece at that time, he had found a soul-mate and they had become fast friends. (S.V. Tempo, in pp. 356–357 of his book «*Revolucija koja Teče*» (The On-going Revolution) *Memoari*, Beograd, 1971, writes: «After the meeting of the CC of the CP of Macedonia, I set out for Greece again. As on the previous occasion Koçi Xoxe came with me. This means that the two of us became 'experts' on Greece. After all friendship had developed between us. Although he did not speak much in the meetings with the Greek representatives, I noticed that Xoxe supported me, not only because of the fact that I was a member of the CC of the CPY, in which he had great faith, but also because of the fact that we shared the same views.»)[15]

His «introduction» was already a formula which we knew by heart:

«On my way back from Greece and since my route ran this way, I came to see you once more before I go to Kosova, Macedonia and Bulgaria. Comrade Xoxe urged me to come, too. 'Come on,' he said, 'otherwise the comrades will be put out'.»

«Comrade Tempo routed the Greek leadership,» put in Koçi Xoxe there and then. «What a debate, what a stern criticism! He really straightened them out! I invited him so he could tell you about it at length.»

«Why did you hold up the comrade on his long journey? Miladin [Popović] asked Koçi Xoxe. «You could have informed us about it if you considered it necessary.»

«Oh, I can never put things the way Comrade Tempo does,» protested Koçi innocently, «he did all the talking.»

Meanwhile, as if he did not notice what Miladin was hinting at, Tempo licked his lips, placed his briefcase on his knees and embarked on one of his usual outbursts. After pouring out a series of criticisms about the line of the CP of Greece (unfortunately he had grounds for criticism . . .), the rest of his spleen he vented on us.

«Why do I tell you these things?!» he asked at one moment like a pedantic teacher, giving us a «superior» look. «I tell you,» he continued, «because I have criticisms of you and your line, too. Your stand towards the Balli Kombëtar is incorrect, it is wrong.»

«How, in what direction?» I asked him.

«To put it bluntly,» he said putting on a very stern mien, «it has been and is an impermissible opportunist stand.»

«The criticism you make is extremely grave, it is an accusation,» I replied to Tempo angrily. «What is the basis for what you say?» . . .

After the fierce quarrel on political issues which we had at Kucaka, we had, what you might call a ludicrous incident with Tempo's wife Milica, who at that time travelled around with him as his secretary. Before he left, «the Balkan brain» wanted to take the only radio transmitter we had. Naturally, we could not give it to him. However, when Tempo was persisting in his request in a reasonably comradely way, Milica intervened and, in a somewhat authoritarian tone, tried to convince us that we had no need for it, while it was very important for Tempo. I lost my temper and I said in an ill-mannered way:

«You keep out of this. It's nothing to do with you, you are behaving like Geraldina . . .» [Wife of the ex-king of Albania, Ahmet Zog.]

She was offended and began to cry. I begged her pardon. Tempo tried to soothe her and told her: «Enver said it only as a joke.» So this incident came to a close.

The first British missions to Albania

Some time after the Yugoslavs, the British sent in their first S O E missions to Albania.

Between spring 1941, when the German occupation of Yugoslavia terminated operations by S O E's predecessor in Belgrade, and the Allied victories in North Africa in late 1942, Britain did little about Albania, except to commission policy papers; one of these was written by Arnold Toynbee – on the territorial dispute between Greece and Albania, which was rather cavalier about Albania's claim.[16] The first senior British official who seems to have taken a serious interest in enunciating a policy which would recognise the territorial unity of Albania was the head of S O E for the Balkans in 1942–3, Lord Glenconner.[17] But at the time Britain was too committed to pandering to the interests of Greek revanchists to follow Glenconner's recommendations.

It was not until spring 1943 that a decision was taken to send a British mission into Albania. The moving forces behind this decision appear to have been mainly two very different characters. One was a British woman called Fanny Hasluck, who had lived in Albania for over a decade prior to 1939.

She was allegedly engaged in anthropological research, in collecting flowers, butterflies and folklore, but in fact, as was proved later, she was working for the British Secret Service. Mrs Hasluck remained in Elbasan until the occupation of Albania in 1939 by fascist Italy. After leaving Albania, this long-time agent of the British Intelligence Service turned up in Cairo and served as instructor there for the British missions that were sent to Albania during the National Liberation War.[18]

The second moving spirit was the redoubtable Major Neil ('Billy') McLean, who was to become the head of the first British mission to Albania (May–October 1943).

Altogether, s o e sent some fifty British officers, plus wireless operators, into Albania between spring 1943 and Liberation at the end of 1944. There were four heads of mission to the partisan resistance: Major (later Lieutenant Colonel) McLean (May–October 1943); Brigadier E. F. ('Trotsky') Davies (October 1943–January 1944); Lieutenant Colonel T. N. S. Wheeler (January–May 1944) (de facto); Major (later Colonel) Alan Palmer (May 1944–February 1945). Brigadier D. E. P. Hodgson headed the British military mission after Liberation.

The first two of these missions were, in effect, missions to the whole of Albania, both geographically and politically (Zog's main supporter, Abas Kupi, was a member of the L N C until September 1943). On 17 December 1943 'Trotsky' Davies sent a formal recommendation urging the British government to recognise the L N C and withdraw support from the right-wing movements. This recommendation, unlike that sent (quite independently) by Brigadier Fitzroy Maclean from Yugoslavia urging recognition of the Partisans there, was not acted upon by London.[19]

In January 1944 'Trotsky' Davies was wounded by a right-wing Albanian band and captured by the Nazis. Thereafter the missions headed by Wheeler and Palmer were, de facto, with the L N C, in the south and centre of the country. In April 1944 McLean and Smiley returned to Albania, to the northern right-wing tribal leaders, along with Julian Amery. There they linked up with Major Alan Hare, the sole survivor on the spot of Davies's ambushed group.[20]

Thus, for the crucial half year from spring 1944 until Liberation at the end of 1944, there were in effect two different missions, pursuing different policies: Wheeler and Palmer, with the Partisans, recommended, as had Davies, that Britain recognise the L N C and withdraw support from Zog's group, the Legality movement, and from the Balli Kombëtar (so-called Nationalists), which were collaborating with the Nazis.[21] Throughout summer 1944 civil war raged between the L N C, on the one hand, and the Zogists and Ballists (members of Balli Kombëtar). But, unlike in Yugoslavia, the British government never made a firm policy decision for either side. In fact, while successive heads of mission with the L N C strongly urged London to back the L N C, McLean and Amery tried to implement an alternative and opposing policy on the ground, with backing from elements in s o e and the Foreign Office. So bad was the confusion in British policy that on 19 July 1944, as the civil war was at its peak, Churchill sent a sharp memo to Eden: 'Let me have a note on this, showing which side we are on. W.S.C.'[22]

Hoxha is thus quite right to claim that powerful British interests were opposing the LNC – and collaborating with known collaborators (which itself ran against official British policy). But, conversely, he is not accurate or fair about the policies advocated by Davies, Wheeler and Palmer, and supported by many British officers in the field (such as Tilman, Riddell and Hibbert).[23] These wrote favourable, but fair reports of LNC activity and political leadership. Hoxha seems not to have understood the reasons why they could not officially disown the activities of McLean's mission in the north, without higher authority.

There were also conflicting priorities as regards war aims. The main stated goal of the British and Americans, whose OSS mission, made up of Americans of Albanian descent, arrived later, in spring 1944,[24] was to defeat the Axis powers – first the Italians, and then the Germans. Hoxha's main goal was to achieve political power, in a liberated Albania. An additional goal of the British was to establish a regime sympathetic to Britain's policies.

It was clear from about the time the first British mission arrived that the Germans were going to be defeated anyway. Serious differences emerged between the British and the Albanians about priorities. German reprisals were extremely harsh (as were Italian) and it was by no means always clear that it was militarily, or humanly, advantageous to inflict relatively minor damage on the Axis forces and bring about severe reprisals on the civilian population. And, while the British wanted to destroy communications to deny them to the Axis, Hoxha argued that these were also the future communications of a liberated Albania.[25] It has even been suggested that there may have been a secret deal between the LNC (Hoxha) and the Germans to allow the latter to withdraw relatively unassailed in return for not attacking the Partisans and for not damaging the country's infrastructure.[26]

Above all, Hoxha wanted to defeat his Albanian foes before liberation. The British regarded this as suspect, or immoral, and at some stages cut arms supplies (the main bone of contention) back, or off, to try to bring the Partisans to heel – without success.

The Anglo-American Threat is designed to demonstrate that Britain, in particular, and the USA harboured malign designs against Albania as a nation, and especially against the radical forces – the Albanian Communist Party (ACP) and the National Liberation Movement, the LNC. Hoxha's personal account has been supplemented by a documentary volume, based on the official British records: *From the Annals of British*

Diplomacy, by Arben Puto (1981), which covers the years 1939 to 1944. Taken together, these two books constitute a unique attempt by a Communist leader and the regime which emerged from a liberation war to describe and analyse the role of Britain in one particular country.

There are several problems with Hoxha's version. The first concerns his reliance on his own memory. He makes a point of saying that he kept notes.[27] But some of the conversations, which took place in war conditions, stretching over 20–30 pages, are inherently rather implausible. Suspicion about their accuracy is strengthened by at least three factors: first, there are errors or misleading elisions (e.g., the suggestion that Major R. Riddell was in Albania before he had actually arrived);[28] second, Hoxha's willingness to rewrite history, and even commit two different versions to print, in the light of later events (e.g., accounts of Shehu written before and after the latter fell from grace in 1981);[29] third, several of the British officers whose conversations are allegedly reproduced by Hoxha have contradicted his version in ways which are convincing to me.

The second main problem with Hoxha's account is that he ascribes a unity and linearity to British policy which did not exist. Hoxha is on perfectly good ground in claiming that Britain, as a regime, had very little interest in, and very little goodwill towards Albania as such. But he suggests a unity of policy-making which the public record shows did not exist. And, further, he does not discriminate adequately between the views and policy recommendations of the different British officers sent into Albania, and particularly between the recommendations of the different British heads of mission.

Hoxha's views are starkly expressed in a passage referring to late 1943:[30]

What conclusions had I reached in regard to the activity of the British? Regardless of the fact that they were fighting against fascist Italy and Hitlerite Germany, regardless of the fact that they were allied with us who were fighting the same enemy, they wanted to weaken our National Liberation War, to weaken and, if possible, eliminate the influence of our Party, to recruit agents and spies in the ranks of the Front [LNC], and especially in the ranks of the communists, in order to weaken and destroy us, to create groups and factions, and thus prepare a terrain in which the British officers would make the law in the ranks of our detachments and turn them into «commandos» to carry out sabotage

actions and gather information in the interests of the British
Empire and to the detriment of the independence of our country.

Their plan was to get to know, to meet and link up with the
supporters of Zog, the heads of the Balli Kombëtar, with the
bajraktars and quislings, and together with them, to create a
military-political force in Albania opposed to the Communist
Party and the National Liberation Front. They wanted to have
this force, which they would lead politically and militarily, ready to
engage in direct fighting against us during the National Liberation
War and especially on the eve of Liberation, in order to seize power
from our hands, or at least, to force us to share power with them.

It was the sacred duty of the Party and of me personally, as its
General Secretary and responsible for the partisan armed forces,
to block, paralyse and destroy these diabolical plans of the British.
We were to carry out this sacred duty with complete success. With
its heroic struggle and revolutionary vigilance, the Party saved the
people and the Homeland from falling into many dangerous traps
which the British pseudo-allies were secretly preparing. The
British imperialists were unable to achieve any of their objectives.

Hoxha shows little affection for the first British head of mission, 'Billy'
McLean:

McLean, who presented himself as the chief of the mission,
seemed quite young, no more than 30 years of age, slim, . . . rather
tall, with very regular features, and a cold, intelligent, clean-
shaven face. He was fair-haired, with intelligent blue eyes, with
the look of a savage cat about them. As we learned later, McLean
was of the Scots Greys Regiment and was a trained agent who had
served in the colonial wars in Palestine and elsewhere.[31]

Hoxha's main attacks on McLean lie in his claims that, first, he intrigued
with the right-wing forces; second, that he did not come through with
nearly enough military supplies; third, that his mission tried to bribe
people in Albania. Towards the end of McLean's stay, he came to tell
Hoxha that the status of the mission was being upgraded and that a
Brigadier was being sent in.

I received him [McLean] in a correct but cool manner. The
British officer, on the contrary, was all smiles as he squeezed my

hand. He laughed, his eyes gleamed like those of a fox; he was intelligent, but he had a black heart. This time the cat had hidden its claws and was purring sweetly. I had formed the opinion that when McLean, the agent of the Intelligence Service, smiled, I should be on my guard, because his smiles hid perfidious aims.

I asked Bill McLean to sit down and offered him my tin of tobacco to roll a cigarette, although I knew that he did not smoke, and never touched our raki. He was continually munching chocolate, which the aircraft dropped him along with his personal supplies. Perfidious Albion had aircraft for such things, but when it came to dropping weapons to us who were fighting fascism, aircraft were not available![32]

'Trotsky' Davies was dropped in with a large support group and supplies in late October 1943. The Nazis had by now taken over the occupation of Albania from the Italians after the latter's surrender to the Allies. Hoxha here describes his first meeting with Davies, which took place at Labinot, near Elbasan, on 31 October 1943.[33]

General Davies came to the meeting in the afternoon of October 31, right on time. He was accompanied by his chief of staff, Colonel Nicholls.[34] I shook hands with him and asked:

«*How are you? How do you feel in Albania?*» I said this in English, because, when I was in the Lyceum I had learned a little English . . .

The General smiled and said to me:

«*I didn't know you spoke English, you speak it . . .*»

«Your information is correct, I don't speak English,» I interrupted him, «but these are a few words I remember from my secondary school days. I speak French. We can speak in the language of Voltaire if you know it.»

He replied with a laugh:

«I have read Voltaire but I don't know the language.»

Davies was a middle-aged man, a bit portly, with a round face and a bulbous red nose (apparently he liked his whisky). His eyes were not as hard and cunning as McLean's. He laughed frequently and knew how to conceal his thoughts and feelings. The most hard-worked word of his vocabulary was «I». He was wearing battledress with gaiters and heavy tan winter boots. He had on a thick khaki field jacket like those they had dropped us for the partisans. On his head he wore a black beret with an RAF badge and there were two or three medal ribbons on his jacket. He was carrying a stick, a real walking stick and not one of those fancy batons British officers like to carry. As to his age, he must have been well on in his fifties.[35]

«Brigadier Davies», I said, «you are the honoured representative of one of our allies, Britain, in the war against the Italian fascists and the German Nazis, and I am eager to hear what you have to say to us.»

«First of all,» began the General, «I want to pay homage to the fight of the Albanian patriots who have voluntarily sacrificed their comfort, their property and their lives for their cause. The Allied Powers consider the Albanian movement, along with the movements of other peoples, of great importance, especially in the Balkans.»

Then, assuming a grave pose, as if to say, «Look with whom you have to do», he continued in a pompous tone:

«I am happy that I was chosen to head the Allied mission . . . I was chosen on the basis of my past as a soldier. (What irony! He might as well have said for merits in suppressing the liberation movement against the British colonial yoke in Mesopotamia and Palestine.) In London and in Cairo I have had discussions with senior officers and leading statesmen. Churchill himself would have met me when I was preparing to leave for here, had he not been at the Quebec Conference . . .»

In order to cut short this arrogant prattle, I interrupted [him. Hoxha talks about the need for cooperation].

«I'm a soldier and not a politician,» said Davies. «Indeed, I must say that I'm not involved in politics at all, because as you know, Mr Hoxha, our army is apolitical.»

«I've heard this from your colleague also,» I said, «but it would be better to say that you try 'to keep the soldier outside politics', or more correctly, to ensure that he unquestioningly carries out the policy of his officers, who are not apolitical, but loyally follow the policy of their government. Excuse me, I don't mean to offend you,» I said to Davies, «but what you said cannot be true anyway, because military questions cannot be separated from political questions. As a soldier, you must know the famous statement of Clausewitz of Prussia on this problem, because he was a soldier, too: 'War is the continuation of politics with other means'. In any case, . . . you will see for yourself that politics are linked very closely with the war. Willy-nilly, you yourself will be involved in politics. It cannot be otherwise.»

General Davies smiled as he continued:

«You communists mix these two questions together. Of course, that is your business, but we British do not do this, because otherwise we would be accused of interfering in the internal affairs of others, while we do not want to interfere.»

«This statement pleases me,» I said. «Apparently the British Empire has changed its policy and this is as it should be, because now the peoples are awakening and the era of interference in the internal affairs of others is almost over. Nevertheless,» I continued without entering into academic discussion, «I'm pleased to note that General Davies and all the other British officers subordinate to him will not interfere in our internal affairs.»

I begged his pardon for interrupting and General Davies continued . . . for some twenty minutes. Then he got on to the main theme:

«I have been sent to you so that, within our possibilities, I can assist the war of the Albanian people who are our allies, and for whom we have always had feelings of good will. I shall lead all the groups of officers of the British missions in your country and they will take orders from me. I'm sure that I will have the support of the Partisan Command which you lead, and will be assisted to acquaint myself with the situation in the country, so that I can inform my superiors who want more complete knowledge of the situation here in order to be able to organise and co-ordinate aid for the Albanian fighters.

«I want to make it clear to you and I tell you frankly, Mr Hoxha,» continued the General, «that both in Cairo and London there's confusion about the question of Albania. There they are not really certain whether the war is being fought, how it is being fought and who is fighting in Albania. In London they say that the Zogites are fighting the war, some say that there is an organisation of nationalist patriots called the Balli Kombëtar, while others say that those who are fighting are communists, the partisans that you lead. I believe that one of the causes for this confusion is that our missions here are few, and thus, for one reason or another, they have not had the possibility to acquaint themselves properly with the situation.

«The reason that they have sent me here to the Partisan Command, Mr Hoxha,» continued this agent of the British Intelligence Service, General Davies with the RAF badge on his beret, «is to clear away the *smog* in London and send a ray of sunshine there from Albania.»

«You're speaking like Shelley, Brigadier,» I said. «It seems to me that your inspiration and the poetic phrases that you use have their source in the heavens, since you are an RAF officer.»

«Oh, no, Mr Hoxha,» he said, «this is just an honorary RAF badge which they gave me because I am a paratrooper.»

«Carry on,» I thought to myself, «I know none of what you're telling me is true.»

Brigadier Davies continued:

«While looking at matters from the angle of the partisan war, since I have been sent to you for this purpose, I would like, with your permission, to make contact also with the other anti-fascist currents which are fighting against the occupiers, for example, with the Balli Kombëtar, the Zogites or any other current, if such exists. You must understand that I shall do this,» continued the General, «in the interests of our common fight, but also in the interest of Albania itself. In this undertaking, I am guided by no interests other than those of the war against Nazi Germany. That is all I have to say, Mr Hoxha,» concluded General Davies with a smile.

«I have listened to you with attention, General», I said. «Now please listen to me. I shall speak at somewhat greater length, regardless of the fact that I am the representative of a small people. Our people, small in numbers, have fought during their whole existence. Your people have fought, too, but the wars of our two peoples have been of different characters. Our country has been invaded many times, but we have always fought the enemies, we have driven them out and we have never mixed our blood with them . . .»

I went on to speak about the regime of Zog and how the external and internal enemies of the Albanian people brought him to power.

«Under his regime the country was utterly ruined,» I continued. «Its independence existed only on paper and the people suffered every sort of hardship. Albania was completely dependent politically and economically on the Great Powers, which used it as a token for barter. There were very few schools, 85 per cent of the population was illiterate. The internal policy of the despot Zog was a policy of suppression of human rights, a policy of corruption, of the club and the noose, against any ordinary patriotic person, against anything new and progressive. Agriculture was completely neglected, and the peasants were exploited to the bone by most ferocious mediaeval methods. Hunger, disease and ignorance prevailed everywhere. Such industry as there was, was quite negligible – only a few workshops, where the workers toiled to exhaustion for very little pay. Our country was left without one metre of railway.

Later on, during the brief period when Davies was heading the British mission, Hoxha ruminates on the behaviour of the British. After criticising the BBC (fairly), Hoxha continues about Davies's manoeuvres in contacting the Balli Kombëtar.[36] This passage also shows Hoxha articulating his doubts about Mustafa Gjinishi, who had been on the raid into Northern Albania in spring 1941 with Oakley Hill and Abas Kupi. This extract exemplifies Hoxha's way of describing his own suspicions – a central theme of his memoirs.

Our partisan war against the Germans and their tools continued fiercely and without interruption. The BBC still remained silent about this war and churned out reports about the «war» that the Ballists and the Zogites were waging. The weeks and months went by and the British dropped us some automatic rifles, but without sufficient ammunition, occasionally dropped some clothing or a few boots, although these were often only for one foot, a thing which made the partisans laugh and say: «Apparently the British want us to march and fight on one foot . . . but we'll get by with our *opinga* [home-made greenhide sandals] with which our ancestors have fought.» The quantity of weapons, ammunition and clothing which they sent us was ridiculously small.[37] Under the pretext of supplying us with weapons, the British officers tried to get into our detachments to learn what forces we had, how they were organised, where they were stationed and where they operated and so on. But they ran up against a brick wall everywhere. All that the partisans would say to the British officers was: «Why don't you drop us weapons?» As usual, the British made all sorts of lying excuses.

The British officers asked for information on the German forces, wanted us to give them the emblems and numbers of the detachments to which the Germans killed in battle belonged, and we gave them any amount of these. They wanted to go all over the place, to check up on things, to make contact with our units and we, of course, did not keep them on a chain. We allowed them to travel through the mountains and gorges, but they were unable to learn what they wanted. They were always accompanied by two or three partisans, an interpreter and one or two of our trusted peasants to look after their mules. Hence, in this direction our comrades were very vigilant. However, sometimes the vigilance slackened and there were instances when the British officers sent to the partisan forces in Dibra escaped from their supervision and managed to link up with the chiefs of reaction in Dibra, for instance, Fiqri Dine and Xhem Gostivari, and even attacked our forces in Peshkopia together with them. I wrote a letter to Comrade Haxhi Lleshi,[38] instructing him to give the British a final warning and tell them that our bullets would make no distinction between the enemy and those who united with the enemy to attack us. Once again it was clear that the British missions were operating to assist the gentry against us . . .

Our prediction that they chose to reside in Biza, because it was a more suitable place from which the General could make intensive contacts with the British missions in the North and would have frequent contacts with Mat, Dibra and Central Albania, was proved correct. Naturally, we kept all their movements under observation — why should we hide this? — but what they talked about and what they decided we did not know. We watched and discovered their decisions during their practical application.

This is how General Davies worked against us, but we were not asleep.

Some time had passed since I had met the General, when Frederik Nosi[39] came one day and informed me that the General had told him that he had finally managed to contact the heads of the Balli Kombëtar and they had agreed to come to a meeting with him in Shëngjergj. «I believe that Lumo Skëndo [Mithat Frashëri, chairman of the CC of Balli Kombëtar], Begeja and some others will be at this meeting,» the General had told him. Therefore, he had instructed Frederik to inform our General Staff about this matter.

I told Frederik to transmit to the General that our Staff would put ten partisans at his disposal to protect him from any German attack, but the General himself must bear responsibility for this meeting with the Ballists, because he had wanted and prepared it contrary to the desire of the political commissar of the General Staff of the National Liberation Army. I instructed Frederik, who knew about the talk I had had with the General, «You must adopt a stand of indifference. Take command of the partisans, go to Ali Shtëpani and tell him to have his men ready for any eventuality, take up your positions, listen carefully to anything which the General may say afterwards, but give the impression that you are not greatly interested. If he tells you to transmit his words to me, tell him, 'It would be better to tell him yourself.'»

General Davies held the meeting with Lumo Skëndo and returned to Biza immediately. He told Frederik, «It was a fiery meeting and Mr Hoxha was absolutely right about certain things, but in the end I managed to convince them that they must fight.» And, as far as I remember, he had even received a document with this promise in writing.[40] Frederik had listened to him with indifference and told him: «The Balli Kombëtar won't fight, it is up to its neck in treachery, they are deceiving you.» Brigadier Davies did not ask Frederik to report to me, because I had told him that the talks which he would hold with the Ballists did not interest me. However, he knew Frederik would inform me.

A little later Frederik came and told me that the General had invited me and the comrades with me to go to dinner at his quarters in Biza. I accepted the invitation and in the afternoon of November 11, accompanied by partisans and taking Mustafa Gjinishi as interpreter and member of the Staff, I set out from Orenja. I arrived at Biza in the evening. There, in front of the main tent, I received a smiling welcome from the General accompanied by his adjutant, Colonel Nicholls of the *Coldstream Guards*, if I'm not mistaken. We shook hands and entered the tent because it was very cool. It was windy at night on that open plateau.

The General was comfortably set up in his field tent. Everything, from the table in the middle, to the upholstered stools, could be folded up for packing. The bulldog with the beautiful collar round its neck was curled up on his bed.[41] Dinner was a cold meal with tinned meat and fish, imported and local cheese, several kinds of local fruit, chocolate, English cigarettes, raki, whisky and wine. The General invited me to sit at the head of the table and we all took our places. He filled our glasses with whisky.

I said to him: «Just a little for me, because I've never drunk it before, but I shall do so in your honour as my host. Pour me a glass of raki because this is what my ancestors, grandfather and father have drunk.»

«You are conservative, Mr Hoxha,» he said.

«I cannot fail to favour the fine things of my people,» I said. «We must love our Homeland more than our lives. For instance, you, General, bring your whisky from Britain by aircraft.»

«Whisky is a very fine drink. I like it very much,» said Mustafa Gjinishi.

«Then drink it,» I said, «but watch out it doesn't go to your head, because I'm not going to carry you to Orenja.»

There was general laughter and we began a free conversation, but as the people say, the tongue automatically goes to the tooth that's aching. All of us were thinking about politics, the main problem was hammering away in all our heads, but we kept off it, because we knew we would quarrel, since on this our interests differed completely. First we talked about literature. I talked about ours and he talked about his. He knew nothing at all about our literature. The culture which I had acquired in France and the many books which I had read had given me some knowledge about a series of British authors.

«We're well acquainted with Shakespeare,» I said, «not only from school, but especially from the brilliant translations which our poet, historian and revolutionary democrat Fan Noli has made of his works.[42] Just as Fitzgerald made Omar Khayyam 'speak' English, our Noli made the great Shakespeare 'speak' Albanian.»

That night in Biza, with the north wind blowing, I talked to the General about the winter nights of *David Copperfield*, about the humour of Jerome K. Jerome, about Swift and Byron, Shelley and Kipling.

«You regard Kipling as a great writer, General,» I said, «but I hate him because he is one of your writers who sings hymns in praise of the colonial conquests of the British Empire in his works. I prefer your great Byron, whom the new generation of English people has neglected, preferring poets and writers of little value. I like Byron, not because I am a romantic, but because he sincerely loved my people, has sung their praises with pure feelings and has, as I have read somewhere, even named his daughter Alba, thus expessing his admiration for the Albanian people. As you know, in his famous *Childe Harold* he sings to the valour, manliness and maturity of the Albanians:

> *Fierce are Albania's children, yet they lack*
> *Not virtues, were these virtues more mature.*
> *Where is the foe that ever saw their back?*
> *Who can so well the toil of war endure?*
>
> . . . .
>
> *Their wrath how deadly! but their friendship sure,*
> *When gratitude or valour bids them bleed,*
> *Unshaken rushing on wherever their chief may lead.*

«These characteristics of our ancestors we have kept alive. We love our friends and welcome them with hospitality, while for enemies we have bullets. You, General Davies, are our friend and ally.»

The General bowed, smiling as he said, «*Thank you.*»

«Byron loved the peoples who fought for freedom. . . . Do you know, General, who were Byron's most faithful followers and his inseparable companions? Two Albanian bodyguards whom his friend, Ali Pasha Tepelena, had given him . . .

«We like Byron and we want the British people to love the Albanian people as he did.»

«You've won my heart, Mr Hoxha,» said the General. «I knew that you were acquainted with French literature, but you seem to be well acquainted with ours, too.»

«We Albanians, General, have a thirst for freedom and for knowledge. We have fought for them both through the centuries. We are fighting for them now and will fight tomorrow, too, if need be,» I said, and we both raised our glasses, mine with raki and his with whisky, and Gjinishi, who was deep in pleasant conversation with Colonel Nicholls, did not lag behind with his glass.

«Have you been through any military schools?» the General asked me.

«Yes, I have,» I answered.

«Where?» asked the General.

«I've been through the military school of my people, which is a school of great experience. You have heard of Gjergj Kastrioti, Skanderbeg,» I said. «He became famous throughout the world because he fought against the Ottoman Turks, against two of their greatest sultans. He led 22 battles and never lost one. Sultan Mehmet-Fatih captured Constantinople, but as long as Skanderbeg was alive, he could not take Kruja.»

«He was from the North,» remarked the General cunningly.

«He was an Albanian,» I replied curtly, understanding the General's allusion (to A. Zog and A. Kupi who were from the North, too), «and he was a prince who relied on the people. He loved the people and they loved him.»

«Yours is a beautiful country,» said the General, changing the direction of the conversation, «that is why Byron loved it. In England we have a picture in which he is portrayed in Albanian dress. When we win the war, Mr Hoxha, I hope you will invite me to come to visit your country,» said the General, trying to give the conversation a pleasant and intimate tone.

«Of course, you must come and get to know it well, because both our country and our people are marvellous. You must not be left with the outdated impression you have formed from the tendentious reports of British consuls who wrote things to your Foreign Office, which were not true and which had ulterior motives, or from the reports of 'collectors' of flowers and butter-flies, who in reality were doing other work. Of course, I'm not referring to scholars such as Miss Durham who travelled Albania, especially the North,[43] to study the life in the Northern Highlands and did not write badly about it. But the times have changed, General. The British Empire no longer has its former strength and power, while in our country, the power of the beys and the bajraktars is declining and the end of this war will put the lid on their grave.»

«Mr Hoxha,» replied the General, «it is true that our Empire is not what it was in Victorian times, but we are a democratic monarchy, you might say ... In our country we have free elections.»

«I know about your system of democracy,» I said, «but in that system the workers 'hold keys of straw', as an expression of ours puts it. It is democracy for the capitalists, for the lords, but not for the workers. When we win we shall establish democracy, but not like that democracy of yours. In our country there will be democracy only for the people, while the 'keys of straw',» I said with a laugh, «will be in the hands of the beys, aghas and the bajraktars, who have always oppressed and betrayed the people.»

«Do you mean you're going to take all their property from them, Mr Hoxha?» asked the General.

«Of course, General. The evil-doers, the enemies, those who have stained their hands with blood, will certainly be handed over to the people's courts, while we'll put the rest of them to work, to sweat and learn how tasty food is when you've earned it with your own toil.»

«That is why they do not want to unite with you, Mr Hoxha, because they are afraid of you,» said the General.

«They have good reason to be afraid. They know what they have inflicted on our people throughout all their existence, that is why they are afraid of us. Nevertheless, we and the people have appealed to them to abandon their course of betrayal. They have not listened and will suffer the consequences. In the National Liberation Front we have people from the wealthy strata, who are patriots, and we and the people respect them for their patriotic anti-fascist stand.»

«Mr Hoxha,» said the General, «I had a talk with Mr Lumo Skëndo and others and I spoke to them straight from the shoulder. I reproached them and said to them, 'As far as I can see, only the National Liberation Front is fighting against the Germans, while you are not fighting.' But they denied this, and all but accused me of being a communist. However, I persisted in my argument and, in the end, I believe I convinced them and they gave me their word that they would fight.»

«They'll fight against us,» I told him.

«Oh, no, Mr Hoxha,» said the General, «against the Germans.»

«In that case, let me assure you that they have deceived you. They have not fought and never will fight the Germans. Remember these words I'm saying to you. They will continue their betrayal of the people to the end, with weapons and every other means, in close collaboration with the Germans.»

Up till the time he fell in the hands of the Germans as a prisoner, General Davies saw for himself the fact that the Ballists and the Zogites did not fire one shot against the enemy occupier.* The traitor organisation of Lumo Skëndo and Ali Këlcyra continued their treachery at a savage level and that is why the British pinned greater hopes on the gang of Abaz Kupi, attached to whom were the wily officers McLean and Amery, of whom the latter, if I'm not mistaken, has been a minister in several Conservative governments since the war.[44]

With such conversation we passed the dinner with the Englishman Davies. About 11 o'clock at night we thanked the General for his hospitality, took our leave and departed from Biza. The wind had freshened and the rustle of the forest seemed to make it even stronger. Mustafa Gjinishi had a great glow from all the whisky he had drunk and no doubt also from that conversation by the stove with Colonel Nicholls, which seemed to have been pleasant. He volunteered nothing about what they had discussed, so I stirred him up a little.

* See p. 375

«Mustafa,» I said, «you speak English very well. It seems to me you've improved on what you learned at the Technical School. I don't understand English, but I have the impression that you speak it more readily and easily than Frederik. When you are translating I believe you translate my expressions faithfully. This evening you left me with Frederik and got the Colonel going. What did he say, Mustafa?»

«Oh, he was talking to me about the war. I asked him about the life and biography of some British generals and ministers like Montgomery, Beaverbrook, Eden and so on,» he replied.

«Both the General and the colonel seem good fellows. The General looks a bit dull-witted, but he finds the way to say the things he wants to. Anyway,» I said, «the important thing for us is that they drop us weapons and stop their propaganda from the BBC which attributes our fight to the Ballists and the Zogites.»

We walked together through the forest, accompanied by our partisans. The wind whistled around our ears. Our automatic rifles were slung from our shoulders. I had an American Thompson, which one of the comrades had brought me as a gift after an action against the Germans and the Ballists. We walked in silence. The combination of the whisky he had drunk, the enthusiasm seething inside him, and that night journey amidst the sighing of the wind in the forest, apparently encouraged Mustafa, who began to tell me about a proposal which the British General had made to him through the Colonel, that representatives of the National Liberation Front should go to London for talks with the British government.

... What Mustafa told me highlighted and confirmed my suppositions about the tasks and aim of the British General. Likewise, it proved more clearly that Mustafa Gjinishi was an agent of the Intelligence Service in the General Staff of the National Liberation Army.

The liaison officer of our Staff with the British officers had informed me about some questions which the General had put to him some days earlier: «How strong is the Communist Party? Does it have links with Moscow? What position has it in the National Liberation Front? Are the Albanian partisans linked with Tito's partisans in Yugoslavia?»

To all these questions our comrade had given the agent of the Intelligence Service the answer he deserved. So this was what the «soldier», who was not «involved in politics» wanted to discover!

He also informed me about the quarrels the General had had with Baba Faja[45] in connection with his «excursions». Baba Faja had warned him several times not to venture outside his territory, because he might strike some Ballist village and, if anything occurred, he would be to blame. However, the General had replied with great indignation: «Wherever I go is my responsibility, not yours. I shall go even to the villages where the Balli Kombëtar has influence without running into any danger.»

His meeting with the chiefs of the Balli Kombëtar and with Abaz Kupi, the questions he had asked and the «excursions» which he tried to make, spoke clearly of what this delegate of the «British Lion», who posed as a proper gentleman, really was.

I advised the comrades of Elbasan to keep General Davies and his staff under special supervision. I instructed Frederik to be very vigilant during their movements and meetings. I instructed the commander and commissar of the zone, who both knew English, to be vigilant, to visit the General sometimes, to encourage him to talk, but to give nothing away. I notified Mat, Dibra, Martanesh and Shëngjergj once again that the orders which I had sent them in regard to the British officers, remained in force. I personally went to Tirana and from there to Babë Myslim[46] in Peza. I inspected the forces of the 3rd Shock Brigade, talked with the comrades of its staff, ordered them to speed up and strengthen its organisation and to be in full readiness to go into action in whatever zone they were allocated to, as soon as I sent them the order.

Ammunition was short in Peza. The representative of the British mission there, a major as tall as a bean-pole, with a bristling little moustache,[47] was telling the same old lies that the arms and ammunition would be coming, perhaps today, perhaps tomorrow. I gave Myslim a sum of money to buy a little maize, salt and a few weapons. I held various meetings with the organisation and regional committee of the Party, summoned Gogo Nushi,[48] and the four of us, Myslim, Gogo, Shule and I, took decisions on the organisation of fiercer fighting actions in the direction of Tirana and the roads leading to it, on the question of supplies and on the dispatch of commissars to other units.

When I finished my work in the zone of Peza, I went up . . . [to] Elbasan . . . I saw that morale was very high everywhere.

On November 28, 1943, I went to Shëngjergj of Tirana district to take part in the ceremony of the formation of the 2nd Shock Brigade. General Davies had come there, too, on the invitation of our General Staff. With his own eyes he saw how poorly the partisans were clothed and armed, and also saw their enthusiasm, drive and determination on the course on which the Party was leading them. But with his miserable bourgeois spirit he was completely unmoved. My patience ran out and I said to him:

« You see, Mister Representative of the Allied mission, very few of them have great-coats, and nearly all of them are without boots, have only sandals made of old tyres or greenhide. Winter is coming and great battles await them. As you see, they are poorly armed, too. You are dropping us nothing. What are you doing about all those promises? »

« I've told you before, » he replied. « We are not going to supply you with clothing and armaments as long as you are fighting amongst yourselves. »

Boiling with indignation I no longer cared what I said to him. I went so far as to warn him: « Either keep your promises or clear out! » In the face of my protest which was an expression of the anger of all the comrades, of all the partisans, the General felt himself in a very tight spot.

In December 1943 the Germans launched a major assault designed to trap the LNC high command (known as the Shtab) and the leadership of the British mission. This is Hoxha's account of the penultimate stages of the march with 'Trotsky' Davies and his number two, Colonel Arthur Nicholls. There is a parallel account of this episode in Davies' auto-biography, *Illyrian Venture*.[49] In fact, Hoxha and the Shtab did manage to break out of the encirclement, and Davies and his group who broke away were ambushed. Davies was wounded and captured. Nicholls escaped with Alan Hare, but died soon thereafter of gangrene and complications. Hare, although suffering from frostbite, survived.

On the march, Davies says to Hoxha:

«Have a mouthful to warm yourself up, Mr Hoxha!» He and his colonel were continually munching chocolate. By way of a joke I said to him:

«Don't eat it all at once, General, because nobody knows how long the partisans' road may be. See, we don't eat on the march.» In fact we had nothing to eat.

When we reached the forest of Qarrishta, the vanguard informed us that we could go no further [in that direction] . . . The Ballist çetas of Aziz Biçaku and others were on the alert and had blocked all the roads, passes and tracks. We had no option but to turn back towards Okshtun.

I informed the General, who had lagged behind, that we could not go on because of the Ballist-German armed reaction and that we had to change course. Apparently the British General had run out of patience, lost his temper and begun to be frightened. He sent his orderly to me to say that the General wanted me to wait so that he could talk to me.

. . . The General came, accompanied by Frederik [Nosi].

«He's angry and scared to death,» Frederik told me.

«We are giving him some bitter medicine to swallow,» I said.

As soon as he arrived, I explained quietly that we could not get through in this direction.

«We shall return to our starting-point and get out in some other direction,» I explained.

«I'm losing my patience, Mr Hoxha,» said the General, red-faced and angry.

«It seems you have forgotten the advice that Kipling gives his son in one of his poems: 'If you can keep your head when all about you are losing theirs . . . You will be a man, my son!' Why have you lost your patience?» I asked.

«We have been all these days and nights in the darkness and the snow which remind me of nights in the mountains of Scotland, roaming through mountains and forests and making no headway.»

«This is war, General,» I continued, «our road is not strewn with rose petals.»

«But I want to break through, to get out of this,» he persisted.

«Where will you go?» I asked. «Will you go alone? What impels you to go?»

The General replied angrily:

«I do not account for what I do to anyone except my superiors.»

I said to him calmly:

«I do not want you to render account to me, but you must understand that we are allies. You have been sent to our Staff and we're responsible for your safety. Whatever occurs must occur to us together, but I assure you that nothing will occur.»

«No,» said the General haughtily, «I shall go to Korça without you.»

«You may want to do so, but I shall not allow it,» I said.

«Why, am I your prisoner?» exclaimed the General raising his voice.

«No, you are not our prisoner, but you are our ally and friend and I cannot allow the Germans to kill you.»

«Since I am not your prisoner and am a representative of Great Britain, I shall go even without your permission,» the General replied.

«Keep your temper, General», I said, «if you put the question in this way, I shall not stop you from going, but only on certain conditions: you must give me a signed document which says that you yourself took the responsibility and left the General Staff of the National Liberation Army without the approval and against the desire of me and our Staff. I am certain that you are going to your death or captivity, therefore I cannot allow you to take Frederik or any other partisan, because I am responsible to the people for the safety of their sons.»

The General was taken aback and, seeing no way out, snorted furiously:

«I shall issue no such document, Mr Hoxha. As anyone can see, it is all up with you. You are lost. The Germans have staged a big, co-ordinated offensive and your forces have been routed. Now there is nothing for it except for us to leave and you to surrender. But your eyes are blinded and you can see nothing. You have no hope; you have lost the war, you are encircled and are left with only two courses: either to kill yourselves or to surrender.»

This was too much for my self-control. I jumped to my feet (Frederik stood up, too) and I said:

«Listen, General! What you have dared to say is the culmination of your treachery and villainy. However, you should know that we shall not surrender and don't think that we have lost the war. We have treated you as allies, but apparently you do not want those who fight fascism as allies. We shall continue our war to total victory. You will have to answer for the betrayal you are committing against our people's war. You are deserting under fire and you know what awaits deserters in the army. Apart from anything else they are called traitors. What you're about to do is deserting under fire, betrayal.

«Who has lost the war? Who should surrender, we? Never! You General are a defeatist, a capitulationist. The Albanian partisans have not lost any war and will not do so ... Do you think, General, that the partisans are in despair because they have to stay in the forests? You are wrong. Our whole existence has been ceaseless war against the enemy ... We are masters of these mountains and these forests and also of houses within the cities. And you advise us to surrender because we have allegedly lost the war?! ... This is an insult to us, General. The Albanian will never tolerate insults. Excuse me, but it seems to me that you have lost your sense of logic.»

The General looked crest-fallen. He stood up, told Frederik to tell me that he begged my pardon and had not intended to insult us and went off to rejoin his group with a nod of his head to me. I returned his nod equally coldly.

I gathered up the comrades and related to them what had happened. «He got what he deserved,» they all said unanimously.

We set out again. The General and his suite followed a little behind us.

Heavy snow continued to fall. It was bitterly cold. The north wind was like a whiplash on our faces. We made slow progress. In the middle of the forest we made a longer stop under the shelter of a tree. As was his custom, Koleka sliced up a loaf and gave each of us a slice of bread and an onion. We ate the food and started out again. The snow was falling so thickly that we could not find the path to Studa Flat. We wandered for hours in the forest and suddenly found ourselves back in the place we had stopped to eat, because we saw the onion skins. Our «guide», who had beaten his breast boasting that he knew «every inch» of the terrain, had lost his bearings, but as usual he tried to avoid admitting it. Then we took the situation in hand ourselves and, using a map and a compass, after many wearisome efforts at last managed to find our bearings. In the end we struck the right road, but the snow continued relentlessly. Night overtook us before we reached Studa Flat. We had been on the march for more than ten hours.

Suspicion: The case of Mustafa Gjinishi

Mustafa Gjinishi had accompanied Abas Kupi and the Kryezius on the big raid into the north early in 1941. Subsequently, he became one of the leaders of the LNC, and was one of the representatives of the LNC at the important meeting at Mukje (or Mukaj) on 1–2 August 1943. At Mukje the LNC, whose chief delegate was Ymer Dishnica, signed an agreement with the right-wing Balli Kombëtar for a united front.[50] Immediately afterwards, Hoxha repudiated the agreement, charging that the LNC delegates had gone beyond their mandate. This is by no means certain. A plausible alternative interpretation is that the LNC delegates interpreted their mandate accurately, but that pressure was brought to bear on Hoxha by the Yugoslavs.

This passage shows Hoxha working away at his own suspicions and is fairly typical of his approach to an issue which preoccupied him during his entire time at the top of the Party.

Mustafa Gjinishi . . . was a clever, dynamic, active fellow, but conceited, wary with us and insincere. He spoke with gestures as though to give himself authority. He wanted to show that he had links and great influence with Myslim Peza, as well as with many circles of «nationalists» and anti-fascists, and gave the impression that his words and advice were listened to in those circles. He told us nothing concrete. Where and who these «bases and suppor- ters» of his were, we discovered later.

Allegedly illegal, he went all over Tirana wearing dark glasses and a blue suit, sometimes with a felt hat, sometimes wearing plus-fours and a cap and a white gabardine coat, and carrying a black satchel containing papers, a Turkish revolver and two Yugoslav grenades . . . He had meetings with a great mixture of people, including beys, some of whom had declared their links with the occupiers, others who had not done so at that time, and some other «candidates», «sympathizers» with the movement, some of them inveterate and resolute anti-communists. Mustafa told us very little about what he discussed, and what intrigues he hatched up with them, even later when the Party was formed, and indeed, even after we admitted him as a member of the Party.

Mustafa Gjinishi was continually asking the comrades and me to put him into the Party. The comrades said to him: «You have to get the approval of Enver with whom you have contact, because he alone can make the recommendation.» However, I hesitated.

«Mustafa,» I said to him one day, «you have positive aspects, but you also have many negative aspects, which I have continually pointed out to you, as a comrade. The Party wants modest, sincere, disciplined people. If you give me your word that you will correct yourself, I shall give you my recommendation.» He said that he would do so and promised that he would keep his word.

Thus, Mustafa Gjinishi was admitted as a party member in the organisation of Peza.

After having secured admission to the Party, Mustafa Gjinishi set to work to climb in its leadership!

In one meeting which I had with the head of the British mission, General Davies, I had Mustafa with me, to serve also as interpreter on this occasion.

When we were returning through the forest to our base, on the way Mustafa said to me:

«We are waging a heroic war, full of sacrifices and nobody abroad hears about it, while the Yugoslavs have a special station of their own which broadcasts, of course, from Moscow.»

«There's nothing we can do about this, Gjinishi,» I said. «. . . we have no Soviet mission here. Nevertheless, we shall continue the war and eventually the world will learn what a great fight our people, led by the Party, have put up.»

«That is so,» said Gjinishi. «These British we have here aren't helping us. Perhaps they have orders, but maybe they are just dull-witted and lacking initiative. They don't understand the great importance of Albania in the Balkans. We ought to find the way to interest the government of our British allies in our war.»

This alerted all my senses.

«I am a bit tired, Mustafa,» I said. «Let's sit down and have a cigarette.» And we lit up.

«How could we interest the British government? Have you thought about this?» I continued the conversation.

«We should send one or two comrades to London on behalf of the Anti-fascist National Liberation Front,» he replied, «to put forward our views there, our requests for arms, for aid, for propaganda only about our National Liberation War, and for the exposure of the Balli Kombëtar and the quislings, because we are getting nowhere with these people of the British mission and merely quarrelling all the time.»

In order to discover more of Mustafa's plan I continued:

«It would be difficult. These people of the British mission have presented us to their superiors as savage enemies of the British. I don't think it can be done.»

«If we demand it,» continued Mustafa, «these people are obliged to present our requests. Let's try it, what have we to lose?»

Mustafa Gjinishi was quite shameless! I understood this at the time he proposed to Myslim Peza that he should meet and talk with Qazim Mulleti and Irfan Ohri. Now he was proposing that we should send a delegation to London.

«No, Mustafa, we must not do such a thing. I don't agree with this idea,» I said, in order to avoid putting him on his guard. «Forget about it, because it would do us no good.»

«Very well,» said Mustafa, «but discuss it with the comrades in any case.»

When I met the comrades I informed them how Mustafa had fallen into the trap and related what had happened:

«The scoundrel! An agent of the Intelligence Service,» exclaimed one of the comrades, and in fact, he was not mistaken.

«Patience,» I advised. «We must not be hasty. We must watch him and get further proof.»

«You are still like Saint Thomas,» the comrade said to me.

«When I say that, I am not concerned about him personally,» I replied, «but I think we still need proof and facts to convince the circle of people around him, to whom we must make it clear what sort of a person he is.» . . .

These were the sort of things Mustafa Gjinishi did. But other even more dangerous actions of his were to come and these would fill the cup.

Every evening London broadcast messages over the BBC for the whole network of agents of the British Intelligence Service, stationed in Europe and other continents where fighting was going on. One night it began to broadcast messages for Albania, too. These incomprehensible messages were given periodically . . . For us the important thing was to discover to whom these messages were addressed and then to try to find out the content. When the members of the British mission were asked directly or indirectly, of course, they maintained a graveyard silence.

. . . One night, when several comrades and I were listening to the BBC, it gave another message for Albania. This time, if I am not mistaken, the message spoke about the figs or wild cherries which were «ripening». The message was addressed to Tafari. I sprang to my feet.

«What's wrong?» said the comrades.

«Tafari is Mustafa Gjinishi,» I said.

«Is that a guess?» they asked me.

«No,» I replied and went on to tell them about something that had happened in the past.

Shortly after we had formed the Party . . . we saw that Anastas Lula and Sadik Premte[51] were continuing their factional work within the Party and their sabotage among progressive elements close to the Party. Because of this we held the Extraordinary Party Conference in which we put these two in the dock and eliminated the «abscess», as is well known.[52] We had called Mustafa Gjinishi to attend this meeting, too, because he was not without involvement, although Qorri and Xhepi were the problem.

It was a long meeting in the home of Zeqi Agolli. We were all illegal. However, it was not easy to get the truth out of Qorri and Xhepi. Almost stupefied by the thick fog of tobacco smoke we were obliged to take repeated breaks to rest in the other room where, besides drinking coffee, we continued to smoke tobacco.

During one of these breaks, Qorri had sat down near me, hanging his head with his face like a cobra and smoking in silence. Mustafa came in, stood in front of Anastas and said to him:

«Qorri, tell us what you have to tell, because you are making us tired.»

Anastas raised his head, looked Gjinishi in the eye, slapped his thigh and said:

«Listen, Mustafa, listen you, 'Tafari'. Don't try to come the big man over me, because I've done nothing. Better confess your own sins which even a river could not wash away.»

That is where I heard for the first time that Anastas Lula called Mustafa Gjinishi «Tafari». I gave it no importance, because the name Ras Tafari or Hailé Selassié had become familiar to us at the time of the war in Abyssinia.

However, when the BBC mentioned the name «Tafari» in its message, my memory clicked at once and I made the connection.

«I'm sure of this,» I told the comrades. «We must call Mustafa and persuade him to admit it.»

«Don't be hasty,» said someone, «we shall certainly ask him, but we must act so that we get the bird into the cage, because there's a danger he may give us the slip. Now he has heard the messages, he may suspect that we are on his trail.»

During those days Mustafa Gjinishi was in Tirana. For some time he had been nagging me for permission to go there, in order to meet Cungu who had control of the trucks of a ministry . . . I sent Nako [Spiru], who was in Tirana, a letter in which, amongst other things, I wrote: «We are not happy about the business of Mustafa. The 'Mukje question',* and the leaflet which was issued, have made us think a great deal about the message from London for Tafari and the Albanian government which the BBC mentions, and which it regrets that we do not have,» etc. I told him also that these things ought to make them reflect a little, too, because the attitude of Mustafa seemed to me precisely the attitude of someone with a worry on his mind, who is constantly haunted by the fear he might be exposed. «We must check up on his connections and movements without fail,» I advised Nako, «hence, we must play our hand very carefully until we discover the dirty linen he is trying to hide.»

. . . We waited for Mustafa to return to Labinot. I summoned him to the room where I worked. It was a dramatic night.

* See p. 375

«Mustafa Gjinishi,» I said, «what was that message the BBC broadcast a few days ago? What connection has this broadcast with you?»

«I know nothing about it, Comrade Enver,» he replied very red-faced, and to give me the impression that he was indignant at this question, although he was unable to hide his alarm, he continued: «Why do you ask me? What do you suspect? I am a patriot, a communist. What sort of question is this that you're asking me?»

He was ill at ease and, like the wily devil he was, he tried to wriggle like an eel.

«Gjinishi,» I said, «tonight you are going to tell the Party everything, or otherwise I shall tell it,» and I reeled off one by one the things we had observed: the very cordial talks with Colonel Nicholls in Biza, the proposal to send representatives to London, the bag of gold that he had given Kaçaçi, and so on.

«Come on, speak, what have you to tell the Party?» I said in a stern tone.

Instead of replying he lit a cigarette.

I lit one, too, as if I wanted to take the conversation more calmly.

«Tell me how matters stand?» I said. «What connection have you with the British? What mischief have you been up to? Because the level of the punishment, which the Party will mete out to you, depends on your explanation of this matter. This has great importance for our Party. Therefore, explain everything to us.»

For hours on end Mustafa turned and twisted like a snake caught by the head and tried to deny everything. Finally, hard-pressed in the face of many facts, willy-nilly he was obliged to confess and, briefly, this is what he admitted: he said he was not a spy of the British, but had «collaborated» with them «for the good of Albania»! He had first made contact with the British in Yugoslavia, where he had met Lt.-Col. Oakley Hill. He had sent him to Albania together with Abaz Kupi.[53]

«My crime,» said Mustafa, «is that I did not inform the Party about this, and about what occurred later. The Party did its utmost to help me, but I thought and acted on my own responsibility and according to the decisions we took with [Oakley] Hill.»

«What were these decisions?»

«These decisions,» he continued, «were that I should organise the war in Albania with the patriots, and possibly also with the communists. You know something of my activity here, but you do not know that a certain Cungu, sent from London, entered and left the country secretly in order to make contact with me. I reported to him on the situation, my activity and what I intended to do.»

«What instructions did Cungu give you?»

«He encouraged me. He told me to continue on this course and opened the prospect that later we would have greater possibilities for work. In confidence, he told me that I should work with great care and persistence to make contact with Mehdi Frashëri and convince him to go abroad. 'Naturally,' continued Cungu, 'later we shall organize his departure and yours for London and there Mehdi will form an Albanian government in exile. With or without Zog at the head . . .»

«And what else?» I put in . . .

«He also gave me the passwords which you have heard from the BBC . . .»

This was the essence of the matter.

There and then I summoned several comrades who were in Labinot at that time and related to them all that Mustafa Gjinishi had told me.

After showing that we took a very stern view of his activity, I said to Mustafa:

«What punishment do you deserve from the Party for these things you have done, for this treachery in the service of a foreign capitalist power?»

«Shooting,» said Gjinishi and he took out his revolver and laid it on the table. «Let the Party make its decision, I shall wait in the yard,» he said and went outside.

After several hours of thrashing the matter out amongst ourselves, weighing up everything: the circumstances of the war, Gjinishi's social circle and acquaintances, the danger he represented, his treacherous activity, his arrogant, big shot character, his complete confession of his activity, we decided not to condemn him to death.

We summoned him and after once more listing all the faults of which he was guilty, one by one, we asked him again if he had anything else to say, whether he felt remorseful and whether he would give the Party his word that he would abandon this course forever. He replied that from now on he would remain «loyal to death to the Party and the National Liberation War». Then we told him that the Party was magnanimous and was going to pardon him once again, but that he must understand clearly that he must atone for these evil things he had done through deeds, through fighting.

Thus we parted with Mustafa Gjinishi on this occasion. However, even in the future he never became a good man, but continued his course of betrayal and remained an agent of the British.

This was a dangerous and diabolical activity which would have brought colossal damage to the people, the Homeland and our National Liberation War, if we had not cut all the threads of it. Nothing had escaped or would escape the vigilant eye of the Party. The British and their agents were not going to have their way in Albania as they hoped.

The Stojnić mission and Yugoslav pressure

At the end of August 1944 a new chief of the Yugoslav Military Mission reached Hoxha's headquarters – Colonel Velimir Stojnić.[54] With the exception of Miladin Popović, all the Yugoslav emissaries are described as double-dealers and intriguers. This passage about Stojnić embraces almost all the main issues at the heart of Albanian–Yugoslav relations in the period when Liberation was approaching.

First of all, Yugoslav advice/pressure about an alliance with the right-wing groups. Hoxha accuses the Yugoslavs of zigzagging on this issue, criticising the Yugoslavs for calling the Albanians too left-wing one minute and too soft the next minute. Hoxha also refers to a serious disagreement with the Yugoslavs about what action to take against the German forces as they withdrew through Albania from Greece. Hoxha claims that Yugoslav tactics would have blocked too many German forces inside Albania and caused unnecessary hardship to the relatively weak Albanian partisans and the extremely poor Albanian population. Another theme concerns Yugoslav monopoly over Albania's communications with the rest of the Communist world, and particularly with the Russians. It is a constant lament of Hoxha that the Yugoslavs blocked his lines of contact with Moscow. This is discussed in more detail below. While there is some truth to this, it seems most unlikely that this is the whole truth. But in order to stick to his own line on this, Hoxha has to write off the first Soviet head of Mission, Ivanov, as a Yugoslav stooge.

Finally, according to Hoxha, the Yugoslavs forced the withdrawal of Miladin Popović, considered too friendly to Hoxha. Simultaneously, the pro-Yugoslav elements in the leadership, headed by Xoxe, manoeuvred to get Stojnić into the Politbureau of the ACP.

The «Stojnić mission»

Velimir Stojnić came to Albania [at] the end of August 1944 as chief of the Yugoslav military mission attached to our General Staff.

«The task of our mission,» he told us at the first meeting in Helmës, «is, first, to transmit in a fraternal way to your General Staff the experience of the Yugoslav Staff in connection with big combined operations now that the German troops are withdrawing from Greece; second, to establish regular liaison between the general staffs and armies of our two countries, to examine the possibilities to co-ordinate our actions in large-scale joint operations in the future, and third, to assist in the further organisation of the sister army of Albania.»

Very quickly, however, from the first conversation with this colonel and his main aide Nijaz Dizdarević, we were to become convinced that their mission was military only in name, in its label and method of operation. Indeed, at the first meeting Stojnić himself told us that he had come also as «instructor of the CC of the CPY» attached to our leadership, but we did not accept him in this capacity and he quite openly expressed his annoyance. The truth is that he came for other «duties». Some of them, those most obvious and which, with the level of our knowledge at those moments, we could recognise most readily, we were to understand at that time. The others were to become clear later, when we went back again and again over all those things which occurred from the moment the Stojnić team arrived in Albania.

Time was to prove that, above all, the «Stojnić mission» was a special mission which was sent by Tito to Albania at the end of the war for sinister political aims, for sabotage and espionage. It came to organise the attack on the CPA and its line, to subjugate the CPA, to turn it into a tool and appendage of the CPY. It came precisely on the eve of the complete liberation of Albania in order to attack the foundations on which the new people's state power was being erected, and to prepare the terrain for turning Albania into the 7th Republic of Yugoslavia.

On account of the special relations we had created with the CPY, we welcomed the new emissary of the Yugoslav leadership warmly and whole-heartedly. He told us about the situation in Yugoslavia, the partisan war and the successes achieved under the leadership of the CPY and Tito. And we, too, at the first meeting, told him in a comradely way about the situation and successes of our army, about the Front and the new people's state power which was being set up.

«Some other day,» he said, «I can also tell you about the organisation and experience of our Communist Party.»

«We shall be very pleased to hear these things,» I said. «Ours is a young party and we need to know the experience of older and bigger parties and to exchange opinions.»

So, at another meeting, Velimir Stojnić talked to us about the CPY . . .

On this occasion, I, too, spoke about the history of our Party from its founding, about how it had extended and the successes it had achieved, etc., etc. As soon as I finished, the colonel threw off his «military» role and said:

«In fact, my main mission is military, but as a party cadre and on the special instruction of the leadership of our party, I shall also talk about party matters and everything else,» and assuming a very serious air, he began to make «criticisms» of us over our line and to list the «mistakes» which our Party had allegedly committed «continually»!

One of the «main» criticisms which Velimir Stojnić had brought was the allegation that the line of our Party had «continually» vacillated from right to left, and he did not fail to link the «opportunism» of our line with the criticisms of Vukmanović-Tempo. In fact, Tempo had advocated fratricidal war, had advised us to attack the newly emerged Balli Kombëtar and had criticised the efforts of our Party to win misled elements away from the Balli Kombëtar. For his part, Velimir Stojnić accused us of opportunism in our line and «proved» this with the fact that representatives of the General Council of the National Liberation Front held talks with representatives of the Balli Kombëtar in the Mukje village near Kruja at the end of July and the beginning of August 1943. At the same time, while describing Mukje as an «opportunist act», using the same «argument», he reproached us for being sectarian, because we had not continued the talks with these collaborators with Italian fascism and traitors to our people.

After listening quietly to this person (whom at that time we considered at least ill-informed about our line), I said to him:

«Not only are you in contradiction with yourself and with Tempo, but you force me to the conclusion that you don't know the situation in our country. You have to understand that the Balli Kombëtar is the front of betrayal, its chiefs are collaborators with the Italian fascists. From the moment that the Balli Kombëtar was formed our Party appealed to its members to unite against the occupiers. This was not opportunism in our line, but a correct application of the line . . . On the eve of the capitulation of Italy new situations were being created in our war, and we had to take advantage of them. To this end, we appealed once again to the members of the Balli Kombëtar to join in the war, both against the Italian occupiers who were on the verge of capitulation, and against the new German occupiers. The chiefs of the Balli Kombëtar responded to our call to hold talks and to decide what should be done later. We had our objectives and they had theirs. They came to the talks with us to gain a little credit after the great discredit they had suffered among the people, while, as I said, we set out with the aim of drawing the Balli Kombëtar into the war against the new occupiers, the savage German Nazis. If the chiefs of the Balli Kombëtar were to continue to play their old game this time, too, then they would be more thoroughly and finally exposed in the eyes of the people and would be abandoned by the misled elements who comprised the base of that organisation. That is why the Mukje Meeting was held. The delegates of our National Liberation Front had been clearly instructed that they were going to Mukje to tell the Balli Kombëtar to join in the war and that beyond this no compromise could be made with them. The chiefs of the Balli Kombëtar had their own plans at Mukje. They not only wanted to create a joint committee, but also wanted parity in the leadership of the Albania of the future . . . And the two delegates of our Party fell for the Balli Kombëtar's trap and accepted its demands, because one of them, Mustafa Gjinishi, as it is emerging, was an agent of the British Intelligence Service, and the other, Ymer Dishnica, was an opportunist. Immediately the Party learned of this betrayal by its delegates, it denounced it. Therefore, Comrade Velimir, I tell you that your criticisms of our Party and its leadership either of opportunism or of sectarianism are without foundation.»

«I insist that your condemnation of Mukje was sectarianism,» repeated Velimir. «You should have found the language to persuade the chiefs of the Balli Kombëtar.»

«Never! That would have been betrayal, betrayal of the Party,» replied Miladin [Popović] very angrily. «Had we done that the Albanian people ought to have lined us up against the wall and shot us. Why did this people and this Party fight? To share power with reaction?»

The debate flared up and went on for a long time. Velimir, Miladin and I did most of the speaking. Koçi Xoxe sat completely silent, but according to the argument, sometimes went red and sometimes pale, while Nako Spiru had no «chance» to engage in the debate: his knowledge of Italian had tied him up with the number 2 in the «Stojnić mission», with the clever and cunning Yugoslav Nijaz Dizdarević, to whom he translated what we said.

«I do not say you should share power,» Stojnić replied indignantly to Miladin Popović. «You ought to have taken part in the meetings envisaged at Mukje, this is what I want to say. Don't try to conceal your sectarianism. It is blatant!»

«In what do you see it?» I asked him.

«In what I said about the way you acted with regard to Mukje. But I have other facts, too. Liri Gega and Mehmet Shehu have made your sectarianism obvious. By what name shall we call what they are doing?»

«They have their own faults and we have criticised them for

these things and we shall look into them more deeply. But don't forget that their close collaborator, indeed, their inspirer in all their distortions and sectarian acts, has been your comrade, Dušan Mugoša.»

«Leave Mugoša out of this,» interrupted Stojnić, «he belongs to us and we shall look into his work. I am referring to your comrades . . . At Peqin Mehmet Shehu kills 50–60 Ballists from the villages of Lushnja, in the North Liri is brandishing a naked sword.»

«You seem to be well-acquainted with our situation!» I said with obvious sarcasm.

«I believe I am! Indeed, I know it very well!» replied Velimir Stojnić arrogantly.

«Comrade colonel!» I put in in a stern tone there and then. «We are friends and comrades, we respect and honour your party and fraternal people, but excuse me, it seems to me you are going beyond your military authority, either as a delegate of the Yugoslav General Staff or as a member of another party. Your interference in our affairs is out of place and your tone is unacceptable.»

«We are communists, first of all,» he said backing down a little. «There is nothing wrong with our talking about these questions. I told you that I have special instructions from Comrade Tito to talk with you about these matters, too.»

«All right,» I said, «we can talk as communists, but bear in mind where you are speaking and why.»

«I beg your pardon,» he replied, blushing. «Perhaps I used some ill-considered expression, but you must understand, I say everything in a comradely way, for your benefit, because we are friends. I have no other aim. But let us leave this for today, we'll talk about it more calmly another time.»

We parted coldly although we smiled and shook hands. However, I could not get what had occurred out of my mind, especially the unexpected accusation of «sectarianism». A year earlier we had made efforts to win the nationalist elements and anyone else to the course of the war against the occupier and for this Tempo accused us of «opportunism», while now, when we had put the Balli Kombëtar firmly in its place, it emerges that we had fallen into «sectarianism». This was intolerable and I said to Miladin:

«I don't understand this. Do these delegates want to help us or do they want 'to catch' us, or saddle us with a 'mistake' at all costs . . . ?!»

Miladin forced a smile, slapped me on the shoulder and said nothing. It was a smile which I had rarely seen on the face of my comrade-in-arms and in hardships. In that smile there was despair, regret, and perhaps also suspicion about what the comrades of his Party were pouring out.

«Let us fight, let us fight and forge ahead,» he said, «and these matters will be cleared up. After all, Tempo and Velo [Velimir Stojnić] and the devil knows who else are neither the CPY, nor the CC of the CPY.»

«I wouldn't want to put that in doubt,» I said.

Those were days full of work, tension and most difficult and varied problems which demanded correct and urgent solutions . . . we were a government in action, a government which had power over most of Albania and from day to day this power was being extended to the towns, villages and regions which were liberated . . . In our way, we had the Anglo-American allies, who, like experienced political gamblers, played new cards day after day to lead us up a blind alley, and around us we had internal reaction which saw that it was losing its case and tried to create a thousand obstacles and difficulties for us. Add to this the lack of experience of nearly all of us in the problems of the organisation and running of a new state, add the marked lack of cadres, and the picture becomes more or less clear.

In the first days of September we had gone down to Odriçan, . . . and from there through many ceaseless contacts we led the whole country. The telephone never stopped ringing, radio messages came from all directions, the coming and going of couriers and comrades was uninterrupted. Sometimes, Velimir Stojnić came, too, for a «consultation», for «assistance» or simply to say *dobar dan* [Serbian, good morning]. He tried to learn everything and poked his nose everywhere. At one moment, when I was exchanging a couple of words with him in passing, the signals officer came to me and said:

«Comrade Commander! They report from Gjirokastra that they are going to blow up the Dragot Bridge. German convoys are approaching from the Drino and the Vjosa gorges, and the Dragot Bridge is a key point. They want your opinion.»

«In no way!» I told him. «Transmit the order immediately not to blow up the Dragot Bridge, but to defend it at all costs.»

«Where is this bridge?» asked Velimir Stojnić all interest immediately.

I went up to the map and pointed it out to him.

«Why shouldn't it be blown up?!» he exploded as if a wasp had stung him. «It's an extremely strategic bridge. If the German columns cross it that will open up a lot of trouble for you and also for us. Let the Germans be cut up and wiped out on the other side, otherwise they'll penetrate all through Albania and even into Yugoslavia.»

«Don't worry,» I told him, «our order is that between Kakavia and Hani i Hotit [respectively the south-easternmost and north-westernmost extension of the border of Albania] no German is to be left alive. And if some are left we shall pursue them, hot foot, over our borders.»

«Then, why not destroy this bridge?!» he asked again. «Blowing it up would greatly hinder their penetration . . .»

«Because the time has come when we need the bridges. A good many of them have been and are being blown up by the Germans and the officers of the British missions are astoundingly zealous about blowing up many others. But now that our military forces have all our roads and gorges and mountains under control, to blow up the bridges means to blow up the property of the people in power. You don't realise that the Dragot Bridge is a strategic point for our operations. As to stopping the enemy columns, I must tell you that the Këlcyra Gorge is near the bridge and our forces have made it impassable for the Germans.»

The chief of the Yugoslav military mission went away displeased. One of [his tasks] was to «influence» us so that during this period we would engage the maximum number of German units which were deployed in Albania, or those withdrawing from Greece, in battle on our territory, and hence, not permit the penetration of Nazi forces into Yugoslavia . . . Albania remained the only «door» for their withdrawal. Hence, through this «division of doors» the mortally wounded Nazi beast was to pour its final ferocity on our territories and forces.

. . . How did Velimir Stojnić and his associates begin their work? They divided their roles. Velimir posed as «competent» on the organisation of the army, the party, the state, the security service, education, culture, etc. In a word, he was «a great brain» and it was «a great favour» that the Communist Party of Yugoslavia did our Party by sending such a man to give us «experience».

For his part, Nijaz Dizdarević was a real fox: clever, but evil and a dyed-in-the-wool intriguer. The things he knew, he knew thoroughly and expressed well. He had been charged to work with our youth and to organise them in resistance against the Party, if it opposed the implementation of the diabolical plans of the Yugoslavs. Nijaz Dizdarević not only became the *éminence grise* of Nako Spiru, but he also played on people's «heart strings» in the interests of the Yugoslav U D B. During the plot, he «fell in love» with a member of the plenum of the Central Committee of our Party, promised to marry her and, when he had gathered all the information he needed, cleared off and left her.

A few days before the arrival of the «Stojnić mission», a Soviet major, Ivanov, had also come to Helmës. As can be imagined, we welcomed him with open arms and with all the honours befitting the representative of the glorious army of Stalin. But it was regrettable that Major Ivanov should represent such an army as the Red Army. He was a clever, cunning type, and as became apparent later, he, too, had come on a military mission, as well as on other «special» missions. I well remember how he sat the whole day near the stairs waiting for Colonel Stojnić, and the fact is that Ivanov was «informed» about Albania and us, its fighters, in the light in which Stojnić described us. Regrettably the Soviet Union was being informed about Albania through the eyes of Stojnić, and not only on the eve of liberation, but also for several years afterwards the Soviets were «acquainted» with us through the tales that Tito, Kardelj, Djilas and others concocted. At every opportunity Major Ivanov continually boosted Velimir Stojnić and Nijaz Dizdarević to «convince» us that «the two Yugoslav comrades have ability». In reality, however, Velimir Stojnić was a young ass, a very ordinary person, who had learned a few formulas by rote and could speak only about them, apart from the instructions which they had given him and which he would draw from his briefcase and quote time after time.

. . . When he saw that Miladin [Popović], as a Yugoslav, did not support them in the criticisms they made, but, on the contrary, opposed them, he sought to remove him from the scene and to isolate me from the comrades in order to attack me more easily . . . We were still at Odriçan when he managed to get rid of Miladin. He passed on to him Tito's order that «Miladin should return as quickly as possible to Yugoslavia and present himself to report».

At first to avoid upsetting me, [Miladin] did not tell me the truth.

«But why precisely at these moments?!» I asked him. «Just a few more weeks and Albania will be liberated. Let us enter Tirana together once more, not illegally, with bombs and pistols in our pockets, as in 1941 and 1942, but freely, as victors, then you can go. I'll gather the people and say to them: 'You see this chap. He is a Montenegrin, a Yugoslav. But he is ours, he's an Albanian, too. His name is Miladin Popović, we call him Ali Gostivari. He is our comrade, our brother, a communist who for four years on end, together with us and with you, fought and made sacrifices, grew up with us, and gave everything he had for this victory, for freedom. Now he is going away. All of you should kiss him and wish him good-bye!'» As I said this Ali Gostivari wept.

«Listen,» I said, «you have to stay a few more weeks to see freedom!»

«I want to so badly, Enver, but . . . I have to go. This is the order from my centre.»

I sensed that he was hiding something from me. I met Stojnić and asked him in the name of our leadership to intervene with his leadership to postpone the order.

«That cannot be done,» said Velimir Stojnić, cold and inexorable. «Comrade Tito issues an order only once.»

. . . Before he left, Miladin was strolling thoughtfully. I caught up with him and when we were approaching the church square in Odriçan he put his arm round my shoulders and said to me:

«Enver, I didn't tell you yesterday because I didn't want to add to your distress, but you ought to know. I'm going because I'm forced to do so in Tito's name. They're not pleased with my work. But I tell you one thing: this Velimir Stojnić and Nijaz Dizdarević are behaving like enemies. Watch out for them! I only hope that I reach Yugoslavia alive and I'm able to meet Tito, because I'm not going to keep quiet and let them go undenounced.»

So they removed Miladin.

Immediately after this a meeting of the Political Bureau was convened.

As soon as we began the meeting of the Political Bureau, Koçi Xoxe got up and said:

«I propose we should invite the delegate of the Yugoslav leadership, Comrade Stojnić, to take part in this meeting.»

Ramadan Çitaku[55] and I, and at first Liri Gega, too, totally opposed this. Nako Spiru was in solidarity with Koçi Xoxe. The meeting of the Bureau about the most important current and future problems suddenly became a battle of words:

«He is chief of the military mission,» said Ramadan Çitaku, «why should he come to the Bureau?»

«He is the representative of a sister army and a sister party!» put in Koçi Xoxe.

«Then let us call Ivanov, too,» I replied. «Indeed, according to this logic,» I added sarcastically, «we should even invite the Englishman as an observer, he is our ally . . .»

Tempers blazed and this was completely unexpected and astonishing to me. Never before had such a scene occurred. Since we were failing to agree, it was proposed to put the matter to the vote. Unexpectedly Liri Gega raised her hand together with Koçi Xoxe and Nako Spiru. Ramadan Çitaku and I were left in the minority.

In this way Velimir Stojnić was given the right to take part, discuss and dictate his will in our Political Bureau.

From these moments begins one of the most unpleasant and gravest processes in the life of our Party, the process of the splitting of our Political Bureau, of «reorganisations» of it and «co-options» to it, and later, of upsetting the whole Central Committee elected in Labinot in March 1943.

Koçi Xoxe and Nako Spiru

Hoxha claims that the Yugoslavs, via Stojnić, relied particularly at the time on three key leaders of the A C P. The first was Sejfulla Malëshova, the leading party intellectual who was also one of the very few Albanian Communists who had been in Moscow before the war. Hoxha dismisses him as a vain megalomaniac and suggests that Malëshova considered that he (Hoxha) had usurped the position which should rightfully have been Malëshova's because of his Moscow past. Hoxha goes on to describe the other alleged two key members of 'the Stojnić faction'. His description of Xoxe acquires historical interest, since he was the main wartime leader who was executed after the break with Tito – and also, according to Hoxha, the person whom the Russians wanted rehabilitated in the 1950s after the death of Stalin.

Immediately after this, Hoxha records a curious incident involving his future wife, Nexhmije Xhuglini.

The other element on whom Stojnić relied heavily was Koçi Xoxe. He was an old member of the Korça Group, a small tradesman who was included in the group of workers because he worked as a tinsmith. At first he loved the Party and communism, but was cowardly, made no efforts to extend his horizon and to raise the level of his knowledge, was one of those few workers of Korça in whom arrogance and haughtiness were obvious and who remained, you might say, «illiterate». Neither he nor Pandi Kristo[56] made any effort to learn. Koçi Xoxe learned a few isolated things and all the time scribbled a few illegible notes which only he could decipher. Even these he did not write on normal paper but on envelopes. This was a mania of his. However, he did not need much paper, because he wrote little or nothing. Koçi was neither an organiser nor a man of action. He had a great opinion of himself and posed as being everything. His only merit was based on the fact that he was a worker and that is why he had been elected to the leadership and I respected him. I tried to help him, but I also criticised him, because he was not brilliant in anything – on the contrary.

The Titoites had been working on him for a long time through Vukmanović-Tempo, since he came to Albania and took Xoxe with him on his «Balkan» travels to Greece. As I said, at that time I saw nothing wrong in Tempo's association with Koçi Xoxe and agreed that they should go together to Greece twice, because of the additional fact that Xoxe knew the Greek language and originated from Negovan. However, Koçi Xoxe returned from Greece completely the man of Tempo and the Yugoslav secret agency.

All the time he was in prison we had respect for Koçi. When he came out of prison and worked together with me in the leadership we were disillusioned. We sent him with the task of leading the struggle in Korça; he kept himself busy with «the base and the rear» and concerned himself with the clothing that was gathered in Lavdar and Punëmira. There he was given every opportunity to work, to create and to organise, but he proved to be an undistinguished comrade of the leadership and made no concrete contribution to the work of the Party, let alone that of the army. With the conceit and pretensions he had, it was inevitable that he would cultivate a great internal discontent. Of course, Tempo was well aware of his spiritual state and it was well known also to Velimir Stojnić who took him over, worked on him, urged him in the direction we mentioned above and made him a weapon against our Party and against me personally. Brainwashed and inflated in this way, Koçi Xoxe emerged as one of the «persecuted proletarians» and «one of the men of the Party with a proletarian heart and great value for the Party». (Later, Ranković, the Yugoslav counterpart of Koçi Xoxe, did not fail to recommend Koçi Xoxe even to Stalin as «a leader with a proletarian spirit», «the most resolute» and «the most clear» in the leadership of the CPA (!), etc.)[57]

The third person whom Stojnić managed to win over was Nako Spiru.

Nako was unlike the other two from a number of aspects. He was intelligent, clear on the line, courageous and a good organiser. I liked and respected him and, after the death of Qemal, recommended him to replace Qemal in the Youth Organisation and in the leadership of the Party . . .

However, just as much as the other two, Nako Spiru was a petty bourgeois in his spirit and he had a number of very marked negative traits. He was extremely ambitious and inclined to intrigues. He had gossip and criticism, both justified and ill-founded, on the tip of his tongue. He did not fail to encourage those he liked to advance and to praise them, he was a person who played favourites and worked to fulfil the great desire he had to surround himself with people who listened to him, obeyed him and carried out the orders he gave. Nako was extremely inquisitive and rummaged around to discover the pettiest personal facts about anyone. Many a time when he came and told me petty personal details, which were none of our business, about this or that person, I was astonished at him and criticised him.

«Where do you hear these things, Nako?» I asked him reproachfully.

«I have my methods and my people who keep me informed,» he replied.

All these were dangerous tendencies for a communist and a leader and, apart from other things, as a result of these tendencies, Nako became involved in that dirty anti-party work which Tito's emissaries hatched up.

The Yugoslavs knew these serious defects and came to know them better. Velimir Stojnić and especially his aide, Nijaz Dizdarević, who was allegedly engaged with the work of the youth, fostered these ambitions in him and compromised him very gravely. They went so far that Nako Spiru was to send Tito and the CC of the CPY secret reports written in his own hand, reports which they used against him later as pressure and some of which they published, including those parts in which, while describing «the deplorable situation of our war, the mistakes and bad situation in the Party», he attacked me, put the blame on me and sought their aid to ensure that I was removed from the post of General Secretary of the Party. This is how far this comrade went in his anti-party work. The Yugoslavs, carefully studying Nako's careerist tendencies, his petty-bourgeois desire for power, his spirit as a carping critic, flattered his pride and ambition and encouraged him in all these directions . . . Nako was to involve himself with all his might in the plot, brutally trampling, not only on the Party, but also on the sacrifices of his own life in the 3 to 4 years of the war.

. . .Naturally, the portrait which I painted above of these elements could never have been made or even imagined with this clarity at Odriçan or even later when we went down to Berat.[58] Irrespective of those shortcomings with which I was acquainted, I considered these people as comrades and treated them as comrades of the leadership of the Party in every step and action which we took. That is why, when I heard the gravest opinions and accusations against the Party from their own mouths, I was taken aback and felt that I was facing a group of comrades who were placing themselves *en bloc* against the line of the Party and personally against me, the General Secretary. Naturally, I did not realise immediately that we were faced with an organised plot . . .

In this meeting of the Political Bureau in which Stojnić launched his accusations, Liri Gega took part, too, but it was her «bad luck» to be used by the Yugoslav agency as the «scapegoat». As I mentioned above, during his «service» in the region of Vlora in the spring and summer of 1943, Dušan Mugoša became well acquainted with Liri Gega, took note of her many weaknesses, especially her ambitious and careerist spirit, and kept close to her to foster these shortcomings in the interest of his work as an agent. To give the devil his due, Mugoša carried out this dirty anti-party work with Liri Gega and with a number of others in masterly fashion. The sectarian actions which were recognised and had already been condemned by our Party were, in the first place, the fruit of the work of Dušan Mugoša as an agent, in which his «pupil» and agent Liri Gega displayed obvious zeal.

For these things, Dušan Mugoša deserved the heaviest condemnation, but in fact he did not leave Albania under a cloud. On the contrary, after performing the role with which his leadership had charged him, by recruiting and fouling whomever he could, Duqi [Mugoša] cleared out and left our Party a «heritage» of «mistakes of sectarianism» which the leadership of the CPY now needed to accuse the leadership of our Communist Party of being «incompetent» and «sectarian».

But in order to make these «accusations» stick and seem to have a concrete basis, the Yugoslavs now had to «attack» their loyal agent Liri Gega, even if only temporarily, as «the embodiment of the sectarian line of the CPA». The wide-ranging attack which was made on our Communist Party was hidden behind «Liri's mistakes».

All this painful anti-party history was to take place during the months of October and November in the liberated city of Berat where we arrived, as far as I remember, a few days after the «platform» meeting at Odriçan.

. . .Two or three days later Pandi Kristo shoulder to shoulder with Sejfulla [Malëshova] and Koçi [Xoxe] and Nako [Spiro], linked together by Velimir Stojnić, were to rise as a solid bloc against me in the Bureau.

The second step of the «Stojnić mission» was achieved. The Bureau of our Central Committee was reorganised behind the scenes and now, in its composition of five members, four were obedient tools of the Yugoslavs . . .

My isolation became complete not only within the Bureau but also outside it . . . the day when the Plenum was to be held was approaching. I saw that it would be extremely difficult to determine the line and the tasks for the future.

. . . During one of these days . . . Nexhmije [Xhuglini-Hoxha] came to me. There were tears in her eyes and with a feeling of concern and despair which she was quite unable to conceal she said to me:

«How is this . . . right on the eve of Liberation you have apparently decided to withdraw me from the leadership of the Youth?»

«Why?» I asked in surprise. «Who told you this?»

«Why pretend you don't know? Nako summoned me and proposed that we take a 'walk'. We walked beside the Osum River and there he told me: 'You came to Berat for nothing . . .'»

. . . 'How do you mean for nothing . . . ?!' I asked him,» Nexhmije told me. «'Comrade Enver sent me a letter and at the end told me that in November the meeting of the CC of the Youth and the Congress of Anti-fascist Women would be held. I waited for you to notify me, but since no notification came either from you or from the comrades in the Women's organisation, I thought your notification must have got stuck somewhere on the way. That's why I came. Why, should I not have come?'

«'No, no, since you have come you'd better stay,' Nako told me, 'but you are not to continue to work with the Youth. You have been appointed to another important task as a member of the

Agitation and Propaganda Commission attached to the CC of the Party and now you are going to work with Sejfulla Malëshova.'»

Nexhmije told me these things and fell silent. I was silent for a moment, too, then I pulled myself together and said with a smile:

«Is that what you are upset about?! We have a great deal to do and we can't all be engaged with the Youth. The sector which Nako mentioned is very important, too, especially now that the Party and people are taking state power.»

I spoke in this way because I did not want her to learn about the great quarrels and splits in the leadership. I did not want her to learn about them, because they were extremely delicate problems and had to be kept very secret, but also because I did not want to upset and worry her when, from day to day, we were expecting the great news of the liberation of Albania.

Inwardly, however, I realised that matters were worse than I had thought. By not calling Nexhmije to attend either the Congress of Women or the meeting of the Central Committee of the Youth, Nako and company wanted to keep her away from me, because she might hinder them in what they wanted to do, might hear what was being said and inform me. This struck me immediately and I asked myself: What is this? Are they up to something behind our back . . . ?

However, I kept my mouth shut, because I could not accuse the comrades of such base activity. I was dissatisfied about their activities and stands and my suspicions were building up relentlessly.

British landings; Anglo-American intrigues and invasions

After the capture of Davies, Lieutenant Colonel Wheeler became de facto head of the British mission. Like Davies, Wheeler strongly recommended recognition of the LNC, and wrote of the courage and determination of the Partisans. Curiously, Hoxha omits all mention of this, although Wheeler's report is extensively – though somewhat inaccurately – cited by Puto.[59]

When Wheeler left at the end of May 1944, he was replaced as head of mission by Colonel Alan Palmer. Hoxha speaks well of Palmer, whom he obviously liked.[60] But Hoxha's account of conversations with Palmer, and with Palmer's liaison officer with the LNC, Captain Lyon, seem unusually inaccurate. Palmer, like Wheeler, supported recognition of the LNC and wrote to Anthony Eden, with whom he was on Christian-name terms, to beware of the views of 'right-wing' British agents like McLean and Amery.[61] Palmer stayed on as head of the British military mission in Tirana for a short period after Liberation.

Although McLean, Amery and conservative elements in SOE head-quarters were trying to keep the Balli Kombëtar and Legaliteti in conten-tion, it is beyond dispute that the LNC did the overwhelming bulk of the fighting against the Axis.

The Albanian regime claims that the liberation struggle began with over 100,000 Italians – and, later, 70,000 Germans – in Albania; that the Axis forces lost more than 26,000 dead, more than 21,000 wounded, and about 20,800 soldiers and officers taken prisoner. Albanian dead num-bered 28,000 out of a total population of 1,125,000 – i.e. 2.48 per cent (much less than Yugoslavia; but conditions were much more favourable to guerrilla warfare in Albania, with almost all areas except the main roads and the cities relatively inaccessible to the occupying forces, in an age before the helicopter).[62]

The Albanian Communist movement can claim two remarkable achievements: first, in exactly three years flat it advanced from the founding of the Party (8 November 1941) to liberating the whole country (November 1944) – a record. Moreover, within this liberation struggle, it also carried out a genuine revolution, in extremely harsh conditions. No less a source than Tito is reported to have remarked that Albania was the only country in Europe, apart from Yugoslavia, which waged a revolu-tionary struggle during the war; other occupied countries only produced resistance movements.[63] Second, the LNC freed the entire territory of Albania (except for the contentious area of Kosovo – and even there it played a major role), without any of the Allied armies making a major contribution to the defeat of the Germans on Albanian soil.

However, apart from the sizeable British contribution in training, arms and supplies (which were averaging 70 tons per month in mid-1944), the British also made several landings in Albania in the second half of 1944. Hoxha suggests that the British were trying to establish a bridgehead and perhaps occupy Albania, or at least exercise enough pressure on Albania to influence or control the complexion of the post-Liberation government.[64] He describes three British 'attempts' at landings, indi-cating that only two actually took place – both in the south. The first of these was by the Long Range Desert Group (LRDG), at Spile, near Himara. The second was by commandos, at Saranda. But there was also at least one landing by the SBS, the Special Boat Service (the naval equivalent of the SAS). And a number of agents were parachuted into the Tirana area just before the capital was liberated, at a time when the RAF was carrying out heavy bombing of the city.[65]

Hoxha puts a sinister construction on these events. The question is: is he right to do so?

In terms of background, it should first be said that Hoxha was writing when it was known that there had been serious discussion of a British landing earlier in Albania – at Durrës in 1943 – as an alternative to the Normandy landings, and specifically as a counter-Soviet move. Although some Western sources now try to write this off as a bluff or a decoy, there is strong evidence that it was reasonable for the Albanians to take it seriously. Recently published Yugoslav sources have claimed that the Yugoslav Partisans entered into negotiations with the Nazis in early 1943, partly to canvas the possibility of joint action against a British or Anglo-US landing in Yugoslavia at that time.[66]

The 1944 landings themselves are much more problematic than the scant references to them in the existing Western literature indicate. The first one at Spile, by the LRDG, an elite SAS-type unit, seems to have been a fairly straightforward joint British–Albanian venture to wipe out the German garrison, successfully. But the second one, at Saranda, in late September, is much more dubious.[67]

What the available records show are more than enough to justify Hoxha's suspicions. The first appearance of the Saranda landing in the archives is a rather anxious telegram dated 29 September 1944 from the Foreign Office to Bari saying: please report on reports that British have landed in Albania. Bari replied the same day: 'Operation referred to *started* [my italics – JH] as a normal raid on September 22nd ... The intention was to harrass [sic] the enemy in the area around Sarando [sic] ...' But, the telegram went on, because it appeared possible to isolate the German garrison on Corfu, the British put in more guns and troops on 24 September – 'and the plan [now] is to continue operations until Sarando is captured.' It continued: '... it is possible that if everything goes well we may be able to maintain a permanent footing on Albanian soil as well as in Corfu.'

The unequivocal threat contained in the above document should be read in connection with several other relevant factors.

First, a document written by the head of the Albanian section of SOE at Bari in October 1944 reports that the main problem between SOE in the field and Hoxha concerned (British) 'special troops', which 'have been infiltrated without their [SOE BLOS'] knowledge or consent'.[68] In other words, not only without Hoxha's agreement, but without the knowledge of the s o e agents in the field.

Second, the explicit call by s o e both 'to build up unobtrusively' pro-British elements and, if possible, to land sizeable forces: the key document of early November 1944 states flatly: 'the ideal means of turning to good account the pro British feeling existing in ALBANIA would be the introduction of British troops' – although it acknowledges this is unlikely.

Third, even more ominous, is overt British support for a US plan of August 1944 to split Albania in half and occupy parts of it.[69] The American plan recommends: 'Sasseno [Sazan] should be seized by the Allies at once' [italics in original]. And goes on: '6. At the very earliest moment American troops to the number of 5000 should be sent to Tirana and Durazzo.' Among the reasons given are: 'c. To forestall the possibility that LNC might . . . deny the right of the Allies to occupy Albania' and 'f. To prevent a too close integration of LNC with Tito, and the Russians.' The US and Britain were explicitly discussing intervention to force power-sharing within Albania and Western control over the political process. Hoxha was not wrong to see this as an early variant of Reagan's 'cry uncle' plus Contras.

After Liberation the British, along with the Americans, Russians and Yugoslavs, maintained a military mission in Tirana, the capital. Hoxha later charged that the British and American missions intrigued with opponents of the new regime. The full files are not open to document these charges, though they are inherently plausible. Especially in the light of the fact that senior members of the wartime mission to Albania – McLean, Amery, Smiley and Hare, plus Oakley Hill and others – shortly thereafter made a major effort to overthrow Hoxha's regime, by backing an invasion in 1949.[70]

Hoxha is surprisingly low-key about this, and devotes remarkably little space to it. Virtually the entire section is given here. Hoxha also suggests that Amery and company may have dabbled in another attempt in 1961, at the time of the break between Albania and the USSR. This cannot be confirmed. It has been denied to the author by a senior former s o e agent, but with the unsolicited proviso that 'We would have had a go if we could.' As late as 1982 Hoxha was claiming that yet another attempt had been made to subvert his regime from abroad.[71]

The Anglo-American military, civilian, and «philanthropic» missions broke their necks. However, the struggle of the imperialists against our country has never ceased.

When they were leaving Albania, the British officer Neel[72] and the American Henderson, declared: «We shall come back in another way.» And truly they continued the struggle in other ways.

The organisation of all the remnants of the Balli Kombëtar and Legaliteti in exile began under the patronage of officers of the CIA and SIS. The American colonel Herbert and the British officers Amery, McLean and others, who were charged with this task, found it very difficult. They understood that they had to deal with a pack of jackals and a herd of rabbits, but . . . it had to be done. Each of the heads of reaction in exile defended the interests of the employer who fed him. Right from the start they began to quarrel, abuse one another and come to blows. Nevertheless, a certain unity was achieved in a so-called «Free Albania Committee», attached to which a «military staff» was set up, headed by the «strategist» Abaz Kupi. However, the quarrels continued and the contradictions became more acute. In exile, the «crabs» were tearing one another to pieces. Quarrels existed not only between the chiefs, but also between the chiefs and the misled individuals, who got caught up in the current of betrayal and who had been promised «paradise» by the «fathers of the nation». They were beginning to understand what they had been reduced to and were beating their heads with their own fists. There were some who repented and wanted to return and a few did so, while the majority, poisoned by bourgeois demagogy, went even further on their course and ended up in the training camps to be used as cannon fodder in the interests of the ambitions of the imperialists and the heads of Albanian reaction . . . We made official requests to the British and American governments for the extradition of war criminals, not only Albanians, but also Italians and Germans, who had stained their hands with blood in Albania and were now under their jurisdiction. Contrary to the declarations and the joint commitments of the allies during the war and the decisions which were taken later on this question, they turned a deaf ear and did not hand them over to us. On the contrary, they kept the chiefs in luxury hotels, while they trained their «fighting men» in special camps and courses in Rome, Munich, London, Athens and elsewhere.

At first, they used aircraft to drop leaflets against us, which the people gathered up, handed over, or burnt. The imperialists did this to prepare the terrain for dropping in Albanian criminals by parachute or infiltrating them into our country through Italy or some other neighbouring country, to carry out sabotage, assassinations, etc. The imperialists had pinned all their hopes on these degenerate elements who, with a dagger in one hand and gold in the other, tried to intimidate our people or bribe them into becoming their followers.

Deceiving themselves that Albania at that time was the weakest link of the countries of people's democracy, the British and American imperialists tried to undermine our people's state power. They had not reckoned on its strength, which was based on the people, on the cleverness, determination, vigilance and swiftness in action of our organs of security and people's defence.

Blinded by their hostility towards our country, and having no accurate knowledge of the Albanian reality, the imperialists soon found themselves in great difficulties. As the criminals themselves testified in court, Oakley Hill, Stirling[73] and others reappeared on the scene at these moments when things were hotting up. We forced the captured agents to make radio contact with their espionage centres in Italy and elsewhere, hence to play our game, totally deceiving these centres, which showed themselves to be completely incompetent and short-sighted. Things went so far that they dropped us whatever we dictated to their agents who had fallen into the trap. The bands of the criminals who were dropped in by parachute or infiltrated across the border at our request, came like lambs to the slaughter, while the armaments and other materials which they dropped or brought with them went to our account. In a word, they came and we were waiting for them. We put them on trial and after all their filthy deeds had been exposed, we gave them the punishment they deserved. The espionage centres which sent these bands became alarmed and tried to alter their methods of action against the new Albania and its glorious leadership — the Party of Labour. But up till now, events have proved that everything they have attempted against us has run into a granite rock and been smashed to smithereens. History has the same fate in store for them in the future, too.

Our famous radio game, the wisdom, justice and the revolutionary vigilance of the Albanian people brought about the ignominious failure of the plans of the foreign enemy, and not the merits of a certain Kim Philby,[74] as some have claimed. Those who tried to bite Albania left not only their teeth, but also their bones in this sacred land. The security organs and our people's defence forces were always in readiness and, assisted by the people, crushed the criminals and assassins. A few escaped by crossing the border to carry the sad tidings to their mentors, while the others were crushed in the vice of the people.

Although the Albanian reactionaries in exile were reduced to a dreadful state, whenever the class struggle inside or outside our country became more acute, they raised their heads. Imperialism gave them the necessary injection and they reactivised themselves. This is what occurred after the betrayal of Titoite revisionism emerged openly in 1948 and it was repeated again in 1961 and later. Precisely when our country was fighting tooth and nail against Khrushchev in 1961, Abaz Kupi was invited to London and welcomed with honours by Amery, the British Minister of Aviation, by the MP McLean, the retired Colonel Smiley and the journalist Kemp,[75] while Amery's wife, the daughter of Prime Minister Macmillan, was present at every activity which was organised for Bazi i Canës [Kupi] by his old friends during his three-day visit. That same year, reaction prepared yet another farce: it «approved» the initiative of Zog's son to proclaim himself «king», and the Americans appointed General Blomberg and the British appointed Kemp as his aides-de-camp.

All this interference and pressure, the unscrupulous provocations, like that in the Corfu Channel,[76] the use of the veto against the rights of our Republic in the international arena, the holding of the gold, and many other hostile acts, are the continuation of the savage struggle which the American, British and other imperialists and world reaction have never ceased for one day or even one minute against our country.

2
FROM LIBERATION TO
THE BREAK
WITH YUGOSLAVIA

Albania after Liberation

By October 1944 the partisan forces were poised to liberate the whole of Albania. The Balli Kombëtar and Legaliteti movements had been both discredited and crushed by the Partisans. The Germans were in full retreat. In late October the Partisans took the town of Berat, in south-central Albania. Here the liberation forces held the Second Session of the Anti-Fascist Council of National Liberation. This body had first met at Përmet in late May 1944, when Hoxha had been elected president of a provisional democratic government. At Berat in October the new governmental structure was decided and issued an eight-point programmatic declaration.[1] Hoxha was elected national president and commandant of the NLA.

Immediately after the Berat Congress, the NLA, under Mehmet Shehu, launched an all-out assault on Tirana, which it took on 17 November, after twenty days of bitter fighting. Quite apart from the psychological and political importance of liberating their own capital, the Partisans thus managed to pre-empt action by the Western allies. The last stronghold, the city of Shkodra, in the north, was freed on 29 November.

After Liberation, the country was run initially by a provisional government, headed by Enver Hoxha, who also held the post of head of the Communist Party. The Anti-Fascist Council for National Liberation immediately issued a series of decrees, confiscating all German and Italian assets and instituting state control over industry and mining. An initial land reform was also instituted, and educational and other reforms enacted.

In August 1945 the National Liberation Front (LNC) converted itself into a political organisation, the Albanian Democratic Front, within which the ACP was the leading force. In elections on 2 December 1945, the Front candidates won 93 per cent of the votes. From this election emerged a Constituent Assembly which proclaimed a People's Republic on 11 January 1946, and abolished the monarchy. On 14 March 1946, the Assembly approved a new Constitution.

Throughout this initial period, the new Albanian regime behaved very much along the lines of the other 'People's Democracies'. However, there were two unusual features. The first was Hoxha's outspoken attempt to maintain good relations with the West. In a speech to the Youth Congress in April 1945, he paid fulsome tribute to the British and US armies, and to

Churchill and Roosevelt personally.[2] The second was that the Albanian Communist Party, even though it had manifestly led the liberation struggle and was the dominant force in the new regime, did not hold any congress or assembly. Hoxha later, and plausibly, attributed this to Yugoslav pressure, linking it to Yugoslav attempts to annex Albania and deny it autonomy. The Albanian CP was the only one in the Communist bloc which was not invited to join the Information Bureau, the Cominform, when it was set up in October 1947.

Hoxha's relations with the West broke down over the period 1944 to the end of 1946 over a number of issues. Apart from real and alleged interference by the US and Britain in the area of espionage, etc., there were two main issues. The first was the attempt by the Western powers to vet – and, Hoxha claimed, interfere in – the postwar elections and the general political process. In particular, the US and Britain charged that the 1945 elections were not free, since there was a single Democratic Front list. Hoxha replied that the wartime struggle had united the nation behind the Front.[3] The second was the question of inheriting responsibility for agreements, debts, etc. incurred by previous regimes. Hoxha argued that the new regime could not be held responsible for these – e.g. oil concessions and suchlike. The West insisted on holding the new government to Zog's signature.

These two basic issues were aggravated by numerous others, some closely related. In particular, the Western powers were extremely reluctant to accept Albania as a member of the anti-fascist coalition, and even tried to exclude Albania on the grounds that it had been an ally of Italy![4] This was deeply resented. The final breakdown in relations came in late 1946 with the Corfu Channel Incident(s). The USA and Britain have had no relations with Tirana since then, though France maintained its mission throughout.

Hoxha visits Yugoslavia, June 1946

In June 1946 Hoxha made his first postwar visit abroad – an official visit to Yugoslavia, then in close alliance with the Soviet Union and acting as de facto supervisor of Albania. Once again, Hoxha is concerned to stress that he had almost no direct contact with Moscow at the time (probably true).[5] His main criticism of Tito is on the personal level – that he lived in luxury, behaved haughtily, and did not spend much time getting into specifics, especially economic issues.[6] Hoxha records a conversation about the Kosovo; his account is plausible, but cannot be verified. It is unlikely that Tito expressed himself in quite such a straightforward way, even on a matter of principle.[7] Hoxha seems also very concerned to present himself as a rather naive, inexperienced actor in international relations – again, perhaps to provide retroactive cover to exonerate himself from charges of having been a key promoter of the close relationship with Yugoslavia in this period.

There is both truth and invention in Hoxha's account of his relations with Tito and the Yugoslav regime. Hoxha's basic charge – that Yugoslavia was out to annex Albania – is correct (as confirmed later by Djilas).[8] His grounds, therefore, for being suspicious of Yugoslav motives seem good. On the other hand, the leap he makes in claiming that because Yugoslavia wanted to annex Albania it also plundered it is not substantiated by the available evidence. On the contrary, Yugoslavia greatly aided Albania in the period 1945–8, in purely economic terms.[9]

In the very close and sincere relations which (as we thought at that time) existed between the Soviet Union and Yugoslavia, and between Stalin and Tito, we saw another reason which rejoiced us about the meeting we were to have with Tito . . . Since it was impossible to have any contact with Stalin at that time (through the Soviet legation, which as far as I remember had just been opened in Tirana, and through no fault of ours, direct Soviet-Albanian relations were very weak), we thought that the meeting with Tito would be, you might say, a transmission and an elaboration of the view of Stalin, too.

. . . The aircraft reached Belgrade . . . we were especially excited in anticipation of meeting Tito . . . for the first time . . . We saw that there were many people there to meet us, soldiers, and a military band. We had never been through such ceremonies; these things were unknown to us, and we would have to take care to make no mistakes in the so-called rules of protocol. We walked forward and Tito came towards us. He held out his hand and gripped ours firmly. We thought that we would embrace as is our custom. But no. Different rules and customs. These things made no impression on us . . . we reviewed the guard of honour. «The soldiers are like ours,» I said to myself, «brave former partisans.» Their uniforms were better than ours and their weapons newer, Soviet ones. Ours had been captured from the enemy. Then, Tito introduced us to the Yugoslav personalities who had come out at the airport . . . Most of them (with the exception of Djilas who had once passed through Albania in transit) we were seeing for the first time.

After we had rested . . . they told us that we were to pay a courtesy visit to Tito in the White Palace. For the Yugoslavs who were constantly hovering around us the question was extremely complicated: How were we going to dress for this visit to Tito? Don't dress in this suit, nor in that suit. Even then protocol had begun its work in «Tito's court». For us, however, the problem was quite simple. We had two suits each: [a] military uniform . . . and a civilian suit. Therefore, we dressed in civilian suits. After all, we were going to visit a comrade who was a communist as we were! And we set out to walk through the park.

Guards dressed in spick and span uniforms, and armed with automatic rifles were placed all round the palace. «Why all these guards?» I asked myself, when I recalled that only two partisans guarded my house and at that time people went freely up and down the street in front of it.[10] However, I quickly found the «reason»: «It's a big country, Tito is a great personality and they are quite right to guard him like this.» In front of the palace there was a guard of honour, in the halls of the palace everything had been foreseen, from a clothes brush down to a man who wiped the dust from our shoes gathered during the walk through the park. «Apparently you have to be all 'dolled up' to see Tito!» I said to myself. «Just think, all these heroes who are wiping your shoes and bowing and scraping all round you, were waging the war and living as partisans up till a year or so ago!»

We entered the great chamber of the palace. Luxurious. Tito was standing alone under a picture at the head of the chamber, dressed in his white marshal's uniform, with gold-embroidered collar and cuffs, with stars on his epaulettes, and a considerable number of medal ribbons on his chest. To the left of him came a series of comrades, one after the other, members of the Political Bureau of the CPY and ministers: antique French armchairs of 17th and 18th century style lined both sides and there were beautiful Persian carpets in the middle of the chamber. From the door of the chamber to its head, till we reached and shook hands with Tito, who did not move from his position, we seemed to walk a kilometre.

After he sat down, they brought in cigarettes and drinks. Tito proposed a toast to the friendship between our two peoples, and to our health, asked some general questions about our country, the weather, the crops, the olives and the oranges. We thanked him, delivered the greetings of our people, Party and army and said good-bye. The first protocol audience with Tito did not last more than half an hour. . .

The day for the discussions was set.

. . . While I was speaking Tito took some notes on a notebook and smoked cigarettes continuously, using a cigarette holder in the form of a pipe. He wore glasses and always sat serious, with furrowed brow as though deep in thought. It seemed that he was listening with attention. From time to time he filled the glass he had in front of him and drank mineral water. When I had finished, we took a break and went to a room where a buffet was richly spread with everything, from cakes and sandwiches to Šlivovica and soft drinks. There Tito began to talk, to crack jokes and laugh with his comrades about unimportant things to pass the time; the interpreters translated to us. Later I found these jokes and talks of Tito with Moša Pijade[11] identical with those of Khrushchev with Mikoyan, who went on and on with such things when they were together.

After the break the meeting recommenced and Tito took the floor. He outlined the international situation at that period, attacking the imperialists and reactionary governments. He put great stress on the «major» role which socialist Yugoslavia played, not simply in the Balkans, but also in Europe and especi- ally in the countries of people's democracy, of course, «after the Soviet Union», as he stressed. We noticed nothing suspicious in what he said, apart from the «majestic» tone in which he said it, the «authoritarian» words and the special importance he gave matters by saying, «I said this to one» and «I said that to another».

. . . He did not dwell at length on the economic problems of Yugoslavia, saying only, «we have many difficulties», and went on to our question, in regard to which he said: «Despite these difficulties, we must assist you to the limit of our possibilities.» Tito said that from their side they would appoint Comrade Boris Kidrić.[12]

. . . After we talked about the development of education and culture in our country and I put forward some requests in this direction, too, especially about sending a number of Albanian students to the University of Belgrade, Tito asked me what I thought about the solution of the problem of Kosova and the other Albanian regions in Yugoslavia. After a moment's silence to sum up our views on this important problem so that I could present them in the most complete and concise way, I said:

«You know about the historical injustices which the various imperialist and Great-Serb reaction have done to Albania. You also know the principled stands of our Party during the National Liberation War and the desire of our people for friendship with the peoples of Yugoslavia.»

I went on to express to Tito the opinion of the Albanian side that Kosova and the other regions in Yugoslavia, inhabited by Albanians, belonged to Albania and should be returned to it.

«The Albanians fought,» I told him, «in order to have a free and sovereign Albania with which the Albanian regions in Yugoslavia should now be united. The time has come for this national problem to be solved justly by our parties.»

President Tito replied:

«I am in agreement with your view, but for the time being we cannot do this, because the Serbs would not understand us.»

After this Tito went on to another problem, that of the so-called «Balkan Federation» and sought my opinion on this matter. [13]

«. . . Whether or not the possibilities for a 'Balkan Federation' are created is one problem, while the solution of the question of Kosova is another problem entirely. As you yourself said, work must be done to solve the question of Kosova justly.»

«We shall work in this direction,» Tito «gave me his word».

However, all Tito's words and pledges were a bluff. . . By seizing on the idea of the «Balkan Federation» he aimed . . . to annex the whole of the Balkans, including Albania, to Yugoslavia.

. . . Tito gave a big reception for us in the White Palace of Dedinje. It was «majestic». We were dressed in «official» clothes, but when we entered the palace what did we see? It was packed with women, men, officers, diplomats. They were all dressed in brilliant uniforms, dress suits, the bejewelled ladies in long silk gowns, deep décolletés, some with furs around their shoulders, the officers with all their decorations. Tito standing at the head of the room where he received us, was dressed in full uniform, with his chest stuck out and covered with decorations; on one finger he wore a ring with a great sparkling diamond. We were completely out of our depth! We made our way among the people who looked us over curiously from head to foot and applauded to the extent required by protocol. Only when we reached Tito and shook hands with him did we say to ourselves that we had escaped that ordeal and in fact we had. We were no longer subjected to the stares of the «nobility» of Belgrade. The central point again became Tito from whom we had stolen the limelight for no more than five minutes. The public of the White Palace no longer took any notice of us and we were relieved.

Tito wandered here and there, talking with one group after another, took me along and introduced me to some of them, but their names went in one ear and out the other. For me it was indescribable torture until we sat down at the table. Tito stood up, produced a sheet of paper which he read in his haughty tone, eulogised us to some extent, was applauded and sat down. After him I stood up, brought out my speech, read it, received some laconic applause and sat down. This ordeal, too, was over but our tortures at this «majestic» dinner had not ended. To take coffee, Tito stood up and all of us followed suit. He took some of us, the Soviet ambassador Lavrentyev and some of his comrades out into the park ... We came to a grotto and went inside ... [After a while:]

«Shall we get up and return to the hall?» he [Tito] said, «because the rain has stopped.» While we were in the grotto a light rain had fallen, just enough to make the path muddy and to my distress, since the legs of my trousers were long, the cuffs of my trousers and the heels of my shoes became smeared with mud. When I glanced at them at the entrance to the chambers which were packed with people because the Marshal was coming, I blushed with shame. There was nothing I could do about it except that I should not move much, but this depended on Tito. I had to drag my feet so that the heels of my shoes would not be seen. And that is what I did. But I went through real torture. It was a blesssing that the eyes of all were on the Marshal.

The room was so hot that we were sweating, people encircled the Marshal and us, but the heat dried the mud on my trousers and shiny shoes and made it more obvious. Finally, Tito said:

«Come along, my friends, I'll show you round the palace where I live and work.»

We thought we were saved! But there in front of us, with a crowd of women with low-cut dresses and jewels sparkling on their necks and fingers and men in formal evening dress following us, appeared a stair «*en colimaçon*» [spiral staircase].

We had to go up it and this time the trick of dragging my feet would not work. What was I to do? Against my desire and allegedly out of politeness I climbed seven or eight steps without turning my back so that people did not look at my feet, but went up backwards facing them and waving to them. I got through this final torture, too . . .

. . . They also took us to Bled, to a luxurious hotel beside the beautiful lake with the same name . . . Later, not on an official visit, I had a meeting with Tito on the shores of this lake, I think it was when I was on my way to the Peace Conference in Paris.[14] . . . We talked on the verandah about the . . . problems which were to be discussed in Paris. Naturally we were in agreement. Tito kept me for lunch. It was a beautiful luxurious summer villa set amongst the trees and flowers. At the edge of the lake below the villa white motor-boats were anchored. Lying at Tito's feet in the room was his big dog (the successor to the unfortunate «Lux»),[15] which seemed to be asleep, snoring sometimes, and sometimes releasing a loud fart. In the end Tito could put up with it no longer and told General Todorović, a former partisan who had also been in Albania: «Put him out!!»

After we finished our talk, before we had lunch Tito proposed to me and Žujović, whom he liquidated later together with Hebrang as Stalinists, that we take a trip on the lake.[16] I did not refuse, although I did not know how to swim if the boat should capsize.

The motor started and the boat began to move. Tito's dog followed us swimming. «At least,» I thought to myself, «this will cool his backside.» From the edge of the lake men, women and children shouted:

«*Heroj Tito, druže Tito, naš Tito!* [Hero Tito, Comrade Tito, our Tito!]»

This impressed itself on me because we had heard this slogan from the Italian fascists when they shouted, «*Duce a noi!*» [The Duce is ours!] I was astonished how they could permit it. On the way back Tito said:

«The dog's tired.» And he called to him, «Climb in!»

The dog scrambled into the boat and since it was the size of a calf, the boat rocked a bit, but we came to no harm, except that when the dog shook himself the suit which I had for the Peace Conference was soaked.

«We will dry it when we get back to the villa,» said Tito.

«It doesn't matter,» I said to him, giving the dog a hard look.

However, all this was a later occurrence, from which, apart from what I have just mentioned, I remember almost nothing, because in fact we did not discuss any weighty problem . . . Let us return again to the first visit, the official one.

When we returned to Belgrade . . . First, we reached agreement over the main content of the Treaty of Friendship and Mutual Aid and decided that the signing of the treaty would be done a little later in Tirana. (This treaty was signed in Tirana on July 9, 1946.)

. . . Another important question was that of a number of joint companies which we agreed would be set up, mainly for the development of our mines. Tito boosted these companies to us, when we finally met to sign the documents, saying:

«We have similar companies with the Soviet Union which are going very well, give results and are helping us in the construction of socialism!»[17]

We agreed to the formation of these companies . . . [for now I] will content myself by pointing out that the aim of the Yugoslavs to plunder us meant that on paper these companies would exist as joint companies, but would be run by them. While all the material would be ours, they would not contribute or bring in anything, but would dominate them and take their production. Of course, the deception did not go on for long. The deception about the «joint companies», which Tito advertised to us so vigorously, was unmasked like all the others.

When all the official documents were ready we signed them at a solemn meeting. Champagne was drunk.

. . . The day for our departure for our Homeland arrived. At the airport they farewelled us with all the ceremony with which they had welcomed us. We climbed into the aircraft and returned to Tirana.

The joy with which I set out had evaporated. I returned with an inexplicable feeling, a mixture of trust and disillusionment over the haughtiness and scandalous luxury of Tito which was clearly obvious even at that time. I asked myself: How are we going to get on and work with Tito?

Hoxha and Stalin

Hoxha had five encounters with Stalin – the first in July 1947, the last in April 1951. He has devoted a book, *With Stalin*, to an account of these meetings.

The book is prefaced by a long article which Hoxha wrote on the hundredth anniversary of Stalin's birth, in 1979. Hoxha's general line is that Stalin can do no wrong. Unmentioned is Hoxha's own criticism of Stalin at the Third Congress of the Albanian Party in 1956 (long since expunged from the official record). Hoxha's enthusiasm for Stalin, at least officially, knows no bounds:

'Stalin was no tyrant, no despot. He was a man of principle, he was just, modest and very kindly and considerate towards people, the cadres, and his colleagues . . . No mistake of principle can be found in the works of this outstanding Marxist-Leninist.' 'Stalin never acted in that way' claims Hoxha, comparing him to Khrushchev with regard to the execution of the former Hungarian premier Imre Nagy. 'He [Stalin] conducted public trials against the traitors to the party and Soviet state. The party and the Soviet peoples were told openly of the crimes they had committed. You never find in Stalin's actions such Mafia-like methods as you find in the actions of the Soviet revisionist chiefs . . . [On] this glorious anniversary, I bow in devotion and loyalty to the Party and the people that gave birth to me, raised me and tempered me, and to Joseph Stalin who has given me such valuable advice for the happiness of my people and left indelible memories in my heart and mind.'[18]

First meeting

In July 1947 Hoxha finally got to Moscow for the first time. The main thing which strikes one about this first encounter (16 July) is the almost incredible banality of the exchanges between the two men. Stalin's level of knowledge about Albania is abysmal (in a later meeting he even seems unsure if the Soviet Red Army got to Albania – something which, if it came from anyone else, would doubtless be taken as a foul insult against Albania).[19] Omitted here are quite long passages where Stalin and Hoxha discuss the ethnic origins of the Albanians and the origins of their language. Several of the Yugoslavs who saw Stalin during this period have commented on the fact that he was rather interested, almost obsessed with the Albanians, even before he met Hoxha. Dedijer records that Stalin told Kardelj in 1947 that Tito had told him (Stalin) that the Albanians were descended from the Basques, to which Kardelj assents. Stalin tries this out on Hoxha – but meets with a firm rebuttal.[20]

In the extracts below, there are two important political issues concerning Albania's history at this time on which some light is shed. The first is that Hoxha says that it was Stalin who suggested that the Albanian Communist Party, which had yet to hold its first Congress, should be called the Albanian Party of Labour, the name which it holds to this day. It is quite possible that this suggestion did indeed come from Stalin, and it probably reflects his view that the Albanian Party, like the Party in (North) Korea, which took the name of the Korean Workers' Party, did not quite merit the appellation of 'Communist', given its relatively unproletarian composition (especially among its leadership) and its far from advanced ideological level. On the other hand, it would be in Hoxha's interest to claim that the idea came from Stalin, who is presented (as in the discussion about Greece reproduced below) as the source of all wisdom and the final arbiter on all issues in the world Communist camp. Secondly, in the discussion about Yugoslav planes landing in Albania without permission, Stalin gives no hint of any anxiety about Yugoslav actions, or any hint of backing for any anti-Yugoslav stance by Albania. Since Hoxha would undoubtedly have mentioned any such remarks, it can safely be assumed Stalin did not criticise Yugoslavia. On the other hand, it is Hoxha's policy studiously to ignore any possibility that Stalin was backing Yugoslavia's attempt to take over Albania.[21]

That same day,[22] full of indelible impressions and emotions, we were received by . . . Stalin, who talked with us at length.

From the beginning he created such a comradely atmosphere that we were very quickly relieved of that natural emotion which we felt when we entered his office, a large room, with a long table for meetings, close to his writing desk. Only a few minutes after exchanging the initial courtesies, we felt as though we were not talking to the great Stalin, but sitting with a comrade, whom we had met before and with whom we had talked many times. I was still young then, and the representative of a small party and country, therefore, in order to create the warmest and most comradely atmosphere for me, Stalin cracked some jokes and then began to speak with affection and great respect about our people, about their militant traditions of the past and their heroism in the National Liberation War. He spoke quietly, calmly and with a characteristic warmth which put me at ease.

... «I have acquainted myself, especially, with the heroism displayed by the Albanian people during the Anti-fascist National Liberation War,» he continued, «but, of course, this knowledge of mine cannot be broad and deep enough. Therefore, I would like you to tell us a little about your country, your people and the problems which are worrying you today.»

After this, I began to speak and gave Comrade Stalin a description of the long and glorious historic road of our people ...

Comrade Stalin expressed his joy over the successes of our people and Party in their work of construction and was interested to learn something more about the situation of classes in our country. He was especially interested in our working class and peasantry. He asked a lot of questions about these two classes of our society ...

«Has the working class of Albania any tradition of class struggle?» Comrade Stalin asked ... [After Hoxha's answer]

Comrade Stalin replied: «In general, the peasants are afraid of communism at first because they imagine that the communists will take the land and everything they have. The enemies,» he continued, «talk a great deal to the peasants in this direction with the aim of detaching them from the alliance with the working class and turning them away from the policy of the party and the road of socialism. Therefore the careful and far-sighted work of the Communist Party is very important, as you also said, to ensure that the peasantry links itself indissolubly with the party and the working class.»

While assessing the policy which our Party had followed towards the masses in general and the peasantry in particular as correct, Comrade Stalin gave us some valuable, comradely advice about our work in the future. Apart from other things, he expressed the opinion that since the biggest percentage of its members were peasants, our Communist Party should call itself «The Party of Labour of Albania». «However,» he stressed, «this is only an idea of mine, because it is you, your Party, that must decide.»

After thanking Comrade Stalin for this valuable idea, I said:

«We shall put forward your proposal at the 1st Congress of the Party for which we are preparing, and I am confident that . . . the Party . . . will find it appropriate and endorse it». Then I went on to expound to Comrade Stalin our idea about making our Party completely legal at the congress which we were preparing.

«In reality,» I said among other things, «our Communist Party has been and is the only force which plays the leading role in the entire life of the country but formally it still retains its semi-illegal status. It seems to us incorrect that this situation should continue any longer.» (The 11th Plenum of the CC of the CPA which met from 13-24th of September 1948 and the 1st Congress of the CPA decided on the complete and immediate legalisation of the CPA.)

«Quite right, quite right,» replied Comrade Stalin. «For a party to be in power and remain illegal or consider itself illegal, doesn't make sense.»

. . . I also spoke about the Soviet instructors we already had and asked him to send us some more . . . then I raised the problem of strengthening our coastal defences.

«In particular, we need to strengthen the defences of Sazan Island and the coast of Vlora and Durrës,» I said, «because these are very delicate positions. The enemy has attacked us there on two occasions. Later we could be attacked there by the Anglo-Americans or the Italians.»

«As for the strengthening of your coastal defences,» said Comrade Stalin among other things, «I agree with you. For our part, we shall help you, but the arms and other means of defence must be used by Albanians and not by Soviet forces. True, the mechanism of some of them is a bit complicated but you must send your people here to learn how to use them.»

In connection with my request about sending political instructors for the army to Albania, Comrade Stalin said that they could not send us any more, because in order to work well, they must know the Albanian language and should also have a good knowledge of the situation and life of the Albanian people. «Therefore,» he advised us, «it would be better for us to send people to the Soviet Union to learn from the Soviet experience and apply this experience themselves in the ranks of the Albanian People's Army.»

Then, Comrade Stalin inquired about the attempts of internal reaction in Albania and our stand towards it.

«We have struck and continue to strike hard at internal reaction,» I told him. «We have had successes in our struggle to expose and defeat it. As for the physical liquidation of enemies, this has been done either in the direct clashes of our forces with the bands of armed criminals, or according to verdicts of people's courts in the trials of traitors and the closest collaborators of the occupiers. Despite the successes achieved, we still cannot say that internal reaction is no longer active. It is not capable of organising any really dangerous attack upon us, but still it is making propaganda against us.

«The external enemy supports the internal enemy for its own purposes. External reaction tries to assist, encourage, and organise the internal enemy by means of agents, whom it has sent in by land or by air. Faced with the endeavours of the enemy, we have raised the revolutionary vigilance of the working masses. The people have captured these agents and a number of trials have been held against them. The public trials and sentences have had a great educational effect among the people and have aroused their confidence in the strength of our people's state power, and their respect for its justice. At the same time, these trials have exposed and demoralised the reactionary forces, both internal and external.» . . .

During the conversation I underlined the fact that some Yugoslav aircraft had landed in Tirana contrary to the recognised and accepted rules of relations among states . . . Although we are

friends, we cannot permit them to infringe our territorial integri-
ty . . .

«Are your people not happy about the relations with Yugoslavia?» Comrade Stalin asked me, and added, «It is a very good
thing that you have friendly Yugoslavia on your border, because
Albania is a small country and as such needs strong support from
its friends.»

I replied that it was true that every country, small or big, needed
friends and allies and that we considered Yugoslavia a friendly
country.

The death of Nako Spiru

Nako Spiru, an old associate of Hoxha from the Korça group of
Communists before 1941, was in charge of economic relations with
Yugoslavia (whose counterpart was Boris Kidrić). Spiru is officially
stated to have committed suicide in November 1947. The generally
accepted interpretation of his suicide is given by Griffith: 'Spiru, increasingly anti-Yugoslav and driven frantic by Xoxe's attacks (and
probably by Hoxha's lack of open support), in November 1947 committed suicide.'[23]

This death (by whatever means) played a major role in the break
between Stalin and the Yugoslavs. When Stalin summoned Djilas to
Moscow in January 1948 for the first of the cataclysmic encounters
leading up to the break, the first thing Stalin raised with Djilas was Spiru's
suicide. Djilas himself later reflects on Spiru's death and, in effect, says he
thinks Spiru did kill himself – because of the pressure Yugoslavia was
putting on Albania.[24]

The original official Albanian version of events was that Spiru killed
himself because of Belgrade's pressure, and Spiru was made into an
Albanian hero after Hoxha's break with Tito. Here, however, in *The
Titoites*, published in 1982, after the demise of Mehmet Shehu, in which
Hoxha is peering with renewed suspicion into every nook and cranny of
the past, Spiru's death is given a new twist. It may be that after Shehu's
death, officially reported as suicide, Hoxha either genuinely thought he
should re-examine all past major suicides, or perhaps should tidy up the
'suicide group' and make them all Yugoslav and foreign agents. The
passage also provides a good example of the difficulty of 'reading'
Hoxha's version(s) of events, since there is an apparent authenticity to
many of the descriptions and exchanges.[25]

The extract opens towards the end of a meeting of the Politbureau during the night of 19–20 November 1947, convened to discuss problems in economic ties between Albania and Yugoslavia and, originally, accusations brought by Tito's emissary in Tirana, Savo Zlatić.

We decided to continue the meeting at 8 o'clock in the evening on the next day.

Before I closed the meeting I added:

«In the coming meeting I shall not permit anyone to speak in this tone[26] and we must be clear that we shall make an analysis of the line of our work and in this context we shall also discuss what Comrade Nako is responsible for and to what extent, but not only in connection with the accusation that Zlatić made and which Koçi raised here against the person of Nako.»

When the meeting was over, I approached Koçi and said to him:

«You attacked him very harshly. You were hasty. The question should have been put forward and judged more calmly and dispassionately.»

«Oh, Enver, we are trying to make things clear to the others . . . the enemies, and we can't make things clear to ourselves! All this time I've been telling you: you are supporting Nako Spiru too much. I beg you, don't support him any more!»

«I'm not supporting Nako,» I said. «I support that which seems to me right.»

And so we parted to meet again the following day or, more precisely, in the evening, because the morning of November 20, 1947 had almost arrived.

There could be no talk of going to sleep. I was convinced not only that all the problems were proceeding at headlong pace on the most mistaken and distorted course, but also that simply from the viewpoint of the most elementary rules of the internal life of the Party we were acting incorrectly. However, I thought that now the stand of Nako Spiru had importance. I was convinced that in essence he was not wrong about the problem which was raised, I was convinced that his collisions with the Yugoslavs in the concrete instance were correct and inevitable collisions. But how and for how long would he stand up to the attack?!

The way he flared up immediately when we told him what the

Yugoslavs had put before us in the address of the Party and in his address, in particular, did not please me at all. I did not like the way he was stunned and bemused later, or the way in which he asked for five days for preparation. In essence, I was of the opinion that he should have not five days, but even more to prepare himself if need be, but I did not like the way in which he asked for them, as if begging for mercy. I knew his impulsive temperament which often made him say cutting things. At those grave moments those defects were especially out of place.

About midday Nako Spiru knocked at the door and came in. He was shaken, demoralized and broken from every point of view.

«I wanted to beg you once again,» he said, «you understand my grave situation. Use your influence so that they give me five days' time.»

«Listen Nako,» I told him, «we have gone through the most difficult times and moments together. We have gone through moments when we were facing the enemy and we knew how to reply to him, but we have also gone through moments when we had the enemy amongst us and it was not easy to distinguish and attack him.»

«Even you think that I'm an enemy?» he said, his shoulders sagging.

«No, I don't say that, and I never have said it. That is a statement, an accusation which comes from someone else, from another party. You were told it openly. Very well then, do you have to cry about it? No, this does not befit you, does not befit a communist. You must refute it. You must give your ideas, your arguments.»

«That's why I came, give me time to prepare myself!»

«I don't decide that – the Bureau has decided it,» I told him. «Listen Nako, why do you need five days? We're among comrades, we should say things just as they are. The only help I can give you in this situation,» I said, «is this: speak openly and sincerely. The day has come, Nako, to lay on the table everything that has been kept secret, covered up for years. The moment has come when, not only you, but all of us must answer those questions which I have continually raised: what is this situation, why has it come about, is it right, where do the causes lie, what must be done?! Now you are placed in the 'dock'. But the criticisms don't rest only on you. They go wider and deeper. Answer what you are charged with with coolness and courage, qualities which I believe are not lacking in you. In this way we, the Party, the Central Committee, will be able to judge correctly and give the proper answer to the accusations.»

«I need time to prepare myself, to remember everything and put it in order.»

«This does not depend on me and you were at the meeting yourself,» I told him. «However, everything won't be over this evening. Let us begin from the analysis and then things will be cleared up one after the other. And there let it come out whether it is you, I, Koçi or anyone else who is right or wrong. That's all I have to say to you.»

«I shall try,» he said and went away.

. . . However, precisely when I thought that the time had come and the conditions were ripe for us to do what should have been done long ago, to do what they did not allow me to do in 1946, the door banged open and Koçi Xoxe came in:

«I told you so,» he shouted, «he's an enemy, a scoundrel. He killed himself and died like a dog. Now he has proved that he's been an enemy and worse than an enemy!»

«Who?» I asked. «What are you talking about?»

«Nako Spiru has killed himself. He ended up as he deserved!»

He spoke in an angry tone in which it was not difficult to distinguish a deep, inner gloating. Thus, the only obstacle to the conspirators' directing their attack against me had been removed from the scene.

For Koçi this meant a big stride forward towards his final aim. Nako Spiru's suicide shook me deeply and I had reason for this. If he considered himself innocent he had no reason to commit suicide . . .

Nako Spiru would have assisted the Party greatly if he had revealed the manoeuvres of the Titoites behind the scenes and the role of Koçi Xoxe. But together with this he would also have disclosed his own faults and, faced with this dilemma, he did not have the courage. He put his «name» above the interests of the Party and killed himself.

Only a few months were to pass and the truth was to be made completely clear. Nako Spiru had opposed the Yugoslavs because they left their man of Berat[27] in the lurch and preferred Koçi Xoxe to him. Then Nako turned his eyes in another direction, to a greater «power» than the Yugoslav power. He linked himself with the Soviets. We regarded these contacts of his as something more than correct and in order, in favour of our cause and socialism, but Nako did not see them in this way. He had not linked himself with them simply out of the feeling of respect and affection. He saw his rapprochement with the Soviets as a means, as a way to impose himself on others, especially on Koçi, with the aim of displacing him and taking his position . . . After his suicide one of the comrades of the Soviet embassy, called Gagarinov, informed us orally that Nako Spiru had sent them a letter in which he said that, «after the grave accusations which the Yugoslav leadership has made against me I am obliged to kill myself . . .» That was all we were told. The Soviet advisers, and especially the main Soviet adviser for the economy, Troitsky, shed tears over the loss of Nako and did not hide their grief over him, but they did not take any action before this act or to prevent his act. I believe that they knew nothing about what was going on, or if one of the people of Nako's circle informed them, the Soviets did not consider it in order to involve themselves in this question. Perhaps it was not without purpose that Nako said in the Bureau, «Have you consulted with the Soviet legation over this analysis?» and for this reason sought five days' time to prepare himself, or to put it better, to send a call to Moscow, «sos! Save me!»

However, it was to be proved subsequently that the other side, the Yugoslavs, acted urgently and it was they who drove Nako Spiru to the base and unpardonable act he committed. Warned by Koçi Xoxe that Nako Spiru might reveal in the Bureau all the threads of the plot that had begun in Berat and continued to operate, the Yugoslavs confronted Nako with the incriminating documents in which he expressed himself against our Party and me. Finding himself in that grave situation, Nako, judging like a petty bourgeois, thought that he would lose my support, too, and considered himself in a hopeless position.

His end finally sealed off the only remaining road for us to get out of the situation which the Yugoslavs had created for us. He took with him [to] his grave the secret of the plot hatched up. At the same time the end of Nako was the most powerful weapon which the Yugoslavs and their agents, Koçi Xoxe and company, were now to use in order to realise their aims. The way was open for them to concentrate the attack on me.

To make more clear what the Yugoslavs were aiming at, on the day following Nako Spiru's suicide, Savo Zlatić said to Tuk Jakova:

«Great attention should be paid to what is happening in your Party, because similar things have occurred in the past in our Party, too. The former general secretary of our Party, Gorkić, turned out to be a traitor . . .»[28]

All this was aimed directly against me . . .

The agents of Belgrade, Koçi Xoxe, Pandi Kristo and others, took up the banner and began the most vicious attack against the Party, against its line and against me. The process of endless «meetings» and «analyses» began in the Bureau in which Koçi Xoxe now openly predominated and directed.

The question of Yugoslav troops in Albania

Throughout the years 1945–7, Yugoslav control over Albania became stronger and stronger. Albania was treated more or less as a province of Yugoslavia. Tirana's subordination to Belgrade was apparent not only in the Yugoslav–Albanian economic agreements, but also in the political field: the Albanian CP was the only ruling Party not represented in the Cominform; and the Albanian CP did not even hold its first Congress until after the break with Belgrade. This was not because, as Hoxha later claimed, the Party was still semi-clandestine; it was because it was treated as an appendage of the Yugoslav CP.

In the middle of 1947 Hoxha finally received an invitation to visit the USSR and meet Stalin (see above pp. 97). During this visit, even according to Hoxha's retroactive accounts, Stalin did not criticise Yugoslavia or its relationship with Albania. But it is clear from Hoxha's accounts that he was bitterly disappointed at Stalin's failure to establish direct links with the Tirana leaders earlier on, and with Stalin's complacent attitude towards what Hoxha claims he already saw as the Yugoslav menace. Stalin's repeated enquiries at the time about the Albanian leaders have been recorded in several Yugoslav memoirs.[29]

About the end of 1947 a proposal emerged to station Yugoslav troops in southern Albania. This much is agreed, but little else. Hoxha's version is that the Yugoslavs suggested putting their troops into Albania (one armed division) because of the danger of an invasion of Albania by Greece. The Yugoslavs say that they already had a regiment of their air force in Albania and that the proposal was to put in two armed divisions – and that these had been requested by the Albanians. Hoxha does not mention the Yugoslav Air Force regiment.[30]

In the present state of knowledge, it is not possible to be sure who decided what. But since the Yugoslav accounts are, on the whole, far more truthful than Hoxha's, it seems that the military units in question were those described by Djilas and Dedijer. In any case, concern about Greece's intentions was eminently reasonable at the time. The right-wing government in Athens was vociferously laying claim to 'Northern Epirus' (i.e. southern Albania).[31] Greece was in the middle of a fierce civil war, in which many Greek Communists and partisans were taking refuge in Albania, which was their main rear base. The US had recently become heavily involved on the side of the Athens regime, taking over from the British. So a fear that there might be an invasion – and that Tirana's forces might not be strong enough to hold out – was not at all unreasonable.

The episode became a decisive one. Hoxha claims that this was the first time that he contacted Stalin to get his backing in a direct confrontation with Yugoslavia. This is quite possible. Yugoslav sources also state that the question of stationing their troops in Albania became a major issue in the break with Stalin. Kardelj has confirmed that Yugoslavia did not consult Moscow about moving its land forces into Albania – on the grounds that Moscow had not complained about the Air Force regiment being stationed there.[32] It is not clear if Stalin (and/or Hoxha) did actually complain about the Air Force regiment and somehow draw the line at the ground forces.

It is also possible that not only is the Yugoslav version correct over the question of who asked to move in the Yugoslav forces, and that it was the Albanians who asked for them, but that Hoxha, far from objecting, supported this and only invented his opposition retroactively, after finding out that Stalin had decided to make an issue of it. Another possible interpretation of Stalin's behaviour is that at the time when the proposal was made to move in the Yugoslav ground troops (about January 1948), he had already decided to abandon the Greek revolution and that he turned the issue of Yugoslav forces in Albania into an anti-Belgrade weapon after previously giving the project at least tacit support.[33]

In this extract Hoxha gives his version of the arrival of the Yugoslav military mission, headed by General Kuprešanin, in January 1948.

As far as I remember, I received them the day following their arrival in Tirana. We exchanged the usual greetings and the General [Kuprešanin] started directly into his theme:

«On the special order of our supreme commander, the Minister of People's Defence, Marshal of Yugoslavia Josip Broz Tito, I have come to you to bring a series of proposals of exceptional importance. What I have to communicate to you, as well as information about my identity, is communicated officially and in detail in this personal letter from Comrade Tito. Allow me to hand it to you!»

He rose to his feet, stood to attention, took one step forward and held out the envelope to me, all solemnity, as if he were presenting his letter of credentials.

«Now allow me to communicate to you orally the purpose of my dispatch here so unexpectedly. The situation around us presents greater threats than ever. We have information that in Greece the preparations are being completed for an attack which will be aimed initially against your southeastern borders.»

He was silent for a moment, and then said to the Yugoslav officer whom he had with him:

«The map!»

Immediately a big map of the Balkans on which arrows, circles, flags and all kinds of other multi-coloured lines struck the eye was unrolled.

«It is envisaged that the attack will begin in this territory,» said Kuprešanin, pointing to the border in the Korça-Erseka zone. «We have information also that simultaneous attacks may begin from the sea. The Greek aggressive forces, supported by the Anglo-American forces and means, will try to smash your defence with a rapid general assault and then penetrate in depth . . . In these conditions, our leadership, extremely worried and loyal to its obligations under the Treaty of Friendship and Mutual Aid, considers that a series of urgent measures should be taken. In regard to the main one, I shall cite textually what Comrade Tito writes to you in the letter I handed to you,» said Kuprešanin. He opened his briefcase, took out a sheet of paper and began to read: «Because of such an unclear situation, I beg you to give us the base in Korça for one division and for the auxiliary technical units. In this way the possibility will be created for you to secure the sector in the direction of the sea better and, in case of a provocation, our units will be able to intervene more quickly.» (From the letter of J. B. Tito addressed to Comrade Enver Hoxha, January 26, 1948.CAP.)

«This is the main and urgent proposal of the Yugoslav leadership,» continued Kuprešanin. «At the meeting they had with Comrade Tito, Comrades Balluku and Themelko[34] agreed and, convinced that you would have no opposition either, I and the group which accompanies me came to begin work immediately. We will leave urgently for Korça to examine the terrain and see where our first division will be deployed . . .»

«I must interrupt you, General,» I told him. «Comrade Tito's proposal is of such importance that it can never be passed over with a casual communication.»

«Everything I said you have there in writing from Tito himself!» replied Kuprešanin.

«This I believe,» I continued, «but we have just heard it. We must study it, discuss it in the leadership of our Party and state and then we shall give you our reply.»

«How is it possible!» exclaimed Kuprešanin in «astonishment». «Your comrades who are engaged directly with the army showed themselves extremely ready and reasonable.»

«No one has authorised our comrades to approve a proposal of any kind whatever without first having the opinion of the leadership of our Party and my opinion as Commander-in-Chief,» I replied. «Moreover, such an action, if not carefully weighed up, may create great problems.»

«The course you suggest could be followed,» persisted Kuprešanin, «but bear in mind the situation. We can wait for your analyses, but will the enemy wait until you are convinced?!»

«Whether or not we are convinced,» I said, «this will emerge in the end. As for the enemy, first, I think that in this situation, they have no possibility to attack us. Second, even if they do attack us, we are capable of dealing with them ourselves.»

«I brought the assessment of our leadership which has ample information about these preparations. Do you not believe this?!»

«You may have this information,» I said, «but one thing is now well known: a general offensive of the patriotic forces has just been launched in Greece and the government army is engaged in fighting them.»

«Let us assume that this is so! What is wrong with our taking preliminary measures?» Kurešanin tried to persuade me.

«There are several things wrong with it,» I said curtly. «First, we, for our part, cannot approve such an action without thrashing it out well in our leadership and I tell you that I, as Commander-in-Chief, do not agree. Second, this hasty action would create great concern amongst our people.»

«Comrade Tito has foreseen this,» the General interrupted me, «and here is what he writes in the letter: 'I think that all these actions should be carried out quietly and unnoticed.' We have instructions to organise everything in secrecy without it coming to the ears of the people.»

«And you believe that this is possible?!» I asked him. «Do you think that the people are goats? Indeed, even if we were to agree to your proposal we could not take any action without first explaining it to the people and convincing them. The people have the right to call us to account and to reject an action which does not seem right to them. Third,» I continued, «such an action would increase the tension of the situation in the Balkans and in the international arena. The enemies would begin to speak in the way that suits them.»

«Comrade Tito has foreseen this, too,» said Kurešanin, «and he writes in his letter: 'The enemy will learn of such a thing, but when our units are established there we have no reason to keep it secret, because this will show that our alliance is not a formal thing, but, on the contrary, that we are definitely determined to defend our borders together.' Indeed, Comrade Tito thinks that after the division is established in Korça,» continued Kurešanin, «if the press asks you or Comrade Tito about it, you should declare that 'this base has been given by agreement for the needs of the security, not only of the Albanian borders, but also of the

Yugoslav borders.'» (All the quotations in inverted commas have been taken from Tito's letter of January 26, 1948. CAP.)

«Comrade General,» I said, «we have discussed this more than was necessary. We heard your communication and we have Tito's letter. Now let the responsibility rest upon us. We shall give you our reply at the proper time. This is for our good and for yours.»

«The best thing would be for the division to be placed as quickly as possible with the aim that reaction should not have any possibility to undertake any act for the occupation of your country!» persisted Kuprešanin.

«But the worst thing would be if, from such a precipitate action, enemies or friends were to accuse us that Albania has been occupied by the Yugoslav troops!» I replied to the General and I saw that momentarily he went completely pale.

With this the meeting came to an end. We parted very coldly with Kuprešanin and as he was leaving he asked me:

«Will you be very long in giving your answer?»

«I believe it will be given at the proper time!» I replied frigidly.

Koçi Xoxe, who had been standing there like a black monk throughout the debate, intervened and said to me:

«The situation is very alarming, Comrade Enver, and we should not put off this internationalist aid of the Yugoslav brothers.»

Kuprešanin's face immediately brightened and he stood staring at me, awaiting my reply.

«If the situation is so alarming,» I told Koçi in a loud voice so that Kuprešanin would hear clearly, «then, let the Yugoslavs deploy their army close to the north of Greece within their own borders.»

General Kuprešanin could not control his anger, he muttered something and departed. Koçi Xoxe, trying to appear «calm» and extremely «concerned about the situation», said to me:

«It seems to me that you were hasty. Comrade Kuprešanin will notify Comrade Tito and open up problems for us.»

«What they are demanding is extremely dangerous and delicate. I gave him my opinion, convinced that the Bureau will be of the same opinion.»

«All right, let us meet and decide today or tomorrow!» implored Xoxe.

«No! The coming of the Yugoslav division is not a matter to be decided hastily here and now. It is a decision of importance for our future and the future of our friendship with Yugoslavia,» I said in such a tone as to convince him that I would not budge from this . . .

«Well, well, but I say we should raise the matter in the Bureau as quickly as possible,» said Xoxe as he was leaving. «We cannot keep Tito waiting.»

Convinced that we were facing a great danger with the bitterest consequences, I decided to carry out an action solely «on my own responsibility» for the first time. Through the Soviet embassy I informed Stalin about what Tito demanded of us and, while awaiting the reply, with great effort I managed to postpone raising in the Bureau the proposal about the dispatch of the Yugoslav division for the time being.

Stalin's reply came very quickly . . . Stalin told us that he did not see any possibility or danger of an eventual attack against us by the Greek army and was in agreement with my opinion that the dispatch of the Yugoslav division to Albania was not necessary.

The Yugoslavs were furious when I communicated to them that not only we, but also the Soviet comrades and Stalin personally did not consider the dispatch of their division in order, but nevertheless, they «retreated» and, temporarily, said no more about this.

3
WITH STALIN

Hoxha's secret visit to Bucharest to meet Vyshinsky after the break with Tito

In June 1948 the Soviet bloc broke with Yugoslavia.[1] Tito and his colleagues were denounced as 'agents of imperialism'. Albania went along with Stalin's decisions – undoubtedly against serious attempts by Belgrade to dissuade Tirana from following Moscow. Hoxha claimed, plausibly, that some key members of the Albanian regime opposed the break with Tito.

Relations between Albania and Yugoslavia played a big role in the earlier stages of the breakdown of relations between Stalin and Tito, as noted above (the question of Yugoslav annexation of Albania, and the stationing of Yugoslav military forces in Albania). But it does not seem that Yugoslav–Albanian ties were ultimately central to the Belgrade–Moscow break. Rather, it was Yugoslav relations with Bulgaria and the attempt to found a Balkan federation with Bulgaria (whose leader, Dimitrov, was a man of considerable prestige in the Communist world) which seem to have brought the crisis to a head. It was Tito's independence, rather than general disagreement with Stalin's foreign policy, which caused the explosion.

The breach with Yugoslavia left Albania in a very vulnerable position, militarily and economically. It was completely cut off from the rest of the Communist bloc by land. On its southern borders the Greek civil war was raging. Some reports suggest that the Yugoslavs considered (and perhaps implemented) plans to raid into Albania from the north and the north-east. As noted above, the Western powers thought this was a good time to try to topple Hoxha.

The Yugoslav writer and former close colleague of Tito, Vladimir Dedijer, has recently claimed that Stalin (who, it is generally acknowledged, did try to stage a coup against Tito in 1948) had a plan to bring about a mutiny in the Yugoslav navy and invade Yugoslavia partly with the help of the Soviet fleet based in Albania (this plot was to be masterminded by the Italian Communist, Vittorio Vidali, who was until his recent death a senator from Trieste).[2]

Economically, too, the breach with Tito left Albania in a very bad spot: Yugoslav credits had made up half the Albanian budget, and, quite apart from the effects of plans to integrate the Albanian economy with that of

Yugoslavia, the country was woefully short of almost all basic goods, starting with food.[3]

As the extract below recounts, after the break Hoxha established contact with the Soviet hierarchy via Andrei Vyshinsky, the Deputy Foreign Minister, in Romania. The Romanian leader, Gheorghe Gheorghiu-Dej, sat in on these meetings. It is interesting that Hoxha did not go to Moscow, and thus did not see Stalin. Why not? One possibility is that it was deemed too risky to get him there. But another is that Stalin may have wanted to keep Hoxha at arm's length for a while, and designated Vyshinsky, the chief prosecutor at the 1936–8 trials, to make sure Hoxha was on the right track. Vyshinsky, who had already performed a major role in establishing the new pro-Soviet regime in Romania in early 1945, was probably en route back to the U S S R from a meeting of the Danube River Commission which had been held in Belgrade at the end of July 1948.

This extract reveals a number of elements. First, it allows Hoxha to state his main grievances against Yugoslavia – suitably rewritten both for Vyshinsky and for the historical record. It also gives a fairly brief outline of the general case against Yugoslavia. Second, it gives a résumé of Hoxha's grievances against Stalin, especially Stalin's failure to keep in touch with Tirana, and to inform Hoxha of doubts about Tito. Third, it gives a flavour of the curious idiom in which Hoxha claims to have conducted his discussions with the Soviet leadership. Vyshinsky is very stilted, yet Hoxha lavishes praise on him. This praise is preconditioned: Hoxha goes into the meeting and nothing will shake his admiration for Vyshinsky. Fourth, Hoxha reproduces some of Vyshinsky's comments about evidence and exposing one's foes. However inherently implausible these may seem, they are the only such record available of Vyshinsky's comments on the Moscow trials, in which he was the key actor – and the awful thing is that it is quite possible that he did actually make such banal and lethal comments to Hoxha. Lastly, the extract shows Hoxha sounding off (one of his own favourite expressions) against the Romanian leadership for their slack approach to the revolution. Hoxha's comments contain a note of brutal puritanism and pompousness.

One morning we set out for Bucharest by Soviet aircraft. We were to travel through Yugoslav airspace, although we had become enemies with them. A hero of the Soviet Union flew the aircraft. The Soviets had sent this pilot to get me, because he knew the route over which the aircraft was to pass and there was greater security for me, if the Yugoslav secret service were to learn of my journey. Only Chuvakhin[4] and I were on board the aircraft.

. . . The weather was fine and sunny, with no clouds and from the aircraft we saw the land of Yugoslavia with the plains which were never to be collectivised, the land unsystemised, as ours was in the first years of Liberation, and as the land of Rumania over which we flew was.

At Bucharest airport we were met by Dej, Ana Pauker, the Soviet ambassador and some other comrades[5] . . . In our country everything was in order, the people's power had been established on sound constitutional foundations, while in Rumania no. It took Rumania some time to liquidate the monarchy and King Michael, the powerful capitalist relations which still existed, the remnants of Antonescu's fascist «Iron Guard», which were still active at the time of my stay [in] Bucharest, etc.[6] The decisive factor in the liberation of Rumania and the liquidation of these dangerous remnants was the Soviet army. All the rest was just tales and boasting of Gheorghiu-Dej . . .

We embraced with Dej, Ana Pauker and the other comrades. My first impression when I met Gheorghiu-Dej at the airport was good, not only because I had heard good things said about him by the Soviets, but also because he had a reputation as a veteran communist who had «suffered» in the dungeons of Doftana . . .

Dej was a tall man, with black eyes, black brows and hair, well dressed and cheerful, who gave the impression of a *perifani* as we say in Gjirokastra about those people who are vigorous and energetic and speak with a sort of pride in themselves, self-satisfied with what they say and do. Ana Pauker was a woman of a quieter nature than Dej, although she seemed energetic, too. She was a big, heavy-featured woman who looked as if she had suffered more in prison than Dej, her hair was grey and cut short as they say *à la garçonne*.

I got into a big Soviet ZIS car together with Dej. The others got into cars, too. When I was [about] to enter the car the driver opened the door for me and I did not notice that it was a [bullet-proof] car. I saw this when I got out and opened the door from inside. Never before had I had the occasion to see such a thing, although I had read in newspapers and books that such cars were used by kings and dictators to protect themselves from attempts on their lives, and by gangsters to protect themselves from the attacks of the police. Once in the car, it seemed to me I was not in a car, but in a real arsenal: both on my side and Dej's side we had a German twenty-round automatic pistol, each with two spare magazines, under our feet we each had another German twenty-round pistol with spare magazines and, of course, the guard and the driver had the same.

I said to Dej as a joke:

«We can fight for 20 days with these weapons ... But my impression was not good, not because Dej had thought about taking measures for defence, but because those measures were excessive. They showed either that the Rumanian comrades were as frightened as rabbits, or that the situation in their country was by no means as calm as they tried to make out.

When I commented on the «arsenal» Dej replied:

«We must be vigilant!»

«Of course, we must be vigilant,» I said to myself, «but not let the enemy terrify us. We must terrify him and make him tremble.» As far as I could see the enemy in Rumania had not been dealt with firmly as in our country.

On the way from the airport to Bucharest, Dej said to me:

«We are not going into the city, but will turn off to a house on the plain outside Bucharest, where we have taken measures for you to stay since you are *incognito* and Vyshinsky has not yet arrived ... There where we're going,» continued Dej, «is a very reliable family, an old base where I have stayed before Liberation. The son of the house is a communist and his mother is a very dear old lady who keeps her mouth shut. You will be very well looked after there.»

«It has not the slightest importance for me», I told him. «I shall be quite all right wherever you have decided I shall stay.»

Nevertheless, these things surprised me and I asked myself the question: «Is the situation so bad for them in the city that they cannot take me to some apartment there? Either they are so insecure that they are unable to protect me, whom nobody knows, or is it that they want to keep the meeting strictly secret?» However, these latter ideas did not convince me ...

[Next day on the way into Bucharest.] In the car, Dej told

me that . . . Chuvakhin and I were to stay in the former king's palace.

«This is like the characters from the Grimm brothers' fairy tales, going from the peasant's cottage to the king's palace!» I told Dej. «Please, don't take me there. I don't like such places. I prefer to stay in an apartment in the middle of the city, amongst the people, because no one knows me and there is no danger for me.»

«No,» said Dej. «You will stay there, because we were embarrassed yesterday, leaving you outside the city, and then that is where the meeting will be held. All the facilities are there.»

I repeated my protest and told him:

«For me it was a great honour to stay with that simple peasant family and you have no reason to be embarrassed.»

However, I had to go, like it or not . . .

[Vyshinsky arrived next day.] He was just as I had heard, a vigorous man, not very tall, with horn-rimmed glasses and bright black eyes that took in everything. He was wearing a blue suit. Vyshinsky shook hands with all of us in turn and when he came to me, apparently as I was the only one he had not met before, he guessed who I was, because he gave me his hand and asked me in Russian:

«How is your health, Comrade Enver Hoxha?»

«*Harasho!* [Well]» I replied.

«The object of this meeting,» said Vyshinsky in general outline, «is to exchange our experience and reveal our joint knowledge about the betrayal of the Yugoslav Titoites, about their undermining activity against our countries, parties and socialism, and to define the method of combatting and unmasking their deviation which is dangerous for communism in general and for the Yugoslav Communist Party and socialism in Yugoslavia in particular.»

. . . With his penetrating style, with arguments and the amazing clarity characteristic of him, Vyshinsky, as the true Bolshevik prosecutor that he was, made their content even clearer to us. This time we did not have the accused before us in the dock, but the fact is that their trial was being held and it was a fair trial, based on sound arguments, an historic trial the justice of which was to be completely confirmed by the passage of time.

«. . . Their activity is identical with the activities of the Trotskyites, Bukharinites and agents of world capital whom we have
unmasked in our trials.

«The unmasking of the enemy has very great importance,»
stressed Vyshinsky. «The Soviet peoples had to be convinced
of the treacherous activity of the Trotskyites, the Bukharinites
and the rightists, therefore we placed importance on this and
managed to achieve that our enemies themselves brought out
the smallest details which are frequently important because
they explain major questions. The truth which proved their
treachery emerged naked before our courts and our peoples.
This had decisive importance. This is the important thing to
achieve,» said Vyshinsky. «After this the number of years to
which the enemy is sentenced has secondary importance. The
people must approve this sentence, must be convinced. This is
what we must do with Tito's renegade group, too. This group
is in power and will defend itself. It will also commit all sorts
of provocations against our socialist states, but we must be
prudent, vigilant and must not fall for their provocations!» he
concluded.

In his speech Dej, amongst other things, pointed out the great
danger of this agency of criminals and murderers; made an
interpretation of the joint decisions which they had taken in the
Information Bureau, told of the arrogance of the Yugoslav «comrades» at this meeting against the French and Italian communist
parties, etc . . .

I, too, took the floor. I had a lot to say about the Titoites. In
our relations with the traitor group of Belgrade there were
loads of facts and data which proved their betrayal of Marxism-
Leninism and the openly state capitalist and colonialist tendencies in the relations which they tried to establish in our
country.

. . . I presented the participation of our National Liberation
Partisan Army in the war for the liberation of Yugoslavia correctly and objectively, as an honourable, correct and undeniable act,
which had a truly liberation character, but always remained an
aid, alongside the Yugoslav National Liberation Army which for
its part, fought heroically. This must not be denied or underrated,

irrespective of the fact that the Tito group betrayed the blood shed by this heroic army which bore the brunt in the liberation of the peoples of Yugoslavia . . .

I refuted the absurd anti-Marxist claim that allegedly the Yugoslavs had created our Party, that allegedly they had «kindled the fire of our national liberation war» . . .

«I must point out,» I told the comrades, «that our contacts with the Yugoslavs during the war were rare, and moreover, when we managed to meet (and I told them about the meetings with Vukmanović-Tempo and Blažo Jovanović), we had differences over principles with them on many issues, since even at that time the Yugoslav tendencies to consider and use our Party as an appendage of their party, and Albania as a province of Yugoslavia were already apparent . . . We sought whole-heartedly to wipe out forever those feelings which the circumstances of past periods, such as the partitioning of Albania, the leaving of Kosova to Serbia, the ceaseless terror and countless intrigues of the Serbs against our country had created . . .»

I went on to inform them about the Yugoslavs' hostile activity in our country in every field, one by one, demonstrating this with many arguments backed by concrete facts which were indisputable and not in the least equivocal . . .

In a round-about way I let Vyshinsky know that we had not been given direct aid from the CPSU and also alluded to other problems, that the Soviet comrades, . . . whom we informed about everything, . . . never expressed any opinion in reference to our contradictions with the Yugoslavs . . .

«Another matter which confused us to some extent,» I pointed out, «was that for a long time our suspicions about the hostile actions of the Yugoslavs did not extend to the top, to Tito, and the whole of their leadership. In this direction it must be admitted that we were not given any information about whether the sister parties had ever drawn the attention of the Yugoslav leadership to its incorrect stands. Indeed, this situation continued right to recent weeks or months, when the letters of the Bolshevik Party, which criticized the Yugoslav leadership, reached us. Before these letters the only signal that things were not going well,» I told them, «was given us when we informed Comrade Stalin about the question of the Yugoslav division which Tito wanted to deploy on our territory . . .»

«Stalin personally criticised Tito for this impermissible act which he wanted to commit against you,» said Vyshinsky.

«This rejoices us immensely,» I told Vyshinsky, «but through the Soviet embassy I was told only that Stalin agreed with our opinions and not with those of Tito and that was all. However, I think that I and the comrades of our leadership could and should have been told something more, should have been told why Tito did these things.

«A similar thing occurred,» I pointed out to the comrades, «over another question, that of the so-called 'Balkan Federation' or 'Confederation',[7] allegedly proposed and settled between Tito and Dimitrov, about which we were never given any information.

«To this very day,» I continued, «we cannot say precisely what this thing was, how it came about, and approval from us was neither sought nor received. Only at the beginning of this year we learned at one moment that the Moscow newspaper *Pravda* criticised this 'idea' of Dimitrov's and he replied to Stalin and *Pravda* that they were right . . .»

I went on to tell the comrades about the pressure exerted on us by the Yugoslavs and Koçi Xoxe to accept the union of Albania with Yugoslavia and about our categorical opposition to this proposal . . . I let Vyshinsky know that at these important moments we were not assisted as much as we should have been . . .

I remember that at this point Vyshinsky interrupted me and said:

«People are tempered in struggle!» . . .

My speech . . . was fairly lengthy . . .

As soon as I had finished, we took a break, after which Vyshinsky gave the conclusions of the meeting . . .

«I stress,» said Vyshinsky finally, «that it is our duty as friends, as comrades, and as internationalists to help the PR [People's Republic] of Albania more, so that it makes up for the time lost, improves its economic situation, and we must not forget, either, that now it is completely encircled by enemy states. The sister Republic of Albania is a worthy member of our powerful socialist camp, therefore, it never should feel itself isolated, and will never be isolated either politically, economically, ideologically or militarily. This is the instruction of Comrade Stalin . . .»

I was very satisfied [with the meeting], first, because matters were made clear to us, but also because of the good assessment which Vyshinsky made of the work of our Party . . .

The day after the meeting, Chuvakhin and I asked Dej for permission to go to visit the city of Bucharest . . . The influence of capitalism and the capitalist way of life had introduced political and moral degeneration to this country. Corruption, bribery, cabarets, transactions, prevailed here.

The Rumanians called Bucharest «the little Paris». I had read Paul Morand's book about Bucharest.[8] . . . When you looked at the city, you formed the impression that it had never seen the war . . .

When we came to the most beautiful and busiest street of Bucharest, where business was brisk, we got [out] of the cars and walked. A member of the Central Committee and five or six security men accompanied us.

What there was to see! The shops were full of strikingly luxurious goods . . . It seemed as if you were not in a city which had just emerged from the war, but in [the] Champs Elysées of pre-war Paris. And all the shops were still the property of the Rumanian bourgeoisie, . . . it made the law in commerce. Chuvakhin and I looked at the shop windows with curiosity and astonishment. As always I thought of the empty shops in Tirana, while Chuvakhin thought of those in Moscow which certainly were not full of goods like these . . .

We went into a big café and sat down to rest. There were many people there, strikingly well-dressed. They looked us over curiously from the corner of their eyes; they did not know us, but certainly recognised the security men who accompanied us. This was one of those cafés which Dej told us were frequented by the bourgeoisie, where he «with his revolver in his belt and surrounded by security men went to provoke them within their own lairs».[9]

He went and «provoked» them in cafés, indeed! But what harm did such a thing do them when they had the economy, the market, their wealth in their hands? This scandalised me and I wondered:

What sort of communists are they? What sort of socialism is this?

Only a few years later they were to show completely what their worth was – Dej, this «stern fighter» against Tito, was the first to become the defender and the supporter of Tito as soon as Khrushchev turned over the page.

When we returned to the Palace for the farewell dinner . . . I spoke about the very good impressions we had of Rumania, of the people, the individuals, but I also spoke about our experience and I expressed my astonishment in the form of a question:

«Why do you not expropriate the bourgeoisie, but allow them to exploit the people?» Dej explained to me that «everything will be done in its own time, because the situation here is different from that in your country,» and other such theories.

Four meetings with Stalin after the break with Yugoslavia

Second meeting with Stalin (March–April 1949)

Hoxha went back to Moscow in the spring of 1949 for the first time after the break with Tito. A large part of the discussion with Stalin was taken up by the Stalin–Tito split. These extracts from the second meeting show Stalin and Hoxha ranging over a very wide range of issues, including policy towards domestic opponents and agents, collectivisation of agriculture, the Greek civil war, Albanian foreign policy (where Stalin urges a cautious line, in contrast with the tougher policies suggested earlier by Yugoslavia); Hoxha claims the British want bases in Albania; finally, Hoxha and Stalin have a preliminary discussion about religion, a topic to which they returned at greater length in another meeting later that same year. This extract also includes a paean to the state security services and their then chief, Mehmet Shehu. One year after Hoxha published this version Shehu was denounced as, among other things, an agent of the Yugoslavs, the Americans and the Russians. A revised edition of *With Stalin* was rushed through the presses in Tirana.

In this extract and elsewhere in *With Stalin* and *The Titoites*, Hoxha presents a picture of Stalin as committed to supporting the Greek Communist movement in the civil war. This is directly at variance with the detailed, and much more credible, accounts given by the Yugoslav leaders who reported that as early as 1948 Stalin said the Greek civil war had to be stopped – i.e. abandoned.[10] Hoxha's claim that Stalin was still expressing strong support for the Greek Left in March 1949 is most implausible – although it is just possible that Stalin felt able to use this ritualistic and completely unreal language to Hoxha. Stalin is also recorded as minimising the danger from Greece. This could be a true report, particularly if Stalin had already signalled his abandonment of the Greek Left. It could also represent a further attempt by Hoxha to downplay the grounds on which the Yugoslavs had based their arguments for stationing military forces in Albania in winter 1947–8.

The extract opens with Hoxha giving Stalin an account of how the pro-Yugoslav figures have been treated.

I went to Moscow again on March 21, 1949, . . . and stayed there until April 11 that year . . .

[I told Stalin that:] We adopted differentiated stands towards those who, in one way or another, were implicated in the anti-Albanian activity of the Trotskyite Yugoslav leadership. Some of them made self-criticism over the mistakes they had committed in good faith, while those who were gravely compromised were already rendering account before the people's court.

«Protect your Homeland and the Party,» Comrade Stalin said. «The enemy must be exposed thoroughly, with convincing arguments, so that the people can see what this enemy has done and be convinced of the menace he represents. Even if such an enemy, utterly discredited in the eyes of the people, is not shot, he is automatically shot, morally and politically, because without the people he can do nothing at all.»

«The trial which is now going on in Tirana,» I told Comrade Stalin, «is being held with open doors and everything that is said in the court room is published in the newspapers.

«At the same time,» I added, «those who have thoroughly understood their mistakes, who have made sincere and convincing self-criticism, we have treated patiently and magnanimously . . . We have even thought we should send one of them to study in the Soviet Union,» and I mentioned one name.

«Really?» Stalin asked me and looked me right in the eye. «. . . Do you still have political trust in him?»

«We do,» I said, «his self-criticism has become more and more profound and we hope that he will correct himself.»

«But does he want to come here?»

«He has expressed the wish to come,» I said.

At this point Chuvakhin added some explanations in support of my opinion.

«Well, then, since you have weighed this matter well, Comrade Enver, let him come . . .»

Continuing the conversation, I told Comrade Stalin that during the same period the Americans, from Italy had parachuted groups of saboteurs into the south and north of Albania.[11] We killed some of these saboteurs and captured the remainder. Foreseeing the difficulties on our southern border and wanting to have the forces available for any eventuality, we first had to undertake a mopping-up operation in north Albania against the groups of political and common bandits who operated within our borders under the direction of agents sent in by Ranković, and we did this. These bands in the service of the Yugoslavs carried out a number of assassinations. Our mopping-up operation ended successfully: we wiped out some of them and all the others crossed over into Yugoslav territory, where they remain to this day.

«Do they continue to send in other saboteurs?» Stalin asked.

«We think that they have not given up. The policy of Tito and Ranković to lure Albanians into their territories in order to organize groups of saboteurs and wreckers with them, met defeat, and at present there are very few defections . . . The imperialists are training groups of wreckers abroad, just as the monarcho-fascists and the Titoites are doing on their part. The Italians are not lagging behind. Our present plan is to rout the remnants of the bandits at large in our mountains for whom we have already made things very difficult, and to destroy their bases, which are among the kulaks, especially. Most of the reactionary groupings in the cities have been smashed by the State Security Forces which have scored many successes. Our Party put things in order in the Ministry of Internal Affairs, a former centre of the Titoites, and the State Security has become a very powerful and much beloved weapon of the Party and our people. General Mehmet Shehu is a glorious leader and he enjoys the continuous aid of the Party and the people in his difficult and delicate task . . .

«Have you set up many farm co-operatives? What criteria do you follow?» Comrade Stalin asked . . .

«In my opinion,» said Comrade Stalin, «you must not rush things in the collectivisation of agriculture. Yours is a mountainous country with a relief that differs from one region to another. In our country, too, in mountain areas similar to those of your country, the kolkhozes were set up much later.» . . .

«As for surpluses of agricultural products,» Comrade Stalin went on, «these the peasants must dispose of as they like, for, if you act otherwise, the peasants will not collaborate with the government. If the peasantry does not see the aid of the state concretely, it will not assist the state.

«I do not know the history and characteristics of the

bourgeoisie of your country,» said Comrade Stalin and then asked: «Have you had a merchant bourgeoisie?»

«We have had a merchant bourgeoisie in the process of formation,» I said, «but now it has no power».

«Have you expropriated it entirely?» he asked me . . .

In conclusion, I mentioned to Comrade Stalin the threats the external enemies were making towards Albania.

He listened to me attentively and, on the problems I had raised, expressed the opinion:

«As for the Greek people's war,» he said among other things, «we, too, have always considered it a just war, have supported and backed it whole-heartedly. Any people's war is not waged by the communists alone, but by the people, and the important thing is that the communists should lead it. Things are not going well for Tsaldaris and he is trying to save himself by means of the Anglo-Americans.[12]

«As for the screams of the external enemies about partitioning Albania,» he went on, «they are just to intimidate you, because I do not think there is any danger in this direction at present . . . In the first place, Albania is a free and independent country, the people have seized power there and they will know how to defend their independence, just as they knew how to win it. Second, the external enemies themselves have contradictions with one another over Albania. None of them wants Albania to belong only to the one or the other. If Greece wants to have Albania for itself, this would not be advantageous to Italy or Yugolsavia, which would raise obstacles to this, and so on in turn. On the other hand,» Comrade Stalin pointed out, «the independence of Albania has been recognised and confirmed by the declaration of the big three — the Soviet Union, Britain and the United States of America. This declaration may be violated, but that is not so easy to do. Hence, come what may, Albania has its independence protected.»

Comrade Stalin repeated several times that if the Albanian Government pursued a cautious, intelligent, and far-sighted policy, then its affairs would go well.

Continuing, Comrade Stalin advised me:

«You must consider the possibilities of establishing relations with Italy, because it is your neighbour, but first you should take measures to protect yourselves against the activity of the Italian fascists.» . . .

«And what about with the United States of America and Britain?»

«For their part,» I went on, «the British want naval bases in our ports, and only then will they recognise us . . .»

«As for the bases the British want to have in your ports, in no way should you agree to this. Guard your ports well.»

«We will never relinquish them to anybody!» I said. «If the worst comes to the worst we shall die rather than relinquish them.»

«You must guard them and not die,» said Comrade Stalin, laughing. «Here diplomacy is needed.»

Then he rose, shook hands with each of us in turn and went away . . .

At a second meeting with Stalin a few days later.

«How many religious beliefs are there in Albania,» Comrade Stalin inquired, «and what language is spoken?»[13]

«In Albania,» I replied, «there are three religions: Moslem, Orthodox, and Catholic. The population which professes these three faiths is of the same nationality – Albanian, therefore the only language used is Albanian, with the exception of the Greek national minority which speak their mother tongue.»

From time to time, while I was speaking, Stalin took out his pipe and filled it with tobacco. I noticed that he did not use any special tobacco, but took «Kazbek» cigarettes, tore them open, discarded the paper and filled his pipe with the tobacco. After listening to my answer, he said:

«You are a separate people, just like the Persians and the Arabs, who have the same religion as the Turks. Your ancestors existed before the Romans and the Turks. Religion has nothing to do with nationality and statehood.»

And in the course of our conversation, he asked me:

«Do you eat pork, Comrade Enver?»

«Yes, I do!» I said.

«The Moslem religion prohibits this among its believers,» he said, «this is an old, outdated custom. Nevertheless,» he went on, «the question of religious beliefs must be kept well in mind, must be handled with great care, because the religious feelings of the people must not be offended. These feelings have been cultivated in the people for many centuries, and great patience is called for on this question, because the stand towards it is important for the compactness and unity of the people.»

Third Meeting with Stalin (November 1949)

Hoxha returned to the Soviet Union in November 1949, travelling via Budapest, where he met the Hungarian leader Mátyás Rákosi. On arrival in Moscow, Hoxha was told by Malenkov that he would have to submit his points in writing and then it would be decided whether he would actually meet Stalin, who at the time was at Sukhumi, on the Black Sea.

The extracts below cover two main issues: the aftermath of the Greek civil war and religion.

On 16 October 1949 the radio of the Greek Democratic Army announced that its forces had decided to 'cease fire'. In effect, the Greek civil war was over. Even before this, Hoxha had taken pre-emptive action: on 26 August 1949, he announced that all armed Greeks in Albania would be disarmed and detained – although he was not able to put this into effect immediately.[14] Cut off from the Soviet Union and the Soviet bloc by hostile Yugoslavia, harassed by the Western powers, Italy and Albanian émigrés, Hoxha had reason to fear that the West might back, or allow the army of the Athens regime to pursue the Greek Democratic Army into Albania and perhaps overthrow his government or seize southern Albania.

As for religion: the discussion below hardly sparkles with brilliant views, but is interesting in the light of the fact that Hoxha later took very tough measures against organised religion in Albania. As of 1967 all religious institutions were closed and Albania now claims to be 'the first atheist state in the world'. It is also interesting that Hoxha decided to publish a text of this discussion, which implies at least medium-term tolerance of religion, after his regime had taken such hard measures against organised religion. Hoxha also gives Stalin's version of his discussion at Yalta with Churchill and Roosevelt about 'How many divisions has the Pope?'

Comrade Stalin asked:
    «Are any of the Greek democrats who were given temporary

asylum in Albania still there? How do you intend to act from now on?»

. . . I replied that «. . . the fact that we are neighbours with Greece brought about many innocent Greek men, women and children, maimed, terrified, and hotly pursued by the monarcho-fascists, came over our border as refugees. Towards all of them we adopted a just and very careful stand: we gave them aid and shelter and established them in centres far from the border with Greece.»

. . . I told Comrade Stalin that the influx of these refugees had created many acute difficulties for us and, apart from carrying out our humanitarian duty, we were being careful to avoid allowing the presence of Greek democratic refugees on our territory to serve as an opportunity for the further incitement of the anti-Albania psychosis of people in the Greek government. This was one of the main reasons why we welcomed the request of Comrade Zakhariades[15] and the Greek refugees themselves to leave Albania for asylum in other countries. «At present,» I added, «following the incorrect stands towards us by leading comrades of the Greek Communist Party and the grave accu-sations they are making against us, our Political Bureau thinks that the departure of those few Greek refugees who still remain in our country has become even more urgent.» I told him that not only the democratic soldiers, but also those Greek leaders who had also been given asylum in Albania recently, ought to leave.

. . . I also told Comrade Stalin about some other mistakes of the Greek comrades . . .

After listening attentively to all I put forward, Comrade Stalin, amongst other things, said to me:

«Like you, we too, agreed to the request of Zakhariades for the departure of the Greek democratic refugees from Albania and have interested ourselves in assisting them to be settled where they wanted to go. We did this because such a stand is humanitarian. Aid for this number of people was a burden even for us, but they had to go somewhere, because they could not stay in a country bordering on Greece.

«The stand which you have adopted towards the democratic

soldiers who crossed your border seems to me correct,» added Comrade Stalin. «As for their weapons which have been left in Albania, I am of the opinion that you Albanians should keep them, because you deserve them.

«It appears,» continued Comrade Stalin, «that the leaders of the Greek Communist Party have not evaluated the situation properly. They have underestimated the strength of the enemy, thinking they had to do only with Tsaldaris and not with the British and Americans. As to the final withdrawal by the Greek comrades, there are people who say that they should not have retreated, but I think that, after what had occurred, the democratic soldiers absolutely had to retreat, otherwise they would have all been wiped out.

«On the other questions the Greek comrades are not right. They could not wage a frontal war with a regular army, because they did not have either an army capable of this kind of war, or a sufficient breadth of territory for this. Overestimating their strength and possibilities, they did everything openly, making it possible for the enemy to discover all their positions and their arsenal.

«Nevertheless, I think you should reach agreement with the Greek comrades. This is my view. What they say about you Albanians having adopted a 'Trotskyite' and 'Titoite' stand towards them are baseless accusations.» . . .

[Later, at dinner the same day.] «There are no cut-and-dried prescriptions about how you should behave on this or that occasion, about how this or that problem should be solved,» he would repeat frequently, according to the various questions I raised.

During the talk with Stalin I pointed out to him the stand of the clergy, especially the Catholic clergy in Albania, our position in relation to it, and asked how he judged our stand.

«The Vatican is a centre of reaction,» Comrade Stalin told me among other things, «it is a tool in the service of capital and world reaction, which supports this international organisation of subversion and espionage. It is a fact that many Catholic priests and missionaries of the Vatican are old hands at espionage on a world scale . . .» Then he told me of what had happened once in Yalta with Roosevelt, the representative of the American Catholic church . . .

During the talk with Roosevelt, Churchill and others on problems of the anti-Hitlerite war, they had said: «We must no longer fight the Pope in Rome. What have you against him that you attack him?!»

«I have nothing against him,» Stalin had replied.

«Then, let us make the Pope our ally,» they had said, «let us admit him to the coalition of the great allies.»

«All right,» Stalin had said, «but the anti-fascist alliance is an alliance to wipe out fascism and Nazism. As you know, gentlemen, this war is waged with soldiers, artillery, machine-guns, tanks, aircraft. If the Pope or you can tell us what armies, artillery, machine-guns, tanks and other weapons of war he possesses, let him become our ally. We don't need an ally for talk and incense.»

After that, they had made no further mention of the question of the Pope, and the Vatican.

«Were there Catholic priests in Albania who betrayed the people?» Comrade Stalin asked me then.

«Yes,» I told him. «Indeed the heads of the Catholic church made common cause with the Nazi-fascist foreign invaders right from the start, placed themselves completely in their service, and did everything within their power to disrupt our National Liberation War and perpetuate the foreign domination.»

«What did you do with them?»

«After the victory,» I told him, «we arrested them and put them on trial and they received the punishment they deserved.» [16]

«You have done well,» he said.

«But were there others who maintained a good stand?» he asked.

«Yes,» I replied, «especially clergymen of the Orthodox and Moslem religion.»

«What have you done with them?» he asked me.

«We have kept them close to us. In its First Resolution our Party called on all the masses, including the clergymen, to unite for the sake of the great national cause, in the great war for freedom and independence. Many of them joined us . . .»

«Very good,» Stalin said to me. «What more could I add? If you are clear about the fact that religion is opium for the people and that the Vatican is a centre of obscurantism, espionage and subversion against the cause of the peoples, then you know that you should act precisely as you have done.

« You should never put the struggle against the clergy, who carry out espionage and disruptive activities, on the religious plane,» Stalin said, «but always on the political plane. The clergy must obey the laws of the state, because these laws express the will of the working class and the working people. You must make the people quite clear about these laws and the hostility of the reactionary clergymen so that even that part of the population which believes in religion will clearly see that, under the guise of religion, the clergymen carry out activities hostile to the Homeland and the people themselves. Hence the people, convinced through facts and arguments, together with the Government, should struggle against the hostile clergy. You should isolate and condemn only those clergymen who do not obey the Government and commit grave crimes against the state. But, I insist, the people must be convinced about the crimes of these clergymen, and should also be convinced about the futility of the religious ideology and the evils that result from it.»

Fourth meeting with Stalin (January 1950): Postmortem on the Greek Civil War

According to Hoxha, it was at their meeting in Sukhumi in November 1949 that Stalin suggested that the Soviet, Albanian and Greek Communist leaders should get together soon to discuss the Greek question. This meeting took place in Stalin's office in the Kremlin early in January 1950. The Soviet side was represented by Stalin, Molotov and Malenkov; Albania by Hoxha and Shehu; and the Greek Communist Party by its new head, Nikos Zakhariades, and Mitsos Partsalides.[17] There is no other published account of this meeting, or even any public acknowledgement that it took place.

According to Hoxha, Stalin asked Hoxha to speak first, to be followed by the Greeks. Hoxha opens by addressing Stalin: 'We have requested this meeting in your presence in order for you to judge whether we are right or wrong in our views.' Hoxha then goes on for 30 pages. The points he raises are essentially the same as in earlier discussions with Stalin. He criticises Zakhariades for supporting Greek claims to Southern Albania ('North Epirus'). He claims that the Albanians forewarned the Greeks about where the main assault against them would be in the crucial fighting in August 1949. Hoxha also records that after spending some time with the Greek Democratic Army (GDA) Shehu had articulated his criticism of the behaviour of the GDA in the final battles, at Vitsi and Grammos. Hoxha concludes by saying that the disagreements between the Greek Communists and the Albanians made it seem a good idea to get the remaining Greek refugees in Albania (independently estimated at some 8500) to leave.[18] Hoxha concludes with a rather slavish appeal to Stalin. He then gives Zakhariades exactly one page to present his case (noting that Zakhariades spoke for as long as or longer than himself).

According to Hoxha, the dispute between the Albanians and the Greeks is put to arbitration by Stalin – and simply settled by Stalin's fiat. This may well be how it actually occurred. Noticeable in Hoxha's account, though, is that there is no real discussion of future strategy.

The meeting closes with an extraordinary vignette. As everyone is getting up to go, Molotov suddenly announced that Zakhariades had been accused of being a British agent! In the account here what is interesting (apart from the fact that Zakhariades is reported as being allowed to state his case – a rare privilege in the Kremlin on such issues) is that there is conspicuously little examination of the facts. Stalin just gives his own personal view and everyone seems to accept this as gospel in a thoroughly servile manner. Partsalides' concluding remarks, religiously reported by Hoxha, may well have been made, but more probably for the Kremlin microphones than for anything else.

«. . . Whether we are right or wrong in these stands and views we have maintained, let Comrade Stalin tell us. We are ready to acknowledge any possible mistake and to make self-criticism.»

Comrade Stalin interrupted me saying:

«You must not reject a comrade when he is down.»

«You are right, Comrade Stalin,» I replied, «but I assure you that we have never rejected the Greek comrades . . . Our Party could not permit the Greek Communist Party to have the centre of its activities in Albania, nor could it permit their troops to be organised and trained in our country in order to resume the war in Greece. Apart from the request made by Comrade Nicos [Zakhariades] himself, that the refugees go to other countries, logic forced us to the conclusion that, in the existing situation, even those who had remained absolutely must leave Albania . . .

«Have you finished?» Comrade Stalin asked.

«I have finished,» I said.

Then he called on Comrade Zakhariades to speak.

He began to defend Varkiza,[19] stressing that the agreement signed there was not a mistake . . .

In order to explain the reason for the defeat, amongst other things, Zakhariades raised the question: «If we had known in 1946 that Tito was going to betray, we would not have started the war against the Greek monarcho-fascists.» Then he added some other «reasons» in order to explain the defeat, repeating that they lacked armaments, that though the Albanians had shared their own bread with the refugees, nevertheless they had raised obstacles, and so on. Zakhariades raised some second-rate problems as questions of principle. Then he mentioned our request . . . that those Greek democratic refugees who still remained should also leave Albania. According to him, this put an end to the Greek National Liberation War.

On this occasion, I want to express my impression that Comrade Nicos Zakhariades was very intelligent and cultured, but, in my opinion, not sufficiently a Marxist. Despite the defeat they had suffered, he began to speak in defence of the strategy and tactics followed by the Greek Democratic Army, insisting that this strategy and tactics had been correct . . .

This is what Nicos Zakhariades said. He spoke at least as long as I did, if not longer.

Comrade Stalin and the other Soviet leading comrades listened to him attentively, too.

After Nicos, Comrade Stalin asked Mitsos Partsalides:

«Have you any opinion to express on what Comrade Enver Hoxha and Comrade Nicos Zakhariades have said?»

«I have nothing apart from what Comrade Nicos put forward,» said Partsalides, adding that they were awaiting the judgement of the Soviet comrades and the Bolshevik Party on these questions.

Then Stalin began to speak in the familiar calm way, just as we have known him whenever we have met him. He spoke in simple, direct, and extremely clear terms. He said that the Greek people had waged a heroic war, during which they had displayed their courage, but that there had also been mistakes.

«As regards Varkiza, the Albanians are right,» Stalin pointed out, and after analysing this problem, added: «You Greek comrades must understand that Varkiza was a major mistake. You should not have signed it and should not have laid down your arms, because it has inflicted great harm on the Greek people's war.

«As regards the assessment of the strategy and tactics you followed in the Greek Democratic War, although it was a heroic war, again I think that the Albanian comrades are right. You ought to have waged a partisan war, and then, from the phase of this war should have gone over to frontal war.

«I criticised Comrade Enver Hoxha, telling him that he must not reject a comrade when he is down, however, from what we heard here, it turns out that the Albanian comrades have maintained a correct stand towards your views and actions. The circumstances which had been created and the conditions of Albania were such that you could not stay in that country, because in this way the independence of . . . Albania might have been placed in jeopardy.

«We complied with your request that all the Greek democratic refugees go to other countries and now all of them have been removed. Everything else, including the weapons, ammunition, etc., which the Albanian comrades took from those Greek democratic soldiers who crossed the border and entered Albania, belonged to Albania,» Stalin emphasised. «Therefore, those weapons must remain in Albania,» he said, «because, by accepting the Greek democratic soldiers, even though it disarmed them, still that country endangered its own independence.

«As regards your opinion, according to which, 'If we had known in 1946 that Tito was going to betray, we would not have started the war against the monarcho-fascists,' this is wrong,» Stalin pointed out, «because you must fight for the freedom of the people, even when you are encircled. However, it must be recognised that you were not in a situation of encirclement, because on your northern flank you had Albania and Bulgaria; all supported your just war. This is what we think,» concluded Comrade Stalin and added:

«What do you Albanian comrades, Hoxha and Shehu, think?»

«We accept all your views,» we replied.

«And you Greek comrades, Zakhariades and Partsalides, what do you say?»

Comrade Nicos said:

«You have helped us greatly. Now we understand that we have not acted correctly and will try to correct our mistakes,» and so on.

«Very good,» Stalin said. «Then, this matter is considered closed.»

When we all were about to leave, Molotov intervened saying to Nicos Zakhariades:

«I have something to say to you, Comrade Nicos. The Central Committee of the Communist Party of the Soviet Union has received a letter from a comrade of yours, in which he writes that 'Nicos Zakhariades is an agent of the British'. It is not up to us to solve this question, but we cannot keep it a secret without informing you about its content . . . Here is the letter. What can you say about this?»

«I can explain this matter,» replied Nicos Zakhariades, and said: «When the Soviet troops released us from the concentration camp, I reported to the Soviet command with a request to be sent to Athens as soon as possible, because my place was there. Those were decisive moments and I had to be in Greece. At that time, however, your command had no means to transport me. So I was obliged to go to the British command where I asked them to send me to my homeland. The British put me on an aircraft, and that is how I returned to Greece. This comrade considers my return home with the help of the British command as though I have become an agent of the British, which is untrue.»[20]

Stalin intervened and said:

«That's clear. This question is settled, too. The meeting is over!»

Stalin got up, shook hands with all of us in turn and we started to leave. The room was a long one and when we reached the exit door, Stalin called to us:

«Wait a moment, comrades! Embrace each other, Comrade Hoxha and Comrade Zakhariades!»

We embraced.

When we were outside, Mitsos Partsalides remarked:

«There is no one like Stalin, he behaved like a father to us. Now everything is clear.»

Thus, the confrontation in the presence of Stalin was over.

Fifth meeting with Stalin (April 1951)

Hoxha's last meeting with Stalin took place in Moscow on 2 April 1951. Molotov, Malenkov, Beria and Bulganin also took part.

The meeting opened with Hoxha giving Stalin a detailed account of the latest round of assaults and incursions made against Albania by the Western powers. He then went on to report on the decision of the International Court of Justice at the Hague on the Corfu Channel Incident.

It seems appropriate to end the Hoxha–Stalin discussions with a short extract about internal security. Did Stalin really talk like this?

In the course of the talk I told Comrade Stalin of the great work being done in our country to strengthen the unity among the people and between the people and the Party, and of the blows we had dealt at the traitor and enemy elements within the country. I told him that we had shown no vacillation or opportunism in dealing with such elements, but had taken the necessary measures to avert any consequences of their hostile activity. «Those who have filled the cup with their criminal and hostile activity,» I told Comrade Stalin, «have been handed over to our courts where they have received the punishment they deserved.»

«You have done well,» Stalin said. «The enemy,» he continued, «will even try to worm his way into the Party, indeed into its Central Committee, but his attempts are uncovered and defeated through high vigilance and a resolute stand.»

4
BATTLING
KHRUSHCHEV

Albania's relations with the Soviet camp between the death of Stalin (1953) and the break with Moscow (1960–61)

Hoxha visited the Soviet Union many times between the death of Stalin in 1953 and the final break with Khrushchev – the last time being in November 1960 for the Conference of Communist and Workers' Parties. He met all the top Soviet leaders and seems to have dealt mainly with Khrushchev, Mikoyan (who was in charge of Soviet-Albanian economic relations) and Suslov (particularly on ideological matters and on events like the 1956 Hungarian uprising). But Hoxha also met the older figures like Molotov, Beria and Malenkov, as well as Brezhnev before his access to the top position, and had lengthy dealings with Yuri Andropov, then one of the Secretaries of the Central Committee.

On the surface, relations between Moscow and Tirana seemed good right up to the late 1950s. According to Hoxha – and this is quite plausible – relations deteriorated soon after Stalin's death, and went into an irreparable decline from the time Khrushchev decided to seek a reconciliation with Tito. Khrushchev's rapprochement with Tito in 1955 and his denunciation of Stalin's crimes in 1956 were the two main issues behind the deterioration of Soviet-Albanian relations, compounded by personality differences between Hoxha and Khrushchev. Once again, there are two sharply variant accounts – Hoxha's and that of the other side.

In his memoirs, Khrushchev has bitter words for the Albanian leaders, especially Hoxha, premier Shehu and Defence Minister Balluku, describing them as 'worse than beasts – they're monsters'. Khrushchev states, with much justification, that: 'The rift which developed between the Soviet Union and Albania stemmed mainly from the Albanians' fear of democratisation.'[1] This is the crux of the matter – which Hoxha refuses to acknowledge (if Khrushchev's concept of democracy leaves much to be desired, Hoxha's leaves even more).

Hoxha presents himself throughout as the guardian of Marxist-

Leninist orthodoxy. But his case is severely undermined by his own steadfast refusal simply to examine historical facts. In particular, Hoxha is incapable of examining what Stalin actually did – and, therefore, what was involved in Khrushchev's denunciation of Stalin and Stalin's methods. He records – with pride! – that when he was given the text of Khrushchev's 'secret speech' he gave it back (after he and Shehu had read it): 'We had no need for that package of filthy accusations which Khrushchev had concocted'.[2] Hoxha even goes to the opposite extreme – he accuses Khrushchev of the very crimes which Stalin committed:

It was the Khrushchevites who strangled the voice of the party, strangled the voice of the working class and filled the concentration camps with patriots; it was they who released the dregs of treachery from prison, the Trotskyites and all the enemies, whom time and the facts had proved and have proved again now with their struggle as dissidents to be opponents of socialism and agents in the service of foreign capitalist enemies.

It is the Khrushchevites who, in conspiratorial and mysterious ways, «tried» and condemned not only the Soviet revolutionaries but also many persons from other countries.[3]

One of the main accusations Hoxha makes is that Mikoyan, Khruschev and others planned to kill Stalin. He claims that Mikoyan told him this himself in February 1960, when briefing Hoxha and Shehu on the Sino-Soviet disagreement as it was blowing up:

Among other things, Mikoyan spoke about Mao and compared him with Stalin, saying:
«The only difference between Mao Zedong and Stalin is that Mao does not cut off the heads of his opponents, while Stalin did. That is why we could not oppose Stalin,» continued this revisionist. «At one time, together with Khrushchev we had considered organising a *pokushenie* [assassination attempt] against him, but we gave up the idea because we were afraid that the people and the party would not understand.»[4]

But Hoxha undermines his case by elsewhere converting Mikoyan's statement of failed intention into an accomplished fact. Writing on the 100th anniversary of Stalin's birth, in 1979, Hoxha writes: 'All this [the Khrushchevites'] villainy emerged soon after the death, or to be more precise, after the murder of Stalin.'[5] He gives Mikoyan as his source.

Hoxha goes on to query the events surrounding the notorious 'doctors' plot' – generally agreed to have been a plot by Stalin. But instead of accusing Stalin of failing to ensure that a proper trial was conducted and for failing to publicise any evidence there was, Hoxha accuses Khrushchev and his colleagues of sweeping the incident under the carpet!

Mentioning the death of Stalin looses Hoxha's mind on a trail of paranoia: he hints that Khrushchev and his colleagues may have been responsible for other deaths.

Immediately after the death of Stalin, Gottwald died. This was a sudden, surprising death! It had never crossed the minds of those who knew Gottwald that this strong, agile, healthy man would die . . . of a flu or a chill allegedly caught on the day of Stalin's funeral ceremony . . . Gottwald, an old friend and comrade of Stalin and Dimitrov, died suddenly. This grieved us, but also surprised us.

Later came the equally unexpected death of Comrade Bierut, not to mention the earlier death of the great George Dimitrov. Dimitrov, Gottwald and Bierut, all died in Moscow. What a coincidence! The three of them were comrades of the great Stalin![6]

One thing Hoxha fails to mention here is that Dimitrov died in 1949 – while Stalin was alive and well and in power. Hoxha cannot resist having a go at Khrushchev. Hoxha describes him at Bierut's funeral:

While the speeches were going on, not far from me, I saw Nikita Khrushchev leaning against a tree, exchanging words with Wanda Wassilewska. Without doubt, he was striking deals over the body of Bierut, whom they were putting in the grave.[7]

However, there are some points in Hoxha's indictment of the post-Stalin leadership (all equally applicable to Stalin, of course) which are *in themselves* fair, even if severely undermined by the unilateral way in which Hoxha presents them.

First, he accuses the post-Stalin leadership of failing to inform the Soviet people adequately both of general events in the world (e.g., the revolution against the Shah in Iran) and of specific actions of the Soviet state. This accusation is both true and important. And Albania has a much better record on this issue than the Soviet Union, or most of the post-revolutionary regimes.

Second, he accuses Khrushchev and Brezhnev of seizing power via a putsch. The charge that there was a glaring lack of democracy in the procedures of the CPSU was fair. But Hoxha's claim is based on the wholly unwarranted assertion that the process of putsches began with an alleged violation by Khrushchev of existing democratic norms. Nor, en passant, can it be argued that the Albanian Party of Labour has been a shining beacon of democratic practice.

Third, Hoxha accuses the Soviet leadership of killing the Hungarian leader Imre Nagy. A correct point, so far as it goes. But the way Hoxha couches it leaves a lot to be desired.

After tempers cooled and the victims of the Hungarian counter-revolution, a deed of Tito in particular, as well as Khrushchev, were buried, Nagy was executed. The way this was done was not right, either. Not that Nagy did not deserve to be executed, but not secretly, without trial and without public exposure, as was done. He ought to have been publicly tried and punished on the basis of the laws of the country of which he was a citizen. But of course, neither Khrushchev, Kadar, nor Tito wanted him brought to trial, because Nagy could have brought to light the dirty linen of those who pulled the strings in the counter-revolutionary plot.[8]

According to Hoxha, economic questions were the main bone of contention in the early post-Stalin years.[9] Hoxha portrays the Armenian Anastas Mikoyan, who was in charge of economic relations with Albania and whom he repeatedly refers to as a 'huckster', as particularly mean-spirited.

Hoxha's main charge is that the post-Stalin Soviet leaders opposed Tirana's plans for a relatively broad-based comprehensive form of development based on industrialisation as well as agriculture. According to Hoxha, the Russians tried to impose 'the international socialist division of labour' on Albania and, under the guise of economies of scale and Soviet generosity, keep Tirana in a position of dependency vis-à-vis Moscow. The question of investing in Albanian oil was at the centre of this debate, along with the question of grain supplies to Albania.

There is undoubtedly a good deal of truth in Hoxha's account. Equally, from Moscow's point of view, Albania was asking a lot. Hoxha conspicuously fails to give the Khrushchev leadership much thanks for the considerable aid which they did give Tirana, at least in the early years. On the other hand, Hoxha's account of Soviet economic pressure, especially over grain, in the final breakdown period, is substantially fair. Moscow did exert enormous economic pressure on Albania, tantamount to black-mail. At the same time, the Russians piled on the pressure over the major submarine base at Vlora. And many Western sources think it likely that Khrushchev made a serious attempt to unseat the Hoxha regime.

Hoxha's first visit to Moscow after Stalin's death: June 1953

Hoxha's description of his first visit to Moscow after Stalin's death is chiefly of interest for his vignettes of the new Soviet leaders, and his suspicion (not entirely unfounded) that there was some confusion in the group. Khrushchev does not seem to have taken part in this first encounter.

The other two main points of interest are that Hoxha states clearly that Soviet aid had never been adequate – and this can only mean during the Stalin period, as well as post-Stalin; nonetheless, as he also remarks, the Albanians always pretended it was. This is one of the many points which Hoxha is capable of making, often with clarity, yet from which he is incapable of drawing the obvious conclusions about the way relations within the socialist bloc are conducted – with silence, evasion, cover-up and apparent harmony, until the moment of rupture when the discourse switches sharply to denunciation and vituperation.

The second point is the rather ludicrous accusation, delivered by Bulganin, but apparently on 'evidence' from Beria, that the Albanian army was politically unreliable, because of the number of right-wing elements in it. It is hard to believe that Hoxha has simply invented this accusation, and one is left with the conclusion that it demonstrates the very low level of knowledge about Albania among the Soviet leadership at the time, as well as indicating the extremely crude mode of discussion between the leaderships of the two regimes.

A few months after Stalin's death, in June 1953, I went to Moscow . . . to seek an economic and military credit.

It was the time when Malenkov seemed to be the main leader.

. . . I had met them all [the leaders] in the time of Stalin. Malenkov looked just the same – a heavy-built man with a pale, hairless face. I had met him years before in Moscow, during meetings I had with Stalin, and he had made a good impression on me. He worshipped Stalin and it seemed to me that Stalin valued him, too . . . now he was at the head of the table, holding the post of chairman of the Council of Ministers of the USSR. Beside him stood Beria, with his eyes glittering behind glasses and his hands never still. After him came Molotov, quiet, good-looking, one of the most serious and most honoured comrades for us, because he was an old Bolshevik from the time of Lenin and a close comrade of Stalin's. We still thought of Molotov in this way even after Stalin's death.

Next to Molotov was Mikoyan, his dark face scowling. This merchant was holding one of those thick pencils, half red half blue (something you could see in all the offices of the Soviet Union), and was keeping the «score». Now he had taken even greater authority into his hands. On March 6, the day the posts were shared out, it was decided that the Ministry of Foreign Trade and that of Internal Trade should be combined in one, and the Armenian wheeler-dealer grabbed the portfolio.

Finally there was the bearded Marshal Bulganin, with white hair and pale blue eyes, sitting a little bit bemused at a corner of the table.

«Let us hear what you have to say!» said Malenkov in a very grave tone. This was not at all a comradely beginning. This was to become the custom in talks with the new Soviet leaders, and no doubt this behaviour was supposed to show the pride of the great state. «Well, say what you have to say to us, we shall listen to you and pronounce our final opinion.»

I did not know Russian well, I could not speak it, but I could understand it. The talk was conducted through an interpreter.

I began to speak about the problems that were worrying us, especially about military questions and the problems of the economy ... The aid which they provided for our army was always insufficient and minimal, regardless of the fact that in public we always spoke very highly of the value of that small amount of aid which they granted us ... I also portrayed the situation of our country in connection with our Yugoslav, Greek and Italian neighbours. From all around our country the enemies were carrying out intensive hostile work of diversion, espionage and sabotage from the sea, the air and the land. We were having continual clashes with armed bands of enemy agents and needed aid in military materials.

My concern was to make my exposé as concrete and concise as possible. I tried not to go on at too great a length and I had been speaking for no more than twenty minutes, when I heard Beria, with his snake's eyes, say to Malenkov, who was sitting listening to me as expressionless as a mummy:

«Can't we say what we have to say and put an end to this?»

Without changing his expression, without shifting his eyes from me (of course, he had to maintain his authority in front of his deputies!), Malenkov said to Beria:

«Wait!»

I was so annoyed I was ready to explode internally, but I preserved my aplomb and, in order to let them understand that I had heard and understood what they said, I cut down my talk and said to Malenkov:

«I have finished.»

«*Pravilno!*» [That's right] said Malenkov and gave Mikoyan the floor.

Beria, pleased that I had finished, put his hands in his pockets and tried to work out what impression their replies were making on me. Of course, I was not satisfied with what they had decided to give us in response to the very modest requests we had made. I spoke again and told them that they had made heavy reductions in the things we had asked for. Mikoyan jumped in to «explain» that the Soviet Union itself was poor, that it had gone through the war, that it had to assist other countries, too, etc . . .

Molotov was leaning on the table. He said something about Albania's relations with its neighbours, but he never raised his eyes. Malenkov and Beria seemed to be the two «cocks of the walk», while Mikoyan who was cold and bitter, did not say much, but when he did speak, it was only to make some vicious and venomous remark. From the way they spoke, the way they interrupted one another, the arrogant tone in which they gave «advice», the signs of discord among them were quite clear.

«Since this is what you have decided, there is no reason for me to prolong matters,» I said.

«*Pravilno!*» repeated Malenkov and asked in a loud voice: «Has anyone anything to add?»

«I have,» said Bulganin at the end of the table.

«You have the floor,» said Malenkov.

Bulganin opened a dossier and, in substance, said:

«You, Comrade Enver, have asked for aid for the army. We

have agreed to give you as much as we have allocated to you, but I have a number of criticisms. The army ought to be a sound weapon of the dictatorship of the proletariat, its cadres loyal to the party and of proletarian origin, the party must have the army firmly under its leadership . . .»

Bulganin went on for a very long time with a «moralising» speech, full of words of «advice». I listened carefully and waited for the criticisms, but they did not come. In the end he said this:

«Comrade Enver, we have information that many cadres of your army are the sons of beys and aghas, of dubious origin and activity. We must be certain about those into whose hands these weapons, with which we shall supply you, will be put, therefore we advise you to study this problem deeply and carry out purges . . .»

This made my blood boil because it was a slanderous accusation and an insult to the cadres of our army. I raised my voice and asked the marshal:

«What is the source of this information which you give me with such assurance? Why do you insult our army?»

The atmosphere of the meeting became as cold as ice. They all lifted their heads and looked at me while I waited for Bulganin to reply. He found himself in a tight spot because he had not expected this cutting question, and he looked at Beria.

Beria began to speak, the movements of his hands and eyes revealing his embarrassment and irritation, and said that according to their information, we allegedly had unsuitable and dubious elements, not only in the army, but also in the apparatus of the state and in the economy! He even mentioned a percentage. Bulganin sighed with relief and looked around, not concealing his satisfaction, but Beria cut short his smile. He openly opposed Bulganin's «advice» about purges and stressed that the «elements with a bad past, but who have since taken the right road, must not be purged but should be pardoned.» The resentment and deep contradictions which existed between these two were displayed quite openly. As it turned out later, the contradictions between Bulganin and Beria were not simply between these two persons, but were the reflection of deep contradictions, quarrels and opposition between the Soviet state security service and the intelligence organs of the Soviet army . . . We could never accept this accusation, therefore, I stood up and said:

«Those who have given you this information have committed slander, hence they are enemies. There is no truth in what you said . . . In our army there are no sons of beys and aghas. Or if there are perhaps ten or twenty individuals, they have abandoned their class and have shed their own blood . . . All the cadres of our army have fought in the war, have emerged from the war, and not only do I not accept these accusations but I am telling you that your informers are deceiving you, are concocting slanders. I assure you that the weapons that we . . . receive from you . . . will be in reliable hands, that the Party of Labour, and no one else, leads our People's Army. That is all I had to say!» and I sat down.

When I had finished, Malenkov began to speak to close the debate. After stressing that he agreed with what the preceding speakers had said, he issued a load of «advice and instructions» for us, and then dwelt on the debate which we had with Bulganin and Beria about the «enemies» in the ranks of our army.

«As for undertaking purges in the army, I think that the problem should not be presented in this way,» said Malenkov, opposing the «advice» which Bulganin gave me about purges. «People are not born ready-formed, and they make mistakes in life. We must not be afraid to excuse people for their past mistakes . . . The term 'purge' of the army is not suitable,» repeated Malenkov and closed the discussion.

Utter confusion: one said irresponsibly, «You have enemies» and «carry out purges», the other said, «We are bringing out laws to pardon them for their past»! . . .

My conclusion from this meeting was unpleasant. I saw that the leadership of the Soviet Union was ill-disposed towards our country. The arrogant way they behaved during the meeting, their refusal to give those few things that we sought, and their slanderous attack on the cadres of our army were not good signs.

From this meeting I observed also that there was no unity in the Presidium of the Communist Party of the Soviet Union: Malenkov and Beria were predominant, Molotov hardly spoke, Mikoyan . . . spouted venom, while what Bulganin said was bullshit.

First encounter with Khrushchev as head of the Party

Hoxha's first meeting with Khrushchev after the latter became First Secretary of the Soviet Communist Party was in June 1954. Hoxha was accompanied by his close friend, Hysni Kapo. Apart from the economic issues under discussion, the chief point of interest is the way that Khrushchev imposes the decision to divide the posts of head of the Party and head of government in all the countries of the bloc. Hoxha, who at the time held both these posts, as well as several others, naturally took the proposal amiss – although he soon stepped down as premier, a post in which he was succeeded by Mehmet Shehu, who held the job for twenty-seven years until his demise in 1981.

Hoxha's portrait of Khrushchev, though unsympathetic, is not implausible.

Knowing from the meeting a year earlier with Malenkov that the new leaders . . . did not like to listen for long, I tried to be as concise as possible in my exposé and put the emphasis mainly on economic questions about which we had sent a detailed letter to the Soviet leadership two months earlier.

. . . Khrushchev spoke immediately after me and right from the start displayed his clownish nature . . . :

«We are informed about your situation . . .» he began. «The report which Comrade Enver gave us here made matters clearer to us, and I describe it as a 'joint report', yours and ours. But,» he continued, «I am still a bad Albanian and I am not going to speak now either about the economic problems or about the political ones, which Comrade Enver raised, because, for our part, we have still not exchanged opinions and reached a common view. Therefore, I am going to speak about something else.»

And he began to give us a long talk about the importance of the role of the party.

He spoke in a loud voice with many gestures of his hands and his head, looking in all directions without concentrating on any one point, interrupted his speech here and there to ask questions, and then, often without waiting for the reply, went on with his speech, hopping from branch to branch.

«The party leads, organises, controls,» he theorised. «It is the initiator and inspirer. But Beria wanted to liquidate the role of the party,» and after a moment of silence he asked me: «Have you received the resolution which announced the sentence we passed on Beria?»

«Yes,» I replied.

He left his discourse about the party and started to speak about the activity of Beria; he accused him of almost every crime and described him as the cause of many evils. These were the first steps towards the attack on Stalin . . .

. . . [At the June 1954] meeting, moreover, to our astonishment, Khrushchev told us:

«When you were here last year, you assisted in the exposure and unmasking of Beria.»

I stared in amazement, wondering what he was leading up to. Khrushchev's explanation was this:

«You remember the debate which you had last year with Bulganin and Beria over the accusation they made against your army. It was Beria who had given us that information, and the strong opposition which you put up in the presence of the comrades of the Presidium, helped us by supplementing the doubts and the facts which we had about the hostile activity of Beria. A few days after your departure for Albania we condemned him.» [10]

However, in that first meeting with us Khrushchev was not concerned simply with Beria. The «Beria» dossier had been closed. Khrushchev had settled accounts with him. Now he had to go further. He dealt at length with the importance and the role of the first secretary or general secretary of the party.

After going all round the question from the aspect of «principle», Khrushchev did not fail to launch a few gibes which, of course, were aimed against Malenkov, although he mentioned no names . . .

While he was speaking I glanced several times at Malenkov who sat motionless while his whole body seemed to be sagging, his face an ashen hue.

Voroshilov,[11] his face flushed bright red, was watching me, waiting for Khrushchev to finish his «discourse». Then he began. He pointed out to me (as though I did not know) that the post of prime minister was very important, too, for this or that reason, etc.

«I think,» said Voroshilov in an uncertain tone, as though he did not know with whom to side and whom to oppose, «that Comrade Khrushchev did not intend to imply that the Council of Ministers does not have its own special importance. The prime minister, likewise . . .»

Now Malenkov's face had become deathly pale. While wanting to soften the bad impression which Khrushchev had created, especially about Malenkov, with these words, Voroshilov brought out more clearly the tense situation which existed in the Presidium. Klim Voroshilov went on with this lecture about the role and importance of the prime minister for several minutes!

Malenkov was the «scapegoat» which they displayed to me to see how I would react. In these two lectures I saw clearly that the split in the Presidium was growing deeper, that Malenkov and his supporters were on the way out . . .

At this same meeting Khrushchev told us that the other sister parties had been told of the Soviet «experience» of who should be first secretary of the party and who prime minister in the countries of people's democracy.

«We talked over these questions with the Polish comrades before the congress of their party,» Khrushchev told us. «We thrashed matters out thoroughly and thought that Comrade Bierut should remain chairman of the Council of Ministers and Comrade Ochab[12] should be appointed first secretary of the party . . .»

However, the congress of the Polish United Workers' Party did not fulfil Khrushchev's desires. Bierut, a resolute Marxist-Leninist comrade, of whom I have very good memories, was elected first secretary of the party, while Cyrankiewicz[13] was elected prime minister.

Soviet pressure for a reconciliation with Yugoslavia

In the summer of 1955 Hoxha was pressingly invited to visit the USSR 'for a holiday'. As he remarks, it was no fun getting there – eleven days or so each way.

On arrival, Mikhail Suslov, the Kremlin's chief ideologue, told Hoxha that the Russians had reconsidered the 1948 condemnation of Yugoslavia. Suslov also indicates the role of the 1948 dispute with Yugoslavia in the downgrading of Molotov. In the account as given here, one key criterion of the status of Yugoslavia (as 'socialist' or not) appears to be the extent of its economic ties with the West (though the level of debate between Suslov and Hoxha is not of a very high order). Suslov also urges Hoxha to consider rehabilitating Albanians condemned at the time of the break with Belgrade, of whom the chief one was the Minister of the Interior, Koçi Xoxe. Albania refused (it remains to this day the only European Communist state which has refused to rehabilitate those condemned in the purges of the time).

Subsequently, Hoxha's *bête noire*, Anastas Mikoyan, makes a post-midnight telephone call pressing Hoxha to meet Svetozar Vukmanović Tempo, the Yugoslav who had been Tito's main emissary throughout the Balkans during the war, and had attempted to persuade Hoxha to accept both a 'Balkan staff' and a Balkan federation. Tempo had been close to Xoxe.

Since Khrushchev in his memoirs states flatly that the key issue in the Soviet break with Albania at the end of the decade was democratisation, it is reasonable to imagine that it figured in Suslov's discussions with Hoxha – but there is no sign of it in Hoxha's account. Instead, Hoxha reduces the issue to that of *rehabilitation*. In doing so, he alters the terms of the debate, placing himself on relatively surer terrain, since (although the other East European leaders condemned at the time were definitely innocent) it is very possible that Xoxe had indeed intrigued with the Yugoslavs to oust Hoxha, and Hoxha can thus put up a plausible defence, even if on spurious grounds.

In the summer of 1955, I received a most pressing invitation to go «for a holiday in the Soviet Union».

In Stalin's time I went there for work and very rarely for a holiday. In Khrushchev's time they began to put such pressure on us to go for holidays that it was difficult to refuse . . . However, I did not like to go because, in fact, I could not rest there and it took a lot of time. To go to Moscow we had to travel eight days by ship from Durrës to Odessa, and the ships (*Kotovksy* and *Chiatura*) were not big and rolled heavily. Two more days were needed for the train trip from Odessa to Moscow and one day by aircraft from Moscow to the Caucasus (to go to Kislovodsk, etc.), that is, a trip of eleven days each way, plus several days of meetings, so you can see what sort of holidays they were.

Once in Moscow the meetings with the Soviet leaders would begin, but these meetings were no longer pleasant like those with Stalin. Now they were held sometimes with smothered anger, sometimes with open flare-ups.

This is what occurred on this occasion. As soon as I arrived in Moscow I had two meetings with Suslov.

In his opening words he told me that we would talk about the Yugoslav problem and stressed in a dictatorial tone:

«The leadership of your party must take careful account of this question, it must not look at the Yugoslav problem in a rigid way.»

I did not take my eyes off him as I listened. Sensing my displeasure, he back-pedalled a little:

«Their mistakes remain mistakes,» he said, «but our objective is to become friends . . . with Yugoslavia . . .

«The main problem is that the Central Committee of the Communist Party of the Soviet Union has examined the Yugoslav question in a realistic light, bearing in mind the traitorous work of Beria, and we made self-criticism about this. Our Central Committee came to the conclusion that the breaking off of relations with Yugoslavia was a mistake, that is, we were hasty.»

«In what way, hasty?!» I said. «At that time, thorough analyses were made, long and thorough discussions were held and the true ideological and political causes of the existing disagreements were uncovered.»

«The main cause for this break,» continued Suslov, «was not the ideological issues, although they were making mistakes, and they have been pointed out openly to the Yugoslavs. The main cause lies in the slanders that were made against the Yugoslav leaders and in our lack of patience. The Yugoslavs' mistakes of principle should have been discussed, backed up by facts, and ironed out. This was not done.

«From all the facts examined,» he continued, «it turns out that there is no basis at all for saying that the Yugoslav comrades have deviated and have sold Yugoslavia, just as it does not turn out that the Yugoslav economy is dependent on foreigners.»

«Pardon me,» I said, «but let us not go back to those things we have analysed and decided in 1948 and 1949. Let us take only your correspondence with the Yugoslav leadership during the last two years. Not only in several of your letters, but the Yugoslavs themselves in their letters, admit that they have created strong links with the West. What are we to think now of your opposite assessment of these matters?»

«A number of mistakes have been made, but they must be examined carefully,» said Suslov, and started to list a series of «arguments» to convince me that the Yugoslav leaders were allegedly not on a wrong road. Naturally he also tried to lay the blame on Beria and Djilas and the efforts of imperialism «to attach Yugoslavia to itself».

«Molotov, too, has maintained a very sectarian stand on this problem,» continued Suslov. «He personally made mistakes in state relations with Yugoslavia while insisting that it was the Yugoslav comrades that made the mistakes. However, the Central Committee demanded that Molotov prove where the Yugoslavs had been wrong, and we criticised him severely for his stand. Finally he, too, expressed his solidarity with the Central Committee».

I began to speak and gave a detailed presentation of our relations with the Yugoslav leadership . . .

[Suslov said] «. . . we must not allow the imperialists to take Yugoslavia from us.»

At the end of this meeting, as though in passing, he said to me:

«During past years you have condemned many enemies, accused of links with the Yugoslavs. Have a look at their cases and rehabilitate those that ought to be rehabilitated.»

«We have never accused and condemned anyone for nothing,» I said bluntly, and as we parted, he instructed me to be «more broad-minded».

It was clear why they had invited me to come for a holiday. However, the Khrushchevites did not content themselves just with this. They had hatched up diabolical plans to compel our Party, too, to follow their course of [re-]conciliation with the revisionists of Belgrade. This time they had put me in a villa outside Moscow, which, as they told me, had been Stalin's villa. It was a simple house, . . . one night we heard a loud knock at the glass door which led to our suite. My wife, Nexhmije, got up quickly, thinking that our son was not well, since he had fallen over that day and had hurt his hand. She went out, immediately returned and said to me:

«It's one of the officers of the guard – Mikoyan wants you on the telephone.»

I was sleepy and asked what time it was.

«Half past twelve,» said Nexhmije.

I put something over my shoulders and went into the study to the telephone. Mikoyan, at the other end of the line, did not beg my pardon for ringing me up after midnight, but said to me:

«Comrade Enver, Comrade Svetozar Vukmanović-Tempo is here in Moscow and I was with him till now. You know him and it would be good if you were to meet; he is ready to meet you tomorrow.»

For a time I remained silent on the telephone, while Mikoyan, who had no intention of asking, said: «Tomorrow then, you agree,» in a tone as if he were giving an order to the party secretary of an *oblast* [region].

«How could I agree to this, Comrade Mikoyan,» I said. «I talked with Comrade Suslov, and expressed the view of our Party about the position of Yugoslavia and Tito.»

Mikoyan began to deliver a standard monologue about «socialist Yugoslavia», about Tito who was «a fine chap», about Beria's mistakes and the sins they had allegedly committed (the Soviet Union and the Information Bureau), and then he concluded:

«You ought to take this step, Comrade Enver. You know Tempo, talk with him and try to iron out your differences, because this is in your interest and in the interest of the camp. You, too, must help ensure that Yugoslavia does not go over to the imperialist camp . . . So, you agree, tomorrow.»

«All right, I agree, tomorrow,» I replied, clenching my teeth in rage. I went back to bed but I was so disgusted over these backstage manoeuvres and faits accomplis . . . that I could not sleep. I had met Tempo twice in Albania during the time of the war and both times we had quarrelled, because he was arrogant and a real megalomaniac . . . What was I to say to Tempo now, after all those things which Tito, Ranković, their envoys Velimir Stojnić, Nijaz Dizdarević and their agents Koçi Xoxe and Co., had done to us? Must we swallow this too?! I tossed and turned sleepless all night thinking about what should be done. The time had not come yet to settle accounts with the Khrushchevite revisionists.

The next day we met Tempo. I began to speak about those things that had occurred.

«Let bygones be bygones,» he said and began to speak about the situation in Yugoslavia.

. . . «Our agriculture is in a very bad state,» he said.

. . . He . . . said that they had been obliged to accept aid at heavy interest rates from the Western countries.

«Now the Soviet Union is helping us and our agreement with the Soviets is going well,» he concluded.

I, too, spoke about the progress which our country had made during this time and the difficulties which we had. I spoke about the commission on Lake Ohri[d],[14] in which the discussions were being dragged on by their side, but he told me he knew nothing about it because «these were the plans of the Macedonians.»

«Nevertheless, we must look more carefully at the question of Lake Shkodra where the benefits will be greater for both sides, especially for your side,» he added.

And that is how the meeting . . . passed. After this meeting, when I met Mikoyan and Suslov, they both said to me:

«You did well to meet Tempo because the ice has been broken.»

According to them, the mountain of ice created between us and the Titoite revisionists could be broken with one chance meeting or contact, but this was not our opinion. There would be no «spring thaw» in the ideological field in our relations with Yugoslavia and we had no intention of plunging into the murky waters of the Khrushchevites and the Titoites.

The first whiff of the denunciation of Stalin

Although Hoxha often suggests that he could foresee the exposure and denunciation of Stalin well before it happened, the first occasion which he describes in detail when he heard the Soviet leaders speak clearly of Stalin's crimes was at the beginning of 1956. Again, there is a ring of truth to the account, particularly in the way Khrushchev swiped at the cabbage head. But perhaps the most interesting aspect of Hoxha's account is what it tells one about Hoxha himself – he never actually asks if the account he is given is true. After a moment's pause he rounds on Khrushchev and Voroshilov with the idiotic question: 'How is it that you did not help him [Stalin] to avoid these mistakes?'

I was in Moscow on the occasion of a meeting of the parties of all the socialist countries. I think it was January 1956 . . . We were together with Khrushchev and Voroshilov in a villa outside Moscow, where all the representatives of the sister parties were to have lunch. The others had not yet arrived. I had never heard the Soviet leaders openly speak ill of Stalin, and I, for my part, continued as before to speak with affection and deep respect for the great Stalin . . . While waiting for the other comrades to come, Khrushchev and Voroshilov said to me:

«Shall we take some air in the park?»

We went out and strolled around the paths of the park. Khrushchev said to Klim Voroshilov:

«Do tell Enver something about Stalin's mistakes.»

I pricked up my ears, although I had long suspected that they were crooks. And Voroshilov began to tell me that «Stalin made mistakes in the line of the party, he was brutal, and so savage that you could not discuss anything with him.»

Voroshilov went on, «He even allowed crimes to be committed, and he must bear responsiblity for this. He made mistakes also in the field of the development of the economy, therefore it is not right to describe him as the 'architect of the construction of socialism'. Stalin did not have correct relations with the other parties . . .»

Voroshilov went on and on pouring out such things against Stalin. Some I understood and some I didn't, because, as I have written above, I did not understand Russian well, but nevertheless I understood the essence of the conversation and the aim of these two and I was revolted. Khrushchev was walking ahead of us, carrying a stick with which he hit the cabbages that they had planted in the park. (Khrushchev had planted vegetables even in the parks in order to pose as an expert in agriculture.)

As soon as Voroshilov ended his slanderous tale I asked him:

«How is it possible that Stalin could make such mistakes?»

Khrushchev turned to me, his face flushed, and replied,

«It is possible, it is possible Comrade Enver, Stalin did these things.»

«You have seen these things when Stalin was alive. But how is it that you did not help him to avoid these mistakes, which you say he made?» I asked Khrushchev.

«It is natural that you ask this question, Comrade Enver, but you see this *kapusta* [cabbage] here? Stalin would have cut off your head just as easily as the gardener will cut this *kapusta*,» and Khrushchev hit the cabbage with his stick.

«Everything is clear!» I said to Khrushchev and said no more.

We went inside. The other comrades had arrived. I was seething with anger . . . It was the time when the notorious 20th Congress was being prepared . . . He [Khrushchev] was creating the figure of a «popular» moujik leader, who was opening the prisons and concentration camps . . . Khrushchev, this digusting, loud-mouthed individual, concealed his wiles and manoeuvres under a torrent of empty words. Nevertheless, in this way, he created a situation favourable to his group.

. . . [But it was] those Khrushchevite ideas and reforms which, in fact, damaged Soviet agriculture so severely that their cata-strophic consequences are being felt to this day. All the boastful clamour about the «virgin lands» was empty advertising. The Soviet Union is still buying millions of tons of grain from the United States of America.

However, the «collective leadership» and non-publication of Khrushchev's photographs in the newspapers did not last long. The cult of Khrushchev was being built up by the tricksters, the liberals, the careerists, the lick-spittles and the flatterers . . . His [Stalin's] place and authority was usurped by that charlatan, clown and blackmailer.

The Twentieth Congress of the Soviet Communist Party (February 1956)

Along with the heads of the other bloc parties, Hoxha attended the famous 20th Congress of the CPSU in Moscow in February 1956, at which Khrushchev delivered his 'secret speech' revealing Stalin's crimes.[15]

Hoxha's brief account betrays a tragic misreading of the entire event. Hoxha returned his copy of Khrushchev's report, and denounced the policy of releasing political prisoners and rehabilitating those unjustly condemned.

The opportunist «new spirit», which Khrushchev was arousing and activating, was apparent in the way in which the proceedings of this [the 20th CPSU] congress were organised and conducted. This liberal spirit pervaded the whole atmosphere, the Soviet press and propaganda of those days like an ominous cloud; it prevailed in the corridors and the congress halls, it was apparent in people's faces, gestures and words.

The former seriousness, characteristic of such extremely import-ant events in the life of a party and a country, was missing. Even non-party people spoke during the proceedings of the congress. In the breaks between sessions, Khrushchev and company strolled through the halls and corridors, laughing and competing with one another as to who could tell the most anecdotes, make the most wisecracks and show himself the most popular, who could drink the most toasts at the heavily laden tables which were placed everywhere.

With all this, Khrushchev wanted to reinforce the idea that the «grave period», the «dictatorship» and «gloomy analysis» of things were over once and for all . . .

. . . On the last day . . . a second report by Khrushchev was read to the delegates. It was the notorious, so-called secret report against Stalin, but which had been sent in advance to the Yugoslav leaders, and a few days later it fell into the hands of the bourgeoisie and reaction as a new «gift» from Khrushchev and the Khrushchevites. After it was discussed by the delegates to the congress, this report was given to us and all the other foreign delegations to read.

Only the first secretaries of sister parties taking part in the congress read it. I spent all night reading it, and extremely shocked, gave it to Mehmet [Shehu] and Gogo [Nushi] to read. We had known in advance that Khrushchev and company had cancelled out the glorious work and figure of Stalin . . . But we could never have imagined that all those monstrous accusations and calumnies against the great and unforgettable Stalin could have been put on paper by the Soviet leaders. Nevertheless, there it was in black and white . . . Our hearts and minds were deeply and gravely shocked. Amongst ourselves we said that this was a villainy which had gone beyond all bounds, with catastrophic consequences for the Soviet Union and the movement, and that in those tragic circumstances, the duty of our Party was to stand firm on its own Marxist-Leninist positions.

After we had read it we immediately returned the terrible report to its owners. We had no need for that package of filthy accusations which Khrushchev had concocted. It was other «communists» who took it away to give to reaction and to sell by the ton in their book-stalls as a profitable business.

We returned to Albania heart-broken . . . but at the same time we returned with a great lesson that we must be more vigilant and more alert towards the activities and stands of Khrushchev and the Khrushchevites.

Comecon (the Council of Mutual Economic Aid, CMEA)

One of Hoxha's most devastating passages is this account of how the Soviet-led Comecon, the socialist 'Common Market', works, and particularly the level of discussion and argument among the bloc leaders. To some extent, the discussion, as recorded here, reflects both the relatively low level of economic development in the countries concerned, the still low level of integration – and, perhaps above all, the usually ignored fact that the Soviet Union is the centre and head of a bloc of countries many of which had then, and still have, a higher standard of living and economy than the 'core' country itself.[16]

The way in which these meetings [of the Council of Mutual Economic Aid] were organised and our friends behaved towards us . . . more and more impelled us to ask ourselves: are we dealing with Marxist-Leninists or hucksters? Ulbricht, Novotny, Ochab, Dej, Kadar, Gomulka, Cyrankiewicz, Zhivkov, and the others,[17] were at one another's throats; each of them complained that he was in dire straits; they all called for «more aid» from their friends, because they had «pressure from below»; they tried to elbow one another out, presented all kinds of «arguments» and figures; they tried to dodge their obligations and to grab as much as possible at the expense of others. Meanwhile Khrushchev or his envoys would get up, deliver lectures on the «socialist division of labour», support one or the other, according to their own interests in a given situation, and demand «unity» and «understanding» in the «socialist family». And in all this wrangling Albania went almost unmentioned, as if it did not exist for them . . .

Socialist Albania was treated with disdain by the others as if we were a nuisance. We were well aware of the situation in our country, were conscious that our economic potential was no-where near that of the other countries; we knew also that these countries had their own big problems and difficulties, but these should never have served as a reason for them to underrate and ignore us. With great efforts, after many meetings and talks, we managed occasionally to squeeze some aid or credit out of them . . . It was precisely sincerity, the genuine internationalist spirit, that was lacking amongst them. When it came to practical fulfilment of their commitments to provide aid for our country, each of them would make excuses:

«We have shortages and needs ourselves,» said Ulbricht, «we have pressure from Federal Germany, therefore we are unable to help Albania.»

«The counter-revolution caused us damage,» was Kadar's justification. «We cannot fulfil our commitment about aid.»

All of them, one after the other, acted in this way. And in the end the «solution» was found:

«The Council of Mutual Economic Aid recommends to the Albanian comrades that the problems raised by them here should be solved with the Soviet government through bilateral meetings.»

Among many such meetings of the Comecon countries, the one that was held in Moscow in June 1956 has stuck in my mind.

. . . Ochab, who had become first secretary of the Polish United Workers' Party, got up and declared:

«We have not fulfilled the obligations with which we have been charged for coal and are not going to do so. We cannot fulfil the plan, its targets are set too high and must be reduced. The coal workers live badly, they work to exhaustion.»

As soon as he finished, Gerö,[18] Ulbricht and Dej got up, one after the other, and levelled every kind of charge against the Poles. The atmosphere was very heated.

«If you want coking coal, invest in Poland,» replied Ochab. «We must improve the standard of living. Things have reached such a state that the Polish workers are about to go on strike and abandon the mines . . .»

«Where should we invest first?!» replied the others. «In the steel plants of the Soviet Union or in your coal mines?!»

«We must examine these things,» said Khrushchev, trying to cool the tempers. «As for the question of workers, if you Poles have insufficient, or those you have walk out, we can bring workers from other countries.»

At this Ochab jumped up.

«It is not fair,» he shouted. «You must help us. We are not going back to Poland without settling this matter. Either reduce the plan or increase the investments . . .»

«Once taken, the decisions must be carried out,» interposed Dej.

«The decisions are not being carried out,» said Gerö, adding fuel to the flames. «We have several factories in which we have been told to produce arms and special equipment, but no one is buying the products from us.»

«They don't take them from us, either,» said Ochab, jumping up again. «What are we to do with them?!»

«Let us not speak here like factory managers,» said Khrushchev to Ochab. «Things can't be discussed in this way. You must look at the profitability. We, too, have changed direction in many plants. For example,» continued Khrushchev, «we have turned some arms plants into plants producing water pumps. I have some suggestions about these problems,» continued Khrushchev, and he began to bring out those «gems» which he had on the tip of his tongue:

«In regard to a number of special products of industry,» he said among other things, «we must do as Hitler did. At that time Germany was alone and he produced all those things. We must study this experience and we, too, must set up joint enterprises for special products, for example, weapons.»

We could not believe our ears! Could it be true that the first secretary of the Central Committee of the Communist Party of the Soviet Union wanted to learn from the experience of Hitler and even recommended it to others?! But this is what things were coming to. The others listened and nodded approval.

«You must provide us with designs,» said Ochab.

«You don't deserve to get them,» shouted Khrushchev angrily, «because the West steals them from you. We gave you the patent of an aircraft and the capitalists stole it from you.»

«That occurred,» admitted Ochab, and pulled in his horns a little.

«We gave you the secret report of the 20th Congress and you printed it and sold it at 20 zloty a copy. You don't know how to keep secrets.»

«Right!» whispered Ochab, and drew in his horns even further.

«We have given you another four top secret documents and they have flown from you,» added Bulganin, numbering them off one by one to his face.

«Yes,» said Ochab, and now his voice could hardly be heard. «Someone stole them from us and fled to the West.»

«The situation in Poland is not good,» continued Khrushchev. «You are following an opportunist policy towards the Soviet Union and the countries of people's democracy, let alone within your own country.»

«In the context of collaboration,» interjected Ulbricht, «we must collaborate with all, especially with the social-democrats.»

. . . «Agreed, collaboration,» shouted Khrushchev, «but not to rise against the Soviet Union and our camp. This is what is happening in Poland.» He turned to Ochab and Cyrankiewicz, who during the whole time had sat smoking French Gauloises, without saying a single word. «You must improve the situation. You must build up the people's trust in you.»

«We have released all the imprisoned social-democrats,» said Ochab.

«You should have kept some of them,» said Saburov ironically. «To whom are we going to drink the toast today, to the social-democrats?!»

Khrushchev provided the answer:

«Let us drink to collaboration!»

It was quite obvious that things in the camp were taking the wrong road. The «demons» which Khrushchev released from the bottle were stirring and poking out their tongues even at their liberator. He tried to manoeuvre, to get them on side, to set the others on to one (this time Ochab was in the dock), and then, when he saw that the quarrel was not dying down, he poured out threats and warnings to all.

The East European countries and their leaders in the late 1940s–early 1950s

In this extract, Hoxha casts a rapid glance over the other East European countries and their leaders. His assessment has three parts to it: the personality of the individual leaders; the regime's attitude to helping Albania; and the general level of culture and openness. On this latter score, Czechoslovakia easily comes out top. Romania comes out bottom all round. The main surprise in the extract is that the East German leader, Walter Ulbricht, generally considered to have been quite subservient to the Russians, should have spoken so forthrightly (if he did).

I knew Gottwald . . . He was a modest sincere comrade, not a man of many words. I felt I could talk to him freely; he listened to me attentively, puffing away at his pipe and spoke with much sympathy about our people and our fight, and promised me that they would help us in the building of industry. He promised me neither mountains nor miracles, but a very modest credit which Czechoslovakia accorded us.

«This is all we can do,» he said. «Later, when we have our economy going, we shall re-examine matters with you.»

. . . I met Ochab several times . . . he was a person who not only could not be compared with Bierut as a man, but also lacked the necessary capacity to lead the party and the country. Ochab came and went like a shadow, without being a year in that position . . . With the death of Bierut the road to the throne of Poland was opened to the reactionary Gomulka. This «communist», brought out of prison, after a number of ups and downs and writhings of a heterogeneous leadership, in which agents of Zionism and the capitalist powers were not lacking, was to be brought into the leadership by his friend Nikita Khrushchev.

Poland was the «big sister» of the Khrushchevite Soviet Union. Then came Bulgaria, with which the Khrushchevites played and are still playing their game shamelessly, to the point that they have turned it into their «obedient daughter».

The Bulgarians were linked closely with Stalin and the Communist Party of the Soviet Union (B) led by him, quite differently from the Czechs, the Poles and the Rumanians, let alone the Germans. Moreover, the Bulgarian people had been traditionally linked with Russia in the past.

. . . Khrushchev . . . exploited this situation . . . and placed at the head of the Bulgarian Communist Party a worthless person, a third-rate cadre, but one ready to do whatever Khrushchev, his ambassador, or the KGB would say. This person was Todor Zhivkov, who was publicised and inflated until he became first secretary of the CC of the Bulgarian CP.[19]

. . . I have gone to Bulgaria several times on business, as well as on holidays with my wife and children. To tell the truth, I felt a special satisfaction in Bulgaria, probably because, although our two peoples are of quite different origin, during the centuries they had co-existed, had languished under and fought against the same occupying power, the Ottomans, and are alike in many directions, especially in their modesty, hospitality, stability of character, the preservation of good traditions, folklore, etc.

. . . After the death of George Dimitrov, Vulko Chervenkov[20] became general secretary of the party. He was a big man, with greying hair and bags under the eyes. Whenever I met him . . . he gave me the impression of a good fellow who walked with his arms flopping aimlessly, as if to say: «What am I doing at this fair? I am serving no purpose here.»

He must have been a just man, but lacking in will . . . He was extremely sparing in words. In official talks he said so little that, if you didn't know him, you would form the impression he was haughty. But he wasn't in the least haughty. He was a simple man. In non-official talks, when we ate together, and met with other Bulgarian comrades to exchange opinions, Vulko sat in stony silence, with his mouth closed, as if he were not there at all. The others talked and laughed, but not he.

Chervenkov was Dimitrov's brother-in-law. He had married

the sister of the great leader of Bulgaria. It is possible that a little of Dimitrov's glory and authority had descended on Vulko Chervenkov, but Vulko was quite incapable of becoming Dimitrov. Thus, just as he came to the head of the leadership of the Bulgarian Communist Party in silence, so he went without any fuss when he was thrown out . . . The revisionist chiefs of [the Romanian] party were the most conceited you could imagine. They «blew their own trumpets» loudly about the fight which they had not fought.

When we began the struggle with the renegade Tito group, Dej became an «ardent fighter» against this group. In the historic meetings of the Information Bureau he was charged with delivering the main report against the Tito—Ranković group.

As long as Stalin was alive and the Resolution of the Information Bureau remained in force, Dej performed like a rabid anti-Titoite. When the revisionist traitors, headed by Khrushchev, usurped power in their countries . . . [and] proclaimed Tito clean and prettied him up, Dej was among the first to . . . change his colour like a chameleon . . .

There was not the slightest warmth and special friendship for a small socialist country like ours, which had fought and sacrificed so much in the war against the fascist invaders, to be seen among the Rumanian leaders. Rumania was the socialist country which proved to be more indifferent than all the others in regard to Albania.

. . . Several times we sought credits from the Rumanians, but they either refused us or gave us some ludicrously small sum. In regard to experience on oil, in industry and in agriculture, for example, they made us promises, . . . but never gave us anything of any substance.

. . . In the other parties, at first, there was a more or less tangible spirit of unity and mutual internationalist aid, and this was reflected towards us in practice. Whereas in the Rumanian party, this spirit of unity and aid was very weak.

In general the Rumanian leaders were prominent both for their megalomania towards «lesser mortals» and for their servility towards «the mighty».

. . . In my opinion, the Czechoslovaks were different from the others. They were more serious than all of them . . . They had respect for our people and our Party. They were not very lively, but I can say they were restrained, correct and kindly.

Novotny and Široky, Dolansky and Kopecky[21] . . . behaved openly and in a modest way with me and all our comrades. That conceit and arrogance, which was apparent in the others, was not to be seen in them.

After the Soviets, it was the Czechs who assisted us most from the economic angle, too. Naturally, when it was a question of granting credits, they were cool-headed and cautious, people who reckoned things carefully. In what they gave us, there was no obvious underestimation, or sense of their economic superiority. Amongst the countries of people's democracy, Czechoslovakia was the most industrially advanced; its people were industrious, skilful, systematic, orderly in work and life. Wherever you went in Czechoslovakia, it was obvious that it was a developed country, with a cultured people who preserved the traditions of their ancient culture. The Soviets used the country as a health resort, and abused it to the extent that they brought it to its present state. The leaders of other countries of people's democracy were envious of the Czech leadership, and made vain gibes about it, but the Czechs displayed much more dignity than all the others. In the meetings of the socialist camp also, what the Czech leaders said carried weight. As far as I could see and judge, within the country, too, they enjoyed respect and sympathy.

When I went to Czechoslovakia I did not feel that heavy sense of isolation which was created in Moscow after Khrushchev took over the reins. As soon as we arrived in Moscow, they allocated us a *dacha* on the outskirts of the city, where we remained isolated for whole days. Officials such as Lesakov, Moshatov, Petrov and some other minor functionary of the apparatus of the Central Committee of the party would be there or would come and go, usually to accompany us, but also to eat and drink. They were all people of the security service, dressed [up] as functionaries of the Central Committee. Of these, Lesakov was my inseparable companion and billiards partner. He liked me and I liked him because, although he was not outstandingly intelligent, he was a good, sincere person. Moshatov came more rarely, appeared to be more important, prepared the journeys or fulfilled any request we might have to buy something, because you could find nothing easily in the market (you had to order everything in advance, because they brought the things ordered from some mysterious source to a special room in the «GUM» store, which had a special entrance for the Central Committee). Petrov was an apparatus man who had long been engaged with the Greeks and our company interested him for this reason. He was a serious comrade and liked us. He had come to Albania several times, especially when we were supporting the Greek Democratic Army in its just war. As if all these were not sufficient, later, other «escorts» were added, such as a certain Laptiev, a young fellow who knew Albanian and who was swell-headed about the «position» they had given him.

. . . I was never free, I always had an escort. They were all Khrushchev's men, informers for the Central Committee and the Soviet security service, without taking account here of the official guards and the bugging devices with which they filled the various villas in which we stayed. But that is another story. Let us pass over the devices and concentrate on the people.

These Soviet employees tried to find out our *nastroyenie* [mood] in order to learn what we were seeking, what we would raise, with whom we would raise it, what the situation was in our country, what we thought about the Yugoslavs, about the leaders of the Greek Communist Party, or any other matter. They knew why they came and we knew who sent them and why they were sent, therefore both sides were friendly, we talked about what interested us and waited for news to come from the Central Committee about when we were to meet. The *chinovniki*[22] did not talk about politics, no doubt because they had orders about this, but even if they had wanted to open some conversation they did not dare, because they knew that every word would be recorded. We talked especially against the Titoite revisionists. You could not visit any collective farm or state farm, or make contact with the comrades or the people, without giving two or three days notice. And if you did go on a visit, they would sit you down at a table laden with drinks and fruit and you would see nothing, no cattle stall or collective farmer's house.

It is fair to say that it was different in Bulgaria. Wherever you went, the atmosphere was more comradely, with less formality and fewer guards.

. . . After the break in relations with Tito, we travelled to the Soviet Union by sea, because the Yugoslavs did not permit us to fly over their territory. Thus, we have had to stay many times in Odessa where we met the famous Yepishev,[23] the first secretary of Odessa and, later, political director of the Soviet army. We saw none of the places of interest there. We did not see the famous catacombs of Odessa because they did not take us to visit them, nor even the historic Potemkin steps, because we would have had to walk down them. We saw these famous steps, which began from the statue of Richelieu, governor of the city at the start of the 19th century, only from the car.

«How is it possible,» I asked Yepishev, «that you keep this aristocratic French adventurer here, precisely at the head of the historic steps?!»

«Oh, he's just been left there,» replied the secretary of the Odessa Party Committee.

But what did we do in Odessa? We were bored, smoked cigarettes, went to the park of the «Kirov» villa, went to a room with an old billiard-table. We did not go to visit any museum or school, the only place he took us was to a vineyard, and there only so that he could taste and drink some of the bottles of selected wines which they kept in the nearby cellars.

This was what usually happened in the Soviet Union. Only at *priyoms* [receptions] would you shake hands with some personality. When you went to a factory or a house of culture in Leningrad, Kiev or elsewhere, everything was organised: the workers were lined up waiting, a speech of introduction was made by a certain Kozlov,[24] who, puffed up like a turkeycock, spoke with his voice made artificially deep in order to show himself omnipotent, and then people appointed in advance and told what they were to say, made speeches of welcome.

It was quite the opposite in Czechoslovakia, where the people, the leaders, and the factory workers would speak freely, ask questions and reply to everything you asked. There you could travel freely whenever you liked, by car or on foot.

I have always taken an interest in the history of nations and peoples. There are many historic places in Czechoslovakia. I visited the place where the Taborite uprising took place and saw those characteristic villages through which Žižka had passed and in which he fought. I visited Austerlitz and from the museum hill I looked over the battlefield and imagined Bonaparte's historic manoeuvre and the sudden appearance of his troops on the Austrian flanks, precisely at the time the sun was rising over Austerlitz. I remembered the battles of Wallenstein and Schiller's famous trilogy. I asked the Czech comrades:

«Is there any museum about this historic personality?»

«Of course,» they said, and took me immediately to a palace, which was the Wallenstein Museum.

I went hunting deer many times.

. . . One day when I was out hunting I found myself in front of a big *château*. I asked:

«What is that building?»

«It is one of Metternich's residences,» they told me, «now it is a museum.»

«Can we visit it?» I asked the comrades accompanying me.

«Of course,» they replied.

We went in and looked at everything . . . I went into Metternich's library, full of beautifully bound books. When we came out of the library, we passed a closed door and the guide told us:

«In here there is a mummy which was sent as a gift from Egypt to the Chancellor of Austria, the assassin of Napoleon's exiled son, the King of Rome.»

«Open it up,» I said, «let us see this mummy, because I am very interested in Egyptology and have read many books about it, especially about the findings of the scientist Carter, Carnarvon's associate, who discovered the undamaged tomb of Tutankhamen.»

«No,» said the guide, «I won't open that door.»

«Why?» I asked surprised.

«Because some misfortune might befall me, I might die.»

The Czech comrades laughed at him and said:

«What are you telling us, come on, open it up!»

The guide stuck to his guns and finally said:

«Here, take the key, open the door yourselves and have a look. I am not going inside and I won't take any responsibility.»

The Czech comrade escorting me opened the door, we turned on the lights and saw the mummy, completely black in a wooden sarcophagus. We closed the door, gave the key back to the guide, shook hands with him, thanked him, and left.

On our way out, the Czech comrade said to me:

«There are still superstitious people who believe in magic like that guide we saw.»

«No,» I said, «the guide is a man of learning and not superstitious.»

. . . The Czechs themselves took me to Slovakia to show me the figure of our National Hero, Skanderbeg, amongst other outstanding historical figures in an old mural on the portico of a monastery. I went to a small spa, at one time called Marienbad, in Sudetenland, to visit the historic house where Goethe lived. Here, in his old age, Goethe fell in love with a very young «Gretchen» and wrote his famous «Elegy of Marienbad».

I mention all these things to show the reality in Czechoslovakia and the good disposition of the Czechs towards us. However, they behaved in the same way with everybody. Even the Soviets felt themselves different people when they went to Czechoslovakia.

In Czechoslovakia I talked in a park for several hours with Rokossovsky and Konev,[25] who in the Kremlin would merely shake hands. I had to go hunting in Czechoslovakia to meet the president of the Presidium of the Supreme Soviet of the Ukraine and for Nina Khrushcheva to invite Nexhmije and me to tea. I had to go to Czechoslovakia to talk to General Antonov and others.

But as I said above, after the death of Gottwald, the Khrushchevites were getting their grip on Czechoslovakia. It seemed that Novotny, as the first secretary of the Czechoslovak Communist Party, adhered to correct positions, but time showed that he was a wavering opportunist element, and thus, in one way or another, he did the work for Khrushchev and Co. He played a major role in carrying through the plans which made Czechoslovakia a dominion occupied by Russian tanks . . .

With the German Democratic Republic they [the Russians]

considered the problem solved, because East Germany was heavily occupied by Soviet troops . . .

With the East Germans we had good relations as long as Pieck was alive.[26] He was an old revolutionary and comrade of Stalin, for whom I had great respect. I met Pieck in 1959 when I was heading a delegation to the GDR. By that time Pieck was old and sick. He gave me a kindly welcome, and listened to me cheerfully when I spoke about our friendship and told him of Albania's progress (he could hardly speak because of his paralysis).

. . . Ulbricht had not shown any sign of open hostility to our Party until we fell out with the Soviets and with him. He was a haughty, stiff-necked German, not only with small parties like ours, but also with the others. He had this opinion about relations with the Soviets: «You have occupied us, you have stripped us of industry, but now you must supply us with big credits and food, so that Democratic Germany will build up and reach the level of the German Federal Republic.» He demanded such credits arrogantly and he got them. He forced Khrushchev to say in a joint meeting: «We must assist Germany so that it becomes our show-case to the West.» And Ulbricht did not hesitate to tell the Soviets in our presence: «You must speed up your aid because there is bureaucracy.»

«Where is the bureaucracy,» asked Mikoyan «in your country?»

«No, not at all in our country but in yours,» replied Ulbricht.

However, while he received great aid for himself, he was never ready to help the others, and gave us a ludicrous credit. When we attacked the Khrushchevites in Moscow, both in the meeting and after it, he proved to be one of our most ferocious opponents and was the first to attack our Party publicly after the Moscow Meeting [1960].

Hoxha visits China (1956)

Hoxha titles the chapter containing this extract 'My First and Last Visit to China'. It also includes very brief accounts of his visits to Mongolia and North Korea.

The description of Mao Tse-tung (Mao Zedong) at the time of the 8th

Congress of the Chinese Communist Party rings true. Hoxha particularly emphasises Mao's habit of interrupting, or not listening to everything his interlocutor had to say – which clearly annoyed Hoxha. The account should be read bearing in mind that it is Hoxha's first passage about his relationship with China, a state with which Albania was in what seemed to be a very close alliance for more than a decade and a half from 1960–61 to 1977, and Hoxha is concerned to demonstrate that he could detect 'revisionism' in Chinese attitudes as far back as 1956.

We knew that at the head of the Communist Party of China was Mao Zedong, about whom personally, as well as about the party which he led, we had no information other than what we heard from the Soviet comrades. Both during this period and after 1949 we had not had the opportunity to read any of the works or writings of Mao Zedong, who was said to be a philosopher and to have written a whole series of works. We welcomed the victory of October 1, 1949 with heartfelt joy . . . [but our] links remained at the level of friendly, cultural and commercial relations, the sending of some second-rank delegation, mutual support . . . through public speeches and statements, the exchange of telegrams on the occasion of celebrations and anniversaries, and almost nothing more . . .

It was said that Mao was following an «interesting» line for the construction of socialism in China, collaborating with the local bourgeoisie and other parties, which they described as «democratic», «of industrialists», etc. . . . All these things were quite incomprehensible to us and however much you racked your brains, you could not find any argument to describe them as in conformity with Marxism-Leninism. Nevertheless, we thought, China was a very big country, with a population of hundreds of millions, it had just emerged from the dark, feudal-bourgeois past, had many problems and difficulties, and in time it would correct those things which were not in order, on the right road of Marxism-Leninism.

. . . At this same period we had also received invitations from the People's Republic of Mongolia and the People's Democratic Republic of Korea . . .

The Political Bureau appointed me, Comrades Mehmet Shehu

and Ramiz Alia, and our then Foreign Minister, Behar Shtylla, as the delegation.

. . . We . . . set out at the end of August 1956.

. . . During those days Tito had been invited to the Crimea «on holiday» and together with Khrushchev, Ranković and others, was putting the nails in Gerö's coffin . . . In Europe the revisionist earthquake was rocking the foundations of everything, with the exception of our Party and country.

Those 3 or 4 days of our visit to Mongolia passed almost unnoticed. We travelled for hours on end to reach some inhabited centre and everywhere the landscape was the same: vast, bare, monotonous, boring. Tsedenbal,[27] who bounced around us as mobile as a rubber ball, harped on the sole theme – livestock farming. So many million sheep, so many mares, so many horses, so many camels, . . . We drank mare's milk, wished one another success and parted.

On September 7 we arrived in Pyongyang. They put on a splendid welcome, with people, with gongs, with flowers, and with portraits of Kim Il Sung everywhere. You had to look hard to find some portrait of Lenin, tucked away in some obscure corner.

. . . During the days we stayed there, Kim Il Sung was kind and intimate with us.[28] The Korean people had just emerged from the bloody war with the American aggressors and now had thrown themselves into the offensive for the reconstruction and development of the country. They were an industrious, clean and talented people.

. . . However, the revisionist wasp had begun to implant its poisonous sting there, too.

. . . Kim Il Sung told us about an event which had occurred in the plenum of the Central Committee of the party held after the 20th [CPSU] Congress.[29]

«After the report which I delivered,» Kim told us, «two members of the Political Bureau and several other members of the Central Committee got up and raised the question that the lessons of the 20th Congress and the question of the cult of the individual had not been properly appreciated amongst us, here in Korea, that a consistent struggle against the cult of the individual had not been waged, and so on. They said to the plenum: 'We are not getting economic and political results according to the platform of the 20th Congress, and incompetent people have been gathered around the Central Committee.'

«In other words, they attacked the line and unity of the leadership,» continued Kim Il Sung. «The whole Central Committee rose against them,» he said in conclusion.

«What stand was taken towards them?» I asked.

«The plenum criticized them and that was all,» replied Kim Il Sung, adding: «Immediately after this the two fled to China.»

«To China?! What did they do there?»

«Our Central Committee described them as anti-party elements and we wrote to the Chinese leadership to send them back to us without fail. Apart from other mistakes, they also committed the grave act of fleeing. The Chinese comrades did not send them back. They have them there to this day.»

We said openly to Kim Il Sung: «Although we have no detailed knowledge of the matters which these two members of the Political Bureau raised, and it is not up to us to pass judgement on your business, since you have told us about this problem, we think that this is a serious event.»

«In our country, too,» we told him, «after the 20th Congress of the CPSU, there was an attempt by anti-party elements to organise a plot against our Party and our Central Committee. The plot was a deed organised by the revisionists of Belgrade, and as soon as we became aware of it, we crushed it immediately.»

We went on to speak about the Party Conference of Tirana in April 1956, about the pressure which was exerted on us, and the unwavering, resolute stand of our Party towards external and internal enemies.[30]

«You are right, you are right!» said Kim Il Sung, while I was speaking.

From the way he spoke and reacted I sensed a certain hesitation and uncertainty that were overwhelming him.

I was not mistaken in my doubts. A few days later in China, during a meeting I had with Ponomaryov,[31] . . . I opened up the problem of the Korean fugitives.

«We know about this», he replied, «and have given Kim Il Sung our advice.»

«You have advised him? Why?» I asked.

«Comrade Enver,» he said, «things are not going very well with the Koreans. They have become very stuck up and ought to be brought down a peg or two.»

«I am not talking about their affairs in general, because I know nothing about them,» I told Ponomaryov, «but about a concrete problem. Two members of the Political Bureau rise against the Central Committee of their own party and then flee to another socialist country. Where is Kim Il Sung at fault in this?!»

«The Korean comrades have made mistakes,» insisted Ponomaryov. «They have not taken measures in line with the decisions of the 20th Congress, and that is why two members of the Political Bureau rose against this. The Chinese comrades have been revolted by this situation, too, and have told Kim Il Sung that if measures are not taken, they are not going to hand over the two comrades taking refuge in China.»

«Astonishing!» I said.

«You have no reason to be astonished,» he said. «Kim Il Sung himself is retreating. A plenum of the Central Committee of the Korean party has been held these days and the Koreans have agreed to correct the mistakes.»

And this turned out to be true. The two fugitives returned to Korea and the places they had had in the Political Bureau. Under pressure, Kim Il Sung bowed his head and gave way. This was a joint act of the Soviets and the Chinese, in which a special «merit» belonged to Mikoyan. He had been sent to China at the head of the Soviet delegation to the 8th Congress of the CPC, and without waiting for the Chinese congress to finish, the man of the Khrushchevite mafia together with Peng Dehuai,[32] whom Mao Zedong gave him as the representative of China, hastened to Korea to tune up the wavering Kim Il Sung to bring him into harmony with the Khrushchevites.

. . . In Beijing, which we reached on September 13, they welcomed us with crowds of people, music and flowers, not forgetting the horde of portraits of Mao Zedong. Liu Shaoqi,[33] Zhou Enlai, Deng Xiaoping, and others whose names I can't remember, had come out to the airport.

We exchanged greetings with them, wished them success in the congress, . . . and could hardly cope with their stereotyped expressions: «great honour», «great assistance», «brothers from the distant front of Europe», «please, offer us your criticism», etc., etc., expressions with which, in a few years' time, we would be full up to our necks. (However, in those days these expressions, which were served up ready-made everywhere, did not make any bad impression on us – we considered them expressions of the Chinese simplicity and modesty.)

Mao Zedong received us during an interval between sessions of the congress in one of the adjoining rooms. This was the first time that we met him. When we entered the reception room, he stood up, bowed a little, held out his hand, and thus, without shifting from the spot, waited to give his hand and a smile to each of us in turn. We sat down.

Mao began to speak. After saying that they were very happy to have friends from distant Albania, he said a few words about our people, describing them as a valiant and heroic people.

«We have great admiration for your people,» he said among other things, «because you have been liberated much longer than we.»

Immediately after this he asked me:

«How are things between you and Yugoslavia?»

«Cold,» I replied, and immediately noticed that he expressed open surprise. «Apparently he is not well acquainted with our situation with the Yugoslavs,» I thought, therefore I decided to explain something from the long history of the relations of our Party and country with the Yugoslav party and state. I gave him a brief outline, dwelling on some of the key moments of the anti-Albanian and anti-Marxist activity of the Yugoslav leadership, expecting some reaction from him. But I noticed that Mao only expressed surprise and from time to time looked at the other Chinese comrades.

«On this question,» said Mao, «you Albanians have not made mistakes towards the Yugoslavs, and neither have the Yugoslav comrades made mistakes towards you. The Information Bureau has made great mistakes here.»

«Although we did not take part in the Information Bureau,» I replied, «we have supported its well-known analyses and stands towards the activity of the Yugoslav leadership and have always considered them to be correct ... Tito is an incorrigible renegade.»

Without waiting to hear the end of the translation of what I said, Mao asked me:

«What is your opinon of Stalin?»

I said that our Party had always considered Stalin a leader of very great, all-round merits, a loyal disciple of Lenin and continuer of his work, a ...

He interrupted me: «Have you published the report which Comrade Khrushchev delivered in the 20th Congress of the Communist Party of the Soviet Union?»

«No,» I replied. «We have not done and never will do such a thing.»

«You Albanian comrades have acted very correctly and the line of your Party is right,» he said. «We, too, have acted as you have done. As long as the Soviet leadership does not publish this report officially, there is no reason for us to act as some have done.»

After a pause, he continued:

«Stalin made mistakes. He made mistakes towards us, for example, in 1927. He made mistakes towards the Yugoslav comrades, too.»

Then he continued calmly in a low voice:

«One cannot advance without mistakes.» And he asked me: «Has your Party made mistakes?»

«We cannot say that there have been no mistakes,» I told him, «but the main thing is that we struggle to make as few mistakes as possible or none at all, and, when mistakes are discovered, we struggle to eliminate them immediately.»

I was too «hasty». The great philosopher was getting at something else:

«It is necessary to make mistakes,» he said. «The party cannot be educated without learning from mistakes. This has great significance.»

We encountered this method of «education» of Mao Zedong's materialized everywhere. During the days we were at the congress, a Chinese comrade told us:

«A terrible fear has existed amongst us. People tried to avoid making mistakes because they were afraid of being expelled from the party. However, with the correct policy of Chairman Mao, that fear has now disappeared, and initiative and drive in creative work has increased among the party people.

«You see that comrade who is speaking?» he said. «He is Li Lisan,[34] one of the founders of our Communist Party. During his life he has made grave mistakes, not just once, but three times on end. There were comrades who wanted to expel this old man from the party, but on the insistence of Chairman Mao, he remains a member of the Central Committee of the party, and now he works in the Central Committee apparatus.»

Meanwhile Li Lisan was making a new «self-criticism» before the 8th Congress.

«I have made mistakes,» he said, «but the party has helped me. Comrades,» he continued, «I ask you to help me still because I might make mistakes again . . .»

But let us return to the meeting with Mao Zedong. After he philosophised about the «great significance of making mistakes», I seized the opportunity to add to what I had previously said about the Yugoslavs and spoke about the work of the Belgrade revisionists through their agents to organise the plot in the Party Conference of Tirana of April 1956.

«In our opinion,» I said, «they are incorrigible.»

Mao's reply, in the Chinese style, was a phrase out of context: «You have a correct Marxist-Leninist line.»

The time had come for us to leave. We thanked him for the invitation, for receiving us and for the aid given us by the People's Republic of China.

«There is no need to thank us,» interrupted Mao, «first, because the aid we have given you is very little,» and he closed one finger. «Second,» he continued, closing the other finger, «we are members of the great family of the socialist camp, which has the Soviet Union at the head, and it is just the same as passing something from one hand to the other, parts of the same body.»

We thanked him once again and stood up. We had several photographs taken together, shook hands again and departed.

To tell the truth, our impressions from this meeting were not what we had expected, and when we came out, I talked over with

Mehmet [Shehu] and Ramiz [Alia] what we had heard. From the talk with Mao we did not learn anything constructive, which would be of value to us, and the meeting seemed to us mostly a gesture of courtesy. We were especially disappointed over the things we heard from the mouth of Mao about the Information Bureau, Stalin and the Yugoslav question.

However, we were even more surprised and worried by the proceedings of the 8th Congress. The whole platform of this Congress was based on the theses of the 20th Congress of the Communist Party of the Soviet Union, indeed, in certain directions, the theses of Khrushchev had been carried further forward by Mao Zedong, Liu Shaoqi and other top Chinese leaders.

We felt that the epidemic of modern revisionism had infected China, too. To what proportions the disease had been spread we could not judge at that time, but the things which had occurred and were occurring in China, showed that at that time the Chinese leaders were hurrying to avoid lagging behind, and indeed, to grab the motley flag of the Khrushchevites with their own hands.

Apart from other things, in the reports which Liu Shaoqi, Deng Xiaoping and Zhou Enlai delivered one after the other at the 8th Congress they defended and further deepened the permanent line of the Communist Party of China for extensive collaboration with the bourgeoisie and the kulaks, «argued» in support of the great blessings which would come to «socialism» from treating capitalists, merchants, and bourgeois intellectuals well and placing them in high leading positions, vigorously propagated the necessity of collaboration between the working class and the national bourgeoisie, and between the communist party and the other democratic nationalist parties, in the conditions of socialism, etc., etc. In fact, the «hundred flowers» and the «hundred schools» of Mao Zedong, which blossomed and contended in the sessions of the congress, blossomed and contended throughout the whole Chinese party and state. This Mao Zedong's theory of a hundred flowers, widely proclaimed in May 1956 by Lu Dingyi,[35] constituted the Chinese variant of the bourgeois-revisionist theory and practice about the «free circulation of ideas and people», about the co-existence of a hotch-potch of ideologies, trends, schools and coteries within socialism. (It turned out later that Mao

Zedong's utterly revisionist decalogue «On the Ten Major Relationships» belongs precisely to this period of the «spring» of modern revisionism.)

Many a time later I have turned back to this period of history of the Communist Party of China, trying to figure out how and why the profoundly revisionist line of 1956 subsequently seemed to change direction, and for a time, became «pure», «anti-revisionist» and «Marxist-Leninist». It is a fact, for example, that in 1960 the Communist Party of China seemed to be strongly opposing the revisionist theses of Nikita Khrushchev . . . It was precisely because China came out against modern revisionism in 1960 and seemed to be adhering to Marxist-Leninist positions that brought about that our Party stood shoulder to shoulder with it in the struggle which we had begun against the Khrushchevites.

However, time confirmed . . . that in no instance, either in 1956 or in the 60's did the Communist Party of China proceed or act from the positions of Marxism-Leninism.

In 1956 it rushed to take up the banner of revisionism, in order to elbow Khrushchev out and gain the role of the leader in the communist and workers' movement for itself. But when Mao Zedong and his associates saw that they would not easily emerge triumphant over the patriarch of modern revisionism, Khrushchev, through the revisionist contest, they changed their tactic, pretended to reject their former flag, presented themselves as «pure Marxist-Leninists», striving in this way to win those positions which they had been unable to win with their former tactic. When this second tactic turned out no good, either, they «discarded» their second, allegedly Marxist-Leninist, flag and came out in the arena as they had always been, opportunists, loyal champions of a line of conciliation and capitulation towards capital and reaction.

. . . After the proceedings of the congress were over, they took us on visits to a number of cities and people's communes . . . they had achieved a series of positive changes and developments. However, these were not of that level they were claimed to be, the more so if account is taken of the exceptional human potential of the Chinese continent, and the desire and readiness of the Chinese people to work.

. . . They had managed to eliminate mass starvation . . . but it was obvious that the standard of living was still low, far from the level, not just of the developed socialist countries, but even of our country . . . we were impressed that their behaviour really was good, correct, but we observed a certain hesitation, both towards us and towards those who accompanied us. It was obvious from their words and their attitude towards the cadres that something from the past was still retained. It was clear that the many centuries of the past, the absolute power of the Chinese emperors, feudal lords and capitalists, of Japanese, American, British and other foreign exploiters, Buddhism, and all the other reactionary philosophies, from the most ancient to the most «modern», had not only left this people in terrible economic backwardness, but had cultivated the slave mentality of submission, of blind belief, and unquestioning obedience to authorities of every rank, in their world outlook. Of course, these things cannot be wiped out all at once, and we considered them as forms of atavism, which would be eliminated from the consciousness of this people, who with their positive qualities and with sound leadership, would be capable of achieving miracles.

Apart from meetings with Mao Zedong and other Chinese leaders . . ., we also had occasion to meet a number of delegations of communist and workers' parties which had attended the 8th Congress of the CP of China.

All of them enthusiastically hailed the «new line» of the period after the 20th Congress.

. . . «We rehabilitated Traicho Kostov, because we could not find any proof of his guilt,» Anton Yugov told us.[36]

He spoke as though with some trepidation. Apparently, he sensed that sooner or later they would bring him down, . . . Dej, the «man of the Information Bureau,» . . . had now made peace with Tito in Bucharest and was preparing to taste his kisses in Belgrade.

«I am going to Belgrade to meet Tito,» he told us . . . «Tito is a good positive comrade, not like Kardelj and Popović,» he continued.[37] (Three months before we had heard this in Russian, and now we had to hear it in Rumanian, too!)

... «Now that I am going to Belgrade myself, would you like me to speak on your behalf?» he asked me.

«If you wish to speak on our behalf,» I told Gheorgiu-Dej, «tell him [Tito] to give up his secret activity and plots against ... Albania. Tell him that before and after the Tirana Conference the Yugoslav diplomats were involved in vicious activity ...» and I told him briefly what had occurred in our country after the 20th Congress.

«Is that so?» he said and I saw that he was put out ... Dej displayed the same sentiments later, too, when I met him after he had made his long-desired visit of reconciliation to Belgrade and had put himself on Tito's side. Some months after that visit I passed through Bucharest where I met and talked with Dej and Bodnaras.[38]

In the course of the talks Bodnaras (Emil, the elder) began to tell me that in talks with him [Tito] the conversation had come around to Albania. «Tito spoke well and with sympathy of your country, of your heroic people,» said Bodnaras, «and expressed his wish for good relations with you», etc. ....

«For our part there will be no conciliation with Tito,» I told Bodnaras bluntly.

During the time that I was sounding off about Tito to Bodnaras, I observed that Dej was scribbling with a pencil on a piece of white paper, without doubt from irritation, but he did not speak at all — my words had a bitter taste for him.

The Hungarian uprising of 1956

Hoxha has no doubts: the 1956 Hungarian uprising was a 'counter-revolution . . . suppressed by counter-revolutionaries who restored capitalism, but in a more camouflaged way . . .' Rarely has the classic Stalinist language of 'masks' and 'disguise' been stretched further.

Hoxha's *analysis* of the Hungarian 'events', as they came to be called in official jargon, is therefore hardly full of surprises. But his account is full of information. It opens with discussions in Budapest with some of the Hungarian leaders shortly before the uprising. It moves on to describe in detail Hoxha's conversations with Suslov. And continues with the role of Yuri Andropov, Soviet ambassador in Hungary at the time. It also contains a hitherto unknown description by Molotov of Mikoyan's role in the Hungarian turmoil.

Hoxha's report of his conversations and his brutal comments on the whole affair (Rákosi's main mistake, according to Hoxha, was not standing firm – whatever that would have involved) allow him to vent his suspicions about too many 'tourists' (always possible spies in Hoxha's view); he also tells us that he ordered the Albanian ambassador in Budapest to set up a machine gun at the top of the embassy stairs and open fire if the building was invaded. Hoxha does, however, in his own perverse way, criticise the Russian decision to execute Imre Nagy, at least in the way it was done.

Hoxha's account in the full version continues with a similar passage on Poland, of less interest, since he did not visit Poland at the time and seems both less interested and less informed about it.

After securing its positions to some extent in Bulgaria, Rumania, Czechoslovakia and elsewhere, the Khrushchevite clique attacked Hungary, the leadership of which was not proving so obedient to the Soviet course. However, Tito, together with the Americans, had his eyes on Hungary.

As was becoming apparent, Hungary had many weak points. There the party had been created, headed by Rakosi, around whom there were a number of veteran communists like Gerö and Münnich, but also young ones who had just come to the fore, who found the table laid for them by the Red Army and Stalin. The «construction of socialism» in Hungary began, but the reforms were not radical. The proletariat was favoured, but without seriously annoying the petty-bourgeoisie. The Hungarian party was allegedly a combination of the illegal communist party (Hungarian prisoners of war captured in the Soviet Union), old communists of Bela Kun and the social-democratic party. Hence, this combination was a sickly graft, which never really established itself . . .

I have been closely acquainted with Rakosi and I liked him . . . Rakosi was an honest man, an old communist and a leader in the Comintern. His aims were good, but his work was sabotaged from within and from without. As long as Stalin was alive everything seemed to be going well, but after his death the weaknesses in Hungary began to show up.

Once, in a talk with Rakosi, he spoke about the Hungarian army and asked about ours.

«Our army is weak, we have no cadres. The officers are the old ones from the Horthy army, therefore we are taking ordinary workers from the factories of Csepel and putting them in officer's uniforms,» he told me.

«Without a strong army socialism cannot be defended,» I told Rakosi. «You should get rid of the Horthy men. You did very well to take workers but you must give importance to educating them properly.»

While we were talking in Rakosi's villa, Kadar arrived. He had just returned from Moscow where he had gone for treatment of an eye complaint. Rakosi introduced me, asked him how his health was now, and gave him leave to go home. When we were alone Rakosi said:

«Kadar is a young cadre and we have made him minister of internal affairs.»

To tell the truth, he didn't seem to me to be of the right stuff to be minister of internal affairs.

Another time we talked about the economy. He spoke to me about the economy of Hungary, especially about agriculture, that was going so well that the people could eat their fill and they did not know what to do with all their pork, sausage, beer and wines! I opened my eyes in surprise, because I knew that not only in our country, but in all the socialist countries, including Hungary, the situation was not like that. Rakosi had one shortcoming, he was sanguine, exaggerated the results of the work. But despite this weakness, in my opinion, Matyas had a good communist heart . . .

In April 1957, when the «anti-party group» of Malenkov, Molotov, etc., had still not been liquidated, I was in Moscow with a delegation of our Party and Government. After a non-official dinner in the Kremlin, in [the] Yekaterinsky Zal, we sat down in a corner to take coffee with Khrushchev, Molotov, Mikoyan, Bulganin, etc. In the course of the conversation Molotov turned to me and, as if joking, said:

«Tomorrow Mikoyan is going to Vienna, to try to cook up the same broth as he did in Budapest.»

To keep the conversation going I asked him:

«Did Mikoyan prepare that broth?»

«Who else?» said Molotov.

«Then Mikoyan can't go back to Budapest again,» I said.

«If Mikoyan goes there again, they will hang him,» Molotov continued.

Khrushchev had dropped his eyes and was stirring his coffee. Mikoyan frowned, ground his teeth and then said with a cynical smile:

«Why should I not go to Budapest? If they hang me, they will hang Kadar, too, because we prepared that broth together.»

The role of the Khrushchevites in the Hungarian tragedy was clear to me.

. . . Possibly the leadership of the Hungarian party, under Rakosi and Gerö, made economic mistakes, too, but these were not what caused the counter-revolution. The main mistake of Rakosi and his comrades was that they did not stand firm.

. . . In June 1956, on my way to Moscow for a meeting of Comecon, I had a talk with the comrades of the Political Bureau of the Hungarian Workers' Party in Budapest . . . [They] told me that they had some difficulties in their party and their Central Committee.

«A situation against Rakosi has been created in the Central Committee,» they told me. «Farkas, who was a member of the Political Bureau, has taken up the banner of opposition to him.»

«The time has come for Farkas to be expelled not only from the Central Committee, but also from the party,» said Bata, the Minister of Defence. «His stand is anti-party and hostile,» he continued. «His thesis is: 'I have made mistakes, Beria is a traitor. But who ordered me to make those mistakes? Rakosi.'» . . .

I told the Hungarian comrades that the situation with us was good and explained how we acted at the Tirana Conference.

«There is proper democracy in the Party,» I stressed, «democracy which must strengthen the situation and unity and not destroy them. Therefore we came down hard on those who sought to exploit the democracy to the detriment of the Party. We have not permitted such things to occur among us.»

Speaking about Togliatti's interview[39] they asked my opinion of it:

«With what he has said, Togliatti is not in order,» I replied. «Of course, we have not raised our objections to him publicly, but we have called in the first secretaries of the party district committees and have explained the question to them so that they will be vigilant and ready at any moment.»

Szalai, a member of the Political Bureau, rose and said:

«I have read Togliatti's interview and it is not all that bad. The beginning is good and it is only the final part which spoils it.»

. . . From this conversation I formed the conviction that their line was wobbly. Apart from this, it seemed that the sounder elements in the Political Bureau were under pressure from counter-revolutionary elements, and therefore they themselves had vacillated. The Political Bureau seemed to be solid, but was completely isolated.

In the evening they put on a dinner for us in the Parliament Building, in a room where a big portrait of Attila hanging on the wall struck the eye. We talked again about the grave situation that was simmering in Hungary. But it seemed that they had lost their sense of direction. I said to them:

«Why are you acting like this? How can you sit idle in the face of this counter-revolution which is rising, why are you simply looking on and not taking measures?»

«What measures could we take?» one of them asked.

«You should close the 'Petöfi' Club immediately, arrest the main trouble-makers, bring the armed working class out in the boulevards and encircle the Esztergom. If you can't jail Mindszenty, what about Imre Nagy, can't you arrest him? Have some of the leaders of these counter-revolutionaries shot to teach them what the dictatorship of the proletariat is.»

The Hungarian comrades opened their eyes wide with surprise as if they wanted to say to me: «Have you gone mad?» One of them said to me:

«We cannot act as you suggest, Comrade Enver, because we do not consider the situation so alarming. We have the situation in hand. What they are shouting about at the 'Petöfi' Club is childish foolishness . . .»

«It seems to me you are taking the matter lightly,» I said. «You don't appreciate the great danger hanging over you. Believe us, we know the Titoites well and know what they are after . . .'

. . . Mine was a voice in the wilderness. We ate that ill-omened dinner and during the conversaton which lasted for several hours, the Hungarian comrades continued to pour into my ears that «they had the situation in hand» and other tales.

In the morning I boarded the aircraft and went to Moscow. I met Suslov in his office in the Kremlin. As usual, he welcomed me with those mannerisms of his, prancing like the ballerinas of the Bolshoi, and when we sat [down] he asked me about Albania. After we exchanged opinions about our problems, I raised the question of Hungary. I told him my impressions and my opinions frankly, just as I had expressed them to the Hungarian comrades. Suslov watched me with those penetrating eyes through his horn-rimmed spectacles, and as I spoke I noticed signs of discontent, boredom and anger in his eyes. These feelings and this disapproval were accompanied by doodling with a pencil on a sheet of paper he had on the table. I carried on speaking and concluded by saying that I was astonished at the passivity and «lack of concern» of the Hungarian comrades.

Suslov began to speak in that reedy voice of his and in essence said:

«We cannot agree with your judgements over the Hungarian question. You are unnecessarily alarmed. The situation is not as you think. Perhaps you have insufficient information,» and Suslov talked on and on, trying to «calm» me and convince me that there was nothing alarming in the situation in Hungary . . . About two months later, at the end of August 1956, I had another bitter argument with Suslov about the Hungarian question. In passing through Budapest when we were going to the congress of the Chinese party, from a talk which we had at the airport with the Hungarian leaders of that time, we became even more convinced that the situation in Hungary was becoming disastrous . . . Suslov maintained the same stand as in the meeting I had with him in June.

«In regard to what you say, that the counter-revolution is on the boil,» said Suslov, «we have no facts, either from intelligence or other sources. The enemies are making a fuss about Hungary, but the situation is being normalised there. It is true that there are some student movements, but they are harmless and under control. The Yugoslavs are not operating there, as you say. You should know that not only Rakosi but also Gerö have made mistakes . . .»

«Yes, it is true that they have made mistakes, because they rehabilitated the Hungarian Titoite traitors who had plotted to blow up socialism,» I interjected. Suslov pursed his thin lips and then he went on:

«As for Comrade Imre Nagy, we cannot agree with you, Comrade Enver.»

«It greatly astonishes me,» I said, «that you refer to him as 'Comrade' Imre Nagy when the Hungarian Workers' Party has thrown him out.»

«Maybe they have done so,» said Suslov, «but he has repented and has made a self-criticism.»

«Words go with the wind,» I objected, «don't believe words . . .»

«No,» said Suslov, his face flushing. «We have his self-criticism in writing,» and he opened a drawer and pulled out a note signed by Imre Nagy, addressed to the Communist Party of the Soviet Union, in which he said that he had been wrong «in his opinions and actions» and sought the support of the Soviets.

«Do you believe this?» I asked Suslov.

«Why shouldn't we believe it!» he replied, and went on, «Comrades can make mistakes, but when they acknowledge their errors we must hold out our hand to them.»

«He is a traitor,» I told Suslov, «and we think that you are making a great mistake when you hold out your hand to a traitor.»

This brought the conversation with Suslov to an end and we left disagreeing with him. From this meeting we formed the impression that, after having definitely condemned Rakosi, the Soviets were fearful and alarmed about the situation in Hungary; that they did not know what to do and were seeking a solution before the storm broke. Without doubt they were talking with Tito about a joint solution. They were preparing Imre Nagy, thinking they would master the situation in Hungary through him. And so it turned out.

The circle around Rakosi was very weak. Neither the Central Committee nor the Political Bureau were up to the mark. People like Hegedüs, Kadar, old men like Münnich and a few young fellows without any experience of the party and struggle, weakened the running of affairs more and more each day and fell into the Titoite–Khrushchevite spider's web.

. . . The decision to remove Rakosi was taken in Moscow and Belgrade.[40] . . . They forced Rakosi to resign, allegedly for «health reasons» (because he suffered from hypertension!), while admitting «his mistakes in violation of the law». At first there was talk about the merits of «Comrade Matyas Rakosi» (thus they «buried» him with honours), then there was talk about his mistakes, until the point was reached of talking about the «criminal Rakosi gang». In the preparation of the backstage manoeuvres which preceded the removal of Rakosi, a major role was played by Suslov, who, precisely at this time, went to Hungary on holiday(!) . . .

Imperialism filled the country with spies and was pouring in arms wholesale from Austria. Radio «Free Europe» urged on the counter-revolution day and night and called for the overthrow and total liquidation of the socialist order. Even earlier Hungary had opened its doors to spies disguised as tourists . . .

The Soviet ambassador in Hungary was a certain Andropov, a KGB man, who was elevated to power later and played a dirty role against us . . . During those days, after the first half-hearted intervention of the Soviet army, Andropov told our ambassador in Budapest:

«We cannot call the insurgents counter-revolutionaries because there are honest people among them. The new government is good and it is necessary to support it in order to stabilise the situation.»

«What do you think of Nagy's speeches?» our ambassador asked him.

«They are not bad,» replied Andropov, and when our comrade pointed out that what was being said about the Soviet Union did not seem to be correct, he replied:

«There is anti-Sovietism, but Nagy's recent speech was not bad, it was not anti-Soviet. He wants to maintain links with the masses. The Political Bureau is good and has credit.»

The counter-revolutionaries acted with such arrogance that they forced Andropov, together with all his staff, out into the street and left them there for hours on end. We instructed our ambassador in Budapest to take measures for the defence of the embassy and its staff, and to place a machine-gun at the top of the stairs. If the counter-revolutionaries dared to attack the embassy he was to open fire without hesitation. But when our ambassador asked Andropov for weapons to ensure the defence of our embassy, he refused:

«We have diplomatic immunity, therefore no one will touch you.»

«What diplomatic immunity?!» said our ambassador. «They threw you out into the street.»

«No, no,» said Andropov, «if we give you arms, some incident might be created.»

«Very well,» said our representative. «I am making you an official request on behalf of the Albanian government.»

«I shall ask Moscow,» said Andropov, and when the request was refused our ambassador declared:

«All right, only I am letting you know that we shall defend ourselves with the pistol and shotguns we have.»

The Soviet ambassador had shut himself up in the embassy and did not dare to stick his head out. A responsible functionary of the Foreign Ministry of Hungary, who was being chased by the bandits, sought refuge in our embassy and we admitted him. He told our comrades that he had gone to the Soviet embassy but they had turned him away.

The Soviet troops stationed in Hungary intervened at first, but were then withdrawn under the pressure of Nagy and Kadar and the Soviet government declared that it was ready to begin talks about their withdrawal from Hungary. While the counter-revolutionaries were wreaking havoc, Moscow trembled . . .

Here in Tirana we did not fail to speak up. I called the Soviet ambassador and told him angrily:

«We are completely uninformed about what is going on in a number of socialist countries . . . You are abandoning Hungary to imperialism and Tito. You must intervene with arms and *far piazza pulita* [make a clean sweep] before it's too late.» . . .

He replied:

«The situation is grave but we shall not allow the enemy to seize Hungary. I shall transmit the opinions you expressed to me to Moscow.»

Everyone knows what happened in Hungary.

. . . The Soviet embassy was surrounded with tanks and Mikoyan, Suslov, Andropov and who knows who else, continued to intrigue inside.

Reaction, headed by Kadar and Imre Nagy, shut up in the parliament building, where they indulged in idle talk, sent out continuous appeals to the Western capitalist states to intervene with arms against the Soviets. In the end, the frightened Nikita Khrushchev was obliged to give the order. The Soviet armoured forces marched on Budapest and fighting began in the streets. The intriguer Mikoyan put Andropov in a tank and sent him to parliament to bring back Kadar, in order to manipulate matters through him. Kadar again changed his patron, returned to the bosom of the Soviets and, protected by their tanks, called on the people to cease the disturbances and appealed to the counter-revolutionaries to hand in their arms and surrender . . .

. . . Later . . . many facts came to light which proved the complicity of the Soviet leaders in the Hungarian events. We, of course, suspected what role the Soviets played . . . However, at that time we did not know precisely how the Khrushchev–Tito collaboration had developed and neither did we know about the secret meetings of Khrushchev and Malenkov with Tito in Brioni.[41]

. . . Some days after order was restored in Hungary, the Soviet leadership informed us of the correspondence which it had exchanged with the Yugoslav leadership over the Hungarian question. The facts which were revealed in those letters disturbed us profoundly,

. . . During those days, after we received the letters, I summoned Krylov:[42]

«I have called you here,» I said, «to clear up some matters which arise from these letters. First, I want to tell you that the allusions which Tito made to 'certain evil men', clearly implying the leadership of our Party, seem to us unacceptable. Such a thing, on his part, does not surprise us because we are accustomed to Tito's attacks. However, we are extremely surprised about the fact that in the reply of the Central Committee of the Communist Party of the Soviet Union there is no clear-cut stand to be seen in connection with these insinuations of Tito's. Have you anything to say about this question?»

«I have nothing to say about this,» replied Krylov, faithful to his manner of playing dumb.

Then I continued:

«Tito should have been told bluntly that we are not evil men and enemies of socialism, as he says. We are Marxist-Leninists, resolute people, who will fight to the end for the cause of socialism . . .»

. . . Krylov was silent, and continuing the talk, I dwelt in particular on another problem which had attracted our attention in these letters. Khrushchev wrote to Tito: «In connection with the removal of Rakosi, you were completely satisfied that the Central Committee of the Communist Party of the Soviet Union tried, as early as the summer of this year, to ensure that Kadar would become first secretary.»

Besides this, the letter clearly indicated their collaboration, not only before the events of October, but also during them . . .

I questioned Krylov about this matter:

«We are not clear about where the Central Committee of the Hungarian Workers' Party was formed, in Budapest or in the Crimea?»

Of course Krylov did not like this question and, biting his words, said:

«This is how matters must stand: the Hungarian comrades have gone to the Crimea and talked with our comrades. There the question has been raised of who should be placed in the leadership. The Central Committee of the Communist Party of the Soviet Union has said that 'it would be good if Kadar were elected.'»

«Does it mean that the leadership of the Communist Party of the Soviet Union was not for Gerö but for Kadar?» I continued.

«That is what emerges from the letter,» replied Krylov.

«Apart from that,» I said, «the Kadar government has been formed in close collaboration between your leadership and Tito. Is that not so?»

«Yes, it seems to be so,» Krylov was obliged to admit.

Continuing the talk . . . I pointed out to the Soviet ambassador:

«The unanimous opinion of our Political Bureau is that these actions . . . are not correct. The Soviet leadership is well aware of our views on all these matters, because we have expressed them to it. Is that not so?»

«Yes, it is so,» said Krylov.

«Have you transmitted all our views to Moscow?»

«Yes,» he replied, «I have transmitted them.»

Postmortem on Hungary (December 1956)

As a coda to Hoxha's description of the actual Hungarian uprising, this extract records some aspects of Hoxha's relations with the Soviet leadership at the end of 1956.

The Hungarian uprising and the events in Poland shook the Soviet regime profoundly. Tito took advantage of his newly strengthened position to stake out in unusually strong terms his own independent and critical position in a speech at Pula on 11 November 1956, to which Hoxha refers scathingly. After the Pula speech, Hoxha received a noticeably warmer welcome in the USSR, even from Khrushchev himself, as well as from more conservative figures like Molotov.

Hoxha here records his impressions of Leonid Brezhnev, before Brezhnev acceded to the leading position in the Soviet Party. This extract also contains Suslov's postmortem remarks on Hungary and Rákosi.

At that period Khrushchev and company were not getting along so well with Tito . . . the welcome for us at that time was more «cordial» and our views, especially with regard to the Yugoslavs, were not opposed, and indeed, even seemed to be approved by the Soviet leaders.

From the moment we left the ship in Odessa we noticed this atmosphere . . .

We travelled from Odessa to Moscow by train. We still had not recovered properly from the journey, when we were informed that . . . [they] had put on a dinner in honour of our delegation. [It] began at about four o'clock in the afternoon. As far as I recall, all the members of the Presidium, apart from Brezhnev, Furtseva[43] and one other, were there. The dinner continued for several hours and Khrushchev and the others strove to create an atmosphere which would seem as friendly as possible. Nearly all who were present proposed toasts (Khrushchev alone proposed five or six) and in the course of the toasts fine words were said about our Party and Albania and I was praised especially. Especially zealous in these praises was Pospyelov who had been at the 3rd Congress of our Party in May.[44]

The toasts proposed were frequently political speeches, especially those proposed by Khrushchev, for whom it was nothing to speak for half an hour in proposing a toast.

. . . That evening Khrushchev did not spare his attacks against the Yugoslav leaders.

«Their positions are anti-Leninist and opportunist,» said Khrushchev among other things. «Their policy is a mishmash. We shall make no concessions to them. They suffer from megalomania,» he continued. «When Tito was in Moscow, he thought that with the majestic welcome put on for him, the people were saying he was right, and that they condemned our policy. In fact we need only have whispered one word to the people and they would have torn Tito and company to pieces.»

Speaking about our attitude to the Titoites, he said, «The Albanian comrades are right but they must keep cool and maintain their self-control.

«Your hair is going grey, but we are bald,» said Khrushchev, concluding his toast.

While the feast continued, «the bald head» told us that Albania was a small country, but had an important strategic position. «If we build a submarine and missile base there, we can control the whole Mediterranean.» . . . It was the idea which was concretised in the Vlora base, which the Khrushchevites used to put pressure on us, later.

. . . I remember that during the evening we had some discussion about Khrushchev's coming to our country . . . Not only Khrushchev, but many other members of the Presidium expressed their desire to come to Albania and someone, I don't remember who, jokingly proposed they should hold a meeting of the Presidium or even of their Central Committee in Albania! There was talk there, also, about the «love» which Khrushchev allegedly had for our country (which he displayed later!) and they nicknamed Khrushchev «*Albanyets*» [The Albanian].

Among many others I remember that Molotov, too, proposed a toast:

«I belong to that category of people who have not given much importance to Albania and have not become acquainted with it,» he said. «Now our people are proud that they have such a loyal, resolute and militant friend. The Soviet Union has many friends, but they are not all the same. Albania is our best friend. Let us drink this toast wishing that the Soviet Union will have friends as loyal as Albania!»

. . . Two or three days later we had a preliminary meeting with Suslov.

. . . Suslov was one of the greatest demagogues of the Soviet leadership. Clever and cunning, he knew how to wriggle out of difficult situations and perhaps that is why he was one of the few who had escaped the purges carried out time after time in the Soviet revisionist leadership. Several times I have talked with Suslov and I always had a feeling of unease and annoyance from the meetings with him. I had even less desire to talk with Suslov now, following the Hungarian events, . . .

Brezhnev took part in this meeting, too, but in fact, he was merely present, because only Suslov spoke during the whole talk. From time to time Leonid moved his thick eyebrows, but sat so immobile that it was difficult to gather what he was thinking . . . I had met him for the first time at the 20th Congress . . . and from the time of that brief, chance meeting he had impressed me as a conceited, self-satisfied man. As soon as he was introduced to us he immediately brought the conversation around to himself and told us «in confidence» that he was engaged with «special weapons». From the tone in which he spoke and the expression of his face, he implied to us that he was the man in the Central Committee dealing with the problems of atomic weapons.

. . . After these events, up till 1960 I had to go many other times to Moscow, where I met the main leaders of the Soviet party but . . . I never saw Brezhnev or heard him speak anywhere. He always remained or was kept in the background, «jn reserve», you might say. After the inglorious end of Khrushchev, precisely this ponderous, stern-faced person was brought out of the shade to carry on the filthy work of the Khrushchevite mafia.

. . . It seems that Brezhnev was brought to the head of the party and the Soviet social-imperialist state, not so much on account of his abilities, but as a *modus vivendi*, to balance and even up the opposing groups which were feuding and squabbling in the top Soviet leadership. But let us give him his due: he is a comedian only in his eyebrows, while his work is tragic from start to finish.

. . . At the start Suslov gave us an exposition about the events in Hungary. He criticised Rakosi and Gerö, who, with their mistakes, had «caused great discontent among the people», while they left Nagy outside their control.

«Nagy and the Yugoslavs,» he continued, «have fought against socialism . . . Now, however, Kadar is following a correct course. In your press there have been some notes critical of Kadar, but it must be borne in mind that he should be supported because the Yugoslavs are fighting him.»

«We are not well acquainted with Kadar. We know that he was in prison and was with Imre Nagy.»

Replying to our complaint that we had not been informed about the development of events in Hungary, Suslov said that the events took place without warning and there was no time for consultations.

«No consultations were held with the other parties, either. Only when we intervened for the second time we consulted the Chinese, while Khrushchev, Malenkov and Molotov went to Rumania and Czechoslovakia,» he said.

«How was time found to consult Tito over the appointment of Kadar, while we were not informed about anything?» I asked.

«We did not consult Tito about Kadar,» he said. «We simply told him that there was no longer any place for Nagy's government.»

«These are issues of principle,» I stressed. «It is essential to hold consultations, but they are not being held. The Consultative Political Council of the Warsaw Treaty, for example, has not met for a year.»

. . . Amongst other things I told him that the term which was now being used, the «criminal Rakosi–Gerö gang», seemed astonishing to us and we thought this did not help in uniting all the Hungarian communists.

«The mistakes of Rakosi created a grave situation and discontent among the people and the communists,» said Suslov.

We asked him to tell us concretely about the mistakes of Rakosi and Gerö, and Suslov listed a number of general things, by means of which he tried to lay the blame on them for all that had occurred. We demanded a concrete example, and he told us:

«For example, the question of Rajk, who was described as a spy without any documentary proof.»

«Were these things discussed with Rakosi? Was he given any advice?» I asked.

«Rakosi did not accept advice,» was the reply.

Khrushchev pleads with Hoxha over Yugoslavia

In April 1957 Hoxha is in Moscow again. Khrushchev is trying to improve relations with Yugoslavia, after a frosty spell during the winter, and in the light of Soviet attempts to convene a world Conference of Communist parties to sign a joint declaration.

This extract opens with a meeting on 15 April between Khrushchev and Hoxha dealing specifically with Albania's attitude to Yugoslavia, and contains some of Khrushchev's thoughts about the different members of the Yugoslav leadership. It moves on to the question of Hoxha's treatment of the latest group of alleged opponents, including Liri Gega and Dali Ndreu, recently executed, and reveals the direct way in which the Soviet leadership attempted to intervene in this matter. Hoxha declines to pass up the chance to state his own approach to such matters in brutal terms.

Finally, Khrushchev engineers another encounter between Hoxha and a Yugoslav representative, Belgrade's ambassador in Moscow, Mićunović. This is one of the rare conversations of which there is a fairly detailed account published by the other party, Mićunović, in his remarkable memoirs.

«Let us examine how the Yugoslavs behave towards us,» he [Khrushchev] continued. «They attack us more than the Greeks,

the Turks and the Italians! But there is something specific, proletarian, about Yugoslavia. Hence, can we break off relations with
Yugoslavia?»

«We do not say this,» I replied.

«You did not say it but from your words it is obvious that you
think it. Certainly Yugoslavia will not become the cause of a war
against our camp, like Germany, Italy or any other country. Do
you consider Yugoslavia as the enemy number one?!» he asked
me.

«We are not speaking about Yugoslavia. We are speaking
about the revisionist activity of the Yugoslav leaders,» I said.
«What are we to do after those things which they hatch up against
us?»

«Try to neutralise their work. What else can you do? Are you
going to war with them?» he asked me again.

«No, we have not made war on them and we are not going to do
so. But if the Yugoslav minister goes tomorrow to photograph
military objects, then what are we to do?»

«Take the film!» answered Khrushchev.

«They will use such a measure as a pretext to break off relations
and put the blame on us,» I said.

«Then what do you want from us, Comrade Enver?» he said
angrily. «Our views differ from yours and we are unable to advise
you! I do not understand you, Comrade Hoxha! Adenauer and
Kishi[45] are no better than Tito, but nevertheless, we are doing
everything in our power for rapprochement with them. Do you
think we are wrong?»

«This is not the same issue,» I replied. «When there is talk about
Tito, the improvement of relations on the party road is implied,
while he is an anti-Marxist. However, the Yugoslav leadership is
not correct even in state relations. What stand are we to adopt, if
the Yugoslavs continue to hatch up plots against us?»

«Comrade Hoxha,» shouted Khrushchev angrily, «you are
constantly interrupting me. I listened to you for an hour without
interrupting you once, while you do not allow me to speak even
for a few minutes, but interrupt me continually! I have nothing
more to say!» he declared and stood up.

«We have come to exchange opinions,» I said. «Then, as soon

as you express an idea, you ask my opinion. Are you annoyed that I reply to you?!»

«I have told you and I am telling you again: I listened to you for an hour, Comrade Hoxha, while you did not listen to me even for a quarter of an hour but interrupted me again and again! You want to build your policy on sentiments. You say there is no difference between Tito, Kardelj, Ranković, [Koča] Popović, and so on! As we have told you previously, they are people and differ from one another. The Yugoslavs say that they are all of the same opinion, but we say otherwise: Tito and Ranković maintain a different, more reasonable, more approachable stand towards us, while Kardelj and Popović are totally hostile towards us. Tempo is an ass . . . , is unstable. Let us take Eisenhower and Dulles.[46] They are both reactionaries, but we must not lump the two of them together. Dulles is a savage war-monger, while Eisenhower is more human.

«We told you at the first meeting: we are not going to attack anyone and not going to provoke any attack. Our attacks and counter-attacks must be made in such a way as to ensure that they are in favour of rapprochement and not alienation.

«We have asked Zhou Enlai to become the intermediary to arrange a meeting between our parties in which the Yugoslavs will take part. (The reference is to Khrushchev's efforts, in collaboration with the Chinese leadership, to organise a meeting of all the communist parties of socialist countries in which Tito was to take part, too. This meeting was organised in Moscow in November 1957, but despite the efforts of Khrushchev and Mao Zedong, the Yugoslavs did not take part in it. For more details see TK, pp. 326–329.) He was pleased to undertake this task. Such a meeting can be held. The Yugoslavs have agreed to it. But it should not be thought that everything will be achieved at such a meeting. However, with opinions like yours, why should we go to such a meeting?! I do not understand what you are aiming at, Comrade Enver! Are you trying to convince us that we are not right?! Have you come here to convince us that we, too, should adopt the same stand as you towards Yugoslavia? No, we know what we are doing! Do you want to convince us that your line is right?! This does not lead to any good solution and is not in the interest of our camp. In connection with the counter-revolution in Hungary we have considered the stand of the Party of Labour of Albania correct, but your tactic in connection with Yugoslavia is wrong. I had thought that you should meet Mićunović (the Yugoslav ambassador in Moscow), not to exacerbate relations but to improve them. However, seeing the way you treat the problem, I doubt that anything will emerge from it. You talk about the provocations of the Yugoslav minister in Tirana. In our country, too, the Yugoslav minister has gone in a demonstrative way to photograph military objects. Our militiaman took his camera and bid him good day!

«Let me repeat: we shall follow the line of improving both state relations and party relations with Yugoslavia. Whether or not we achieve it, that is another matter, but the fact is that we shall have a clear conscience and will serve our party and all the other parties well. We must not make matters worse. The Rumanian comrades are right in describing you in *Scînteia* as 'quarrelsome'.»[47]

«We are opposed not only to this grave insult, but also to the spirit in which a sister party, such as that of Rumania, deals with this problem in its central organ,» I told Khrushchev. «To be quarrelsome means that you make unprincipled attacks. We have never acted with anyone in this way. *Scînteia* itself and those who wrote that article are inciting unjust and unprincipled actions . . .»

Having received his answer for his «agreement» with *Scînteia*, Khrushchev continued, but in a somewhat lower tone:

«Take things quietly, comrades, always quietly, and we shall triumph. Do you know what Stalin used to tell us?» he continued. «'Before we take decisions we should take a cold shower, as the Romans did.' This is what Stalin advised us to do, but he never took a shower himself. Let us do what Stalin did not do!»

Having said these things, he was silent for a moment and then launched off into his accusations again:

«You do not take a shower before taking decisions, either,» he said. «You condemned Dali Ndreu and Liri Gega.[48] We consider this action of yours a grave mistake, very grave.»

«We have discussed the question of these agents on another occasion,» I said. «Nevertheless, if you wish, I can give you endless details about their anti-party and anti-Albanian activity.»

«Nevertheless, nevertheless!» shouted Khrushchev. «They should not have been condemned so severely. The Yugoslavs are furious.»

«Of course! They were their loyal agents,» I said, and I could see that Khrushchev had been just as infuriated by the verdict of our court as the Yugoslavs were.

«When we heard what you intended to do we sent an urgent radiogram to our ambassador in Tirana, Krylov. We told him that the decision of your court must be annulled without fail. Apparently, you did not listen to him. That order was ours.»

«I am hearing this for the first time and I am astonished that you could have given such an order,» I said, trying to control my anger. «However, you ought to know that during the trial the criminal activity of these dangerous agents was proved to the full. Our people would not pardon a soft stand towards them. We do not pat enemies on the head, but give them what they deserve, according to the laws for which the people have voted.»

Khrushchev was squirming in his seat.

«After Tito's speech at Pula,» put in Ponomaryov, «we sent a radiogram to Krylov, that he should tell you to keep cool in your reply, that we would publish an article and it should not appear as an organised action. We also told him what you should do about Dali Ndreu and Liri Gega.»

«He told us about the article,» I replied, «but we could not leave matters without replying to Tito, and therefore we wrote it. As for Dali Ndreu and Liri Gega, I know that your ambassador asked us after we arrested them and we told Krylov about the activity of those agents. He did not mention any kind of order, and it was just as well he did not. However, even if he had told us about it, we could never come out against the decision of the people's court.»

Turning to his comrades, Khrushchev said: «Our ambassador has not carried out his task. That action should have been stopped.»

This individual always openly took our enemies under his protection, imagining Albania as a country in which his orders, and not the laws of our state, had to be applied. I remember that another time he said to me:

«I have received a letter from a person called Panajot Plaku, in which he asked me to help him.»[49]

«Do you know this man?» I asked him. (I knew that he was well acquainted with the traitor and agent of the Yugoslavs, Panajot Plaku, a fugitive in Yugoslavia, who wanted to go to the Soviet Union.)

«No,» replied Khrushchev, «no, I do not know him.» . . .

«He is a traitor,» I said, «and if you accept him in your country we shall break off our friendship with you. If you admit him you must hand him over to us to hang him publicly.»

«You are like Stalin who killed people,» said Khrushchev.

«Stalin killed traitors, and we kill them, too,» I added.

Since there was nothing else he could do, he retreated. He still hoped to make us submit by using other ways and means. After pouring out all he had to say, he fell silent, laid his hands on the table, softened his stern tone and began his «advice» again.

The tactic of the «stick» was finished. At the discussion table Khrushchev again resorted to the «carrot».

«You must understand us, comrades,» he said, «we speak in this way only with you, because we love you greatly, you are close to our hearts,» etc., etc. And after all this he made a gesture of «generosity»: he excused us from repaying the credits, which the Soviet Union had provided for our country up to the end of 1955 for its economic and cultural development. Of course, we thanked them . . . However, we all clearly understood what «motives» lay behind this «generosity» of Khrushchev. He wanted to «smooth us over», to relieve the tense atmosphere which had been created during the talk, to some extent, wanted to bribe us . . . However, he was soon to be convinced that we were the sort of people who would even accept to eat grass but would never bend the knee to him or any other traitor.

A few days after this «generous» gesture, Khrushchev also invited Mićunović[50] to a big dinner for our delegation. He saw him standing somewhat apart and called to him:

«Come over here! Why do you stand so far off?!»

He introduced us and laughing said to us:

«Try to understand each other!» And off he went, glass in hand, leaving us «to understand each other». We quarrelled.

I reeled off to Mićunović all the things I had told Khrushchev at the meeting and said to him:

«We have been and are ready to improve our state relations and, for our part, have made every effort, but you must give up your anti-Albanian activity once and for all.»

«You call us revisionists,» said Mićunović. «How can you have relations with revisionists?»

«No,» I said, «we shall never have relations with revisionists, but I am speaking about state relations. We can and should have such relations . . .»

«When you speak of revisionism you have us in mind,» said Mićunović.

«That is true,» I said . . .

Mićunović stuck to his point of view. The debate was becoming heated. Watching us from a distance, Khrushchev sensed the mounting tension and rejoined us.

Mićunović began to repeat to him what he had said to me previously, and continued to make accusations against us. However, at that dinner we had Khrushchev «on our side».

«When Tito was in Corfù,» he said to Mićunović, «the King of Greece said to him: 'Well, shall we divide up Albania?' Tito did not reply, while the Queen pointed out that they should not talk about such things.»

Mićunović lost his head and said:

«That was only a joke.»

«Such jokes should never be made, especially with the monarcho-fascists, who have been claiming Southern Albania throughout their existence. And you have made similar 'jokes' before this too,» I told him. «We have a document of Boris Kidrić in which he has included Albania as the 7th republic of Yugoslavia.»

«This was something done by one individual,» replied Mićunović.

«One individual, true, but he was a member of the Political Bureau of your party and chairman of the State Planning Commission,» said Mehmet [Shehu].

This was too much for Mićunović and he walked away. Khrushchev took me by the arm and asked me:

«How did this come about? Did you quarrel again?»
«How else could it go? Only badly, as with the revisionists.»
«You Albanians astound me,» he said. «You are stubborn.»
«No,» I said, «we are Marxists.»

Further Soviet Pressure for Reconciliation with Tito
and Rehabilitation of Xoxe

Khrushchev had made the 'recovery' of Yugoslavia a prime goal of his administration, and it was undoubtedly extremely galling, and disruptive, that Albania refused to fall into line with the other bloc countries. In this extract Hoxha ranges over a number of issues, mainly connected with this subject.

He first refers to the still mysterious visit of the Soviet Defence Minister, Marshal Zhukov, to Albania in autumn 1957. Zhukov, who had provided the crucial backing for Khrushchev earlier in the year when an attempt had been made to oust the First Secretary,[51] was dismissed from office while in Tirana. This account is the only known record of Zhukov's activities and talks in Albania (it was unusual for the Communist states to dismiss senior officials when they were out of their own country).

Discussion of the Zhukov affair leads Hoxha on to one of his many discussions of Soviet entertainment habits, and the extensive use made by the Khrushchev regime of hospitality as a means to conduct business, with the emphasis on gross overeating and heavy drinking, common to most of the Soviet leadership of the time. Once again, the account is plausible, but Hoxha consistently fails to mention that this was also Stalin's way of conducting business, and that Stalin's colleagues, including Molotov and Beria, often got drunk (Stalin himself did not, usually).

Khrushchev also makes another attempt in July 1957, to bring Hoxha together with some of the Yugoslav leaders – here Kardelj and Ranković, two of Tito's senior colleagues. Hoxha gets in a short slanging match with Ranković which leads nowhere, except mutual recrimination.

Hoxha also recounts further pressure from Suslov in spring 1956 for the rehabilitation of Xoxe, this time attributing some of the pressure to Tito. He ends up with his most comprehensive description of his number one ideological enemy – 'revisionism'.

For years on end the «great merits» of Zhukov were publicised, his activity during the Great Patriotic War was used to throw mud at Stalin, and as Minister of Defence his hand was used for the triumph of Khrushchev's putsch . . . During those days Zhukov was on a visit to our country. We welcomed him warmly as an old cadre and hero of the Stalinist Red Army, talked about problems of the defence of our country and the socialist camp, and did not notice anything disturbing in his opinions. On the contrary, since he had come from Yugoslavia, . . . he told us: «With what I saw in Yugoslavia, I don't understand what sort of socialist country it is!» From this we sensed that he was not of one mind with Khrushchev. On the very day that he left, we learned that he had been removed from the post of Minister of Defence of the USSR for «mistakes» and «grave faults» in his application of the «line of the party», for violations of the «law in the army», etc., etc. I cannot say whether or not Zhukov was guilty of mistakes and faults in these directions, but it is possible that the reasons went deeper.

In one meeting at Khrushchev's, their attitude towards Zhukov had made an impression on me. I can't remember what year it was, but it was summer and I was on holiday in the south of the Soviet Union. Khrushchev had asked me to lunch. The local people there were Mikoyan, Kirichenko,[52] Nina Petrovna (Khrushchev's wife), and some others. Apart from me, Ulbricht and Grotewohl were there as foreign guests. We were sitting outside, eating and drinking on the verandah. When Zhukov came, Khrushchev invited him to sit down. Zhukov seemed out of sorts. Mikoyan got up and said to him:

«I am the *tamada* [master of ceremonies], fill your glass!»

«I can't drink,» said Zhukov, «I am not well.»

«Fill it, I say,» insisted Mikoyan in an authoritarian tone, «I give the orders here, not you.»

Nina Khrushcheva intervened:

«Don't force him when it harms him, Anastasiy Ivanovich,» she said to Mikoyan.

Zhukov said nothing and did not fill his glass. Khrushchev changed the subject by cracking jokes with Mikoyan.

Can it be that the contradictions with Zhukov had begun to arise as early as that, and they had begun to insult him and to show him that others were giving the orders and not he? . . . Could it possibly be that information about Zhukov's views on Yugoslavia reached Khrushchev before Zhukov returned to the Soviet Union?

In any case, Zhukov was eliminated from the political scene despite his four «Hero of the Soviet Union» stars, a series of orders of Lenin, and countless other decorations.

. . . After Stalin's death, many banquets were organised, because, at that period it was usually only at banquets that one met the leaders of the Soviet Union. The tables were set day and night, laden with food and drink to the point of revulsion. When I saw the Soviet comrades eating and drinking, I was reminded of Rabelais' Gargantua . . . Soviet diplomacy was carried out through *priyoms*.

. . . [One] time (at a reception, of course, as usual), I happened to be seated near Kirichenko . . . Nexhmije was with me, too. It was July 1957, the time when Khrushchev had fixed things up with the Titoites and was flattering them, as well as exerting pressure on them. The Titoites seemed to like the flattery, while as to the pressure and the stabs in the back, they gave as good as they got. Khrushchev had informed me the night before, «in order to get my permission», that he was going to ask me to this dinner at which Zhivkov and his wife, as well as Ranković and Kardelj, with their wives, would be present. As was his custom, Khrushchev cracked jokes with Mikoyan. This is the way they combined their roles, with Khrushchev accompanying his arrows, trickery, wiles, lies, and threats with jibes at «Anastasiy» who played the «king's jester».

When he finished his introduction with jokes with the «king's jester», Khrushchev, in proposing a toast, started to give us a lecture about the three-sided friendship that ought to exist between Albania, Yugoslavia and Bulgaria, and the four-sided friendship, between the Soviet Union, Albania, Yugoslavia and Bulgaria.

«The relations of the Soviet Union with Yugoslavia have not proceeded in a straight line . . . Meanwhile the relations of Yugoslavia with Albania and Bulgaria have not yet been improved, and as I told Ranković and Kardelj earlier, the Yugoslavs must stop their undercover activity against those countries.»

«It is the Albanians who do not leave us in peace,» interjected Ranković.

Then I intervened and listed for Ranković the anti-Albanian

actions, sabotage, subversion, and the plots which they organised against us. That night we had Khrushchev «on our side», but he soft-pedalled his criticisms of the Yugoslavs.

«I don't understand this name of your party, the 'League of Communists of Yugoslavia',» said Khrushchev, waving his glass. «What is this word 'League'? Besides, you Yugoslavs don't like the term 'socialist camp'. But tell us, what should we call it, the 'neutral camp', the 'camp of neutral countries'? We are all socialist countries, or are you not a socialist country?»

«We are, of course, we are!» said Kardelj.

«Then come and join us, we are the majority,» replied Khrushchev.

Khrushchev was on his feet throughout all this discourse, interspersed with shouts and gestures, and full of «criticisms» of the Yugoslavs . . .

Kardelj and Ranković replied coolly, making great efforts to appear calm, but it was very easy to understand that internally they were boiling . . .

The dialogue between them was dragging on, frequently interrupted by the shouts of Khrushchev, but I was no longer listening. Apart from the reply I gave Ranković, when he made the accusation that we had interfered in their affairs, I exchanged not one word with them.

. . . The process of large-scale rehabilitations, disguised as the «correction of mistakes made in the past», was transformed into an unprecedented campaign in all the former countries of people's democracy.

. . . We felt the pressure mounting against us from all sides, but we did not waver a fraction from our course.

This could not fail to anger Tito and company, first of all, because, exalted by the decisions of the 20th Congress and what was occurring in other countries, they expected a cataclysm in Albania, too.

Taking advantage of our correct behaviour and the facilities we had provided for them to carry out their task, the Yugoslav diplomats in Tirana . . . started to arouse and reactivate their old agents in our country.

. . . The Soviet leaders, who posed as our friends to the death and men of principle, did not fail to exert pressure on us openly.

On the eve of the 3rd Congress of our Party, which was held at the end of May and the beginning of June 1956, Suslov quite openly demanded that our leadership should «re-examine» and «correct» its line in the past.

«There is nothing for our Party to re-examine in its line,» we told him bluntly. «We have never permitted serious mistakes of principle in our line.»

«You should re-examine the case of Koçi Xoxe and his comrades, whom you condemned earlier,» Suslov told us.

«They were and still are traitors and enemies of our Party and people, enemies of the Soviet Union and socialism,» we replied bluntly. «If their trials were reviewed a hundred times, they would be described only as enemies a hundred times.»

. . . Then Suslov began to speak about the things that were occurring in the other parties and the Soviet party in regard to looking at this problem with a «more generous», «more humane» eye.

«This has made a great impression on and has been welcomed by the peoples,» he said. «This is what should occur with you too.»

«If we were to rehabilitate the enemies and traitors, those who wanted to place the country in the chains of a new slavery, our people would stone us,» we told Khrushchev's ideologist.

When he saw that he was getting nowhere with this, Suslov changed his tack.

«All right,» he said, «since you are convinced they are enemies, that is what they must be. But there is one thing you should do: you should refrain from speaking of their links with the Yugoslavs and should no longer describe them as agents of Belgrade.»

«Here we are speaking of the truth,» we said. «And the truth is that Koçi Xoxe and his collaborators in the plot were downright agents of the Yugoslav revisionists. The Soviet leadership knows them very well. Perhaps you have not had the chance to acquaint yourself with the facts and, since you persist in your opinion, let us present some of them to you.»

Suslov could hardly contain his temper. We calmly listed some of the main facts.

. . . Suslov snorted, «But there is no other way you can repair your relations with Yugoslavia.» . . .

. . . About 15 to 20 days after the 3rd Congress of our Party, in June 1956, I was in Moscow for a consultation . . . he [Khrushchev] admitted with his own mouth the pressure which Tito had exerted on him for the rehabilitation of Koçi Xoxe and other enemies condemned in Albania.

«With Tito,» said Khrushchev among other things, «we talked about the relations of Yugoslavia with the other states. Tito was pleased with the Poles, the Hungarians, the Czechs, the Bulgarians and the others, but he spoke very angrily about Albania, thumping his fist and stamping his feet. 'The Albanians are not in order, they are not on the right road,' Tito told me, 'they do not recognise the mistakes they have made and have understood nothing from all these things that are taking place'.»

In fact, by repeating Tito's words and accusations Khrushchev found the opportunity to pour out all the spite and ire he felt against us . . .

«When Tito spoke about the Albanian comrades he was trembling with rage, but I opposed him and said to him, 'These are the internal affairs of the Albanian comrades, and they will know how to solve them,'» said Khrushchev, continuing his «report», trying to convince us that he had had a great «quarrel» with Tito. However, we were now well aware of the meaning of the never-ending kisses and quarrels between these two heralds of modern revisionism.

. . . When Khrushchev betrayed, he [Tito] strutted like a «peacock» and posed as Khrushchev's «teacher». Tito was quite right to demand a great deal from him, and did not hang back in this direction. He aimed to make Khrushchev obey him . . .

Tito and Khrushchev were two revisionists, two agents of capitalism, who had things in common, but also contradictions, which were expressed in the zig zags and erratic behaviour of that time, which continue to this day, between Tito and Khrushchev's heirs.

There was nothing Marxist-Leninist in their actions and stands. They were guided by counter-revolutionary aims and had assumed the leadership of revisionism, which is capitalism in a new form, the enemy of the unity of peoples, the inciter of reactionary nationalism, of the drive towards and establishment of the most ferocious fascist dictatorship which does not permit even the slightest sign of formal bourgeois democracy. Revisionism is the idea and action which leads the turning of a country from socialism back to capitalism, the turning of a communist party into a fascist party, it is the inspirer of ideological chaos, confusion, corruption, repression, arbitrarity, instability and putting the homeland up for auction. This tragedy occurred in the Soviet Union and the other revisionist countries. Khrushchev and the Khrushchevites, incited and assisted by American imperialism and world capitalism, created this situation.

The 1957 Moscow meeting of Communist parties

After the tumultuous events of 1956 the Khrushchev leadership made strenuous efforts to convene a meeting of all the Communist parties in the world, and this finally met, after much difficulty, in Moscow, in November 1957, on the occasion of the fortieth anniversary of the Bolshevik Revolution. The heads of the twelve ruling Communist bloc parties attended, including Mao, on his last visit to the Soviet Union. Altogether sixty-four Communist parties were represented.

Hoxha's account is mainly of interest for his description of the behaviour of Mao, who appeared strongly to back the Soviet Union's right to head the 'camp', but who in fact was also staking a major claim for China's role in the world Communist movement.[53] It is also an interesting reminder of Mao's views on Stalin, publicly expressed, and of his ability to pay tribute to Khrushchev, even if for opportunist reasons.

Finally, in a passage not reproduced here, Hoxha puts his finger on a key weakness of Khrushchev's position, although he does not take his criticism to its logical conclusion. Hoxha notes that Khrushchev's economic claims, especially as regards the USSR's ability to compete with the USA, were wildly unrealistic – and that this, in effect, put the competition between socialism and capitalism on a false basis (compare his remarks about Rákosi's insane overoptimism and lying about the economic situation in Hungary and similar, even more extreme, exaggeration of an almost mystical kind by Lin Biao in 1969).[54]

From the place he sat Mao Zedong brought out his «arguments».

«Our camp must have a head, because even the snake has a head, and imperialism has a head,» he said. «I would not agree that China should be called the head of the camp,» Mao went on, «because we do not merit this honour and cannot maintain this role, we are still poor. We haven't even a quarter of a satellite, while the Soviet Union has two. Then, the Soviet Union deserves to be the head because it treats us well. See how freely we are speaking now. If Stalin were here, we would find it difficult to speak like this. When I met Stalin, before him I felt like a pupil in front of his teacher, while with Comrade Khrushchev we speak freely, like equal comrades.»

And as if this were not enough, he continued in his own style:

«With the criticism against the cult of the individual, it seemed as if a heavy roof, which was pressing down on us and hindered us from understanding matters correctly, was lifted from us. Who lifted this roof from us, who made it easier for all of us to understand the cult of the individual correctly?!» asked the philosopher, who was silent for a moment, and there and then supplied the answer: «Comrade Khrushchev, and we thank him for this.»

However, at the same time, in order to avoid angering Gomulka, who was opposed to this thesis, Mao, as the equilibrist he was, added:

«Gomulka is a good comrade and must be supported and trusted!» . . .

Palmiro Togliatti got up in the meeting and proclaimed his ultra-revisionist theses:

«We must go further with the line of the 20th Congress to turn the communist parties into broad mass parties . . . Now we need great independence in working out slogans and forms of collaboration,» he continued, «therefore we are opposed to a single leading centre.» . . .

Jacques Duclos,[55] who was sitting beside me, could not contain himself:

«I am going to get up and attack him openly,» he said to me . . .

After . . . Togliatti [spoke], tempers flared up. Jacques Duclos rose to speak:

«. . . We do not agree in the least with what Togliatti said. His views open the way to opportunism and revisionism.»

«Our parties have been . . . hindered by sectarianism and dogmatism,» interjected Togliatti.

At one moment Mao Zedong got up to calm the tempers, speaking in his style of allegories and implications. He said:

«On every . . . human issue one must go into battle, but also towards conciliation. I have in mind the relations between comrades: when we have differences let us invite each other to talks. In Panmunjom we had negotiations with the Americans, in Vietnam with the French.»[56]

After several phrases of this type, he came to the point:

«There are people,» he said, «who are 100 per cent Marxists, and others who are 80 per cent, 70 per cent or 50 per cent, indeed there are some who may be only 10 per cent Marxists. We ought to talk even with those who are 10 per cent Marxists, because there are only advantages in this.»

He was silent for a moment, looked around the room as though a little lost, and continued:

«Why should we not gather, two or three of us, in a small room to talk things over? Why should we not talk, proceeding from the desire for unity? We have to act with both hands, with the one we must fight against those who make mistakes, and with the other we must make concessions.»

Suslov got up and was obliged to maintain a «principled» stand, to stress that the struggle against opportunism and revisionism is important, as is the struggle against dogmatism, but «revisionism constitutes the main danger, because it leads to splits, damages unity,» etc., etc.

. . . Our delegation had its Marxist-Leninist say about all the problems raised at the meeting.

. . . In the face of the struggle which was waged in the meeting against opportunist views . . . the revisionists retreated. As a result, the 1957 Moscow Declaration, in general, was a good document.

At this meeting, revisionism, right opportunism, was defined as the main danger in the international communist and workers' movement.

This infuriated the Yugoslavs. They had held long debates with Khrushchev's men before the meeting, especially over this thesis.

«What are you worrying about?» said the Khrushchevites, trying to calm them. «Your name is not mentioned. We shall speak about revisionism in general, without any definition.»

«Yes,» replied the Yugoslavs, «but look at the articles by Enver Hoxha, which you publish even in *Pravda*![57] When Enver Hoxha speaks against revisionism, he has us in mind and mentions us by name. But even when we are not mentioned by name, everybody understands that we are implied, and that is why we do not take part in the meeting or sign the declaration of parties of socialist countries.»

And they did not sign this declaration.

Mao Zedong expressed his deep regret:

«They are not going to sign the 12 parties declaration,» he said. «As a rule, there ought to be 13 countries, but the Yugoslav comrades stood aside. We cannot force them. They are not going to sign. I say that in ten years' time they will sign the declaration.» (Mao was wrong only in the time he set. In fact, not ten years, but twenty years later a «declaration» was signed with the Yugoslavs in Beijing. The Maoists signed their submission to Tito.)

Khrushchev visits Albania (May 1959)

In May 1959 Khrushchev paid his only visit to Albania, together with the Soviet Defence Minister, Marshal Malinovsky.[58] Prior to the visit the Albanian regime agreed to a Soviet request for an embargo on attacks on Yugoslavia while Khrushchev was in Albania.

This is the only known account of what transpired between Hoxha and Khrushchev on this occasion.[59] Once again, according to Hoxha, the Russians put pressure on the Albanians to integrate, or subordinate their economic plans more to Comecon imperatives. Hoxha has a go at Khrushchev for philistinism. Khrushchev and Malinovsky discuss the strategic advantages of the Albanian coast for a submarine base (presumably one of their main objectives on the trip). And Hoxha outlines the beginning of Soviet economic pressure, which was to build up steadily, along with political pressure, until the final rupture of all relations at the end of 1961.

One extremely important fact which is conspicuous by its absence here (indeed also in the 1600 pages of *Reflections on China*) is that Khrushchev and Malinovsky were in Albania at the same time as the Chinese Defence Minister, Peng Teh-huai, who was purged shortly afterwards, largely on the grounds of his contacts and alleged collusion with the Russians. Peng held a meeting with Khrushchev in Tirana in late May.[60] It is not known what transpired at this meeting, but it is a curious fact that the Chinese Defence Minister was in Albania at the same time as both Khrushchev and the Soviet Defence Minister at a time when the key base at Vlora was very much under discussion not just between Tirana and Moscow, but within the whole bloc.

I mentioned oil, and informed him [Khrushchev] that in recent days we had struck a new gusher of oil.

«Is that so?» he said. «But what quality is it? I know you have bad, heavy oil. Have you calculated how much it will cost to process it? Then, where will you sell it? Who needs your oil?»

I went on to speak about our mining industry.

. . . When I finished, Khrushchev began to speak:

«Comrade Enver's exposé made the situation in your country clearer to us,» he said. «However, in regard to your needs, I want to tell you that we have not come to examine them. We have not been authorised by our government to discuss such matters. We have come to get to know you, to exchange opinions.»

Then laughing, he cracked a joke which was not simply a joke:

«We think that things are going well with you. Albania has advanced, and if you offered us a loan we would accept it with the greatest of pleasure.»

«We have ample stones, sea and air,» put in Mehmet [Shehu] in the same tone.

«We have much more of those than you. Have you any dollars?» asked Khrushchev, and then, in a different tone:

«Enough of this,» he said. «The truth is that you have made progress, but you are not satisfied. We gave you a credit last year and now you want another one. But we have a popular saying: 'Cut your coat according to your cloth'.»

«We have the same saying,» I said, «and we know it and implement it well.»

«But,» he said, «you are asking for credits again.» He shrugged

his shoulders, was silent for a moment and resumed his jocular
tone:

«Or is it that you gave us a good lunch and thought it a fine
opportunity to ask us for another credit? If we had known this we
would have brought our own lunch.»

«The Albanians have a special respect for a guest,» I said.
«Whether they have plenty [or] whether they have nothing, they
always provide for their guest. They treat him with every respect
when he comes to their home and even swallow something that
they do not like.»

«I was joking,» he said and burst into a laugh. But it was more a
snarl than a laugh. Wherever he went he criticised us . . .

He criticised the work to drain the Tërbuf swamp. In Vlora he
summoned the main Soviet oil expert in our country and he, no
doubt «well prepared» by the Soviet Embassy in Tirana, delivered
a report in our presence which was extremely pessimistic, saying
that Albania had no oil. However, a group of Albanian oil experts
also came there and refuted what the Soviets said with many facts
and arguments.

. . . «Fine, fine,» repeated Khrushchev, «but yours is a heavy oil
and contains sulphur. Have you calculated things properly? You
will process it, but a litre of benzine will cost you more than a
kilogram of caviar. You must look closely at the commercial
aspect. It has not been decreed that you must have everything
yourselves. What are your friends for?!»

In Saranda he advised us to plant only oranges and lemons for
which the Soviet Union had great need.

«We shall supply you with wheat. The mice in our country eat
as much wheat as you need,» he said, repeating what he had said
in Moscow in 1957. He also gave us a lot of «advice».

«Don't waste your land and marvellous climate on maize and
wheat. They bring you no income. The bay-tree grows here . . .
Plant thousands of hectares of bay because we shall buy it from
you.»

He went on with peanuts, tea and citrus fruit.

«These are what you should plant,» he said. «In this way
Albania will become a flourishing garden!»

In other words he wanted Albania to be turned into a fruit-growing colony which would serve the revisionist Soviet Union, just as the banana republics in Latin America serve the United States of America . . .

He even criticised our archaeological work as «dead things». When he visited Butrint he said:

«Why do you employ all these forces and funds on such dead things! Leave the Hellenes and the Romans to their antiquity!» . . .

Khrushchev was truly an ignoramus in these fields. He could see only the «profitability»:

«Why are these things of value to you? Do they increase the well-being of the people?» he asked me. He called Malinovsky, at that time Minister of Defence, who was always at hand:

«Look, how marvellous this is!» I heard them whisper. «An ideal base for our submarines could be built here. These old things should be dug up and thrown into the sea (they were referring to the archaeological finds at Butrint). We can tunnel through this mountain to the other side,» and he pointed to Ksamil. «We shall have the most ideal and most secure base in the Mediterranean. From here we can paralyse and attack everything.»

They were to repeat the same thing in Vlora a day or two later. We had come out on the verandah of the villa at Uji i Ftohtë.

«Marvellous, marvellous!» Khrushchev cried and turned to Malinovsky. I thought he was referring to the truly breath-taking landscape of our Riviera. But their mind was working in another direction:

«What a secure bay at the foot of these mountains!» they said. «With a powerful fleet, from here we can have the whole of the Mediterranean, from the Bosporus to Gibraltar, in our hands! We can control everyone.»

It made my flesh creep to hear them talk like this, as if they were the masters of the seas, countries and peoples. «No, Nikita Khrushchev,» I said to myself, «we shall never allow you to set out to enslave other countries and shed their peoples' blood from our territory. You will never have Butrint, Vlora, or any inch of Albanian territory, to use for those evil purposes.»

The fictitious «peace» was being more and more thoroughly rocked to its foundations. Khrushchev and his followers . . . tried to make us yield by exerting economic pressure, while secretly orchestrating a discrimination against our leadership by means of their specialists who were working in all sectors in our country, such as in oil and . . . in the army, where we had advisers, etc. The Soviet Embassy maintained contact with all these «experts», and gave them the necessary instructions.

. . . Those experts who remained sincere with us were removed by the embassy, one after the other . . . Those who remained in Albania, of course, had received orders to sabotage the key sectors of our economy, especially the oil industry and geological prospecting. As was proved later, the Soviet oil «experts» had recruited some agents from the ranks of our geologists and, as they themselves eventually admitted, had charged them with the mission of keeping from our Party and Government accurate data about the discoveries which they made, . . . of using all the means of sabotage, so as to make us start drilling in the wrong places, of violating the rules of prospecting and extracting technique and wasting hundreds of millions of leks, etc. . . . These oil «experts» and «geologists» made two reports: an accurate one, with exact and positive data on discoveries of different minerals, and a false one, which said that the prospecting had allegedly yielded negative results . . . The first report was sent to Moscow and Leningrad through the KGB centre, which was called the Soviet Embassy in Tirana, and the second report was sent to our Ministry of Industry and Mines. This whole vile business was discovered and proved after the Soviets cleared out of Albania.

Mikoyan informs the Albanians of the Sino-Soviet dispute

In February 1960 Hoxha was back in Moscow. He received a summons to see Mikoyan. Hoxha specifically insisted on bringing his close colleague, premier Mehmet Shehu, along, as he wanted a friendly witness to what Mikoyan might say. Later on, in *The Titoites*, after Shehu had been denounced as a Soviet agent, Hoxha rewrote the story.[61]

. . . We went to meet Mikoyan in his villa in Leninskie Gori. After the usual greetings, Anastasiy entered directly into the theme of the talk:

«I am going to inform you about the disagreements we have

with the Communist Party of China, I stress, with the Communist Party of China. We had decided to tell these things only to the first secretaries of the sister parties. Therefore, I ask Comrade Mehmet [Shehu], not to misunderstand us, but this is what we had decided and not that we did not trust him.»

«Not at all,» replied Mehmet. «Indeed I can leave.»

«No,» said Mikoyan, «stay!»

... Mikoyan spun his tale in such a way as to create the impression that they themselves stood in principled Leninist positions and were fighting the deviations of the Chinese leadership. Amongst other things, Mikoyan used as arguments several theses of the Chinese which, in fact, for us, too, were not right from the viewpoint of the Marxist-Leninist ideology. Thus, Mikoyan mentioned the pluralist theories of «one hundred flowers», the question of the cult of Mao, the «great leap forward», etc.

... «We have Marxism-Leninism and do not need any other theory,» I told Mikoyan, «while as to the 'one hundred flowers' we have neither accepted this view nor have we ever mentioned it.»

... Just as we were parting he [Mikoyan] asked us: «Please don't discuss these matters I raised with you, even with the members of your Political Bureau.»

Shehu visited by Kosygin in hospital in Moscow (June, 1960)

One of the most bizarre episodes in Hoxha's entire account concerns a visit paid by Soviet premier Kosygin to Albania's premier Shehu, who was in hospital in Moscow. Hoxha describes this episode twice: the first time in the passage reproduced below; a second time in the Titoites written after the death of Shehu.[62] The episode is also described twice by Khrushchev in the published version of his memoirs – and Khrushchev, like Hoxha, has radically rewritten his version on the second occasion (for reasons that are not clear).[63]

In Hoxha's first version, Shehu puts up a spirited and principled defence against Kosygin's manoeuvres, naturally. In Hoxha's second account, he says he does not know what Kosygin said to Shehu (presumably because he only had Shehu's word for what transpired), but that Shehu was subsequently called to a meeting, together with his wife,

Fiqrete Shehu, with the Soviet leaders Mikoyan and Andropov, which lasted four hours.

When Comrade Gogo Nushi was returning to Albania from Beijing, in Moscow Brezhnev, who at that time had become chairman of the Presidium of the Supreme Soviet, sought a meeting with him. Gogo met Brezhnev, who spoke to him at length about the differences with the Chinese.[64]

Four to five days before the meeting in Bucharest began, when Hysni [Kapo] and I were discussing the stand he was to take in the congress of the Rumanian party, we received a radiogram from Mehmet [Shehu], who had been for some days in Moscow for medical treatment. In the radiogram Mehmet informed us about an unexpected «visit» which Kosygin had paid him. When he saw him come in, Mehmet was surprised and thought it was a courtesy visit, although somewhat late.

«Comrade Mehmet, I have come to talk about a very important matter,» said Kosygin, without even bothering to inquire about his health, although he knew very well that Mehmet had gone there for medical treatment.

«Go ahead,» said Mehmet.

Kosygin spoke for an hour and a half about the contradictions they had with the Communist Party of China. Mehmet listened and listened and then said:

«All these things you have told me are very grave. We are astonished that they have been allowed to become as serious as this.»

«We are not going to make any concession to the Chinese,» said Kosygin ... and added, «We were very pleased with the courageous, heroic stand of Comrade Belishova in the talks with the Chinese in Beijing. The counsellor of our embassy in Beijing informed us of what she had told him after the talks with the Chinese.»

Mehmet still had no knowledge of these actions and intrigues of Liri Belishova, but he told Kosygin coldly and bluntly:

«I do not know what Liri Belishova has told you because I have been here. I know that when we talked with Mikoyan, he instructed us not to discuss these matters with anyone. Our opinion has been and is that these things should be settled between your two parties. But since they are not being settled in this way, then they should be placed before the meeting of the parties . . .»

Kosygin got up scowling and when he was about to go out the door, Mehmet dealt him a slap:

«Comrade Kosygin,» he said quietly, «you did not give me the opportunity to ask you – how is your health?»

Kosygin turned back, and, as if to excuse himself, he, too, asked Mehmet how he was feeling.

«I am very well,» said Mehmet, without prolonging the subject, and immediately after this conversation he stopped the treatment and made arrangements to return home by aircraft the following day.

Soviet pressure builds up

Particularly after the Bucharest Meeting (June 1960), Soviet pressure on Albania was stepped up. According to Hoxha (confirmed by independent sources) this pressure was both economic and political. Once again, some leading Albanian political figures, this time Liri Belishova and Koço Tashko, were denounced as having sided with the enemy – and executed (Khrushchev says he thinks Belishova, a resistance heroine who had had one eye gouged out by her fascist captors during the war, was strangled).[65]

Hoxha had declined to attend the meeting in Bucharest, which was attended by all the other party heads from Eastern Europe. Albania decided to send a powerful delegation to Moscow for the preparatory commission which was to draft the documents for the Meeting of Communist and Workers' Parties to be held in November 1960, where the breach between Tirana and Moscow finally became irreparable.

The Albanians have published a volume entitled *Albania Challenges Khrushchev Revisionism* covering the period from the Bucharest Conference through the November 1960 Moscow Conference and its immediate aftermath.[66] This volume contains the verbatim records of most of the key meetings between the Albanians and the Russians, as well as radiograms and letters between Hoxha and the Albanian delegates at the key meetings. The texts published by the Albanians have not been disowned by the Russians.

The open fight began. The Soviet Embassy in Tirana, through its KGB agents, intensified the pressure, interference and sabotage in the dirtiest forms. The Soviet militarymen and civilians working in Albania committed provocations against our people ... The officials of the Soviet Embassy in Tirana, with ambassador Ivanov at the head, tried to recruit agents and provoked our officers by asking them, «Who is the army with?», and tried to work on certain elements to put them in opposition to the line of the Party.

... The provocations of the Soviet revisionists ran into an insurmountable barricade, an immovable rock. The only treacherous elements who opposed the monolithic unity of our ranks were Liri Belishova and Koço Tashko, who surrendered to the pressure of the Soviets ... The Party and the people unmasked them and condemned them with hatred and contempt.

The provocations which the Soviet Embassy in Tirana organised ceaselessly were now co-ordinated with the external pressures which were exerted on our Party and country by the Soviet revisionist leadership and its allies ... the Khrushchevites abandoned every scruple, going so far as to threaten our country with [a] blockade to starve us. These rabid enemies of socialism and of the Albanian people in particular, refused to supply us with grain at a time when our bread grain reserves would last us only 15 days. At that time we were obliged to use our hard currency to buy wheat in France. The French merchant who came to Tirana sounded us out to find what was the reason that impelled Albania to buy grain from the Western countries when it had the Soviet Union as its «great friend». Of course, we told the bourgeois merchant nothing. On the contrary, we told him that the Soviet Union had supplied us with grain, with maize, but we had «used it for the livestock».

«Why worry yourselves about bread grain,» Khrushchev had said to us. «Plant citrus-fruit. The mice in our granaries eat as much grain as Albania needs.» And when the Albanian people were in danger of being left without bread, Khrushchev preferred to feed the mice and not the Albanians. According to him, there were only two roads for us: either submit or die.

... However, the great rift in our relations with the Soviet leadership could not be covered up for long, especially when the Khrushchevites themselves were revealing it more and more each day.

The Soviet and Bulgarian ambassadors in Yugoslavia applauded the hangman Ranković during those days, when, at a rally in Sremska Mitrovica, he described Albania as «a hell enclosed with barbed wire»,[67] the Bulgarians published a map of the Balkans and «by mistake» included our country within the boundaries of Yugoslavia; in Warsaw, Gomulka's men forced their way into [our] embassy . . . and attempted to kill the Albanian ambassador; Khrushchev tolerated and whetted the appetite of the Greek monarcho-fascists, like Venizelos,[68] when they played the worthless card of the annexation of the so-called Northern Epirus, etc., etc. During those days, these and tens of such things occurred from all directions against our Party and country.

. . . However, our Party and people stood firm on the correct Marxist-Leninist line. We told the communists and cadres what was occurring . . . and the masses of the Party closed their ranks around the Central Committee.

. . . At all costs they [the Russians] needed our submission, or at least, «reconciliation» with us.

To this end, during the time that the Soviet Embassy in Tirana was operating through provocations, Moscow, through Kozlov, wearied itself sending letter after letter to the «Central Committee and Comrade Enver Hoxha». In these letters they demanded that I should go to Moscow so that we could talk and reach agreement as «the friends and comrades we are» . . .

They wanted to drag us to Moscow and to operate on us in the «workshops» of their Central Committee in order to «convince» us. However, we knew with whom we were dealing and our answer was curt: «Comrade Enver Hoxha cannot go to Moscow except for the meeting of the Communist and workers' parties. We told you what we had to say in Bucharest; we shall state our views and our stand at the coming meeting of the parties.» . . .

. . . The battle began in the commission which was to prepare the draft declaration for the meeting. There the Soviets had Suslov, Pospyelov, Kozlov, Ponomaryov, Andropov, and some others. A «solid» delegation this, saturated with «big brains» to impress us. Apart from us[69] and the Chinese, almost all the other delegations were made up of low-ranking, third- or fourth-rate people. It was clear that everything had been co-ordinated and agreement had been reached, so that they had nothing further to discuss.

The Moscow meeting of Communist and workers' parties (November 1960)[70]

Hoxha went to the November 1960 Moscow meeting – his last public journey outside Albania. He was accompanied by premier Mehmet Shehu, his old friend Hysni Kapo, and Ramiz Alia. On this occasion Hoxha truly succeeded in putting himself and Albania on the world map. His denunciation of Khrushchev made headlines round the world and even his harshest enemies usually concede that Hoxha turned in an able performance and showed personal courage.

According to Hoxha, the Chinese delegation, headed by Liv Shaoqi, but for which the speeches were made by Deng Xiaoping, came to Moscow ready to compromise with Khrushchev, if it seemed advantageous. Hoxha tries to make it appear that it was Albania, not China, which really took the lead in breaking with Moscow. This gives him a chance to accuse the Chinese, retroactively, of failing to back up Albania against the Russians. But, while there can be no dispute about the fact that Hoxha's assaults on the Soviet leaders and their East European colleagues were by far the most virulent and violent, there is little evidence to support his claim that he took the lead, not the Chinese.

Hoxha's account is interesting for two other things. First, is his insistent description of the personal degeneration of the Soviet leadership, portrayed as sodden with drink and food (as well as being insufferably dull). Second, is his vivid description of Soviet bugging – and of Albania's defiant methods of dealing with them. '

After Enver Hoxha and Mehmet Shehu have quarrelled with virtually the entire top Soviet leadership – including Khrushchev, Kosygin and Yuri Andropov (then an important functionary in the Party apparatus) – Hoxha and Shehu flee Moscow before the end of the Conference, apparently in fear of their lives. They decline to leave by plane (easier to have an accident) and take the train to the point of exit nearest to Albania from the bloc – preferring the safety of travelling as much as possible of the way in the capitalist West. After getting out of Hungary, they make their way to the safety of Austria and Italy. Hoxha never officially left home again.

We were convinced that we were going to a country where we would have to be very careful because they would behave like enemies and would record every word and every step of ours. We had to be vigilant and prudent. We were convinced, too, that they would try to break the code of our radiograms . . .

In passing through Budapest we were met by several of the main «comrades» of the Hungarian party, who behaved correctly with us. Neither they nor we made any allusion to the problems. We boarded the train for the Ukraine. The staff of the train looked at us coldly and served us without speaking at all, while men who were certainly security officers patrolled the corridors. We had not the least desire to open the slightest conversation with them because we knew who they were and what they represented.

At the Kiev station, two or three members of the Central Committee of the Ukraine had come to meet us. They gave us a cool reception, and we remained as cold as ice, even refusing to drink their coffee . . . At the Moscow station they had brought out a guard of honour, a band played anthems and soldiers paraded with martial step, just to keep up the custom as for all the delegations. No young pioneers came out to welcome us with flowers. Kozlov offered us his cold hand, accompanied with an artificial smile from ear to ear, and in his deep voice bid us welcome. But the ice remained ice.

As soon as the anthems and the parade were over we heard cheering, clapping and enthusiastic calls, «Long live the Party of Labour!» We saw that they came from several hundred Albanian students who were studying in Moscow. They had not been permitted to enter the station, but finally they were allowed in to avoid causing a scandal. Paying no attention to Kozlov and Yefremov, who never left us, we greeted our students who were shouting with joy, and together with them, we cheered for our Party. This was a good lesson for the Soviets to see what sort of unity our Party and people have with their leadership. The students did not leave us until we climbed into ZIL cars. In the car Kozlov was unable to find anything to say except «Your students are unruly.»

«No,» I said, «they are great patriots and love the Party and their leadership whole-heartedly.»

Kozlov and Yefremov accompanied us to the residence which they had allocated to us at Zarechie, some 20–25 km outside Moscow. This was the villa where I had stayed many times with the comrades and with Nexhmije when I came on holiday. They told me once, «We have reserved this villa for Zhou Enlai and you, we put no one else here.» Even in the villa they had united us with the Chinese. As we proved later with the special detector we had brought with us, they had filled the villa with bugging devices.

. . . One Sunday when I was in Moscow with Mehmet at the time of the 21st Congress, Polyansky, then a member of the Presidium of the Soviet party and now ambassador in Tokyo, invited us to lunch at his dacha outside Moscow . . . Everything was covered in white because snow had fallen. It was cold. The villa, too, was white as snow, beautiful. Polyansky told us:

«This is the dacha where Lenin used to rest.»

With this he wanted to tell us, «I am an important person.» Here we found Yefremov and another secretary, from the Crimea, if I am not mistaken . . . It was ten o'clock in the morning. The table was laden as in the fables about the Russian czars.

«Let us sit down and have breakfast,» said Polyansky.

«We have eaten already,» we said.

«No, no,» he said, «we shall sit down and eat again.» (Of course he meant «drink».)

We did not drink but we watched them drinking and talking. What colossal amounts they ate and drank!! We opened our eyes wide as they downed whole tumblers of vodka and various wines. Polyansky, with his intriguer's face, was boasting without the least shame, while Yefremov with the other secretary, and another person who came in later, drank and without the slightest sign of embarrassment [at] our presence, poured out their sickening praises on Polyansky. «There is no one like you, you are a great man, the pillar of the party, you are the Khan of the Crimea,» etc., etc. The «breakfast» went on in this way until one o'clock. Mehmet and I were bored to death. We did not know what to do. I thought of billiards and in order to get away from this roomful of boozers I asked Polyansky:

«Is there a billiard table in the house?»

«Yes, of course,» he replied . . .

We went up to the billiard room. We stayed there an hour and a half or two hours. The vodka, *pertsofka* and *zakuski* [peppered vodka and hors-d'oeuvres] were sent up to them in the billiard room. Then we asked permission to leave.

«Where are you going?» asked Polyansky.

«To Moscow,» we replied.

«Impossible,» he said, «we are just about to have lunch.»

We opened our eyes in amazement. Mehmet said to him:

«But what have we been doing up till now? Haven't we eaten enough for two days?»

«Oh, no,» said Yefremov, «what we ate was just a light breakfast . . .»

They took us by the arm and led us back to the dining room. What a sight met our eyes! The table had been loaded all over again. The Soviet state of proletarians paid for all this food and drink for its leaders so they could «rest» and enjoy themselves! We told them: «We cannot eat any more.» . . . Mehmet had a good idea when he asked:

«Have you got a cinema here? Could we see a film?»

«We have, indeed,» said Polyansky and rang the bell, ordering the projectionist to prepare to show a film.

. . . I remember it was a Mexican colour film. We had escaped from the *stolovaya* [dining room]. The film had not been running for more than ten minutes, when, in the darkness, we saw Polyansky and the others stealing quietly out of the room back to the vodka. When the film was over we found them sitting there drinking.

«Come along,» they said, «now we shall eat something, because it tastes fine after the film.»

«No,» we said, «we can eat and drink no more. Please allow us to return to Moscow.»

Very reluctantly they allowed us to get up.

«You will have to sample the beautiful Russian winter's night,» they told us.

«Let us sample even the winter,» I said to Mehmet in Albanian, «but let us get away from this drinking den and these boozers.»

We put on our overcoats and went out in the snow. We took only a few steps and a ZIM drew up: two other friends of

Polyansky, one, a certain Popov, whom I had known in Lenin-grad . . . We embraced in the snow.

«Please come back,» they said, «just for another hour . . . ,» etc., etc.

We refused and left. However, I paid a price for this. I [caught] a chill, developed a heavy cold with a temperature and was absent from sessions of the congress . . .

Now let us come back again to our arrival in Moscow before the meeting of the parties.

Kozlov, then, accompanied us to the villa. On other occasions, usually they took us to the house and left. But this time Kozlov wanted to show that he was a «friendly comrade». He took off his coat and went straight into the *stolovaya*, which was full of bottles, snacks and black caviar.

«Come along, let us have something to eat and drink,» said Kozlov, but this was not what he was really concerned about. He wanted to talk with us to learn with what opinions and predis-positions we had come.

He began the conversation by saying:

«Now the commission has finished the draft and we are virtu-ally all in agreement. The Chinese comrades are in agreement, too. There are four or five matters on which a common opinion has not been reached, but we can bring out an internal communiqué about them.»

Turning to Hysni [Kapo] for his approval he asked, «Isn't that so?»

Hysni replied:

«No, it is not so. The work is not finished. We have objections and reservations which our Party has presented in the written statement we forwarded to the commission.»

Kozlov frowned, he did not get the approval he wanted. I intervened and said to Kozlov:

«This will be a serious meeting . . . Everything must be reflected in the declaration. We shall not accept internal notes and adden-da. Nothing in obscurity, everything in the light . . .

«It doesn't need a great deal of talk,» said Kozlov.

Mehmet jumped up and said in a derisive tone:

«Even in the UNO we speak as long as we like. Castro spoke

there for four hours, while you apparently think you can restrict us!»

Hysni said:

«You interrupted our speech twice in the commission and did not allow us to continue to speak.»

«These things should not occur,» I added. «You ought to know that we do not accept such methods.»

«We must preserve unity, otherwise it is tragic,» said Kozlov.

«Unity is safeguarded by speaking openly, in conformity with the Marxist-Leninist line and norms,» replied Mehmet.

Kozlov got his reply, proposed a toast to me, helped himself to something to eat and left.

The whole period until the meeting of the parties began was filled with attacks and counter-attacks between us and revisionists of all ranks.

Their tactic was to do everything in their power to prevent us from speaking out at the meeting . . . they resorted to slander, alleging that the things we would raise were unfounded, would cause «division», that we were making «tragic» mistakes, that we were «at fault» and should change our course, etc., etc. The Soviets made great efforts to brainwash all the delegations of sister communist and workers' parties . . . For their own part, they posed as «infallible», «blameless», «principled», and as though they held the fate of the Marxist-Leninist truth in their hands.

. . . In the reception put on in the Kremlin on the occasion of November 7, Kosygin approached me, his face as pale as wax, and began to give me a sermon about friendship.[71]

«We shall safeguard and defend our friendship with the Soviet Union on the Marxist–Leninist road,» I told him.

«There are enemies in your party who are fighting this friendship,» said Kosygin.

«Ask him,» I said to Mehmet, who knew Russian well, «can he tell us who are these enemies in our Party?»

Kosygin found himself in a tight spot. He began to mumble and said:

«You did not understand me well.»

«Enough of that,» said Mehmet, «we understood you very well, but you lack the courage to speak openly. We shall tell you openly in the meeting what we think about you.»

We walked away from that revisionist mummy.

(During the whole evening the Soviets acted towards us in such a way as not to leave us alone in peace, but isolated us from one another and surrounded us, according to previously prepared stage directions.)

A little later the Marshals Chuikov, Zakharov, Konev, and others, surrounded Mehmet and me. As instructed, they sang another tune: «You Albanians are fighters, you fought well, you resisted properly until you triumphed over Hitlerite Germany,» and Zakharov continued to cast stones at the German people. At that moment Shelepin[72] joined us. He began to oppose Zakharov over what he said about the Germans. Zakharov got angry and, disregarding the fact that Shelepin was a member of the Presidium and chief of the KGB, told him: «Go away, why do you butt into our conversation? You want to teach me what the Germans are? When I was fighting them, you were still drinking your mother's milk,» etc.

In the midst of this talk of the haughty marshals, full of vodka, Zakharov, who had been director of the «Voroshilov» Military Academy, where Mehmet and other comrades were sent to learn the Stalinist military art, said to Mehmet: «When you were here you were an outstanding student of our military art.» Mehmet cut short his words and said: «Thank you for the compliment, but do you want to say that this evening too, here in [the] Georgievsky Zal, we are superior and subordinate, commander and pupil?»

Marshal Chuikov, who was no less drunk, intervened and said: «We want to say that the Albanian army should always stand with us . . .» Mehmet replied there and then, «Our army is and will remain loyal to its own people and will loyally defend the construction of socialism on the Marxist-Leninist road; it is and will remain solely under the leadership of the Party of Labour of Albania, as a weapon of the dictatorship of the proletariat in Albania. Do you still not understand this, Marshal Chuikov? So much the worse for you!»

The marshals got their reply. One of them, I don't remember, whether Konev or some other, seeing that the talk was getting out of hand, intervened: «Let us end this talk. Come and drink a glass to the friendship between our two peoples and our two armies.»

Along with this . . . Khrushchev and the Khrushchevites attacked us openly in the material which they sent to the Chinese . . . They distributed this material to all delegations, including ours. As is known, in this material, Albania no longer figured as a socialist country as far as the Khrushchevites were concerned. Apart from this, during a talk with Liu Shaoqi, Khrushchev had said: «We lost Albania, but we did not lose much; you won it, but you did not win much, either. The Party of Labour has always been a weak link in the international communist movement.»

. . . A few days before I spoke at the meeting, Khrushchev sought a meeting with me, of course, to «convince» us to change our stand. We decided to go to this meeting in order to make it quite clear to the Khrushchevites once again that we would not budge from our positions. Meanwhile, however, we read the material of which I spoke above. I met Andropov, who during those days was running back and forth as Khrushchev's courier.[73]

«Today I read the material in which Albania does not figure as a socialist country,» I told him.

Without a blush, Andropov, who had been one of the authors of that base document, asked me, «What connection does this letter have with Albania?»

«This letter makes my meeting with Khrushchev impossible,» I replied.

Andropov frowned and murmured:

«That is a very serious statement, Comrade Enver.»

«Yes,» I said, «very serious! Tell Khrushchev it is not he who decides whether Albania is or is not a socialist country. The Albanian people and their Marxist-Leninist Party have decided this with their blood.»

Once again Andropov repeated like a parrot:

«But this is a material about China and has nothing to do with Albania, Comrade Enver.»

«We shall express our opinion in the meeting of the parties. Good-bye!» and I ended the conversation.

. . . We could count on 7 to 10 parties which would adhere

more to our side, if not openly, at least by not approving the hostile undertaking of the Khrushchevites.

As it turned out, the Chinese delegation had come to the Moscow Meeting with the idea that the tempers could be cooled, and initially they had prepared a material in a conciliatory tone ... Deng Xiaoping was to deliver it. As was becoming obvious, they had prepared a stand of «two or three variants» ... However, when the Khrushchevites launched even more vicious attacks, ... the Chinese were obliged to put aside the conciliatory spirit and to take a stand in reply to Khrushchev's attacks.

There was a tense atmosphere when the meeting opened. Not without a purpose, they had put us near the speaker's rostrum so that we would be under the reproving finger of the anti-Marxist Khrushchevite «prosecutors». But, contrary to their desires, we became the prosecutors and accusers of the renegades and the traitors. They were in the dock. We held our heads high because we were with Marxism-Leninism. Khrushchev held his head in his two hands, when the bombs of our Party burst upon him.

Khrushchev's tactic at the meeting was cunning. He rose and spoke first, delivered an allegedly moderate, placatory speech, without open attacks, with phrases put together to set the tone for the meeting and create the impression that it ought to be calm, that we should not attack one another (they made their attacks in advance), that we should preserve unity (social-democratic), etc. With this he wanted to say: «We don't want quarrels, we don't want splits, nothing has happened, everything is going well.»

In his speech Khrushchev ... attacked the Communist Party of China and the Party of Labour of Albania, as well as those who were going to follow these parties, but without mentioning any names. With this tactic in his speech he wanted to warn us: «Take your pick, either general attacks without any names, but with everybody understanding for whom they are intended, or if you don't like it that way, we shall attack you openly.» In fact, of the 20 puppet delegates who spoke, only 5 or 6 attacked China, basing themselves on the Soviet material.

... After him, 15 or 20 others, carefully brain-washed and prepared, got up one after the other and spoke on Khrushchev's line: «Nothing has occurred, there is no problem amongst us,

peace reigns, everything is going well.» . . . «They had synchro-
nised their watches,» as Zhivkov had said in one of his speeches,
and which Khrushchev cited in Bucharest as an «historic» saying.

. . . The Soviets and Khrushchev were terrified of our speech
and wanted at all costs to convince us, if not to abandon our ideas,
at least to soften our stand. They sent Thorez[74] to mediate when
they saw that we refused the meeting with Khrushchev. Thorez
invited us to dinner, gave us a lecture about «unity» and advised
us to be «cool and restrained» . . . But he strove in vain. We
refused every proposal and he threatened us:

«The meeting will attack you.»

«We fear no one because we are on the right path,» we replied.

When they saw that they had failed with Thorez, the Soviets
persisted with requests that we should meet Mikoyan, Kozlov,
Suslov, Pospyelov and Andropov. We accepted. At this meeting in
the villa in Zarechie, the Soviets presented matters as if nothing
had occurred, as if they were not to be blamed at all . . . Allegedly
it was we who were worsening the relations with the Soviet Union
and they asked us to tell them openly why we were doing this![75]

We rejected these accusations.

. . . For their part, Khrushchev's men, with utter shamelessness,
denied everything, including their ambassador in Tirana, whom
they called «*durak*» [fool], when they attempted to lay the blame
for their faults on him. They wanted to get on good terms with us
at all costs so that we would shut our mouths. They even offered
us credits and tractors. But after exposing them, we told them, «If
you do not admit and correct your grave errors, all your efforts are
in vain.» The following day Kozlov and Mikoyan came back
again but they achieved nothing.

The time for our speech was approaching and they made their
final effort – they asked that we meet Khrushchev in the Kremlin.
Apparently Khrushchev was still kidding himself that he could
«convince us», and we accepted the invitation, but not at the hour
he set, in order to tell him that «not you, but we decide even the
hour of the meeting» let alone other things. Apart from this,
before we met him we wanted to send him an «oral message». We
checked the residence they had allocated us with our detector and
found that they had bugged us with microphones in every part of

it. The only room unbugged was a toilet. When it was cold and we could not talk outside we were obliged to talk in the toilet. The Soviets were intrigued to learn where we talked and, when the idea struck them, they sent someone to put some microphones in the toilet, too. One of our officers caught the Soviet technician when he was carrying out the «operation», allegedly to repair a defect in the toilet, but our man told him: «There's no need because the toilet functions well.»

Our embassy, also, was filled with bugging devices and, knowing this, after we set the time of the meeting, we left the Kremlin and went to the embassy. We set up our apparatus and it signalled that they were bugging us from every direction. Then Mehmet sent Khrushchev and the others «a message» lasting ten to fifteen minutes, describing them as «traitors», saying, «you're eavesdropping on us», etc., etc. Thus, when we went to the Kremlin, the revisionists had received our «greeting».

The meeting[76] was held in Khrushchev's office and he began as usual:

«You have the floor. We are listening.»

«You requested the meeting,» I said, «you speak first.»

Khrushchev had to accept.

. . . When he saw that he had his back to the wall, Khrushchev hopped from branch to branch, from one theme to the other, and it was impossible to discuss with him the major issues of principle . . . He wanted the submission of the Party of Labour of Albania and the Albanian people.

«You are not in favour of putting our relations in order,» said Khrushchev.

«We want to put them in order, but first you must acknowledge your mistakes,» we told him.

The talk with us irritated Khrushchev . . . When we told him openly of his mistakes and those of his men he jumped up:

«You are spitting on me,» he screamed. «It is impossible to talk to you. Only Macmillan has tried to speak to me like this.»

«Comrade Enver is not Macmillan, so take back your words,» both Mehmet and Hysni snapped back at him.

«Where shall I put them?»

«Stick them in your pocket,» Mehmet said.

The four of us got up and left without shaking hands with them . . .

As we were leaving the meeting room, Mehmet went back and said to Khrushchev: «The stone which you are throwing against our Party and people will fall on your own head. Time will show this!» and he closed the door and joined us.

This was our final talk with these renegades.

I am not going to dwell on the content of [my] speech[77] . . . I merely want to underline the way in which Khrushchev's followers reacted when they heard our attacks on their boss. Gomulka, Dej, Ibarruri, Ali Yata, Baghdash[78] and many others mounted the tribune and competed in their zeal to take revenge on those who had «raised their hand against the mother party». It was both tragic and ludicrous to see these people, who posed as politicians and leaders «with a load of brains», acting in this way as mercenaries, as *hommes de paille* [men of straw], as puppets manipulated by the strings behind the scene.

In a break between sessions Todor Zhivkov approached me. His lips and chin were trembling.

«Can we have a discussion, *brat* [brother]?» he asked me.

«. . . I said what I had to say and you heard me, I believe. Who has sent you to talk, Khrushchev? I've nothing to discuss with you, go up on the tribune and speak.»

He went waxy pale and said:

«I certainly shall get up and give you your answer.»

When we were coming out of the Georgievsky Zal to go to our residence, Anton Yugov, at the head of the stairs, said to us in a shocked tone:

«Where's this road leading you *bratya* [brothers]?»

«Where's Khrushchev's road leading you, because we are on and always will proceed on Lenin's road,» we told him. He dropped his head and we parted without shaking hands.

After I delivered the speech, Mehmet and I left the residence in which the Soviets had put us and went to the embassy, where we stayed for the rest of the time we were in Moscow. When we left their residence a Soviet security officer told Comrade Hysni in confidence, «Comrade Enver did well to go, because his life was in great danger here.» The Khrushchevites were capable of anything and we took our own measures. We sent the comrades of the embassy and the collaborators of our delegation out to the shops to buy food supplies. When the time we decided to leave came, we did not agree to go by aircraft, because an «accident» could happen more easily. Hysni and Ramiz stayed on in Moscow, as they had to sign the declaration, while Mehmet and I left the Soviet Union by train and ate nothing that came from their hands. We arrived in Austria, went down by train through Italy and from Bari returned safe and sound to Tirana on our own aircraft and went directly to the reception organised on the occasion of the 28th and 29th of November.[79] We felt a great joy because we had carried out the task with which the Party charged us successfully, with Marxist-Leninist determination. The guests, too, were unrestrained in their enthusiasm and united firmly as a fist, as always.

. . . After the Moscow Meeting our relations with the Soviet Union . . . grew continually worse until they, unilaterally, broke off relations entirely.

On November 25, in the final meeting which Mehmet and Hysni had in Moscow with Mikoyan, Kosygin and Kozlov, the latter made open threats. Mikoyan said to them: «You cannot live a day without economic aid from us and the other countries of the socialist camp.» «We shall tighten our belts and eat grass,» Mehmet and Hysni told them, «but will not submit to you. You cannot conquer us.» The revisionists thought that the sincere love of our Party and people for the Soviet Union would play a role in favour of the revisionists of Moscow. They hoped that our many cadres who had been trained in the Soviet Union would return united as a block to split the Party from the leadership. Mikoyan expressed this, saying: «When the Party of Labour hears of your stand it will rise against you.» «Come and attend some meeting of our Party when we raise these problems,» Mehmet told him, «and you will see what sort of unity exists in our Party and around its leadership.»

The final break

The final break was not long coming. Soviet pressure was increasingly centred on the important naval and submarine base at Vlora. Although Hoxha's account is one-sided, there is little reason to doubt that its main substance is roughly true, since it is highly plausible that the USSR would have made strenuous efforts to maintain a presence at this base, its only one in the Mediterranean proper (indeed, it is remarkable that they gave it up so easily). Once again, as with so much of relations in the socialist bloc, events are both tragic and ridiculous, with the Russians even complaining about an Albanian child relieving itself. It is also clear from Hoxha's account that the Soviet leadership sent a string of very senior officials down to Albania either to put pressure on Tirana, or to try to find a solution to the dispute (or both). Hoxha also knew how to put on the pressure and, if his account is to be believed, threatened the Soviet command directly if they tried to remove more than he conceded.

The account then moves on to describe the Fourth Congress of the Albanian Party of Labour in February 1961. The Soviet delegation was headed by Pospelov, who had attended the Third Congress in 1956; number two on the Soviet delegation was Yuri Andropov. By this time Hoxha had purged the Party of any pro-Soviet and wavering elements, and it is likely that the Congress went, in his words, 'like clock-work'. It seems probable that the USSR did try to oust Hoxha,[80] and it is also possible that some of the Western powers and Greece tried to make a move, on the supposition that Albania without Soviet support would be highly vulnerable.

Hoxha's account closes with the Party allegedly united round him, and the break with the Soviet Union complete, Moscow having broken diplomatic relations at the end of 1961. For the next sixteen years China was to be (or seem to be) Albania's closest friend, many thousands of miles away.

. . . The Vlora base was the pretext for a quarrel. There was no doubt that the base was ours . . . By clear official agreement signed by the two governments . . . the Vlora base belonged to Albania and, at the same time, was to serve the defence of the camp. It was stated in the agreement that the Soviet Union would provide twelve submarines and a number of auxiliary ships. We were to train the cadres and we trained them, were to take over the ships and we did so, as well as four submarines. Our crews were trained and were waiting ready to take over the remaining eight.

. . . Especially after the Bucharest Meeting, the Soviet experts, advisers and other militarymen at the Vlora naval base stepped up the frictions, quarrels and incidents with our sailors. The Soviet side stopped all supplies of the materials they were supposed to provide for the base according to the agreement concluded; all the work commenced was suspended unilaterally and the provocations and blackmail were increased . . . Countless acts of the filthiest vandalism were carried out by the Soviet personnel at the base on orders from above, and despite this, «to be in order», they tried to accuse our people over the acts of hooligans they committed themselves. Their shamelessness and cynicism reached the point that the «chief representative», Andreyev, sent a note to the Chairman of the Council of Ministers of the People's Republic of Albania in which he claimed that «unpleasant acts were occurring at the base» from the side of the Albanians. And what were these «acts»? «Such and such an Albanian sailor threw his cigarette butt on the deck of the Soviet ship», «the children of Dukat tell the Soviet children 'Go home' », «the Albanian waiter in a club told our officer, 'I am in charge here and not you' », etc. General Andreyev even complained to the Chairman of the Council of Ministers of the Albanian state that an unknown child had allegedly relieved himself secretly near the building used by the Soviets.

. . . Keeping cool, we vigilantly watched the development of the situation and continually instructed our comrades to act cautiously and patiently, but never to submit and never fall for the provocations of Khrushchev's agents.

«In order to avoid disorder and incidents, the Vlora base should be placed completely under the command of the Soviet side!» proposed the Soviets.

. . . In order to give their proposal the colour of a joint decision, in March 1961, they exploited a meeting of the Warsaw Treaty, at which Grechko[81] insisted that the Vlora base should be left entirely in Soviet hands, and placed «under the direct command» of the General Commander of the Warsaw Treaty, that is, of Grechko himself.

We firmly and indignantly opposed this proposal and, although the decision was adopted by the others, we declared:

«The only solution is that the Vlora base must remain in the hands of the Albanian Army. We will not permit any other solution.»

Then the Khrushchevites decided not to hand over to us the eight submarines and other ships which, according to the agreement, belonged to Albania. We insisted that they were ours and demanded that the Soviet crews should be withdrawn and everything handed over to our sailors, as had been done with the first four submarines. Besides the «chief representative», Andreyev, the Soviet revisionists also sent a certain rear-admiral to Tirana. This whole team was comprised of officers of the Soviet security service, sent to organise disturbances, sabotage and diversion at the Vlora base.

«We shall not give you the ships,» they said, «they are ours.»

We confronted them with the state agreement and they found another pretext.

«Your crews are not ready to take them over, they are not completely trained.» . . .

Just a few months before the situation became tense, the Soviets themselves had declared that our crews were ready.

. . . At the first meeting[82] we had with Mikoyan and his colleagues in Moscow, on November 10 [1960], as soon as he started speaking, he tried to frighten us:

«Your officers are behaving badly with ours at the Vlora base. Do you want to leave the Warsaw Treaty?»

. . . Two days later Khrushchev made the same threat.

«If you like, we can dismantle the base,» he shouted.

«. . . Are you trying to threaten us with this?» I said.

«Comrade Enver, don't raise your voice,» Khrushchev interrupted, «the submarines are ours.»

«Yours and ours,» I said, «we are fighting for socialism. The territory of the base is ours.»

. . . When we returned from Moscow, the provocations at the base were increased and in order to exert pressure on and impress us, the Soviet deputy foreign minister, Firyubin, came to Tirana with two other «deputies»: the first deputy-chief of the General Staff of the Soviet Army and Navy, Antonov, and the deputy chief of the Supreme Staff of the Soviet Navy, Sergeyev.

They came allegedly «to reach agreement», but in fact they brought us an ultimatum:

The Vlora base must be put completely and solely under Soviet command, which was to be subordinate to the commander-in-chief of the Armed Forces of the Warsaw Treaty.

«We are the masters here,» we told them clearly and bluntly. «Vlora has been and is ours.»

«This is the decision of the Command of the Warsaw Treaty,» threated Firyubin, the former Soviet ambassador in Belgrade, at the time of the Khrushchev—Tito reconciliation.

We gave him the reply he deserved and, after trying to frighten us by saying, «We shall take the ships and the imperialists will gobble you up,» he left, accompanied by the two other generals.

After them, the commander of the Black Sea Fleet, Admiral Kasatonov, came to Tirana with the mission of seizing not only the eight submarines and the floating dock with Soviet crews, which were also the property of the Albanian state, but even the submarines which we had taken over earlier. We told him bluntly: Either you hand the submarines over to us according to the agreement, or within a short time (we set the date) you must withdraw immediately from the bay, with only those ships on which your crews serve.

. . . The admiral wriggled and tried to soften us, but in vain. He did not hand over the submarines, but went to Vlora, boarded the command submarine and lined up the others in fighting formation. We gave orders to close the Sazan Narrows and to train the guns on the Soviet ships. Admiral Kasatonov, who had wanted to frighten us, was frightened himself. He was caught like a rat in a trap and if he attempted to implement his plan he might find himself at the bottom of the sea. In these conditions the admiral was obliged to take only the submarines with Soviet crews, and he sailed out of the bay back home with his tail between his legs. A great evil was removed from our land, once and for all.[83]

In the last year in particular, the Soviets at the Vlora base committed innumerable vile and revolting acts . . . They holed the reservoirs, smashed the beds and windows in the buildings where they lived and worked, etc. They tried to take away everything, down to the last nut and bolt, but did not succeed in their aims.

The Soviet revisionists were furious . . . They were compelled to recall ambassador Ivanov and sent a certain Shikin[84] in his place. He was to try to prepare the final act of the hostile work of the Soviet revisionists – to split the Party.

. . . We calmly continued our course: we invited delegations from the . . . other communist and workers' parties [to the 4th Congress]. From the Soviet Union came Pospyelov and Andropov, from Czechoslovakia a certain Barák,[85] who was Minister of the Interior and was later jailed as a thief, etc.

. . . The congress opened in an atmosphere of indescribable enthusiasm and unity of the Party and our people. The opening day was turned into a real people's celebration. The people, singing, dancing and carrying flowers, escorted the delegates to the entrance of the building where the congress was to be held. This was the initial reply which the Khrushchevite, Titoite and other revisionists received right at the start. They would continue to receive other crushing blows inside.

It had never crossed the minds of Pospyelov, Andropov and their lackeys that they would find themselves in the midst of such a fire, which warmed and strengthened our hearts and seared and blinded them.

Pospyelov's speech, with which the revisionists hoped to create the split in our congress, was not applauded at all. On the contrary, it was received with silence and contempt by the delegates to the congress. From his box, Andropov openly directed his puppets as to when they should clap, when they should remain seated, or rise to their feet. It was a ludicrous spectacle. They discredited themselves completely.

. . . The representative of the Communist Party of China at the congress was Li Xiannian, who sat in stony silence through the sessions when he saw the enthusiasm of the delegates. From the tribune he said some good words addressed to our Party, but «advised» us to be patient and cautious and not break off the talks with Khrushchev. We went about our own business.

When they saw that our ranks were very solid, without any sign of a breach, the Khrushchevites intensified their interference, pressure and blackmail. They provoked us everywhere.

«What is this?!» Andropov angrily asked one of our comrades . . . «Why do the delegates cheer so much for Enver Hoxha?!»

«Go and ask them!» said our comrade. «But tell me,» he continued, «for whom should they cheer, apart from Marxism-Leninism, the Party and its leadership?! Or do you intend to propose that we should put someone else at the head of the Party?!»

The blow went home and Andropov pulled in his horns. The Greek delegate and Rudolf Barák of Czechoslovakia were brought into action . . .

In the meantime, the Soviet journalists had also gone into «action» . . .

But they achieved nothing. The congress went like clock-work . . . [But] they found the «shortcoming»:

«There are many ovations and consequently the sessions go on for more than one hour and a half,» an alleged journalist of TASS, just arrived from Moscow . . ., «protested» angrily.

«What can we do? Should we tell the delegates not to applaud?!» asked our comrade accompanying him, in a sarcastic tone.

«The time-table should be respected, an hour and a half and *tochka* [full stop],» said the «journalist».

«However, it's not the journalists, but the elected presidium that presides over the congress,» replied our comrade. «Nevertheless, if you consider it reasonable, make some protest against ovations . . .»

Before they departed after the congress, Pospyelov and Andropov sought a meeting with us.[86]

«We want to talk about some matters which have to do with our mutual comradely relations,» said Pospyelov, who spoke first. «We want to strengthen the friendship between us, to have a strong friendship.» . . .

«You have seen our situation,» I said, «therefore tell Mikoyan what you saw at the 4th Congress of our Party and tell him to what degree our Party is 'split'!»

The aim of these scoundrels was to tell us that, among other things, all the agreements and protocols on credits, which they had accorded us for the five-year plan, would have to be re-examined. To this end they demanded that I should go to Moscow . . .

«There is no reason for me to go to Moscow and I do not want to go . . . Now you must choose: either the road of Marxist-Leninist friendship or the road of hostility.» . . .

They became more furious and more shameless in their actions. As is known, at that period we discovered and smashed the plot of several imperialist and revisionist foreign powers, which, in collaboration with their agents in our ranks, wanted to launch a military aggression against our country and people. At the 4th Congress of the Party we announced that the plot had been discovered and that the conspirators, Teme Sejko and others, would render account to the people's court. The conspirators admitted everything with their own mouths.[87]

Precisely at this time, our «friends», members of the Warsaw Treaty, headed by Khrushchev, apart from their threats, declared to us: «A special commission of the Warsaw Treaty should come to Albania to verify how well-founded were the things you said about the plot»! Their perfidy had gone as far as this . . . For this, too, we gave them the reply they deserved.

Khrushchev was left without another move. Then he came out openly against us. At the 22nd Congress of his party, in October 1961, Khrushchev publicly attacked and slandered the Party of Labour of Albania.

We replied at once, openly, to his base anti-Albanian attacks and through the press made known to the Party and the people both Khrushchev's accusations against us and our stand towards those accusations . . .

Then Khrushchev undertook his final act against us – the only thing left undone – unilaterally, he broke off diplomatic relations . . .

. . . Thus the relations of socialist Albania with the revisionist Soviet Union came to an end. However, our struggle against the Khrushchevite and Brezhnev revisionists will not cease. We will go on attacking them until they are wiped from the face of the earth.

. . . One day the Soviet people will sternly condemn the Khrushchevites and will honour and love the Albanian people and the Party of Labour of Albania, as they loved us in better times, because our people and Party fought unflinchingly against the Khrushchevites, who are our common enemies.

5
DECODING
CHINA

Reflections on China

'We have to try to see clearly into this dark Chinese forest.'[1]

Between 1960–61 (Albania's break with Moscow) and 1977–8 Albania and China were in what seemed to be a very close alliance. It was one of the oddest phenomena of modern times: here were two states of vastly differing size, thousands of miles apart, with almost no cultural ties or knowledge of each other's society, drawn together by a common hostility to the Soviet Union.

Hoxha himself visited China only once, in 1956, for the Eighth Congress.[2] Reflections on China take up two volumes of about 800 pages each, covering the years 1962–77. The 'reflections' consist of several different types of items: accounts of Hoxha's conversations with senior Chinese officials visiting Albania; accounts of his talks with Albanian officials who visit China; extended musings on the condition of China, its history and culture, with speculation on the role of Confucianism and Buddhism in the formation of Mao's thinking; plus comments on major world events such as the Vietnam War and various statesmen like Fidel Castro and Kim Il Sung.

The two volumes of Reflections on China are in a different gear from the earlier volumes of direct personal memoirs. Hoxha represents Reflections on China as being a straight reproduction of diary notes he kept at the time.[3] It seems quite probable that the published text is indeed the outcome, in some form, of a diary kept at the time (the volume Reflections on the Middle East 1958–1983, published in Tirana in 1984, carries the same subtitle: 'Extracts from the Political Diary'). However, it is manifest that some editing has taken place. First of all, the entries, although prolific, are very spasmodic: there are gaps of nine months at a time, and many major events pass unmentioned. So what the two volumes on China definitely are is a selection of items, mainly relating directly only to China itself or to Sino-Albanian relations.

The second question is: has Hoxha rewritten or touched up his text? As his other works show, Hoxha has few compunctions about revising his texts, using hindsight to put himself in the best light. But here Hoxha probably has not rewritten much. He did not have to, since the black and white figures were already established. And he obviously does not feel he has to be ashamed of not understanding China, since he repeatedly refers to its arcane practices, secrecy and deception. But one area where some editing must have taken place is in Hoxha's account of the role played by those senior Albanian figures involved in relations with China who were subsequently denounced and eliminated. In particular, the Defence Minister, Beqir Balluku, and the chairman of the State Planning Commission, Abdyl Këllezi, do not show up in the text until they are denounced in the mid-1970s as plotters and traitors.[4] If Hoxha was keeping a systematic diary, they must have figured well before this, and in quite a different light.

Hoxha allows himself a few predictions. One of them, dated 20 December 1977, envisages that 'China will seek a second string to its bow, that is, it will also seek rapprochement with the Soviet Union'.[5] This may be written with the hindsight of 1979, but could equally well be what Hoxha genuinely thought in 1977.

If there is a central theme to the whole 1600 pages, it is the problem of deciphering China's actions through a thick smokescreen of secrecy, compounded by the real political confusion in China during much of the period. In late August 1976 (in fact a particularly murky moment), Hoxha writes in his diary: 'The news reaching us from China is like the rumble which comes from the bottom of the sea which, although not visible, exists in fact.'[6] In the very first entry published in *Reflections on China* (3 April 1962), at a time when Tirana had broken publicly with Moscow and the Sino-Soviet split was at an acute point, Hoxha writes that in spite of the importance of consulting about 'revisionism', 'up to now, the Chinese have not had any contact at all with us to discuss these things. Were our enemies to know that between us there is no consultation at all about the fight against the modern revisionists, they would be astonished. They would never believe it. But that is how things stand.'[7]

As Sino-Albanian relations degenerate, the Chinese will not even answer official letters; their ambassador in Tirana either disappears, or refuses to talk, or, in Hoxha's words, just produces the same old 'baloney'. Even at the top level, senior Chinese officials talk to Hoxha in slogans — which, naturally, drives him into a rage. One of the most amusing episodes occurs at the time when Mao's designated successor, Lin Piao, has disappeared, but before the Chinese have officially announced this. When China recovers its seat at the United Nations (on a resolution whose lead sponsor was Albania), the Albanians seize the opportunity to confirm Lin's disappearance by checking with the Chinese envoy in Tirana about to whom their telegram of congratulations should be addressed.[8] The rigid ritual of the Communist world is thus neatly turned to their advantage.

Related to the theme of secrecy are the questions of how to present a disagreement and when to go public. Hoxha presents the decade and a half of 'alliance' with China as years when Albania had to muzzle itself quite a lot, with the occasional bust-out to signal disapproval of China's actions (e.g. over Khrushchev, p. 257). Secrecy also requires a great deal of effort to decode what the other party is actually saying or doing. Hoxha is an old pro at deciphering red gibberish and ornate editorials in the world Communist press. He is alert to every nuance, airport greetings and farewells, presents, toasts at banquets (and their absence), line-ups for photos, who laughs on state-controlled TV. The diary is rich in accounts of his attempts to decode both published statements and acts, on the one hand, and (something not so widely known) the private communications of the Chinese to the Albanians which were also in 'code'. In the end, Hoxha is reduced to watching the TV of his hated Yugoslavia and capitalist Italy.

Hoxha's picture of China's behaviour is a dark one at both the personal and the political levels. In Hoxha's account, it was Albania, not China, which led the fight against Soviet and Yugoslav 'revisionism'. Right from the start he presents China as 'wobbly' and trying to find a compromise with the USSR. Hoxha can justifiably claim to have been more consistent than the Chinese in his attitude to both the USSR and Yugoslavia. But he can also be shown to have been far more inflexible. What Hoxha calls a compromise might also be called seeking a *modus vivendi*. Hoxha claims that Deng Xiaoping was a key figure in seeking compromise with the Soviet Union right from the time of the Moscow Conference in November 1960.[9] But Hoxha shows no understanding of the relationship between antagonism and compromise in the Chinese political tradition.

Hoxha spends a good deal of time ruminating on Mao, and particularly on his cult of personality. He gets off a few very good points on this theme. According to Hoxha, Mao was never a Marxist, but merely cloaked himself in the mantle of Marxism-Leninism to disguise an amalgam of atavistic Chinese philosophical trends. Although Hoxha expresses his view that Mao was a genuinely great figure, he also attributes the burden of China's vacillating political line to him.[10]

Having lived through honeymoons and then violent ruptures with both Yugoslavia and the Soviet Union, Hoxha can spot the syndrome third time round. He describes in some detail the economic and, ultimately, political pressure which China placed on Albania and compares it with that exercised by Khrushchev. But Hoxha's version of events is here both particularly ungenerous and, by omission, particularly inaccurate. First of all, Chinese aid to Albania over the period in question was very large and especially far-sighted and generous, in the sense that it was designed to allow Albania to build a relatively comprehensive and self-reliant industrial base. As late as mid-1975, while Hoxha was condemning leading Albanian figures for colluding with the Chinese, China was signing an agreement to provide Tirana with large amounts of aid at zero interest.[11]

Hoxha suggests that China's economic pressure was accompanied by political and military pressure. He claims that the Chinese first of all tried to push Tirana into a military alliance with Yugoslavia and Romania, after the Soviet invasion of Czechoslovakia in 1968, when Albania withdrew from the Warsaw Pact *de jure*. Later, he claims, China resorted to espionage and sabotage. Hoxha's ultimate claim (rather vaguely worded) is that China tried to bring about a coup in Tirana via the Defence Minister, Balluku, and the Planning Commission chairman, in the mid-1970s.

Both Tirana and Peking published considerable documentation on their mutual relations at the time of the break in 1977–8. On the economic front, the Chinese established the case that they gave Albania considerable help. But there was a political dimension to the dispute, which greatly exercised Hoxha. Although he claims in the diary that the political differences with China stretched back to at least 1960, if not 1956, the real crunch came with Mao's invitation to Nixon and the enunciation of the 'Three Worlds Theory' in the early 1970s. Albania's condemnation of the 'Three Worlds Theory' in July 1977 (undoubtedly penned by Hoxha) remains the key moment in the break.[12]

As in the other volumes, there are many interesting revelations. Among these are: a long account of China's reports to the Albanians about the two visits of Soviet premier Kosygin to Peking, in 1965 and 1969, during the former of which he met Mao; and a stage-by-stage account of what the Chinese told the Albanians about the Lin Piao affair; there are also detailed résumés of Hoxha's talks with senior figures, including Chou En-lai (and an account of Chou's apologies over defective equipment supplied to Albania); the current Chinese President, Li Hsien-nien (Li Xiannian) is portrayed in particularly sombre tones. Finally, Hoxha furnishes details on the nitty-gritty of the ultimate disintegration of the alliance – surveillance, espionage, etc.

Hoxha's account in his diary is not always consistent with the facts – this is especially the case over China's economic aid. But in certain areas he is both acute and correct. Early on he identifies a strong streak of chauvinism and even xenophobia in China's behaviour. By summer 1976 his anger and resentment are being expressed in terms like the following:

'The Chinese (I am speaking of the leadership and not of the people, or the mass of the communists) are cunning and hypocritical. When they need you, they butter you up, when they do not need you, and you disagree with them, they leave you stranded.'[13]

But Hoxha's dogmatism blinds him to the real internal effects of the 'Gang of Four' and their policies – and to the liberating effects of the post-Mao policies associated with Deng Xiaoping. For Hoxha, Deng is a rightist. Instead of welcoming the undoubted political liberalisation brought about under Deng, Hoxha condemns not only Deng's 'revisionism' but even claims, contrary to the facts, that political repression worsened under Deng.

Likewise, Hoxha is evasive about the relationship between political developments in China and changes in Albania, which also had a form of 'Cultural Revolution' – although a good case can be made out for claiming that it was markedly different from that in China, and much more consistent with the principles of Marxism and the practice of Leninism.[14]

Not long before he died, Hoxha had assimilated China's behaviour to his preset pattern. On the fortieth anniversary of Liberation, in November 1984, Hoxha told the Albanian people: 'The Titoites, the Soviet revisionists and those of the countries of Eastern Europe, and Mao Zedong's China had ulterior, hostile, enslaving aims. We tore the mask from them and told them bluntly that Albania was not for sale for a handful of rags, or for a few rubles, dinars or yuan.'[15]

Friday July 5, 1963

A meeting which will not yield any result

The delegation of the Communist Party of China, headed by Teng Hsiao-ping, has arrived in Moscow. It was given a pompous farewell in Peking as if it were going to a wedding, while in Moscow it had an icy reception like a funeral.

We shall see what this worthless, formal meeting will yield . . .

Thursday July 11, 1963

Today the Chinese are saying about Khrushchev what Khrushchev said yesterday about Tito

Chen Yi[16] talked to our ambassador in Peking, Reiz Malile, and in substance told him that «the Moscow meeting might be broken

off to be continued later, in successive sittings. Such a thing»,
stressed Chen Yi, «is in the interests of both sides». After venting
his spleen on Khrushchev, he said: «We must try to prevent him
from going over to the imperialists, to prevent him from capitu-
lating, because there is the question of the Soviet people», etc., etc.
«We shall go on exposing him all the time», etc., he said in
conclusion.

Vacillations can be seen among the Chinese comrades, they are
up one minute and down the next and leave the impression that
they are not clear on their tactics, but very wobbly; and are often
intimidated by the pressure of the Soviets . . . The Chinese are
saying about Khrushchev today what Khrushchev said about Tito
yesterday . . . in the end they kissed and made up with Tito . . .
Too bad about the Chinese!!

Thursday January 9, 1964

Chou En-lai's visit is over
Today Chou En-lai left our country.

. . . What is very important . . . is that now the Chinese comrades have no illusions about Khrushchev, that, like us, they
consider him an inveterate traitor. However, Chou En-lai's exposition of the tactics which we should use in the struggle against
revisionism was a bit long-winded . . . We expressed our opinion
openly to Chou En-lai, stressing that we would make no concession to Khrushchev, would reach no compromise with him . . . On
this question, Chou En-lai did not express himself very clearly, as
we did, but he approved our stand. He agreed on those opinions
we expressed about Khrushchev and, finally, on the pretext that
perhaps the interpreter might not have given a good translation,
did not fail to add that, when he spoke about a compromise (and
this not on the question of a compromise with Khrushchev), he
had in mind a Marxist-Leninist compromise . . .

Chou En-lai received our ideas on the perspective plan for the
coming five-year period favourably. He . . . promised that China
would assist us in the processing of oil, chromium, copper, iron
nickel, etc. . . . Chou En-lai was interested in the problem of
labour power, which has been a continual worry to us. He

considered correct the great care we exercise to avoid draining the population from the villages and to use the labour power in the cities as much as possible . . . [He] found our orientation towards the further development of grain growing in the mountain regions also in case of a war situation interesting . . .

Friday April 17, 1964

The lackeys decorate Khrushchev. The Chinese leadership sends him a telegram of congratulations
In Moscow . . . Khrushchev's lackeys awarded him decorations from the «Gold Star» to the «Order of the Lion» on his birthday . . . The lackeys are trying to keep up the bankrupt's prestige. **Telegrams of hosanna are reaching Khrushchev from all sides, but the most unpleasant and completely wrong one is that from the Chinese comrades. The Chinese telegram of congratulations was written with their feet and not their head . . . Their act is a political and ideological class mistake** . . . and we shall find the opportunity to tell them so, if not directly, certainly indirectly. **Today we shall strip Khrushchev of his title of «Honoured Citizen» of the city of Tirana, with the motivation that a traitor such as he deserves.** Thus, this important political act will be a «decoration» in our style for this revisionist and, at the same time, an answer to the telegrams which the Chinese, Koreans, Vietnamese, and others sent him . . .

Tuesday September 15, 1964

The Chinese stand: «they take the first step, we take the second»
. . . The Chinese comrades must have had pent up dissatisfaction towards Stalin, because this was apparent in Mao's statement to the Moscow Meeting,[17] when he said that when he first met Stalin in Moscow, he was «in the role of the school-boy. And though ours were fraternal parties, we were not equal. Whereas,» Mao added, «now that we meet Khrushchev, we are like brothers.»
. . . I don't know how Stalin treated Mao, but I, personally, met Stalin many times, and he always tried in every way to give me the

feeling of an equal comrade, to create an intimacy. He received me in his home and himself handed me the dish, he sent away the waiters, and we got up and served one another, as in our own homes: Stalin has taken me by the arm and walked with me in his garden, tired himself on my behalf many times, taking the greatest care of me, even over the hat I should wear to avoid getting a cold, and going so far as ... to show me where the toilets were if I needed them.

... Since Stalin adopted the stand of a proletarian comrade towards me, imagine what a friendly stand he must have adopted towards Mao, as the leader of the Communist Party of a big country like China.

... Could it be that, with what Mao said, he wanted to say to Khrushchev that now, after the death of Stalin «our two countries and two parties are on an equal basis and we two, hand-in-hand, should lead the revolutionary movement»? (This did not suit Khrushchev because, regardless of the bouquets they threw at him, he sat glowering and worried.) Or did he want to say to Khrushchev, «You are a new boy, and I am going to help set you on the right course»?

Despite Mao's «modest tone» at the Moscow Meeting, still «his reasonable and correct speech» gave you the impression of a «far-seeing», «infallible», «direction-giving» speech.

... [The Chinese] also decided on ten basic theoretical articles about which they told us that they would print one every fifteen days. Fourteen months have gone by since then and the tenth article has not yet come out, while the modern revisionists, without exaggeration, have written thousands of articles.

Hence rigid, hieratic, olympian tactics, according to the moves of the enemy, but in fact, they don't even follow the moves of the enemy.

Why is this? For tactical reasons? For objective reasons? For subjective reasons? Because the Chinese comrades have failed to define a consistent line?! This is astonishing! Many actions are carried out for form, in order to put the blame formally on one or the other. The Chinese comrades contradict themselves in many of their attitudes. **On the one hand, the Chinese comrades have picked up the final stone against Khrushchev, and say to him, «We** are going to put you in your grave», on the other hand they say to him, «Dear Comrade . . . , many happy returns!»?!

When they address him as «Dear Comrade . . .», the Chinese comrades justify this as done «to get closer to the Soviet people». (Interesting, to try to approach the Soviet people by addressing this traitor as «Dear Comrade . . .»!)

Today they say: «We must struggle for the creation and consolidation of the anti-imperialist front **including even the revisionists**»! Tomorrow Mao makes the famous statement about border claims on the Soviet Union (!!)[18] (with which they want to form an anti-imperialist alliance), and he draws a reply from Khrushchev who tells Mao: You are a Hitler, and if you lay a finger on our borders, I have invented a new bomb which will wipe you out completely.

Yesterday Tito was a traitor to the Chinese, later he was rehabilitated, then he became a traitor again, and now, according to Li Hsien-nien, this great traitor has become a «minor devil».

There are many things like this. The Chinese are very slow to react, and also understand things very slowly . . .

The Chinese comrades say that they have a correct appreciation of time, but they consider it something endless, from positions of passivity, in the sense that it can pass freely, quietly, thinking that «it is working for us». Therefore, they are not concerned about any delay, hence, for them it will be very good if others, too, move at their pace . . .

Although Chou En-lai tried to belittle my opinion that imperialism and revisionism are trying to isolate China and that we should break this isolation, I think that the Chinese comrades ought to have this question constantly in mind. They have to break not only their political and ideological isolation, but also their cultural, commercial and other isolation. All this must be done on the Marxist-Leninist course, without violating principles, without weakening the security of the homeland and the general line, but also without exaggerating the «world» value of Chinese culture and without underrating the culture of other peoples . . .

Tuesday October 6, 1964

Ominous signs

Certain unprincipled stands of the leadership of the Communist Party of China, especially some expressed recently, cannot fail to cause us worry:

The question of the Sino-Soviet, Sino-Mongolian borders, and the borders of the European people's democracies, defined after the Second World War. (All this expressed by Mao to the Japanese socialists.)

We wrote a letter to the Chinese comrades on the border problem . . . they told our Party and Government delegation, which is in Peking at present, that they would reply to us in writing. But from the talks with Teng Hsiao-ping it emerges that they have been mulling this problem over . . . The Chinese comrades regard this as a correct ideological action, which harms Khrushchev and does not help him to use it against the Chinese. This is serious. However, their failing to maintain a Marxist-Leninist stand on this problem, and failing to publish at least everything that Mao discussed with the Japanese, shows that they are in a difficult position, are hesitating, and thus they are allowing the enemies to speculate about this stand . . .

Teng Hsiao-ping also said that they **disagree with us when we say that Stalin acted correctly, in those circumstances, on the borders of Europe** . . .

The Chinese comrades are taking an unprincipled stand towards the Rumanian line. In this direction there are ominous signs.

Chou En-lai said:

a) «We (the Chinese) understand the Rumanian comrades, who want to take credits from the Americans, because otherwise they will be ruined.»

b) «We understand the Rumanian comrades in their friendly relations with Tito, because they want to escape the Khrushchevite pressure and attack.»

At Bucharest, Li Hsien-nien developed the thesis that «we should make approaches to the Rumanians, because they are very determined in their opposition to Khrushchev and Khrushchev is

the major devil, while Tito is a minor devil». This slogan has become very widespread in recent times among the Chinese cadres, including their ambassador in Tirana.

In his talk with our comrades, Teng Hsiao-ping was much more explicit on this question . . . He said openly:

a) «The Rumanians listen neither to us, to you, nor to Tito.»

b) «The Rumanians are resolute anti-Khrushchevites, therefore, we (the Chinese) have decided to collaborate closely with them.»

c) «We shall put aside the ideological questions with the Rumanians.» . . .

This is very serious . . . Are these fortuitous, accidental, immature, not well-calculated stands, or traps set by the modern revisionists to lead the Chinese comrades into blind alleys? They could be all these things. Let us now try to draw some preliminary conclusions to see into the future more clearly.

The enemies of our enemies can be our true friends when they are on the same ideological and political line with us.

The enemies of our enemies can be temporary allies with us on certain questions, but we must not give way to them on principles and we must make this clear to them, must not conceal our line and principles from them.

The enemies of our enemies can be our enemies, and the two sides must remain and be fought as our enemies . . .

Saturday October 31, 1964

In no way can we reconcile ourselves to these views of Chou En-lai

. . . The views which Chou En-lai expressed[19] and the manner in which he expressed them to the ambassadors are full of anti-Marxist «great state» and «big party» sentiments, which must be condemned, . . . There is no trace of Marxist honesty, or political maturity, let alone ideological maturity, about the hidden aims of the actions which the Chinese have in mind.

Such an immature, vacillating stand of the Chinese, with frequent, marked and astonishing oscillations, sometimes to the left and sometimes to the right, comes as no surprise to us . . . **the**

Chinese comrades did not want to go so far in the struggle against the modern revisionists, and had not envisaged such an extension of the struggle against them . . . it is clear that they are tired of this struggle, which was a heavy burden for them, that they want to pull out, and that is why they judged the downfall of Khrushchev as the most appropriate moment for them to retire «with honour».

. . . In short, **for them the fall of Khrushchev is everything** . . . from this scandalous performance of Chou En-lai's we must draw other logical conclusions which, regrettably, confirm their betrayal.

What are they?

1 — To assemble the ambassador of Rumania, and finally, even the ambassador of Cuba, together with us, means to say to them: «You, Rumanian comrades (who up till yesterday were on the road of betrayal), and you, Cuban comrades (although you never failed to pour all those praises on Khrushchev), fully deserve the honour of being called those who brought down Khrushchev. We, the popes of Peking, consider you as such. Amen!»

2 — «As to you Albanians, we do not even ask your opinion about these situations, or what you think about the proposals we are making. **You must do as we say immediately. Put aside any claim you have on the 'Soviet comrades', it doesn't matter that the 'Soviet comrades' have done all these things to you for five years on end, up to the point that they called you spies of imperialism and broke off relations with your state, but you should bow your heads and hurry to Canossa!»** What a dirty feudal, fascist mentality! No bourgeois could speak in such a way. Even bourgeois dignity and standards do not permit such disgraceful arrogance. As is known, we immediately slapped back our reply, scorching their faces like a branding iron.

3 — All this was a provocation against us, and on the other hand, it was a scene prepared to tell the Soviets, the Rumanians, the Cubans and others of this ilk: «From now on, I am breaking with the Albanians, I am no longer in solidarity with them, on either the political or the ideological issues. From now on, the Albanians are acting on their own, and they must bear the responsibility for everything they do!!»

. . . 5 – Regardless of the servility, the lack of dignity which they display in begging the Soviet revisionists to invite them to the celebration of the October Socialist Revolution or to meetings (as the Soviet renegades please), their begging to go to the celebration of the revolution in Moscow, conceals in itself a base hankering after «fame». Their intention is to go to Moscow and say to the world, say to the Soviets: «See, we have come as the cosmonauts of Peking, as the victors who brought down Khrushchev, **we are the 'brilliant', 'infallible brain' of the communist movement. All have been brought down, all were wrong – Stalin, Khrushchev and the others. Mao, alone, saw and sees things correctly. Hence, now it is completely right to say: Marx, Engels, Lenin, Mao!»**.

Saturday November 21, 1964

The defeat of Chou En-lai in Moscow
Chou En-lai went to Moscow like Napoleon and returned like Napoleon. He suffered an ignominious defeat. I feel very sorry for the great Communist Party of China and the fraternal Chinese people that are being discredited by a person such as Chou En-lai. The revisionists of Moscow provoked him, discredited him and humiliated him. If it were just a matter of Chou En-lai, who has opportunist and capitulationist views, I would say: «Serve him right», but this is not a subjective matter. This is a matter of the Communist Party of China and what it represents in the international communist movement . . . the Chinese comrades had four meetings with the Soviets and came away shaven and shorn. The Soviets received them very coldly, and told them: «Don't think that we are going to change our line, which was not built up by Khrushchev alone»; . . . «you Chinese must correct your mistakes». Apart from this, from what we hear, the Soviets went even further. **Malinovsky**[20] **said to Chou En-lai: «We overthrew Khrushchev, why do you stick to that old galosh, Mao Tsetung?»**. Chou En-lai did not reply, but later invited Brezhnev, Kosygin, Mikoyan to a banquet, and said to them: «Malinovsky provoked me, is this what you think, too?». Mikoyan replied to Chou that Malinovsky had made a mistake. (Mikoyan said the same thing when the Vietnamese told him that Malinovsky had spoken

against Albania.) Brezhnev «explained» to Chou that Malinovsky had allegedly been drunk and must make a «self-criticism». Chou En-lai informed these gentlemen, «I shall report this matter to Mao Tsetung».

The Soviets demanded from Chou En-lai that they cease the polemic, and he did not promise them anything. Malinovsky also offended Marshal Ho Lu[21] by saying to him: «Why have you not come in your old suit, since you pretend you are modest, but have put on this suit of such excellent stuff?» . . .

Saturday February 13, 1965

Mao Tsetung takes a firm and correct stand towards the revisionist Kosygin

From official reports which the Chinese comrades give in connection with the talks between Mao and Kosygin, when the latter returned from Hanoi, we observe with profound satisfaction that Mao has resolutely cut this dirty revisionist down to size.

Briefly, Kosygin demanded from Mao that the Chinese comrades should take part in the meeting of parties on the 1st of March . . . He asked Mao to stop the polemic between them, or «at least not to make it bitter, but gentle»; Kosygin also asked him to say when the representatives of the Communist Party of the Soviet Union could meet those of the Communist Party of China for talks, and sought his opinion on when the meeting of the 81 communist and workers' parties could be held. He also urged him not to support the new Marxist-Leninist parties and groups that . . . are being created, etc.

As can be seen, Kosygin presented a number of demands to Mao, cunningly, with false humility. But Mao rejected them with irony and scorn.

Mao told Kosygin, «As for the meeting of the 1st of March, our comrades (Chou En-lai) have told you not to hold it, while I tell you to hold it, without changing either the date or the name, and whatever you call it, and whenever you hold it, you will be exposed. We shall not go to that meeting, while as for the bilateral talks, the conditions are not ripe. You must openly acknowledge the mistakes you have made towards Albania, must also acknowledge a series of mistakes towards China», and these Mao listed to him one by one.

As to the polemic, he told him, it would go on for ten thousand years, because polemics never killed anyone, but simply cleared up problems. Kosygin told Mao, «If the polemic is bitter it will harm us», but Mao replied, «If it is not harsh it will have no effect, whereas it has to scald somebody and something.» . . .

When Kosygin spoke on the questions of «unity», Mao said to him: «You must admit your mistakes towards the Albanians, must retract the accusations you made against them at the 22nd Congress.» . . . Apart from this, and in connection with unity, Mao said to him: «You must retract your letter of the 14th of July 1963, and the anti-Chinese reports and decisions of the plenum of the Communist Party of the Soviet Union of February 1964; you must admit that the decisions of the 20th and 22nd Congresses are wrong, just as the struggle against the cult of the individual of Stalin and your idea about peaceful co-existence, about the state and the party of the whole people, about disarmament, and the solution to several other problems which are worrying mankind, are wrong. We are not in agreement with all these views,» continued Mao, «and as long as you do not change your stand there can be no unity between us. All you need do is admit that you have been wrong, and then,» Mao told him, «unity can be achieved. Therefore, first of all, admit that you have been wrong towards Albania and China.» . . .

Mao also spoke to Kosygin about the struggle that must be fought against imperialism, Kosygin interrupted and said: «I do not agree with such an assessment, because wherever there are revolutionary struggles, the Soviet Union gives them great help». But Mao, with cold irony, continued his interrupted idea, saying, «Even when I say that you do very little to help them, I say this out of politeness.»

. . . In this talk Kosygin saw clearly that China and Albania are in complete unity. Indeed, as they tell us, Mao put our question and demands in the forefront . . .

In Korea, likewise,[22], we believe that the Soviet revisionists' results will not be fundamental . . . The Korean comrades have hesitated to . . . attack the Soviet revisionists, and therefore

Kosygin is taking advantage of this, he is trying to find breaches, to give the Koreans aid in order to use it as a «gob-stopper», etc. In my opinion the Korean comrades should be more determined.

Tuesday August 9, 1966

The cult of Mao Tsetung[23]

Marx condemned the cult of the individual as something sickening. The individual plays a role in history, sometimes indeed a very important one, but for us Marxists this role is a minor one compared with the role of the popular masses, [and] . . . **also in comparison with the major role of the communist party, which stands at the head of the masses and leads them.**

However, we see with regret that in recent months, in regard to this question in particular, the Chinese comrades have set out on a wrong anti-Marxist course. **In reality they are turning the cult of Mao almost into a religion,** exalting him in a sickening way, without giving the least consideration to the great harm this is doing to the cause, not to mention the ridicule it gives rise to . . .

What emerges from the Chinese propaganda on this question? «Mao is the sun that illuminates the world», «Mao is a great genius without comparison in the history of mankind», «the thoughts of Mao are the acme of Marxism», «Mao knows everything», «Mao has done everything», «if anyone wants to solve anything, at any time, in any country, let him read the works of Mao, let him be inspired by the ideas of Mao». These are some of the least exalted descriptions we can record, but in the Chinese press they are using such exalted expressions, speaking of such gestures and occurrences that one is impelled to think and ask: Are we dealing with Marxists or with religious fanatics? Because truly, from what we are seeing with our eyes and hearing with our ears, in China they are treating Mao as the Christians treat Christ. What is said about Mao by the Chinese or foreigners, by good people or flatterers, by ordinary people, sincere or hypocrites, all this is being raised to theory by the Chinese propaganda in a sickening chorus.

. . . The question arises: Why all this unrestrained propaganda? Whom does it benefit, and is it necessary to carry on such propaganda about a renowned personality like Mao Tsetung, whom not only the Chinese communists, but also those of other countries recognise? I cannot explain this otherwise than as the deafening beating of the drum which conceals some hostile work, either immediately or in the long term.

. . . The struggle for a proletarian culture and against bourgeois culture and its influence is something correct which must be carried out by all of us. But in this Cultural Revolution which is going on in China we observe certain things which make an impression. The main issue is that «proletarian culture begins and ends in China», «nothing else in the world is any good». For the Chinese propaganda, the positive and progressive aspects of human thought have no value at all, only the «ideas» of Mao Tsetung and everything which comes from Chinese hands is of value! Such a spirit . . . is not healthy and contains great dangers, just as the excessive persecution of the intellectuals there might have repercussions . . .

The Chinese comrades who, in many things, show themselves «cautious», «slow to move», who have made «re-education» a principle, who have the theory of «a hundred flowers» and «a hundred schools», have now begun to attack things with big axes. We agree that the axe should fall where it is necessary and with great force, we agree that the broom, indeed a big broom, must be applied, but, as we see it, at least from the propaganda that is coming out, the broom is sweeping away every work, every literary creation, regardless of the overall progressive spirit of the work, the time at which it was written, and the role it has played in those circumstances. While as for progressive world literature and progressive culture in general, for the Chinese comrades this has no value at all, it is barren country to them.

Perhaps I am mistaken, but all these things are not on the right road and damage our great cause . . .

To allow the students to display a terrible xenophobia, as is being done in China, means to make a great mistake which has nothing at all to do with proletarian internationalism . . .

Saturday August 20, 1966

What is going on in China?
A great puzzle!! Astonishing events, dangerous to the great cause of communism, which worry us immensely, are taking place. We have a problem with many unknown factors to solve, we have to try to see clearly into this dark Chinese forest. With Marxist judgement and with the numerous, but at the same time very fragmentary data of the official Chinese press which we have, we shall try to arrive at certain guiding conclusions . . .

In my opinion, this Cultural Revolution in China did not begin in the way a serious party, which has its feet on the ground, ought to have begun it. The army touched it off, then Peking University, and later its flames spread everywhere. Chinese propaganda presented this as a revolution launched from below, by the revolutionary masses, and said that it developed in a «spontaneous» way, but in reality it is organised. But by whom? We shall try to answer this later, because it is difficult to do so now. However, we must say that now emerges the figure of Lin Piao, the leader of the army, who has been sick for years on end . . . Lin Piao comes out with an article which says, «Everyone should read and study the works of Mao Tsetung, and these must guide us». This article became the pivot and the banner of the Cultural Revolution and the struggle against the «black gang».

The question arises: How is it possible, and is it in order and Marxist-Leninist that for such a Cultural Revolution one person of the Political Bureau and the Central Committee, even if he is Minister of Defence, or the first secretary, or the chairman of the party himself, should become the standard-bearer, while the party and its Central Committee remain in the shade?! No, this is not in order, this is not Marxist-Leninist. Only the Central Committee of the Party can take such decisions . . . The Central Committee . . . did not issue the call for this Cultural Revolution, nor did it lead it . . . the revolution was developed in spontaneity and disorder, and this was called the «revolutionary method». Only now, several months after the beginning of the revolution has the Central Committee finally met (the 11th Plenum, after four years! Scandal!!) and issued a «set of rules» about how the Cultural

Revolution should be carried out. What else did this Plenum of the Central Committee discuss? A great mystery . . .

When I said to Chou En-lai,[24] after his exposition (which was very general in connection with the participants in this conspiracy) that Peng Chen and company were agents of imperialism and the capitalists, he jumped up saying: «I have never described them in this way in the exposition I made to you.»

From these things we can draw certain preliminary conclusions: since the Central Committee of the Communist Party of China meets once in four years, the Chinese leadership is not in order, it has violated the norms of the party, the norms of democratic centralism, the norms of collective leadership. The Political Bureau has set aside the leading role of the Central Committee, . . . and in the Political Bureau itself unrestricted individual leadership has prevailed, uncontrolled, or very weakly controlled, even by Mao Tsetung himself. The fact is that in this whole business of propagating Mao's ideas only his old writings are mentioned, and the quotations, too, are drawn from his old writings. There are no new ones.

Has Comrade Mao exercised effective leadership since the last congress in 1956, or has he just been asked «in passing» and only «given inspiration»? This we do not know concretely. But I suspect that, wittingly or unwittingly, such a method of work . . . has left Mao on the sidelines and has turned him into a mere symbol . . .

Recently the name of the party has been completely overshadowed by the name of Mao Tsetung. «Mao Tsetung has done everything», «his ideas guide everything», the party exists thanks to these «ideas», «without Mao there is no party, no socialism». And all these terrible distortions (you only need to read Hsinhua [New China News Agency] to find them) are being made in Mao's presence. Mao approves them. Why? This is astonishing!

. . . Behind the fanaticisation of the masses about the person of Mao Tsetung . . . there is something very dangerous and Mao is making a colossal mistake in failing to take stern measures about this.

. . . The works of Mao should be read, should be studied, but in the way this is developing in China I think there is nine times more noise than work. What I am afraid of is **lest the noise is covering up some work which is being done on the quiet.** This will be a catastrophe. **The modern revisionists have all sorts of arrows which they use, both short range and long range.**

Tuesday September 20, 1966

The 'Red Guards' are acting without leadership or control
... I think that they absolutely must inform our Party about these decisions ... The «excuse» that the Chinese ambassador in Tirana has been away from his post for four to five months «to do his physical labour» in China, is unacceptable! Does he need so long to do his «physical labour»? During this period the personnel of the Chinese Embassy in Tirana are remaining as silent as mummies, keeping to the premises.

Perhaps in these difficult situations the Chinese comrades need the cult of Mao, because only his great personality can cure the situation in the party and in the country. In this case such a thing could be justifiable for the internal situation, but such a line must not be imposed indirectly on friends and comrades whom they don't even keep informed of the development of the situation at home.

Saturday September 24, 1966

We must avoid being taken by surprise
... Seeing our correct reaction, that we cannot follow them in their dubious excesses, the Chinese, through their people in Tirana, have begun to carry out the first provocations, which remind us of the old methods of the Titoites and the Khrushchevites. The Chinese go through our country and buttonhole people, one after the other, «to interview» them on what they think about the Cultural Revolution, about Mao, and the «Red Guard». These «interviews» have two aims: first, they are to be printed in Peking to serve in the «great orchestra», and second, to urge our people to speak about these problems and to create suspicions that «the Albanian leadership is opposing the 'ardent' desire of

people in Albania». Naturally, these «Chinese correspondents» have not achieved their objective . . .

Today the Chinese students who are studying in our country sought permission to prepare «an exhibition to show what foreigners are saying about Mao Tsetung». This is an open provocation against us, who do not agree to shout hosannas for Mao. Our youth put them in their place, carefully but clearly.

These are the «first needlings» . . . In this situation the need arises to re-examine . . . without any publicity, . . . the 4th Five-year Plan, . . . in the [light] of . . . the possibility that China might cut off the credits or create difficulties for us, so that if «they leave us in the lurch» it will be possible for us to complete them ourselves . . .

Monday September 26, 1966

The army is recommended as a model for all, even for the Party
. . . In May this year, when a delegation of ours was in China, Mao said to our comrades, among other things: «**They say that I am a philosopher, a thinker . . . , no, this is not true, I am an armyman . . .**».

Another thing. Mao also told our comrades about the cadres of the Communist Party of China: «**Things have gone so far that our district secretary will sell himself to the enemy for a pound of pork . . .**».

These are a few isolated facts, but in the light of events and in the darkness in which we are groping, they might help to make things clear and guide us. Perhaps this is what occurred: In recent times Mao has not been greatly involved in leadership, has shut himself up in his ivory tower, or has been isolated by others, who come from time to time to give him general information . . .

Friday July 14, 1967

The foreign policy of China – a policy of self-isolation
Since the beginning of the Cultural Revolution, if not earlier, the Chinese comrades **have been developing an ill-defined foreign**

policy, or to put it better, their foreign policy leans mostly towards self-isolation . . .

Their general tactic is: «Struggle with all, hostility with all». Such a tactic is extremely sectarian and leads only to the course, «either with me or against me»; «if you do not think and act as I say or as I act, then you are against me».

. . . Besides other things, a certain lack of modesty can also be seen on the part of the Chinese . . . They present matters in a distorted way: «He who is with the ideas of Mao Tsetung is a Marxist-Leninist; he who allows himself to ask certain natural, fair questions is suspect and can even be considered an anti-Marxist».

These stands have their source in the exaggerated «cult of the individual» that some dazibaos,[25] which we, of course, believe are uncontrolled (but for the time being these are the official reference materials we have), put Mao even above Marx, Lenin and Stalin. These posters say: «Mao Tsetung thought is the culmination of Marxism» . . .

We have respect for Mao, but being Marxists, we cannot fail to think that if all his revolutionary work is analysed, unclear points will certainly emerge . . .

For example . . . : What has Mao been doing during these eighteen years and why has he allowed the party to be weakened? Why has he left it in the hands of revisionists, who have eroded it from within? During this whole «dark» period, has Comrade Mao been isolated, has he been in the minority, or has he, too, been swimming in opportunist waters . . . ?

This whole situation, all this development, is being kept in the dark, being hidden. The newspapers and dazibaos carry only quotations from the works of Mao prior to 1942! But why only before this date . . . ?

Look at what they say: «In a district of Japan, a hundred communists revolted under the banner of Mao Tsetung». «The Communist Party of Burma is fighting inspired by the ideas of Mao Tsetung», regardless of the fact that it is an old party with experience in struggle. «A faction of the faction of the Indian Communist Party, guided by the ideas of Mao Tsetung, is fighting together with the peasantry for land in the Punjab», and so on.

The only thing they have not said directly (although they are trying to say it indirectly) is that the ideas of Mao guide also the Party of Labour of Albania, the struggle in Vietnam, etc.

In words they say: «We learn a great deal from the Party of Labour of Albania», but they have never sent a party delegation to our country to see our experience, let alone to gain from it. Naturally, this is their business, but it does not correspond to what they say . . .

For Chen Yi it was a great success that «the authorities of the Republic of Mali allowed the distribution of some books with the quotations of Mao»! This is lamentable. The bourgeoisie in France is printing these quotations itself and selling them freely on the market. As everyone knows, the French bourgeoisie has tight control over the authorities of Mali, who know very well how to keep China far away from their people . . .

Monday July 24, 1967

Chinese diplomacy has fallen asleep

. . . 2 — **What do the Chinese comrades think about . . . Cuba? Is it not time that, while safeguarding our principles, they moved a little from their rigid positions towards it at these moments** when Castro has contradictions with the Soviets, with the capitalists of the Latin American countries, and with the United States of America, as always? We know Castro for what he is . . . But the fact is that with the country in a very difficult economic situation, in his own way he is resisting both the Soviets and the Americans to some extent, and issuing calls for «world revolution». Castro does not accept our views and neither do we ever accept his views. But, while his views do not influence us, our views might influence him.

The fact is that he is showing signs of approaches to us, and feeling the need for us . . . We ought to make a move. What do the Chinese intend to do in these situations so that we can co-ordinate our actions?

In all the anarchist activity of Castro, there are certain stages which must not be forgotten . . . Castro is not a purist but neither is he like some Korean or Rumanian leaders. Castro has a pronounced sense of resistance . . .

Saturday July 29, 1967

China and international events
China has shut itself away . . .

For a long time our embassy in Peking has been completely without work, without meetings. Even at any chance meeting with some functionary of the Ministry of Foreign Affairs, this person says nothing to our comrades, either because he does not know anything, or because he is afraid to speak, or because the Chinese live by the general slogan of isolation. Meanwhile the Embassy of China in Tirana is completely non-existent. It has been without an ambassador for a year, and all the others who are there are «dead» silent, they simply go for walks, make visits, say nice words about our country, but as to their own country, what is going on there, not one word, absolutely nothing.

The Chinese press and Hsinhua news agency are also saying nothing about the events in their country, but are juggling with quotations and the same themes which they have dealt with over and over again for two years. But even these are written with such «perfection» that you can get nothing out of them . . . Those who write these «pot-boilers» have become masters at saying nothing by repeating the same thing all the time . . .

World opinion wants to know what is going on in China . . . Progressive opinion, which is waiting impatiently, sympathetically, is becoming fed up with stale phrases and with commentaries on quotations . . . [it] is being left to the bourgeois press and radio to brainwash it with every kind of slander, intrigue, fabrication, etc. Thus, in the absence of the reality (which China itself ought to make clear), the fabrications of enemies become implanted and confusion, coolness and distrust concerning what China is doing, are created. The very line which China has adopted says to the world: «Don't concern yourselves so much about us», or «praise us», «praise Mao, but it doesn't matter if you don't know what is being done here». This means to scorn external opinion about internal matters . . .

Thursday October 24, 1968

Chou En-lai's proposal of a Yugoslav–Albanian «defensive alliance»[26]

According to reliable facts which we have, it emerges that at a time when the situation between Yugoslavia and the Soviet Union and the situation between the Soviet Union and Albania were becoming acute (September–October 1968), the top Yugoslav leadership discussed the possibility of concluding a Yugoslav–Albanian defensive alliance. It was said that this proposal should come from the Yugoslav side. However, after much discussion and being convinced that it would be rejected by the Albanian side, this matter was left unmentioned.

The astonishing thing is that this idea of the Yugoslavs coincides with the proposal of Chou En-lai. It is certain that the Yugoslavs must at least have suggested it to the Chinese, if they have not discussed it together, in secret.

Even the latter is possible, because the proposal Chou En-lai referred to was accompanied with his opposition to the strategic and tactical principles of our defence. Such a thing became clear to us, because Chou did not display readiness to supply us with heavy weapons; he suggested to us that at the very first attack of the enemy we should give way to it and take to the mountains to wage partisan war; he suggested to us that we should co-operate with Tito, and finally, in order to intimidate us, he capped it all by saying: «Following the presidential elections in the United States of America, by spring or summer of 1969, you may be in danger».

In other words Chou En-lai said to us: Hurry up, link up with Tito, form a unity and alliance with him, for that is your road to salvation.

Monday September 15, 1969

Chou En-lai met Kosygin

We suspected that Chou En-lai might have met Kosygin in Hanoi at Ho Chi Minh's funeral.[27] Chou En-lai is capable of such political pirouettes . . .

When Chou left Hanoi before Kosygin arrived there, we rejoiced and said: «A resolute stand. Now the Chinese do not even want to set eyes on Kosygin», let alone shake hands with him . . .

After Ho Chi Minh's funeral, Rita [Marko][28] was invited . . . to Peking. To Rita, or to us here in Tirana they said nothing. On the day of Chou En-lai's meeting with Kosygin in Peking, the 11th of September 1969, Rita also had a meeting with Kang Sheng[29] and others. Just as they were leaving, Kang Sheng told Rita, «It is possible that Kosygin, on his return from Hanoi, will stop at Peking airport, indeed it is possible that right now, while we are here, Chou En-lai is talking with Kosygin at the airport». Rita said in astonishment: «How is such a thing possible? What will they talk about?!» Kang Sheng replied with the greatest shamelessness: «We know nothing». And after these words, which had deliberately been left to the end of the meeting, they parted . . .

From the first radiogram Rita sent us, it turns out that Chou En-lai informed him that, with Kosygin, he had talked about these things:

1 – **The border problems should be settled,** and until they are settled:

a) the status quo should be maintained;

b) the attacks should be stopped;

c) the two sides should withdraw their troops from the disputed zones . . .

2 – **The problems connected with railways, rivers, seas and airspace should be solved** . . .

4 – **Ambassadors should be exchanged.**

The pre-conditions of the Chinese for these talks:

1 – **The ideological polemic is not to be stopped.**

2 – **The Chinese atomic bases must not be attacked by the Soviets because then it would be all-out war.**

According to Rita's radiogram Chou En-lai added: «Kosygin accepted these things in general, and he will present them to the leadership . . . The Soviets asked for the talks because their internal situation is one of great crisis; Kosygin is the 'dove' who has handed in his resignation on three occasions. Through these talks, they want to exert pressure on the United States of America . . . Since the Chinese comrades do not inform us, we must work things out on the facts which we possess.

The Americans spread a «sensational» report: **the Soviet Union is going to attack China and especially the Chinese atomic bases.** The bourgeois press and chancelleries continue to inflate this report. The bloody Soviet provocations on the Chinese border[30] and the massing of hundreds of thousands of Soviet troops (?!) over the whole length of the Sino-Soviet border, support this report.

Can the Soviet revisionists have taken such a decision?! Anything is possible, but I think that this is a Soviet-American bluff to intimidate China . . . the . . . Soviet Union is preparing for war, but it is not yet ready to wage it, especially with China . . .

In my opinion, the Chinese were terrified and wavered in the face of this colossal blackmail frame-up. Unsound analysis of the international situation and unrealistic interpretation of the facts which they possess have brought them to this . . .

For three whole years Chinese diplomacy has been sound asleep. Now it has just woken up and the first sensational thing it did was to give its hand to the Russian czar, Kosygin. However you turn and twist this, Comrade Chou En-lai, you will never convince us. We know the difference between chalk and cheese . . .

Thursday September 18, 1969

The echo of the Chou En-lai–Kosygin meeting
. . . The meeting created a sensation, and as such, it is more in favour of the charlatans than of the Chinese . . .

Soviet television transmitted Kosygin's meeting with Chou En-lai. **I saw this broadcast with my own eyes. When they were farewelling one another especially, they all but kissed, they shook hands like two friends who hadn't seen each other for four years and who had been longing to meet and could scarcely bear to part. Scandalous!! . . .**

Friday September 19, 1969

The Chinese have been frightened by the Soviet blackmail
Today Comrade Rita [Marko] arrived from Peking and reported
to us concretely. **As in the first period of the Cultural Revolution,
. . . Chou En-lai had mounted the revisionist-opportunist horse
and was tearing ahead, full of enthusiasm, at a headlong gallop.**
Indeed he was striking out right and left with success. His
comrades, beginning from Kang Sheng, sat and listened and never
interrupted. This means that they were all in accord with what
Chou En-lai was reeling off.

When Rita expressed his opinion that the meeting with Kosygin
was a wrong action, Chou En-lai replied to him angrily, in an
uncomradely way, **«You are extremist».** There is no doubt that
this revisionist definition of Chou En-lai's was aimed at all our
leadership.

In his exposition, Chou En-lai did not take even the slightest
precaution **to conceal his opportunist views, . . . arranged es-**
pecially in this way to give us to understand that we should reduce
the tension with the Soviet Union.

Here is his reasoning:

1 – The Soviet Union is going to attack us, has massed troops,
but now is not in a situation to act.

2 – The Soviet leaders are fools. Nixon has said this, too.

3 – The Soviet generals and marshals are incompetent. Nixon
has said this, too.

4 – The Soviet leadership is divided into «hawks» and «doves».
The Soviet Union is for peace, we must reduce the tension, assist
the «doves» . . .

5 – The Soviet Union has lost its authority and control over its
satellites. (Hence China ought to help it to regain them.)

6 – The Soviet Union was discredited at the Moscow Meeting.
(Hence China ought to help it recover.)

7 – The Soviet Union must exert pressure on the United States
of America. (Hence China ought to help it do this.)

After listing all these things Chou En-lai concluded that the
reduction of tension is useful.

The question arises: For whom is it useful? According to Chou

En-lai, for China. According to us, for the Soviet Union and the revisionist faction in China, as well as for modern revisionism throughout the world. Even children understand this, let alone political people . . .

Chou En-lai tried to conceal this rotten course with phraseology, with slogans or historical events of the past . . .

Two things are clear:

1 – The Chinese are afraid and are making concessions in principle.

2 – The Chinese have been frightened by the Soviet blackmail, while the Chinese revisionist wing, disguised behind the Cultural Revolution, knows this is a bluff . . .

There is a great deal of talk in China about measures to prepare for war, as well as about sharpening vigilance. This is very good. Chou En-lai said this, too. But what vigilance can you call it when, first of all, you have completely lost your political and ideological vigilance?

Chou En-lai was so irritated during his talk with Comrade Rita and defended his opinion with such heat that, although he had invited Rita to a banquet, he did not propose any toast to our leadership. Could this have been an oversight? I don't believe so. It was pressure. When he «forgot», why did Kang Sheng not remind him?! He had many ways to do so.

The following morning both Kang Sheng and Li Hsien-nien, each of them individually, took Rita aside at the airport when he was about to leave and begged his pardon on behalf of Chou En-lai, who at the banquet the evening before «had forgotten» to propose a toast to the health of Comrade Enver, etc. They get up to such tricks . . .

Wednesday October 1, 1969

A talk with the Chinese ambassador

After the Chinese ambassador had delivered his speech and proposed the toast to the 20th anniversary of the proclamation of the People's Republic of China, I opened the conversation with him about the meeting which was held in Peking between Chou En-lai and Kosygin. Apparently he expected this, because I observed that his interpreter, who, when I was speaking a little earlier, translated everything directly, without taking notes, brought out his pen and notebook when I began to speak on this question. So much the better, but it depends how faithfully my words were translated.

Naturally, I prefaced my remarks before launching into the theme. I said more or less: Comrade Rita reported to us about the conversation he had with Comrade Chou En-lai in Peking. **We tell you sincerely, as comrades, that we do not find this unexpected meeting which Chou En-lai had with Kosygin in Peking correct or opportune . . .**

I told him that we had to be vigilant towards the Soviet revisionist enemies and American imperialism, that we had to be armed, and that every evil should find us well armed and together . . .

I also expressed to the ambassador our opinion that, in these situations, at this juncture, the Soviets are not yet prepared for war against China. Today they are bluffing, exerting blackmail, in this direction.

The ambassador heard me out and thanked me in his reply. He did not know what else to say, only that, «At first I (the ambassador) did not really understand the Cultural Revolution. Later on I was convinced and have confidence in Comrade Mao, Lin Piao and Chou En-lai. We Chinese learn a great deal from you, Comrade Enver. Our friendship . . .», etc., etc.

The dinner continued very well, very cordially.

Wednesday October 8, 1969

For the Chinese the czars of the Kremlin have become «fine fellows»!
Yesterday the Chinese issued a communiqué in which they announced that they are ready to begin talks with the Soviets, at the rank of deputy ministers, in Peking . . .

I think that our press and radio should ignore the Chinese communiqué . . . just as they ignored the Chou En-lai–Kosygin meeting. This is because if we publicise it, we shall have to publish all that follows, and there will be no small amount of that . . . Or other variant, to publish a very, very short report. However, we have time to think about this.

Wednesday December 3, 1969

Li Hsien-nien did not hold any political conversation with our comrades

Li Hsien-nien came and will depart as dumb as a fish.[31] He did not open up even the very slightest political conversation with our comrades. We thought he would say something in the meeting he had with me, but he said nothing, although I gave the conversation a political and very friendly turn. He . . . finally said with utter shamelessness: «When I went to Rumania, at the airport they asked me: How are the talks with the Soviets going? And I replied that the Soviets don't want these talks to be made public.» After saying this and nothing more, Li Hsien-nien looked at his watch and asked to be excused because, he said, «You are very busy». The same thing occurred at all the manifestations, . . . either he has been advised to adopt this stand, or he is afraid to speak because he has taken a beating in the Cultural Revolution. But if the latter is the case, why send us this mummy?! We asked him to hold talks, but he refused this, too, saying: «From our side we have nothing new.» Seeing how things stood, we dropped the matter. But we have the better of them in everything. They remained disgraced and equivocal.

This evening we put on a farewell dinner for Li Hsien-nien, who spoke in the usual formulas. No idea was put forward, no problem was raised on his part . . .

Friday December 5, 1969

Evil and provocative aims

In Fier, the deputy-leader of the Chinese delegation (the army-man) committed a base provocation. With utter shamelessness, he said to Haki [Toska]: «You dress well and eat well, while look at us, we dress in cotton suits.» And Haki replied to him as he deserved. «This suit I am wearing,» he said, «is neither wool nor cotton, but synthetic. Your suit is cotton drill and if you will allow me (and he pulled up the trouserleg a little), these that you are wearing (long underpants), and that singlet you have under your shirt are of wool, while I (Haki pulled up the leg of his trousers) do not have such things. Under my shirt (and he undid one button of the shirt), as you see, I have only a sleeveless cotton singlet. Neither do I have a woollen pullover. Hence your clothing is more expensive than mine. As to what we eat,» he told him, «if you draw conclusions from the dinners which we put on for friends like you, I can say that when I have gone to China, the Chinese comrades did not know what to do to make me eat more, and the tables were loaded. But you are wrong on the two questions which you raise, because not only are we against luxury, but we are extremely economical and rational in the use of things.» . . .

This Chinese delegation has been the most negative, the worst, with evil and provocative aims. But we did not lose our aplomb.

Saturday December 6, 1969

Li Hsien-nien and his delegation
We expected that a delegation worthy of the deep, pure, and sincere feelings, the great love we have for People's China, its Communist Party and Chairman Mao, would come to our great celebration of the 25th anniversary of Liberation from our «great, beloved, Marxist-Leninist» ally.

What did they send us? Who came at the head of the delegation? A gloomy individual, a person who is criticised so severely by the Cultural Revolution, that we are astonished that he remains where he is (only in China do these «miracles» occur even when such «revolutions» are being carried out) . . . This person was Li Hsien-nien, the friend and righthand man of Chou En-lai, who certainly not only saved him from the purges, but kept him where he was before, and indeed increased his «renown» and power even further . . .

He behaved towards us much worse than Chou En-lai himself would have behaved, because [Chou] is very clever, very diplomatic . . .

Tuesday January 6, 1970

No smoke without fire
The Chinese comrades in Peking told our comrades, «Now some of our ships will come to Albania from the northern ports of China, via the Taiwan Straits»!! Our comrades said: «But how?! The American 7th Fleet and the Chiang Kai-shek navy are patrolling there . . .» But the Chinese comrades replied: «We must follow the teachings of Mao and not fear the imperialists», etc. It seems that the meetings of the Chinese and American ambassadors in Warsaw have yielded some first result. There is no smoke without fire . . .

Tuesday February 17, 1971

Chen Po-ta is denounced as a traitor
. . . Suddenly, after all this glorification and these major duties, he [Chen Po-ta] is declared a traitor![32]

We ask the question: What sort of cadres policy is this? We cannot be convinced that the activity of Chen Po-ta was not known . . . Then why was he still kept as Mao's secretary, and even worse, how is it possible that this opportunist, Trotskyist, etc., etc., was placed at the head of the Cultural Revolution, which had as its aim precisely the radical purging of such people? . . .

This situation is inconceivable to us. Such a policy of taking enemies, placing them at the head, praising them, and then unmasking them, is beyond understanding, however Machiavellian it may be . . .

Thursday April 15, 1971

The «ping-pong policy»
As Chou En-lai said two days ago, China «has turned a new page» in its relations with the United States of America. It commenced this policy with its invitation to the American table-tennis team[33] . . .

They went and received a «fine warm welcome», indeed the French news agency AFP even made a comparison, saying that the reception was warmer than one that could have been given to a team from Albania, which has been and is the most loyal friend of China. Naturally, the bourgeois news agencies are making a mountain out of a molehill, wanting to prove that «something big is going on in China» But the fact is that this event has the importance not of a normal sports activity, but of a new political event . . .

Nixon, on his part, was, one might say, quick and eager to respond to Chou En-lai . . . At the same time, according to news agencies, the United States of America withdrew its oil prospecting teams from the China Sea.

Thus, as can be seen, the ice is being broken. There is more to this than meets the eye. The Foreign Ministry of China, through our ambassador in Peking, informed us about this event, while assuring us that nothing has changed or will change in the policy of China towards American imperialism, Soviet revisionism, and world reaction . . .

Sunday May 23, 1971

Ceausescu is to visit China

. . . Ceausescu's Rumania is being sold at auction for credits. This means «death through credits» . . .

The Chinese whisper in our ear: «We know them, they (the Rumanians) are revisionists, we know that socialism is not being built in Rumania, . . . but . . .»

In my opinion this «but» conceals and permits the Chinese comrades to make many political mistakes in their attitude towards Rumania.

In the first place, the «diploma», which Ceausescu is seeking from China to prove that he is a «communist», should not be given to him . . .

It is not correct for credits to be given to Rumania so that the new parasitic Rumanian bourgeoisie can live in great affluence, when the Chinese people are struggling and making great sacrifices . . .

These things may not have an effect in China, but they have an effect in socialist Albania, encircled by savage enemies . . . we

shall watch Ceausescu's journey to China, shall also keep an eye
on the dose of receptions and speeches of the Chinese comrades.
But the stand of our press will be cold and the announcement will
be made in the form of a very simple news item. Let the Chinese
understand our attitude towards the Rumanian revisionists,
whose copper we have no intention of «gilding».

Wednesday June 2, 1971

The Chinese and Ceausescu
**Ceausescu went to China at the head of a delegation of . . . 80
people. Not even the cook was missing!**
**. . . Mao received Ceausescu. Hsinhua reported only that he
said to him: «Rumanian comrades, we should unite to bring down
imperialism.» As if Ceausescu and company are to bring down
imperialism!! If the world waits for the Ceausescus to do such a
thing, imperialism will live for tens of thousands of years . . .**

Durrës, Wednesday July 28, 1971

China, Vietnam, Korea, and Nixon's visit to Peking
. . . The Chinese were against the talks of the Vietnamese with the
Americans.[34] They had told them this many times, and have told
us officially, too . . . [though] China's stand towards the war of
the Vietnamese people and its aid did not alter . . .

We were not in agreement with the talks which the Vietnamese
began with the Americans. We have told the Vietnamese comrades of our opinion on several occasions . . .

Irrespective that China and Albania were not in agreement with
the Paris talks, in the final analysis, this was the business of the
Vietnamese . . . We remained consistent in our support for Vietnam's war, but not China . . .

**The conclusions of Chou En-lai's talks with Kissinger[35] fell like
a bombshell on us Albanians, on the Vietnamese, the Koreans, not
to mention the others . . .** When Chou En-lai summoned our
ambassador, at three in the morning, to inform him laconically
about the «good news», which was to be published a day later, he
told him that he would call him back to inform him more

extensively on the matter, so that he could inform the comrades in
Tirana, because, he said: «I have just returned from Hanoi where I
brought the comrades up to date. Now I am going to Korea to
inform Kim Il Sung, and when I return, I shall inform Sihanouk
and will call you, too.»[36]

We, naturally, were to be informed after the Prince of Cambodia! . . .

The Chinese are making another major mistake to justify this
shitty business of theirs. In the information which he gave our
ambassador, Chou En-lai said: «We foresee that the war in
Vietnam will continue: therefore, as we told the comrades in
Hanoi, they should fight and, at the same time, we should
talk» . . .

The Chinese have begun to praise Korea a great deal. They have
begun to call Kim Il Sung a great leader, while yesterday they told
us officially, «He has no value at all; he has been a corporal in the
Chinese army», etc. *O tempora, o mores!* [Latin in the original].
What will our ears hear and our eyes see!! This is only the
beginning, but a very ominous beginning.[37] . . .

Tuesday October 26, 1971

*Our congratulations on the admission of China to the United
Nations Organisation*[38]
We must send our congratulations to China on its admission to
the UNO. I told Nesti [Nase] to go to congratulate the ambassador
of China on this occasion and to get his opinion (allegedly so we
would not make any mistake) in connection with the telegram
which we shall send to Mao, Dung Pi-wu[39] and Chou En-lai, in
place of Mao, Lin Piao and Chou En-lai as usual, and he should
say, «We are doing this to give importance to the aspect of state
relations, too». The Chinese ambassador, relieved, replied: «Your
idea is very good». Nesti said to him again: «Is it necessary for you
to consult Peking on this question?» The ambassador replied:
«No, no. What you have thought to do about this matter is very
good.» Hence, without their telling us a thing, it is indirectly
confirmed that something has occurred with Lin Piao . . .

Monday January 3, 1972

What is going on with the Lin Piao group?[40]
... The disappearance of Lin Piao from the scene is now an undeniable fact ... The Chinese are saying nothing, but only imply, «these are our internal matters of no interest to foreigners». **This may be correct in principle to some degree and for a certain time, but on such a major question, when the whole head of the army is lopped off, ... something should be done to stop the speculation. Let people hear what has occurred and put their minds at rest. In any case, the friends of China should not be left in the dark to guess at what is going on ...**

Up till now it is the Chinese drivers or the Chinese interpreters at our embassy, «party members», who give us «official» versions of what has happened, versions which vary. They all say to us: «What we are telling you, they have told us in the Party and have advised us not to tell anybody, but you are our loyal friends. We believe that your ambassador knows about it; but please keep it secret in any case.»

Then should we suppose that these people who come and tell us are sent by the leadership, or do they take the initiative themselves, considering us their closest friends and supposing that we have been informed? However, up till now we must say that the Chinese are fanatical about keeping secrets.

... **The essence of what they say is the same in general, but between versions there are differences and contradictions, obscure things, things with double meanings, in a word, these are Chinese tricks.**

... The most reliable version, which we must consider semi-official, concocted for our benefit, is that of the Chinese translator of the press office of our embassy (appointed by the Chinese Foreign Ministry), who, we are certain, is a member of the Communist Party of China.

... When our comrade asked this interpreter what has become of Lin Piao, whom news agencies say has been killed, he replied: **«We know nothing. This is all they have told us.»** Then he continued, «Wu Fa-hsien,[41] Marshal of the Air Force, was bad, because he had left the command of the airforce in the hands of

Lin Piao's twenty-four year old son. Lin Piao's wife, Yeh Chun,[42] whom Lin had made a member of the Political Bureau, was a foreign spy, possibly for the Soviets. Lin Piao . . . sang the praises of Mao, but secretly plotted against him. Mao discovered the plot and now the situation is brilliant, the evil ones have been purged».

It's just like a detective story, with plots, blown-up trains, spies in the service of foreigners, etc., etc.

These events, as they are related to us, are rocambolesque [incredible] adventures, intended for naive and absolutely gullible people who do not understand politics at all. If the Chinese leadership really puts these things to the party in this way, as these people tell us, this is simply to impress the members of the party and not to explain the truth to them . . .

Anything is possible, but it takes a bit of swallowing that there could be such leaders, who for years on end had been considered loyal to the policy of Mao Tsetung and to Mao personally, but who one fine morning turned out to be conspirators, who attempted to «blow up the train» in order to kill Mao, to seize power, and take his place.[43]

The question arises: Why should Lin Piao murder Mao and why take his place, when he himself occupied precisely the main position after Mao, this act looks like an episode from «James Bond». Since the aim was to seize power, why were such unreliable methods chosen, when they were people intimate with Mao and could more easily liquidate him with other methods? No, the train had to «be blown up, and Mao personally had to discover the conspiracy and give the order for its liquidation» — all this was necessary «to make an impression on the people» . . .

I think that somewhere in all this there must be political questions, and this is the nub of the matter. First of all they must have had contradictions over line, debates, opposition. On what were the «ideas of Mao» opposed «by Lin Piao and the leftists»? We are not told this.

Mao and Chou En-lai constructed a «new strategy» on the occasion of Nixon's going to Peking, and this they told even us, officially. Were Lin Piao and the «leftists» in agreement with Nixon's visit, were they in agreement with this «new strategy of Mao and Chou»? This they do not tell us, . . . indeed, they do not tell even their own people, their own party about it. Why do they not tell them? Certainly because there is a strong current in the party and the people against Nixon's visit to Peking. **Then, I think, the Chinese leadership wants to get over this period, till Nixon has come and gone, with this version which they have given about the «Lin Piao group». In this way, the attention of the party and the people will be distracted from the political event of Nixon's coming, and they will concentrate on the plot, and afterwards «we shall see what we shall do».** When Nixon leaves Peking and according to the results achieved, new definitive versions can be adopted, then «the situation will be ripe», the investigations will be ended, and one day before the whole world hears the «definitive version of the conspiracy» they will even tell us, Albanians, «their closest comrades-in-arms» . . .

Who is Lin Piao in fact?[44] For us he is the most unknown person. It is true that he was a commander to whom the liberation of Peking was entrusted. He may have been a fine commander, but nothing else . . . he was inflated «like a balloon» by the others, by Mao, and was «conspicuous» by his absence . . . **Nothing was said about him except eulogies, but he was neither seen nor known, and nobody talked with him.** The pretext found for this was, «he is sick». **But what sort of sickness was this? The answer was mysterious: «He is allergic to water». But on the other hand, he was the second man in the «hierarchy».**

Our comrades, who have gone one after the other to Peking officially many times . . . have very rarely seen the face of Lin Piao. They have done no more than shake hands with him, and have never had any conversation with him . . . It is possible that Lin Piao was nothing much . . .

Now, with the condemnation of Lin Piao, . . . they will saddle him with the blame for all these mistakes of principle, will say that Lin Piao alone was to blame for the fact that the armymen took over the running of the party . . . Hence, it will turn out that all these are Lin Piao's men and the clean-up with the broom, which will no doubt be done, will be presented dressed up with «principled slogans», about the «preservation of the norms» of the party, but the reality will be entirely different . . .

Thursday February 24, 1972

Mrs Nixon advertises China
Even Nixon's wife is joining in the propaganda. She is advertising
«Chinese cooking, Chinese goods, Chinese art, Chinese silk
pyjamas, and people's communes». Pat Nixon has become
another Anna Louise Strong.[45]

Tuesday March 21, 1972

*Nixon's journey to China, the Sino-American talks, the final
communiqué* [46]
... Chinese propaganda maintained «absolute silence» about
this event, as if «it were of no great interest». **Of course, this did
not represent the reality** ... Superficially, it seemed as if the
Chinese were not taking preparatory measures, but this was not
true: they cleaned up the city, painted the shops and houses,
especially in those streets and zones through which Nixon would
pass, removed all the «dangerous» slogans which might annoy the
«notable» guest, filled the shops with all kinds of goods, displayed
books of «Chinese and foreign classics», which up till yesterday
had disappeared from circulation, in the bookshops. **All these
things were done under the guise of the Chinese «New Year». But
no one swallowed this. These things were not done for the «Year
of the Rat», but for «the coming of the ... Paper Tiger».**
    ... Chou En-lai seemed very «stiff», of course, because he
knew that the whole world was watching him, while Nixon was
grinning like a horse, happy, laughing, regardless of the fact that
the streets through which he passed were empty, certainly by
order ...
The «external cold correctness of the Chinese», which was
apparent at the airport and in the streets, through which the
cortège passed, was nothing but a *trompe l'oeil* ...
The President of the United States of America had hardly rested
after his journey, when he was received by Mao Tsetung, and in
his working office at that. As far as we know, this had never
occurred before. Mao Tsetung has always received other friends
and guests, even the closest friends and guests of China, at the end

of their visit . . . In this way Mao wanted to display his special warmth and gratitude to Nixon for these contacts and talks, wanted to display intimacy . . . on the table where the President leaned his elbows, there was a pile of books, in order to let Nixon know that he was dealing with a «great thinker». Mao Tsetung also wanted to show Nixon that it was he, Mao, who opened this «new era in the world», which is the «question of Sino-American relations», and on the other hand to tell the Chinese people that this «policy of friendship» with American imperialism «is my policy, and not Chou En-lai's». If this policy does not turn out well, «we have experience and lay the blame on Chou».

The communiqué issued after the Mao—Nixon meeting, said only «the talks were sincere and frank», hence, it was neither fish nor fowl, while the Chinese television spoke in another language. Mao and Nixon appeared on the small screen happy and laughing, clasping each other not by one but by both hands. Kissinger was lolling, smiling and happy, in an arm-chair, as if in his own home. Chou En-lai was *aux anges* [in seventh heaven] laughing and chuckling so loudly that he became embarrassed and covered his mouth with his hand. Hence, the atmosphere was more than friendly, and this atmosphere only the Chinese tele-vision, that is, a controlled television, had captured, and then it was shown on the small screen, and this was done by Chou not without a purpose, but so that history would fix this «historic moment», so that the Americans would see it and the Chinese people, too, would be orientated by this «brilliant proletarian strategy and tactics» of Mao Tsetung.

After this «very significant» act of Mao's, the atmosphere, which had appeared constrained, improved, the ice was broken, «a hundred flowers began to bloom», and «they set out on the long march».

The banquet put on by the Chinese was magnificent . . . It was clear that even Nixon was surprised, and indeed, more or less implied: «It seems I have been wrong. I thought you really were communists» . . .

Chiang Ching, Mao's wife,[47] has changed her style of dress and *coiffure*. She has had her hair cut short in «urchin» style, flung her cap with the red star in the waste paper basket, and replaced her military uniform of revolution with gowns of black cashmere or fine woollen fabric. At every performance Chiang Ching sits beside Nixon.

Nixon's going to Peking, the welcome he received there, and the Sino-American joint communiqué constitute a victory for American imperialism and for Nixon personally ... China «financed» American imperialism with credibility in the eyes of the peoples ...

Monday April 17, 1972

A talk of Chou En-lai without political problems
At the beginning of April, a government delegation of ours went to Peking to sign an agreement on the credit which China is providing [us] for agriculture.

They received our delegation very well in Peking. Three thousand people had come out to the airport with music, banners and portraits.[48]

... We thought that Chou En-lai, as the clever «politician» he is, would not miss this opportunity, but we were wrong. Chou En-lai received the delegation ... [He] opened and closed the conversation, while the head of our delegation merely interposed a few unimportant things. Chou did not talk to him at all about political matters (although it is usual of him to talk at length about these matters) and said nothing about Albania (except to ask after the health of our comrades ...).

Chou's talk was a self-criticism towards us in other directions. He said, «The tractors which we sent you have defects in the crankshafts, and the Mig-19 aircraft also have defects: therefore, don't use them until we send a team to check and repair them. The trucks and jeep which we have sent to Vietnam and the sugar-cane harvesters we have sent to Cuba have also turned out to be defective», etc. ... it is clear: Chou En-lai did not want to enter into political questions, although he does this with great pleasure ... We get the message.

What conclusions can we draw?

It is not a normal thing for Chou En-lai not to deal with political matters in a talk with one of our comrades. Did he have political problems of first-rate importance which he should have dealt with? Yes!

a) **The relations with the United States of America are new relations**. We think that he should have said how far, or in what directions, these relations will be developed . . .

b) **The problem of Vietnam.** There, the great military offensive by the Vietnamese side has begun . . .

However, Chou En-lai was silent about the victories of the Vietnamese people in this war. Why? Because relations between the Chinese and the Vietnamese are not good, because of the course the Chinese are following towards Nixon, whom the Vietnamese rightly call the greatest war criminal . . .

d) **He did not make the slightest mention of the Soviet revisionists, either, Why?**

The problem which Chou touched on briefly was that of the «ultra-left trend», which has caused «great harm to China and wanted to establish capitalism there». Of course, Chou was referring to the Lin Piao group without mentioning the name. This is their old tactic. What he told us Albanians «in confidence» does not tell us much. What has this trend done? It wanted to establish capitalism!! But how? Merely by sabotaging the aircraft? Can a sister party be satisfied with only this? Either inform it properly, or don't inform it at all!!

As for the sabotage of the aircraft and the helicopters, this is not a new problem. The main Chinese military comrades, indeed the very top ones, some of whom were purged with the «ultra-left group», told our comrades who were in China in 1968–1969 about this. That is, the sabotage on the aircraft was discovered when Lin Piao was «omnipotent». However, on their part, this may be considered, «an act of conspirators», and indeed their main action . . .

On the question of Kang Sheng, which they frequently repeat to us, they want to say that «he is sick and has not been purged with the ultra-left group». However, this «influenza» or «bronchitis» seems to be going on for a long time. It is more than a year since Kang Sheng appeared in public. This is their affair, but it seems to us that on this question, too, they are not serious . . .

Saturday April 22, 1972

The Vietnamese offensive and China

. . . In recent days our ambassador in Hanoi had a talk with the Chinese military attaché in Vietnam. He told him: «We (the Chinese) know nothing about these offensives, because the Vietnamese do not inform us. We do not know whether this is a serious action which will be carried through to the end, or an adventure which will cost them dear. The Soviets have a finger in this offensive» . . . But there may also be the other aspect, that the Chinese consider this offensive of the Vietnamese an adventure, making an analogy with the war in Korea, when the Korean [People's] army advanced as far as Pusan, and the Americans counter-attacked and reached the Yalu river on the border with China.[49]

Are these the reasons that make the Chinese call the Vietnamese offensive an «adventure»? Together with this, can they be thinking that the Soviets . . . have pushed the Vietnamese into this adventure in order to bring the war to the borders of China by provoking a new attack à la MacArthur in Vietnam, and this will give the Soviets cause not only to spread propaganda against China, but also to implicate it in a war with the United States of America, or to get a foothold, themselves, in Vietnam and encircle China from the south? All these variants are possible . . . when the agreement on Nixon's going to China was announced. Precisely from this time on, the Americans did not give much more importance to the Conference in Paris. Why? There is no doubt, it must be thought that Nixon was going to talk about Vietnam in Peking . . . Here lies the source of the conflict.

However, this conflict must have taken place within the Chinese leadership, too, that is, between Mao and Chou En-lai on the one side, and Lin Piao and the armymen, or the «extreme leftists», as they have described them, on the other side. We have to suppose that Mao and Chou were in favour of Nixon's going to Peking and for softening the policy towards the United States, as well as for the settlement of the Vietnam problem to some degree with talks, while Lin Piao and the other comrades were against Nixon's visit, against this softening of the policy with him and for the further development of the fighting on the part of Vietnam. It must be for this that they have been accused as «ultra-leftists».

The Chinese conceal this main question and tell us contradictory things which don't hold water . . . a series of such stupidities. The Chinese raise many natural shortcomings and mistakes in work to principles, and blame them on the «extreme leftists». Such things can't be swallowed!

Now the Chinese comrades tell us that «the Vietnamese are two-faced people».

Our ambassador in Peking informs us today that a reception was given recently for an African personality. Present at the dinner was Chou En-lai, who tried to give the guests the impression that they have «very good» relations with Vietnam. But it turned out the opposite. He rose from the table, went towards the diplomats and beckoned to the two Vietnamese ambassadors, of the North and the South,[50] to approach, but they did not move from their place. Chou En-lai went over and began to talk to them. They listened to him with marked indifference, which struck the eye of all those who were watching. In the end, the two Vietnamese ambassadors, maintaining that same indifferent stand, implied to Chou that they did not understand what he said, so that Chou was obliged to summon a translator. This incident struck the eye of all present and made a big impression . . .

Durrës, Saturday July 22, 1972

The «Lin Piao plot»
At last, after nearly eleven months, the Chinese comrades . . . have given us some official information about the «ultra-leftists» or the «Lin Piao plot» . . .

They also told us: Chairman Mao was not in agreement with the assessments and glorification Lin made of Mao's ideas and work. All that glorification, which built up Mao to the skies, was anti-Marxist, because it put him above Marxism-Leninism, because the Chinese soldiers and officers hung portraits of Mao round their necks, because they bowed before the portrait of Mao every morning and made self-criticism before this same portrait (as before icons of Christ).

We Albanians condemned all these things as anti-Marxist and idealist craziness when we heard of them . . .

But again the question arises: How was Lin Piao allowed to do all these things?! How was this man, who had made mistakes, placed at the head of the party and boosted so much?! . . . They say that they did not understand! But these things were sticking out a mile, even we understood them from away over here, though we did not know many things and had no knowledge of the directives issued, so they should have understood them.

The fact is that the Communist Party of China was not «on its feet», if it was not liquidated, it was paralysed . . .

Then to fail to prevent Lin Piao from fleeing means to have astounding ideas about the class enemy and the class struggle. This speaks of the megalomaniac idea of the great state which says: «Let this enemy get away, even if he is Lin Piao; he will expose himself.» This is true, but it is not right to think that he can do no harm.

The Chinese comrades present Lin Piao as very «cunning», but he did not show himself at all cunning in his plot and his treachery. His plans to kill Mao and Chou En-lai do not seem to be all that refined; on the contrary they are clumsy: a coup d'état with a hundred men, as in Latin America.

According to what the Chinese say, Lin Piao emerges as a simple agent of the Soviets, whom they have put in a tight corner and told: Act at all costs, kill Mao, seize power, because «China has joined the United States of America». However, the Ussuri incident occurred before Nixon's visit to Peking[51] . . .

The other question, again somewhat obscure to us, is the attempt by Lin Piao to flee by aircraft. It seems a very careless flight, completely unorganised. How was it possible that Lin Piao, the Minister of Defence of China, Vice-Chairman of the party, on whom «they have no facts», did not know that his daughter had denounced him five hours before he was to flee?! How is it possible that «the secret agent of the Soviets», as he has been described, who entrusted the arrangements for his flight to his son, a conspirator, the Deputy-Commander of the whole Chinese Air Force, should select an aircraft without a crew, without sufficient fuel, without a radio, which would crash in Mongolia and be burned up like a child's toy?! Such actions do not seem in the least like those of the putchist plotters who, as they told us, were going to kill Mao and Chou En-lai and take everything in hand with a hundred men. It seems surprising that Lin Piao took off so precipitately, while his main collaborators and *pezzi grossi* stayed behind and did not move at all. Astonishing!! However such amazing things occur in China, therefore they should not surprise us this time, either. We have believed them a thousand times before, so why not now! . . .

What about the other version: Could they have forced Lin Piao to flee and liquidated him on the way? Kamikaze!

Let us suppose the version according to which Lin Piao had expressed opposition to the line which was being followed, we do not know in what directions, but we must assume on the policy which began to be followed towards the United States of America. His opponents taxed him with being pro-Soviet and dangerous. Then it was decided to liquidate him. They had no facts about a conspiracy, but they fabricated facts and in this way a plot was hatched up against him. He was summoned urgently to Peking, boarded an aircraft and, when he saw that he was not landing in Peking, asked: Where are we going? When later they saw they were in Mongolia, he and his people brought out their revolvers and killed themselves. What went on inside? The aircraft came down and was burned out. Nothing was learned.

A Canadian newspaper reported that «Kissinger had told the Canadian Prime Minister that expertise had proved that bullet marks were found in the wreckage of the aircraft.» How true is this? Are the Soviets telling the truth or telling lies? It could be true, it could be a lie. The Soviets have the key to this mystery! But it is advantageous to them to give such a version, which makes what we supposed above more plausible. Why? – comes the question. Why was there shooting within the aircraft?! Who opened fire and why?! Did only Lin Piao fire?! And if we accept this version, he started shooting because he saw that they were taking him outside China, to Mongolia (and not to the Soviet Union, as the Chinese say), against his will.

All these versions are suppositions dictated by the unclarity of the facts which the Chinese themselves provide. Officially we accept all that the Chinese say, but time will explain every-thing.

Durrës, Sunday July 30, 1972

Two facts about Lin Piao
All the ambassadors of China, wherever they are, are making contact with our ambassadors and informing them about the betrayal of Lin Piao. It is the same version that was given us officially. There is only a single nuance, on the part of the chargé d'affaires of the Chinese Embassy in Chile, who told our ambassador there. «The friends of Mao killed Lin Piao and the aircraft was shot down in Mongolia.» This is the first time we have been told this by the Chinese side and it is in conformity with a news item of a Canadian newspaper, . . . [that] signs of bullets fired within the aircraft had been found. This means, according to them, that there must have been an armed clash in the aircraft.

Is the chargé d'affaires at the Chinese Embassy in Chile basing himself on this and drawing the conclusion, or does he have this information from his centre? This we do not know. The other Chinese ambassadors are not speaking about such a thing . . .

January 15, 1973

Some anti-Marxist statements by Chou En-lai
. . . A few months ago Chi Peng-fei, the Foreign Minister of China, made more or less this statement: «China, Korea, Vietnam, Cambodia, Laos, and the other countries of Indochina are one big family . . .», etc. Here, naturally, the words «bloc», «camp», «socialist countries» did not appear, but there is a flavour of a «yellow family», an «Asiatic grouping», which is not Marxist-Leninist.[52] . . .

Chou's statement at the banquet with Mobutu[53] is flagrantly anti-Marxist. He included China in the «third world». This means to deny socialism, to conceal the true individuality of China and the character of its socio-economic order from the eyes of the world . . .

This thesis is anti-Marxist. **We Albanians do not agree. Albania** is socialist and socialist it will be, even if it must remain alone . . .

General Mobutu and his clique are reactionaries, the murderers of Lumumba[54] and other progressive individuals in their country. China receives the representative of this anti-democratic African clique with great honours, and in order to please him, Chou En-lai declares: «China is part of the third world». In other words, he tells the Congolese people: «I, China, am Mobutu's friend, support Mobutu, because he is a democrat, progressive», etc., regardless that Mobutu suppresses the people and the proletariat . . .

April 20, 1973

The bourgeois 'wasps' gather honey and release their poison in the garden of 'a hundred flowers'

. . . [The Chinese] are publishing nothing about us, apart from the welcoming and farewelling of football and volleyball players and Chinese acrobats.

. . . Chou En-lai himself has intervened personally with our embassy for measures to be taken against a few Albanian students who were associated in a purely comradely way with some Chinese girls. And this occurred many years before the Cultural Revolution, thus they cannot attribute these views to Lin Piao. **Between that time and this, what «flower-strewn» roads and what «flowers» have blossomed and will blossom in the land of China «blessed» by Confucius!**

What rubbish will be introduced into China! How many of them will marry! How many legal and illegal societies will be created! How many churches and cathedrals will be opened! How much of this rubbish will be granted Chinese citizenship and how much of it will enter the ranks of the Communist Party of China and fight for the CIA, the Soviet KGB and for world capitalism, under the banner of Mao!

Truly, the centre of the Trotskyite International will be created there. All this garbage will pour into China disguised as «leftist», «Maoist» and people «persecuted» in their own countries. They will find aid and support in China, and with a comforting support and the «seal of Mao» they will . . . struggle against genuine Marxist-Leninists . . .

From this a very dangerous activity of «Maoist» revisionists will begin. We must be very vigilant . . .

China has good relations with Tito, Ceausescu and Carrillo. Without doubt it will extend these relations with the other revisionist parties and the «Maoist» Trotskyites. **The bourgeoisie will issue the slogan that its «wasps» go to gather the honey and release their poison in the garden where «a hundred flowers blossom» . . .**

Durrës, Friday July 13, 1973

A formal delegation
In Durrës[55] I received the delegation of the Chinese army which had come on the occasion of the 30th anniversary of our People's Army . . .

I asked the leader of the delegation how he had enjoyed his trip around Albania, although it was short and by aircraft, and what impressions our army and the people with whom he had contact, had made on him. Of course, he told me nothing, just a few well-known formulas used by every Chinese whom we have met. It is difficult to talk with such members of delegations, because you get no response . . . All your ideas, all the conversation you try to make, run into an impenetrable wall (apparently), because you do not see any reaction, any reasonable reply, apart from tasteless, stereotyped platitudes.

. . . I began to speak about economic questions in order to come round to other problems of the army and policy. I noticed that while I was speaking, the leader of the delegation was staring at the ceiling, at the pictures and the walls. Then I used another tactic to stir him up: in the middle of the talk I stopped and asked what he thought, how China judged this or that problem. But Shu Yu never budged from his muteness.

Nevertheless, I expressed my opinions on many questions and the members of the Chinese delegation took notes. At least, let those who will read these notes draw the conclusion, if they like, that the sending of such formal delegations without individuality (judging from their silence) has no value. Even what they were to write in the book of impressions at the museums which they were to visit in our country, they had brought from Peking carefully numbered. This cannot be stomached!

When I finished my remarks, the leader of the Chinese delegation began to speak in platitudes. He said that this summer they would hold the congress of their party and that they had decided not to invite representatives from the fraternal parties. I replied that this was their affair, but we regretted not taking part in the congress of their party, at which Mao would certainly speak. No reaction at all. Then he spoke about the «great victory» of the Vietnamese people, and so on. In the middle of his talk I said that this was not a great victory, since Thieu was still in Saigon and powerful, etc.[56] No impression, no reaction, or to put it better, with his attitude he implied, «I have come to express our formulas and nothing more». He did not say a word about Cambodia. I spoke about it.

In the end he issued the «sledge-hammer slogan» which, according to them, «justifies» their opening up towards the USA, that the Soviet Union is more dangerous but is not regognised as such by the others . . . After he had uttered these formulas, the Chinese kept looking at his watch in order to get away as quickly as possible, because he was afraid the conversation might be drawn out, but I kept him and talked in a friendly way «à bâtons rompus» (jumping from one theme to the other) until finally I let him go and farewelled him with warm words, despite his mummy-like attitude . . .

July 29, 1973

Why did the Chinese postpone the calling of their Party Congress?
. . . For us there are many problems in the foreign policy of China which are obscure . . . What is occurring and what is being done with the Americans? Two whole years have gone by and nothing is being whispered . . . Nixon came and went, many delegations of American senators, bankers, scientists, tourists, football players, artists, and spies of every type come and go to China. What do all these do?! What do they say?! What results from all this traffic?! Not a word is being whispered! Only Chou En-lai and those close

to him know all about this. And Nixon, too, of course. The world knows only that these people go to China, are welcomed with banquets and then leave. A nasty great mystery which lays the Chinese open to suspicion and condemnation . . . When Brezhnev meets Nixon, of course, they take secret decisions, but some of them at least are published. The Chinese publish nothing. What did this mysterious policy bring the Chinese? No good among public opinion, only great harm. The world thinks: What is this China?! What is it up to?! . . .

Will the Chinese comrades explain this line and these results to the congress of their party? We can rack our brains in vain at a time when it is very easy for the Chinese «to settle» this matter: either to present it to the congress as a flower-garden, or to tell it nothing. Such a solution may seem surprising, but this is nothing to wonder at with the Chinese comrades, because they can say both to the congress and to the world: «We do not have to declare anything today, tomorrow you will see what you will see. You should trust us, because we are never wrong, never deviate, leave us in peace to work in secrecy because something will emerge from the darkness so brilliant that it will dazzle the world»! . . .

Monday December 23, 1974

No, Chinese comrades, with the Yugoslavs we are not «like the teeth with the lips»

Yu Chang, Deputy Foreign Minister of China, who was in our country for the celebration of the 30th anniversary of Liberation as a member of the delegation led by Yao Wen-yuan[57] went from here on a «friendly» visit to Belgrade . . .

When he returned to Peking, Yu Chang had a meeting with our ambassador, Comrade Behar [Shtylla].[58] . . .

In these talks, they did not fail to discuss the stand of Albania towards Yugoslavia, with the Chinese allegedly using our statements . . . **And «our friend» Yu Chang told Behar [Shtylla] in conclusion that he had told the Yugoslavs that this was how the friendship should be between the Yugoslavs and the Albanians, because the two sides were «like the teeth with the lips».**

The «Chinese Pope» gave his blessing to the «Yugoslav—

Albanian friendship» with a base revisionist Confucian parable. It is hard to know whether he said this from stupidity or because he was carried away in the «flood» of stereotyped formulas which they use, or because he wanted to tell the Yugoslavs: «We have a hand in this policy and approve it» . . .

How asinine! What perfidy! This «biblical» figure of the Chinese means that, according to him, we are at one with the Titoites in head, in heart and in body, that we follow the one policy and the one ideology! How can one call this foolishness? How can you call these things a slip of the tongue?! . . .

To hell with Yu Chang and the comrades who think like him in China . . .

Tuesday June 17, 1975

Strong Chinese economic pressure has begun, but we shall never give way
After the façade of the welcome, after the usual speeches with stereotyped formulae, Chou En-lai received Adil Çarçani and the other comrades of our government delegation for fifteen minutes at the hospital. He asked after our health, and as they were leaving, said: «**Tomorrow I am to have an operation, therefore I received you beforehand. I am having this operation to extend my life**». This could be the case but it could also be . . . «Farewell, don't ask to meet me again» . . .

The reply of the Chinese to our requests for credits and aid for the coming five-year period was despicable: the Chinese are according us only 25 per cent of the credits we sought, of which 50 per cent for projects and 50 per cent for materials. Military requirements are also included in these credits. This amount of aid is just enough to avoid saying we shall not accord you any.[59]

The reasons the Chinese give for this are a mockery: «**We are a very poor country**» However, five years ago, when they were a «**very much poorer country**» they accorded us a credit several times greater . . .

The Chinese make a friend of any state, any person, whether Trotskyite, Titoite, or a Chiang Kai-shek man, if he says, «I am against the Soviets». We are opposed to this principle. We know how to deepen the contradictions between the enemies of socialism, and we deepen them as much as we can, but first of all respect our principles. We always call a spade a spade . . .

It is clear that this stand from their side is part of a great imperialist-revisionist plot . . . **Their pressure . . . took concrete form in the military and economic plot headed by Beqir Balluku, Petrit Dume, Hito Çako, Abdyl Këllezi, Koço Theodhosi, Lipe Nashi, etc.**[60] The aim of these traitors was the liquidation of the Party, and its Marxist-Leninist leadership in order to turn socialist Albania into a revisionist country . . .

Agents of whom were the traitors we unmasked? This is not important.[61] They were mainly agents of the Soviets and the Yugoslavs, but the Chinese, too, have a hand in this . . . **Not only were Beqir Balluku and his group old agents of the Soviets, but they were also linked with the Chinese. The inimical strategic plan that Beqir Balluku was preparing was drafted on the suggestion of Chou En-lai. Beqir, himself, told us: «Chou proposed this plan to me», while we rejected his proposal as hostile. Beqir Balluku worked secretly in the direction that Chou En-lai proposed to him, that is, for «retreat to the mountains» and for «alliance with Yugoslavia and Rumania».**

. . .All these things occurred at that time when Beqir Balluku was organising the military plot and Abdyl Këllezi and Koço Theodhosi were sabotaging the oil industry and the economy in general. Can we call this co-ordination in aims and in time fortuitous? But when we liquidated the traitors' military putsch, when we struck the blow at Abdyl Këllezi and company, didn't the Chinese show us their wolfish snarl?

. . .I believe China has a hand in this plot, but which China? This is the hand of revisionist China . . .

Wednesday June 25, 1975

A hostile course of Chou En-lai and his group against Albania
The Chinese have finally determined the amount of the economic aid which they will accord us for the coming five-year plan. The commission of the two sides has met. The «famous» Li Hsien-

nien, well-known for his anti-Albanian feelings, headed the Chinese commission.

In a frank and friendly way, Adil [Çarçani] presented our opinion about the aid which . . . China accorded us . . .

Li Hsien-nien, this enemy of socialism in Albania, Chou En-lai's running-dog, gave Adil a disgraceful, brutal, hostile reply, saying: «Your proposals are not accepted. We shall not even examine them; our decision is definitive and approved by our whole leadership, including Mao Tsetung.» «We shall not budge a single yuan from what we have decided,» said Mr Li Hsien-nien. In other words, with this reply he wanted to say: «Take it or leave it; it is all the same to us, whatever you say.»

To the request that our opinions, which Adil also handed to Li Hsien-nien in writing, should be communicated to Comrade Mao Tsetung, Li Hsien-nien replied: «I shall give it to him, but don't expect any reply.» According to Li Hsien-nien, this meant: either **«Mao is firmly opposed to deigning to give a reply to the Albanian requests»**, or «I'm taking this exposition of yours, which I have no intention of giving Mao but will throw into the waste-paper basket.» . . .

Chou lost the fight to overthrow us from within and, since it was impossible to operate otherwise, he used the weapon of the economic blockade. He and his group think like revisionists, that we will be isolated, will die of hunger and will be brought to our knees. They think: **«There is nothing the Albanians can do».** And Chou En-lai repeated to Adil Çarçani his old diabolical plan: **«Unite closely with the other countries of the Balkans, regardless of the disagreements you have.» The dirty scoundrel, the pseudo-Marxist enemy! We have not been brought to our knees and we are not intimidated** . . .

Monday September 29, 1975

Rumania and China have the one line
What are these Rumanian revisionists with Ceausescu at the head, whom the Chinese love and support so much? . . .

There is no doubt that throughout history the Rumanian bourgeoisie has been renowned for its «love affairs». It has made «love» to all and sundry at all times. The bourgeoisie has done this with bourgeois France for example, the new revisionist bourgeoisie . . . is doing this with . . . all that give it money. This is clear to everybody, except the Chinese . . .

If there is the slightest trace of anti-Sovietism in Ceausescu, this comes from the fact that he is an adventurer of the Khrushchevite, Titoite, or similar type, who has got a job as a pander, indeed very likely with the knowledge and aid of the Soviets and the pander lives unharrassed by them in return for the services which he performs for them. He lives on the money he gets from the United States of America, the Federal German Republic and all those who pay him. The Ceausescu regime is a regime of corruption, bankruptcy, of personal and family dictatorship.

. . . The Rumanians are friends of the Americans . . . Ceausescu and Bodnaras became the «god-fathers» of the Sino-American friendship, which is similar to the Soviet–Rumanian, or Soviet–American relationships. They abuse one another for appearances' sake, but behind the wall they indulge in political, commercial and other sodomy.

. . . What is Ceausescu's anti-Sovietism based on? On nothing important . . . It is totally involved in Comecon, but raises some opposition, kicks out a little, but even the Bulgarians, who are as intimate with the Soviets as «their underpants», do this in Comecon . . .

Wednesday October 1, 1975

We must not merely expose the American imperialists but must fight them, too
Last evening, all of us from the Political Bureau and the Government had dinner with the Chinese ambassador on the occasion of the 26th anniversary of the proclamation of the People's Republic of China. The «Dajti» Hotel was packed with guests, a lavish banquet! China is ready to open its purse for lunches and dinners, but is tight-fisted when it comes to fulfilling some needs for our plan . . .

Naturally, during the talk we raised some problems. As always, the Chinese ambassador used the well-known platitudes and slogans, in other words, «baloney». He had just come from China and told us that «the biggest meeting which the State Council has organised» had been held in Tachai, and thus he began the well-known formulas about Tachai.[62] I said, «We have read that Teng Hsiao-ping and Chiang Ching delivered important speeches at Tachai. Could you tell us something about the content of these speeches, because *Renmin Ribao* tells us nothing?» The ambassador replied, «The same meeting was repeated in Peking, too». In other words with this he wanted to say, «I know nothing more» or «I am not authorised to tell you more than this». Despite this, I asked him, if he had the possibility to send us the speeches «so that we could benefit from their importance». «Without doubt,» he said. Of course, we will be waiting for them till . . . the millennium, like the other materials . . .

I told him about the hostile work of the agents of the Soviets and the Titoites, Beqir Balluku, Abdyl Këllezi . . . I stressed that these traitors were in the service of the Soviets, were saboteurs, slanderers, liars, etc. The Chinese ambassador listened and said only: «Like Liu Shao-chi and Lin Piao».

Then I continued the conversation about some key problems of the international situation and the aggressive role of the two superpowers . . .

Then the Chinese ambassador brought out the formula: «Chairman Mao teaches us to prepare for war, therefore we must store grain».

I replied: «What Mao says is right. Preparations for the time of war require grain, but also require modern weapons . . . There is only one road open to Albania to get weapons, that of our great ally, the China of Mao. If this road is closed to us, and it will be closed to us in time of emergency, socialist Albania will be fighting in encirclement».

The ambassador produced the other well-known formula: «We are very far behind because of the hostile work of Lin Piao».

This was too much for my patience, and I said: «This situation must be overcome without fail and as quickly as possible. Otherwise Mao's idea that war cannot be waged properly with conventional weapons cannot be fully applied. You Chinese judge matters correctly when you say that the Balkans is a point under threat of imminent attack by the Soviets. On this we agree with you . . . therefore we are greatly activising our defence. The Party has charged Mehmet [Shehu] with the task of the Minister of Defence. We shall not allow the enemy to set foot on our territory alive, but it will be superior in the air and on the sea, therefore we need weapons suitable to cope with these modern means that the enemy possesses» . . .

The «clever» Chinese ambassador turned the conversation back to the experience of Tachai!

Thus our conversation ended . . .

Thursday January 1, 1976

The zigzags of the Chinese line
. . . Another thing, which could lead one to a wrong judgement of the Chinese line, is their great secrecy about events. The Chinese leaders keep these events hidden with the greatest jealousy, and when something is announced, still it is only partial information, unclear, often incomprehensible and astonishing! The «explanation» about some event (I am referring to important events) comes unexpectedly, and this is proclaimed as the «perfect line» for years on end; then for one or two years it is mentioned with allusions, and later it is declared «openly» that it has been reactionary. «Openly», they say, for after two or three years of «speaking openly» about the mistakes and the people who have made the mistakes, it is announced that «the mistakes have been corrected and the people have been rehabilitated» . . .

Thursday January 22, 1976

The Chinese are not propagating the correct line of our Party
Volume 19 of my works has been printed and distributed in many languages.[63] The whole foreign world, friends and enemies of Albania are talking about the correct line and courage of our Party in its exposure of the Khrushchevite revisionists, and the struggle it has waged against them in defence of the purity of Marxism-Leninism and, in particular, in defence of the Communist Party of China. In China alone, nothing has been or is being said . . .

What is written in the Chinese press about our country is worthless. First of all, the press there does not forget to reprint the good things that are said in our country about China, while the other news amounts to banal accounts: This meeting was held, that rally was held, so-and-so spoke there, so-and-so spoke here, so-and-so arrived in Albania, so-and-so left Albania; they also publish sports news. But there is never mention that «this or that delegation of this or that Marxist-Leninist communist party went to Albania» . . . the political and ideological discussions between our two parties have long been reduced to absolute zero . . .

In regard to economic relations and aid to the army, these, too, have been reduced to the absolute minimum. Despite this, in appearance, the Chinese are bluffing and want to show that «Albania is their most loyal ally».

What significance should we place on these stands? Can the explanation be that the Chinese have been informed by their people with delay? This does not hold water . . .

Can it be that the Chinese need time to translate and study our materials? This does not hold water either, because they have a battalion of translators . . . why are they acting in this way? What is going on? There is no explanation other than this: there is sabotage from the Chinese side, they are not in agreement with the political line of our Party.

They do not want to propagate the correct line of our Party for these reasons:

. . . b) because the megalomania of the big party and great state exists;

. . . e) because they want us to curry favour with them, to speak and act the same as they do . . . They want us to become their servile minions. This, naturally, will never occur;

f) because they did not like the internal measures which we took against the enemies of the Party and state – Beqir Balluku, Hito Çako, Petrit Dume, Abdyl Këllezi, etc. Why? To what extent did the Chinese have a finger in their plot? One thing we do know: the Chinese comrades liked the line of the traitors of our country;

g) because the Chinese want to drive us from our Marxist-Leninist positions, want us to unite with the traitors Tito and Ceausescu, and to throw us into the revisionist cesspool . . .

Tuesday October 12, 1976

The tragedy of China[64]

... Mao Tsetung spoke with revolutionary catchwords about the «revolution», the «class struggle» and other questions of principle, but in practice he was a liberal, a dreamer, a centrist in the direction of the manipulation and balancing of the various currents which existed and intrigued within the Communist Party of China and the Chinese state. With such characteristics, Mao Tsetung was easily influenced by one or the other current; sometimes supported the one, sometimes the other.

What is obvious and true is that Chou En-lai was the greatest «Iago» in the Chinese Shakespearean drama. He was a rightist, he was a mandarin, a bourgeois and pseudo-Marxist. In the manipulations which Mao made, Chou En-lai manoeuvred with mastery. When the ship of one reactionary current with Chou En-lai on board was foundering, he rapidly abandoned that ship and ducked under the banner of Mao ...

Saturday October 23, 1976

This is what must have happened with «the Four»

Reading a report about a circular of the CC of the CP of China with a critical eye, in my opinion, it turns out that **all the things the Chinese are saying are make-believe and lies.**

... An ambassador of China to a Western state, after talking to our ambassador about the «plot of The Four», allegedly giving him confidential information, said: «**I am telling you in confidence that Chang Chun-chiao**[65] **is an agent of the Kuomintang and that Mao Tsetung long ago knew what evil people the four conspirators were, but he himself allowed them to come to Peking and to be appointed to the Central Committee and even to the Political Bureau**». What inquitous things they are concocting about these four! But how stupid they are!! Don't they understand that in this way they are exposing Mao himself? Or are they doing this deliberately ... precisely to «dethrone» Mao in retribution for what they have suffered from his vacillations and to further their ultra-revisionist and reactionary plans for the future. Understand these Chinese tricks if you can!

The revisionist putchists have gone so far as to describe Chiang Ching, in particular, as a «street-walker» and to distribute pamphlets against her in which they write in such filthy terms as to call her a «prostitute». The question arises: How could this «prostitute» have remained the wife of Mao Tsetung for 33 years, have borne him children,[66] been elected a member of the Central Committee and the Political Bureau of the Central Committee of the Communist Party of China? Where were these «valiant spirits» who are now spreading such monstrous slanders, which even the filthiest pornographic literature of the West is unable to match? It is self-evident that these people are agents of imperialism who are trying to discredit Mao, personally, by means of Chiang Ching, while allegedly upholding his banner, of course, just until they get over their difficulties. Even those few good things which Mao did for China, the revisionist putchists are sullying with such activities . . .

Thursday December 2, 1976

A party in disarray
We can describe the question of the Communist Party of China as something mysterious. In appearance it seems like a legal party, and so it is . . . Despite all this, however . . . [it] is a party which lives and acts as in illegality. Its congresses have been held rarely, the meetings of the Central Committee and those of the Political Bureau have also been held rarely and in the greatest secrecy, as if it were war time. Only the 8th Congress was held openly, with delegations invited from the sister parties, and the reports allowed to be distributed to them.[67] . . . *Renmin Ribao* merely writes long propaganda articles which hardly anyone can read, because they are filled with shibboleths, with quotations, with the same slogans that Mao Tsetung issued before liberation . . .

Our impression is that the Communist Party of China lives by slogans and acts on orders. Outside, even the people of the Chinese leadership, with the exception of Chou En-lai, speak to us and the others in quotations and slogans even about the most

varied and complicated situations. It seems as if «silence» has
been made the watchword, «give nothing away but try to get what
you can». This may be true, and there is something behind all this,
that is, either an unhealthy secrecy is being maintained even
towards comrades and friends, or the education by the party is so
stereotyped that nobody knows anything apart from the formulas
which are served up through the press and the radio. Both these
things are true.

**An incontestable fact is that the Communist Party of China,
with this «great» chairman and with these «outstanding» leaders,
still to this day has not a written, officially approved history of the
party**[68] . . . Where do the generations in China learn the history of
their communist party, with its good points and its mistakes?
Nowhere . . . Could they have some history of the Communist
Party of China which they are keeping secret? Such a thing is
impossible. Then why is it not written? . . . **It is difficult to write
the history of their party because it is hard for them to analyse its
line and struggle** . . . If they write such a document, those who
have to do this must assume the responsibility for its content . . .
Those who could write it, cannot write it from the Marxist-
Leninist angle, because they are not Marxist-Leninists.

. . . What is more, the history of the great liberation war of
China has not been written either . . . I am speaking of a scientific
history, and not of isolated articles in which the facts are written
like the legends of mediaeval «knights» and the leading knight is
Chairman Mao. We know that the war was waged, then why is
this rich history not written for people to study it? In my opinion
the reasons are the same as those I gave for the history of the
party . . .

December 6, 1976

Unstabilised leadership
. . . The right will retain «Mao Tsetung thought» in order to
propagate anti-communism in the world and will keep Mao
embalmed in a mausoleum. The Chinese right put Mao in a
mausoleum to elevate him to the same rank as the great Lenin . . .
   But, as I said above, the quotations of Mao cut both ways.

Apart from those which are known, the rightists are using other spoken or unspoken quotations of Mao, which they arrange just as they please, as serves them best. Where are these spoken and unspoken ideas of Mao found? In the air, in the memory of this or that person, or in records, formal or informal? Now Hua Kuo-feng has taken a decision and created a commission for the publication of Mao's works. The world at large knows only the four volumes of Mao's works written before liberation. After liberation there was almost nothing published, no report, no speech of Mao's. Astonishing!! Why did Chairman Mao, whose cult was built sky-high, not allow any of his jewels to be brought to light?! Or, were they jewels or charcoal and ashes?! Now Hua Kuo-feng is to bring out these jewels, but when and how is not known. He will feed the world with «dock leaves» . . . as for the genuine communists, they are not going to swallow them![69] . . .

March 9, 1977

The Chinese opportunists want the Communist world to sing to their glory
. . .The «famous» Keng Piao,[70] who is engaged in international matters in the Central Committee of the Communist Party of China, once told our ambassador in Peking: «We do not want the representatives of the Marxist-Leninist communist parties to come to China, but we can do nothing about it, because we cannot throw them out, . . . they are a hindrance to us» . . .

Tuesday June 7, 1977

Why is Tito going to China?[71]
. . . Tito . . . **will be welcomed with great enthusiasm and pomp by another renegade from Marxism-Leninism, Hua Kuo-feng.** Under his rule at present, and nobody knows for how long, Hua Kuo-feng has a population of 800 million, a whole continent, and the renegade Tito . . . will feel himself at home in Pyongyang and Peking. In Pyongyang, I believe that even Tito will be astonished at the proportions of the cult of his host [Kim], which has reached

a level unheard of anywhere else, either in past or present times, let alone in a country which calls itself socialist.[72]

. . . In fact Tito should be given his due. Regardless of the fact that he is a vile traitor, he is clever at intrigue, at double-dealing, at forming and dissolving combinations . . .

I think that Tito's work in China will be in favour of American imperialism and [to] the disfavour of Soviet social-imperialism.

. . . Tito will receive a pay-off from the three sides, from the two old superpowers and the new, rising superpower, which is «gold plating» the emblems of the «socialist» Republic of China . . . Mao himself was pro Tito and against Stalin, irrespective of the fact that he declared the opposite, that Tito had become incorrigible and must be ranked with Hitler and Hirohito. His successors, or Hua Kuo-feng, to whom Mao Tsetung allegedly said, «With you in charge, I feel at ease», «corrected» this renegade . . .

Meanwhile, Kim Il Sung thinks that the visit to Korea of Tito, whom he considers a great man, will give him even greater credit in the eyes of his own people in order to strengthen his personal cult. Kim Il Sung has great hopes in Tito and will welcome him with great cordiality and pomp, because he knows that Tito is the envoy of Carter, of the Americans.

. . . Tito is going to Korea to carry out negotiations on behalf of American imperialism with Kim Il Sung and not to get credits . . . [North] Korea is so deeply in debt itself that it is unable to meet its repayments.

In regard to the «third world», Kim Il Sung pretends to be not only a member, but possibly, also, its leader. He also has pretensions that the «Juche»[73] ideas, i.e., Kim Il Sung thought, should be spread throughout the world with great speed. All these pretensions do not upset Tito who, as we know, poses as the leader of the «non-aligned world» . . .

Saturday June 18, 1977

The Chinese are engaged in espionage and sabotage activity
Our ambassador in China reports that the Chinese have begun to put pressure on our students with the aim of making them their agents. This occurred with one of our students at the University of

Peking to whom one of the teaching staff made such a prop-
osition. Our student replied to him immediately with great indignation and went quickly to the embassy to report this occurrence.
This is villainous hostile work. We had foreseen this . . .

Such is the «close», «immortal» friendship and other piffle
which the Chinese say in connection with us . . . But they are
doing something else, too. In the course of conversation they go so
far as to try to learn from our students where their parents work,
how many people each has at home, what work they do.
Apparently, they are building up a file on every Albanian who
goes to China for study or work . . . The Chinese are doing this
here, too, in our country. The Hsinhua correspondent is the head
of their agency. We have formed the conviction that the employees of the embassy, right down to the interpreters, are not
career diplomats or party cadres, but agents of the Chinese
intelligence service . . .

In China, the officials . . . remain as cold as ice to our people . . .
There are Chinese ambassadors abroad who are so brazen, so
shameless as to make you vomit. They say to our ambassadors,
«There is no friendship like that between China and Albania; it
will be everlasting; there is no force which can break this
friendship, we love Albania heart and soul», and other such
rubbish . . .

Just like the Soviets, the Chinese too, are carrying on subversive
work in all states throughout the world where they have diplomatic representations.

I think that both the Soviets and the Chinese have this work of
subversion even more highly developed than many capitalist
states . . .

Saturday July 9, 1977

A basket of crabs
Between the Korea of Kim Il Sung, the Yugoslavia of Tito and the
China of Hua Kuo-feng a silent, allegedly ideological, conflict has
broken out. This conflict really has no aspect of an ideological
conflict, but is over who is to seize the banner of false ideologies.
Each of these three fighting cocks wants superiority in the group-

ings of «worlds» which they have invented together with the
imperialists, that is, the «non-aligned world», the «third world»,
and the «developing world».

. . . Since [North] Korea is one of the states which cannot live
without foreign aid, it now finds itself at the crossroads because its
creditors are no longer providing it with loans, for the reason that
it has not paid its debts. World capital is no longer interested in
investing in Korea.

Despite this the Korean press demands that the world should
bend the knee to Kim Il Sung and shamelessly declares that he is
the «greatest leader the world has seen up till now»! . . . Kim Il
Sung . . . is trying to bring about the unification of the two Koreas
under his flag.

This «great leader» of long standing has this day-dream, and in
order to give himself authority he has planned welcomes and
farewells to top personalities in Pyongyang, as well as all kinds of
international seminars and meetings. For example, there are plans
for a big meeting of the youth of the «third world» in which the
youth of the «non-aligned world», the youth of the «developing
world» and the devil and his son are to take part. Of course, one
can guess what such a meeting, which will be a «meeting of the
youth» only in name, will turn out to be, while in that «net» cast
so widely there will be all kinds of fish and crabs, people of every
tendency and ilk, from sold-out agents to vagabond onlookers
who are ready to take «free» trips all over the world not to learn,
of course, but just for pleasure.

Our people, of course, explain the stand of our Party to all and
tell them that we . . . will not in any way take part in this
masquerade which will be held in Pyongyang, because our Party is
a serious party . . .

Durrës, Thursday August 11, 1977

Politics is no bed-time story
I am not going to dwell at length on the great effect which the
article «The Theory and Practice of the Revolution» has had in the
world . . .

Now China has mobilised all its hangers-on, the pseudo-

Marxist parties which it finances, which are concocting muddled articles to defend the Chinese theses which cannot be defended. The Chinese have sunk so low as to wind up a lackey in support of their anti-Marxist stands, using a certain Hill from Australia, a person with two faces (or better to say, with many faces, because we do not know whom else he serves . . .) who posed as a friend of our Party . . . [There is no evidence for this – Ed.]

As to the «reasoning» in support of the Chinese theses, it makes one weep, like some of the lamentable articles in the newspaper *Renmin Ribao*.[74] . . .

Durrës, Monday August 15, 1977

Articles with stale «theorizing»
I have been reading four or five Chinese articles which, taken together, make up a single article entitled, «The Division into Three Worlds by Chairman Mao Is a Marxist-Leninist Definition». This . . . is the only allegedly theoretical article which the «great» Communist Party of China is publishing about the theory of «three worlds» and is a reply to the *Zëri i popullit* article, «The Theory and Practice of the Revolution». It is truly an article to be derided and laughed at, because, in this exposé or analysis, if we can describe it as such, there is absolutely no ideological argument, nothing but a line-up of some general political statements.

August 21, 1977

The main ideas of the 11th Congress of the Communist Party of China[75]
. . . Meanwhile Yeh Chien-ying, the representative of the army, which brought to power the clique of Hua Kuo-feng, of Teng Hsiao-ping, himself and Chou En-lai, praised Hua Kuo-feng. Indeed he said explicitly that . . . «Hua Kuo-feng is the man who will lead us until the beginning of the 21st century», etc.

What does such a declaration show? It shows the dishonesty of what Yeh Chien-ying said earlier, namely, that the coming of Hua Kuo-feng to the head of the party was done in complete order . . . his statement that Hua Kuo-feng would stay at the head of the party for another 30 or 40 years, means that there will be no democratic elections in the Communist Party of China, means that Hua Kuo-feng was appointed by Yeh Chien-ying and the army, and it is in their hands whether he stays in power ... Of course, these Chinese leaders, like Mao, Yeh Chien-ying or Hua Kuo-feng live to a great age, like the cardinals of the Vatican who die about ninety because they have nothing much to worry them and take things easy.

... [But] putsches will take place in China one after the other, and this Mao Tsetung has not foreseen badly. Perhaps he was mistaken in the periodicity of putsches, but he foresaw them.

... But the main thing about the Congress was its closing session in the form of a deification. The histories we have read about ancient Rome and Byzantium say that the emperor Constantine, while going to war against Maxentius, saw in the sky a cross on which these words were written: «*In hoc signo vinces*» («Under this sign you will triumph») ... **At this congress, Hua Kuo-feng had arranged his hair like that of Mao Tsetung; he had allowed that thick black hair of his, as straight as a porcupine's quills, to grow, had cut it and combed it cunningly and given his head the form of Mao Tsetung's with his forehead uncovered like Mao's. Hence, for this, too, we could say: «*In hoc signo vinces*». With his haircut, Hua Kuo-feng assumed the appearance of Mao Tsetung, and with this sign «he will triumph»** ...

Tuesday August 30, 1977

Tito «meets» Mao in the mausoleum

Last evening I saw the Italian and Yugoslav television broadcasts in connection with Tito's visit to Peking ... I noticed great confusion at the airport, one could not make out where Tito and Hua Kuo-feng were. They both appeared a couple of times, then all that could be seen were the flowers of the people and the school pupils that had gathered at the airport. A great confusion of people, police, Hsinhua correspondents, rushing around, pushing one another, and not allowing the main personages to appear, struck the eye. Tito appeared briefly with Hua Kuo-feng tagging along behind. The great nervousness of the Chinese was obvious.

Apparently they were afraid that something might happen to Tito, therefore they had filled the airport with plainclothesmen. Even when the limousine drove into Tien An Men,[76] a lack of order and discipline was apparent. The scene was quite different in Korea, where nobody moved from the footpaths and the squares. They danced, pranced and waved their flowers and every movement was done in an orderly way . . .[77]

Thursday September 8, 1977

The revisionist wind of Tito is blowing towards the East
This evening I saw the return of Tito from the Soviet Union, Korea and China, on Belgrade television . . .

We criticised Khrushchev. All the water of the Volga river cannot cleanse him of his sins; and it is the same with Tito. Now that Tito has gone to China not just the Amur but even the Yangtze cannot wash him clean, or the new Khrushchev of China, either.[78] On the contrary, the whole of China is becoming aware of the stench of Hua and Teng. The Titoite wind of the West is blowing towards the East . . .

Thursday September 8, 1977

Revisionist manoeuvres. Anti-Marxist structure
. . . The question of Chinese communism has been an enigma to me . . . This doubt arose in my mind immediately after the Bucharest Meeting, and it was aroused because of the timorous stand the Chinese adopted there.[79] From the Chinese side, the first to speak at Bucharest was Peng Chen. Teng Hsiao-ping came from China to the Moscow Meeting with a report very conciliatory towards the Khrushchevites. But Khrushchev's activity compelled Teng to change this report and make it somewhat more severe . . .

There is deception, also, in the use of the Marxist terminology with which Mao Tsetung and the clique around him disguised their capitalist and revisionist bourgeois activity. When we read the four volumes of the works of Mao Tsetung we drew some conclusions and these conclusions were positive. Indeed . . . it is not easy to find there any problem treated theoretically in an incorrect way. Mao issued many slogans which appeared simple but also seemed vague, philosophical, Marxist. In fact, the reality of the development of Chinese society was completely different. Then, what was occurring? **Why were Mao's writings not in accord with the actions of this all-powerful man? This is the question, the unknown factor of this problem, and there is no other way to explain this enigma except with the fact that when these four volumes of the works of Mao were compiled and prepared for publication they were, of course, edited by competent people**[80] **who understood Marxism and who must have given a Marxist-Leninist colour to Mao's revisionist aberrations.**

Sunday November 27, 1977

There is no way we can soften our words against Chinese revisionism
. . . China has pretentions to becoming the dominant power in the world. It dreams of overtaking not only the Soviet Union, but also the United States of America, but its loins, as they say in Gjirokastra, hence its real strength, especially its economic and military strength, are insufficient for it to be able to realise the hegemonic policy which it dreams of . . .

Friday December 2, 1977

Communists are being killed in the world – the Chinese revisionists couldn't care less
The news agencies report that the chairman of the Communist Party of the Philippines, together with a group of other comrades of the Central Committee of the Party, has been arrested by the dictator Marcos.

The Communist Party of the Philippines is a militant party but it is being completely sabotaged by the Chinese revisionists. Why should the murderer Marcos not do such a thing when Mao Tsetung himself had established close links with the executioners of the Communist Party of the Philippines? The dictator Marcos and his beautiful wife, with her dress cut so low that her tits almost hung out, were received two or three times in audience by Mao. They were praised and congratulated by him . . .

The Philippine dictator is wreaking havoc against the Marxist-Leninists of the Philippines . . . But the Chinese revisionists couldn't care less.

They did the same thing with the Communist Party of Indonesia led by Aidit, when Suharto massacred 500,000 people.[81] . . . The Chinese couldn't care less about the other parties of the Far East either . . .

Thursday December 8, 1977

Gloomy Chinese panorama
. . . All the reactionaries affected by the Cultural Revolution have been returned to their former positions and have the key posts under their control. Not only are they all reactionaries, revisionists, Trotskyites and capitalists, but they are also old. Thus, the leadership of China, both of the party and the state, is again in the hands of reaction, the old reaction with no drive, but with evil hearts and a spirit of vengeance, which is now attacking the younger generation and throwing them out in the street . . .

As we are told, suspicion reigns among the people, who dare not speak even to one another because they are denounced to the organs of police and the army and immediate measures are taken against them. The country is so big that nobody knows where these people are taken. Are they shot, hanged, or put into concentration camps? Their relatives know nothing. These are facts which are told to our people by Chinese friends.[82] . . .

Monday December 26, 1977

Can the Chinese revolution be called a proletarian revolution?
. . . Mao Tsetung was not a Marxist-Leninist. He did not betray himself, as you might say. We say that Mao is a renegade, is an anti-Marxist . . . We say this because he tried to disguise himself with Marxism-Leninism, but in fact he was never a Marxist.

In general, we can say that in some directions the revolution in China had certain features of a tendency to develop on the socialist road, but the measures taken stopped halfway, or were annulled . . . All these things must be understood by the Chinese people, and they must be understood outside China, too, because, unfortunately, the whole development of that country . . . has gone down in history as a proletarian revolution, which in fact it was not, has gone down in history as if China is a country which is building socialism, which is not true, either.

. . . In one of my notes, I had said that the myths must be exploded, and I had in mind that precisely the myth of Mao Tsetung, that myth which has described him as a «great» Marxist-Leninist, has to be exploded. **Mao Tsetung is not a Marxist-Leninist but a progressive revolutionary democrat, and in my opinion, this is the angle from which his work should be studied.**

. . . The views of Mao Tsetung should not be studied merely from the edited phrases in the four volumes which have been published, but **must be studied in their practical application,** and they have been applied in a period not like that of the bourgeois-democratic revolution [in] France, when, in its own time, the bourgeoisie was a progressive class. The ideas of Mao Tsetung developed in the present period of the decay of imperialism, the final stage of capitalism, hence, at a time when proletarian revolutions are on the order of the day . . . The theory of Mao Tsetung, «Mao Tsetung thought», which emerged in these new conditions, was bound to cloak itself with the most revolutionary and most scientific theory of the time — Marxism-Leninism, but in essence it remained an anti-Marxist theory, because it is opposed to proletarian revolutions and goes to the aid of imperialism in decay.

Therefore, in the ideology of Mao Tsetung we shall find reflected all the aspects of the ideas which capitalism and imperialism have invented during the many years of the period of their decline and decay. «Mao Tsetung thought» is an amalgam of ideologies, beginning from anarchism, Trotskyism, modern revisionism à la Tito, à la Khrushchev, «Eurocommunism» à la Marchais-Berlinguer-Carrillo,[83] and finally down to the use of Marxist-Leninist formulas. In all this amalgam we must also discern the old ideas of Confucius, Mencius,[84] and other Chinese philosophers, which had a very great influence on the formation of Mao Tsetung's ideas and his cultural-theoretical development. Thus it is hard to define a single line or, so to say, a clear line of the Chinese ideology. Even those aspects of it which may be said to be a kind of distorted Marxism-Leninism, have an Asiatic seal and character, have the specific character of an «Asiatic communism», are a sort of «Asiacommunism» the same as «Eurocommunism», . . . In the Chinese ideology we shall find heavy doses of nationalism, xenophobia, religion, Buddhism, marked hangovers of feudal ideology, not to mention many other hangovers which exist and were not systematically combated, not only during the period of the national liberation war, but especially during the period of the establishment of the state of people's democracy . . .

6
MEHMET SHEHU AND HIS STRANGE END

Who Was Shehu?

For well over three decades Mehmet Shehu was the most prominent figure in Albania after Enver Hoxha. He was generally recognised as by far the most able military leader during the war. In 1948 he became the country's second Minister of the Interior, replacing the disgraced Xoxe. After the death of Stalin, when the posts of premier and head of the Party were divided, Shehu replaced Hoxha as premier in July 1954 – a post he held until his death in December 1981. After the purge of Balluku in 1974, Shehu also became Minister of Defence. He represented Albania frequently at the United Nations in New York. He made several trips to China. And he accompanied Hoxha on many important journeys, including that to the Moscow Conference in November 1960.

Shehu was born in 1913, the son of a devout Muslim Sheh of the Halveti sect.[1] He studied at the American Technical School in Tirana and then at the Naples Military Academy, from which he was fired by the fascists. He commanded the Fourth Battalion of the 'Garibaldi' International Brigade in the latter part of the Spanish Civil War. He spent the years 1939–42 in a camp in France, where he joined the Italian Communist Party. On his return to Albania he rapidly rose to become the main partisan military commander; he headed the First Shock Brigade from the moment of its formation in summer 1943 – though he was passed over, inexplicably, for the position of Chief of Staff. He led the armed forces which liberated Tirana in November 1944.

Until his death, Shehu was consistently portrayed as the key hardliner, both personally and politically. He was often described as 'brutal' and 'ruthless'; one source claims that Shehu personally slit the throats of seventy Italian prisoners in one single incident (killing prisoners was, however, universal practice on both sides in Albania during the war). Khrushchev states in his memoirs that Tito told him (Khrushchev) that Shehu had personally strangled Xoxe.[2]

What caused the breach between Hoxha and Shehu is not clear. (Interestingly, such a breach was predicted during the war by two of the British officers most closely associated with Shehu.) Hoxha says that Shehu committed suicide 'in a nervous crisis' on 18 December 1981 after being subjected to severe criticism for arranging the betrothal of his son to a woman whose family allegedly contained 'six to seven war criminals', and thus attempting to create a scandal which would undermine the

Tirana regime.[3] After Shehu died, Hoxha claims, it was discovered that he was a multiple agent.

Hoxha's lengthy account is mainly interesting for two reasons (apart from his self-blinded willingness to lay out at such length his paranoia and to fail to weigh the implications as regards his own lack of vigilance). First, Hoxha avoids mentioning any policy difference with Shehu; Shehu's behaviour is simply attributed to the fact that he was a long-time foreign agent. Secondly, after describing Shehu's alleged *political* machinations from the 1930s onwards, Hoxha couches his account of the final crisis in the classic terms of an Albanian folk tale – 'bad' betrothals, 'scandal' and shame. He ropes in the whole Shehu family: 'Mehmet Shehu had turned, or was to turn, his whole family into a nest of agents, a family of vipers.' And Hoxha refers to 'the hostile and immoral elements of his [Shehu's] own family'. In traditional Albania such things led to a showdown by the only means possible – a shoot-out. Many Western sources think this is what happened – although Hoxha, of course, dismisses this version.

Hoxha devotes about forty pages to a retroactive re-examination of Shehu's entire career. Having been at the American school, Shehu must have been an American agent.[4] So if he went to Spain, he must have been sent. Being three years in a camp in France is also suspect, of course, so there he was recruited by . . . British intelligence. He was taken out of the camp by . . . the Gestapo (and the SIM [Italian Military Intelligence], of course!), and brought back to Albania. He naturally also became an agent of the Yugoslavs during the war – and the Yugoslav envoy, Dušan Mugoša,[5] even arranged the betrothal of Mehmet with his future wife (and co-agent), Fiqrete Sanxhaktari. Later on, Shehu conspired with the Russians. And he also colluded with the Greeks, although he is not specifically called a Greek agent. Shehu is linked to almost every one of the many major plots, real and alleged, which dot Albania's postwar history. For example, Hoxha claims that in September 1960, on his way to the UN, Shehu met and conspired with Tito, Harry T. Fultz ('of the American CIA') and Randolph Churchill ('an Intelligence Service agent' masquerading on the passenger list as a journalist) on board the *Queen Elizabeth*.[6] But how to explain Shehu's unwavering public adherence for over three decades to the Hoxha line? Deep cover, of course. Hoxha even has a suggestion that the Western (US, British and Yugoslav) intelligence services encouraged Shehu to push for the alliance with China as a way to facilitate the weakening of socialism in Albania.

There are three main points. The first is that Hoxha criticises Shehu for 'sectarian' behaviour during the war. This appears to be an attempt to

make Shehu (and Liri Gega) scapegoats for acts of cruelty which undoubtedly occurred.

Second, Hoxha's claim that Shehu was a British agent. Hoxha backs up
this allegation with two sorts of quotations: one from (alleged) communications, e.g. the letter to Mugoša quoted in note 5; the other
quotations are from British official documents (SOE), some of which are
in the PRO. These quotes are genuine. In my opinion, they do not
demonstrate that Shehu was a British agent, but they do raise important
issues.

The key document is a report from Force 399 (SOE HQ) in Bari, dated
11 November 1944, summing up the consensus after debriefing twelve
British agents just out of Albania. In a section titled 'British Influence', the
document claims that 'the majority of the country have an underlying
pro-BRITISH outlook and would welcome a BRITISH occupation.' It
goes on: '. . . there are clearly some who appreciate what Britain has done
and who are fundamentally against the present Party policy, but unable
to express their views openly . . . It is . . . important to consider the
potential opposition within the Movement and its possible leaders.' The
second (of five) names then listed is that of Shehu, described in these
terms: '. . . a personally ambitious and vain man, who has been kept
down by the Party for some time. He is undoubtedly the most respected
and important military figure within the movement. He has recently been
subordinated to [Dali] NDREU, Comd [commander] 1 Corps. He is a
Communist but his personal ambition exceeds his layalty [sic] to the
Party.' The document ends with the words: '. . . every effort should be
made to prevent the elimination of those pro-British elements already
known to us and to endeavour to build these up unobtrusively.' Interestingly, the third name on the list is that of Haxhi Lleshi (q.v.), described as
'a friend of Mehmet Shehu's'.[7]

In itself, this does not prove anything except that the British were still
indulging in wishful thinking. But it is important background, particularly when taken in connection with other information. SOE agents in
Albania spoke much more highly of Shehu than of any other Partisan; he
was the only Albanian under whose command British officers placed
their men. It is therefore, prima facie, highly likely that the British (or
some British) tried to 'recruit' Shehu, even if only in the sense of trying to
establish good working relations with him. This supposition is strengthened by the fact that the SOE group working with Shehu in mid-1944
stated *at the time* that they envisaged a break between Shehu and Hoxha.

It is also important that in the middle of the civil war, the British officer
on the spot, Major Smith, reported that 'Shehu believes possibility of a

compromise exists' – which ran counter to Hoxha's stance at the time.

In the present state of knowledge, it is impossible to state with certainty what Shehu's relationship with the British was – either then (when it might have been close), or later (when it might have been nonexistent). But there is another, unexplored, angle to the affair. Hoxha's book in which he quotes the British documents dates from 1982. In 1981 Tirana published the book *From the Annals of British Diplomacy* by Arben Puto. This is 230 pages long, and it shows that Puto got *past* the file containing the information about Shehu (this file was then open; moreover, there are other interesting items in the file). But that file is not quoted in Puto's book. It seems certain that the Albanian researcher found this information about Shehu – which was undoubtedly dynamite, given Hoxha's suspicious mind; that he brought photocopies back to Tirana, which were handed over to Hoxha; and that it was the discovery of this document which detonated Hoxha's suspicions which, as we now know, rested on almost forty years of fractious relations with Shehu.

The third key point is that Hoxha links the break with Shehu to the riots and disturbances in the Kosovo in 1981. If there was a real political issue on which Hoxha and Shehu disagreed (and any such disagreement has only one outcome in Albania: the elimination of the loser, then invariably described as an 'agent' of foreign powers) the Kosovo seems the most plausible candidate (the other two would be the succession[8] and possible relinking with the West or the Soviet bloc after the break with China). Hoxha does link the Kosovo disturbances to the 'plot' to eliminate him, but he conspicuously fails to mention a political disagreement with Shehu over how to handle the Kosovo issue, which must have been a major topic within the Albanian regime.

Hoxha's re-examination leads him to some difficult conclusions. In particular, he has to confront the fact that, according to him, every single Minister of the Interior since Liberation was a foreign (mainly Yugoslav) agent. This, naturally, is why nothing was discovered for so long. Hoxha conspicuously fails to raise the question of his own dereliction of duty as head of the Party in allowing such a state of affairs to last for almost forty years. After a lucid critique of the official Chinese fairy tale about Lin Biao's 'plot' to kill Mao (which he likens to 'James Bond'), Hoxha, apparently blithely unaware of the irony, writes his own version of the 'plot' to 'get Enver'.

There is a saying in the Balkans: 'Behind every hero stands a traitor.' With his elimination of his oldest colleague, only a few years before his own death, Hoxha showed that whatever other faculties were flagging, his powers of suspicion were not. The classic Balkan drama was staged once again – Hoxha's last great show.

. . . Mehmet Shehu came to Albania and fought not as a communist and partisan, but as a mercenary sent by the Anglo-Americans to serve their plans for the future of Albania. *

After his suicide, a programme written by his own hand in 1942, at the time when he came to Albania, was found in his safe. This was nothing but a bourgeois-democratic programme which made no mention at all of socialism and the communist party, but of many parties, just as the Anglo-American missions and the reactionary groups which supported them tried to bring about in the period immediately after Liberation. We are now in possession of documents which fully prove that Mehmet Shehu was an agent of the [British] Intelligence Service, too. In these documents figure his name and some coded pseudonyms such as BAB-008, etc. From them it emerges that Mehmet Shehu had even received money for his services and the centre instructed to leave him at peace, which meant that he was one of those potential agents that are left, in the language of spying agencies, «dormant» so as to be used when needed. *

Following the death of Stalin, the team that came to power condemned Beria, the chief of the Soviet KGB, for many violations of the law. We asked Mehmet Shehu to examine whether mistakes had also been made in the organs of our Ministry of Internal Affairs of which he was the head. Mehmet Shehu was afraid that his links with the Soviet KGB or with the Western secret agencies had been discovered and he might suffer the same fate as Beria. He went to the Soviet ambassador Levichkin . . . and sought Soviet protection, because, according to his statements, «Enver Hoxha regards me with suspicion»[9] . . . Levichkin advised Mehmet Shehu to come to me and make his position clear, while ensuring him that he, Levichkin, would protect him . . .

Meanwhile,[10] our Party pursued the course of Marxism-Leninism and Mehmet Shehu «endorsed» its line, indeed, he greatly advertised his role in these situations and, of course, in the

* See p. 376
* See p. 376

eyes of the Americans and the Yugoslavs posed as if it was he that inspired this course . . . The Americans and the Yugoslavs knew this, while all the Western secret agencies were in agreement that their «boy» should thunder against them with such statements as «We are dancing in the wolf's mouth», etc., etc. They accepted any abuse, content that their agent was climbing higher and higher and might turn the helm of our Party and state towards the West . . .

The events of Czechoslovakia in August 1968 came about and the Party decided to denounce the Warsaw Treaty, to take our country out of this ill-famed treaty *de jure*, although *de facto* we had withdrawn from it at the end of 1960 . . . Mehmet Shehu . . . presented this to his patrons as his personal victory. The American agency (and those linked with it . . .) thought that Albania was left isolated and undefended, and since China was far away, it considered that the time had come when our country would turn its face towards the West.

The trump card of the Western and Titoite agencies, Mehmet Shehu, was brought into action. In 1972[11] he went to Paris for an operation, accompanied by the same team that accompanied him to the UNO, plus his wife Fiqret Shehu. There he made contact with a top figure of the American CIA, who said to him: «What are you doing? You are getting old, you must act!»

Mehmet Shehu reported to him about the situation and the plots which were being prepared (by Beqir Balluku and Abdyl Këllezi and company). The CIA recommended that he should act, but without compromising himself. It proposed three variants for the elimination of Enver Hoxha: 1) through a motor accident; 2) through shooting with a rifle from a distance; or 3) with delayed-action poison . . .

In Paris Mehmet Shehu was also given a sophisticated radio receiver-transmitter which his eldest son, who was an electronics engineer, installed in his house . . .

In fact, Mehmet Shehu had turned, or was to turn, his whole family into a nest of agents, a family of vipers . . . in 1972 he was directed by the American CIA to work out concrete plans to overturn the situation in Albania in favour of the West, to set in motion and urge in this direction the agents known or unknown to him, regardless of whose they were, Yugoslav, Greek, British, Italian, and others, but avoiding compromising himself . . .

[Major] demonstrations took place in Kosova at the beginning of 1981 . . .

Apart from the slanders that these demonstrations had allegedly been inspired by Albania, the Yugoslavs had to take immediate measures to «discredit» the «Stalinist» Albanian leadership in order to disturb and overturn the sound situation in Albania, as well as to confuse the patriotic-revolutionary forces in Kosova.

The [Yugoslavs] demanded that their agent Mehmet Shehu act . . . they demanded that Mehmet Shehu send his wife urgently to Paris. The demonstrations [in Kosova] took place in March, while she went to Paris in April 1981. There an envoy gave her the poison which had to be administered immediately to Enver Hoxha . . .

In the conditions under which I travelled the motor accident was ruled out, while the attempt with a rifle was too sensational and with unforeseeable dangers . . .

Mehmet Shehu was afraid, . . . Therefore, he appealed to his major patron, the American CIA [arguing] . . . that they should not act hastily, as the Yugoslavs demanded, because they were not well prepared; the poisoning or physical liquidation of Enver Hoxha could be put off until March 1982 (during the winter holidays), while up till that time they could undertake some action which might cause a split in the Party and encourage the liberal element . . .

In this context Mehmet Shehu arranged the engagement of his son to the daughter of a family in the circle of which there were 6 or 7 fugitive war criminals . . . Such an engagement could not fail to attract the attention of the public. And it was done precisely with the aim of attracting public attention and causing a sensation. If it were accepted by the Party, it would lead to splits and liberalism among others, too, in the Party, the Youth organisation, etc. If it were not accepted by the Party, measures would be taken against Mehmet Shehu, not imprisonment, of course, but demotion, removal from his position or even expulsion from the Party. This would cause a sensation and the Yugoslavs could use it to . . . discredit the leadership of the Party of Labour of Albania and especially Enver Hoxha, who, as they have repeated over and over again, is «eliminating» his collaborators, as Stalin did.

However, the plans did not work out as Mehmet Shehu had intended. The Party intervened immediately, the engagement was broken off, Mehmet Shehu was criticised by the comrades for this major political mistake, he was required to make a profound self-criticism to find the sources of such an error and it was left that this would be done after the 8th Congress of the Party. [The 8th Congress of the PLA took place on November 1–8, 1981.] He did not expect this. He tried to make «some other mistakes»: he completely neglected his report for the 8th Congress of the Party, presented it late and with flagrant political errors and the Political Bureau rejected it . . . In the Congress he purposely sat like a «repentant sinner» and this was so obvious to the delegates and the TV viewers that they began to ask one another why.

Meanwhile, the question of Kosova was becoming dangerous . . . The Yugoslavs saw that nothing happened [in Albania] either before the Congress or after it . . . This was of no benefit to the Titoites . . . who were . . . wanting disorder to occur in Albania at all costs. Therefore, on the eve of the meeting of the Political Bureau, . . . the Yugoslav embassy in Tirana . . . sent its agent and contact man Feçor Shehu[12] to Mehmet Shehu to transmit the «ultimatum» of the UDB that «Enver Hoxha must be killed at all costs, even in the meeting, even if Mehmet Shehu himself is killed.» So hard-pressed were the [Yugoslavs] . . . that they decided to «destroy» their trump card, their superagent, provided only that something spectacular would occur which would «shake socialist Albania and the Party of Labour of Albania to their foundations»!

At ten o'clock at night, on December 16, 1981, Feçor Shehu went to Mehmet Shehu's home and transmitted the order of their secret centre.

On December 17, the discussion commenced in . . . the Political Bureau. All the comrades, old and new, took part in the discussion, and resolutely condemned Mehmet Shehu's act of engaging his son to a girl in whose family there were 6 to 7 war criminals.

They expressed their dissatisfaction with Mehmet Shehu's self-criticism . . . (On the day following the suicide, all these contributions to the discussion, which had been tape-recorded, were heard just as they were made by the whole Plenum of the Central Committee and the meetings of party activists.)

The criticisms by the members of the Political Bureau were strong, open and Bolshevik, but only «the recording of a serious reprimand on his registration document» was demanded as sanction. This was the spirit in which I, too, had prepared my contribution . . . However, because the meeting went on late, my contribution was not delivered that day.[13] Thus, it was left that the meeting would continue the following day. At the end of the discussion on the first day, I said to Mehmet Shehu:

«Reflect deeply all night and tomorrow tell us in the Political Bureau from what motives you have proceeded. Your alibi for the engagement does not hold water, something else has impelled you in this reprehensible act.»

What I said alarmed Mehmet Shehu, . . . The «bold» Mehmet Shehu thought all night about how to escape from the tight spot, . . . Apparently, he judged matters in this way: «I am as good as dead, the best thing is to save what I can,» and he decided to act like his friend Nako Spiru, to kill himself, thinking the Party would bury this «statesman», this «legendary leader», this «partisan and fighter in Spain» with honours, would not sully his reputation but would say that «the gun went off accidentally» (as he suggested in the letter which he left), and thus, at least, he would not lose his past and his family would not suffer.

Together with his wife he flushed the poison down the WC and charged his eldest son with dismantling and removing the compromising parts of the radio which he had installed for him.

Fiqret Shehu . . . agreed to the suicide of her husband coolly and cynically, provided only that their «historic» past and she and her sons were saved.

However, they had reckoned their account without the innkeeper. As soon as they informed me about Mehmet Shehu's final act, within moments I proposed that his suicide should be con-

demned, . . . and the Political Bureau expressed its unanimous
condemnation of the act of this enemy.[14]

The UDB and the CIA were left biting their fingers. The foreign
news agencies related the fact as we had given it, that Mehmet
Shehu «committed suicide in a nervous crisis». Here and there
some comment secretly paid for by the Yugoslavs was made.
However, even the Yugoslavs were unable to exploit this act in
their official press apart from charging a student newspaper in
Zagreb to write about the «drama» which had occurred at the
meeting of the Albanian leadership (according to the version
which the UDB had planned). According to this newspaper,
«. . . Mehmet Shehu fired some shots with a Chinese revolver of
this or that type and calibre (!), but Enver Hoxha's comrades
killed him. The fate of Enver Hoxha is not known . . .»

A scenario modelled on westerns with gunfights which occurred in the saloons [at] the time![15] . . .

Here I must point out that the dangerous plot of Mehmet
Shehu, just as other plotters and plotting groups before it, were
discovered through the strength and vigilance of the Party and its
leadership and none by the State Security. Why? Because Koçi
Xoxe . . . was minister of internal affairs until 1948. Then, he was
succeeded by Mehmet Shehu to be followed later by Kadri
Hazbiu[16] and, more recently, by Feçor Shehu. Unfortunately . . .
none of them was suspected to be an agent, while the three of
them, just like Koçi Xoxe, were active agents, mainly of the
Yugoslav UDB, who covered up the dirty linen and crimes of one
another.

After the final traumatic blow we dealt them, the foreign secret
services, and the Titoite UDB among them, in their rage and
despair turned to forms and methods which we had long experience of . . . : they tried to feel our pulse and shake us through a
group of hired mercenaries and bandits! . . . But we, too, were
quick to riposte to them: if in the 50's there were cases when we
needed even 4–5 days, and at times even more, to detect and wipe
out their bands of saboteurs now we needed no more than 5 hours
to discover and wipe out the terrorist band of Xhevdet Mustafa,
which was sent by the UDB.[17] . . . We are well aware that even
after this the foreign secret services . . . will not sit idle. However,

they will never catch us asleep. We will never be lacking in vigilance.

Let everyone understand clearly: the walls of our fortress are of unshakeable granite rock.

APPENDICES
NOTES
BIOGRAPHICAL NOTES
INDEX

Appendix I. The Kosovo Question[1]

The Kosovo is an area in south-west Yugoslavia in which the vast majority of the population (77–78 per cent) is of ethnic Albanian origin. The area is at present an 'autonomous province' within Serbia, one of the six republics making up the Federal Republic of Yugoslavia.

The Kosovo and its inhabitants have been a subject of dispute and contention for a long time. The main issues are:

1. *Historical rights and wrongs*;
2. *The stances adopted during the Liberation struggles*;
3. *What to do now?*

1. Albanians can claim to be the oldest identifiable ethnic group in the territory, going back at least to the middle of the second millennium B C. Slavs arrived much later, at the beginning of the second millennium A D. The Kosovo has traditionally been the richest agricultural area occupied by ethnic Albanians and – most importantly – it was the centre of Albanian nationalism in the nineteenth century: the League of Prizren, established in 1878, was the key force in the Albanian national movement against the Turks.

However, the territory, although with few Slav inhabitants, was also the cradle, as Serbs see it, of the Serbian empire, and the site of the most important battle against the Turks, on Kosovo field in 1389.

Albania was dismembered by the great powers in 1913. Kosovo ended up later as part of Yugoslavia, wherein the Albanian population was extremely badly treated, and many emigrated to Turkey and elsewhere.

2. During the Second World War the Kosovo was integrated into a 'Greater Albania' under Italian occupation when Yugoslavia was dismembered after the German occupation of Yugoslavia in April 1941. The evidence is that much of the population of the Kosovo supported the left-wing partisan forces of both Albania and Yugoslavia, both of whom operated in the area. But the Germans also raised a 'Skanderbeg s s' of some 12,000 men in the area.

Enver Hoxha and the Albanians have claimed that during the war the partisan forces and the radical political movement clearly expressed their wish that the population of the Kosovo be allowed to exercise the right of self-determination after the war was over. Initially, it seems, the Yugoslav C P backed this position, but in mid-1943 altered its stance and argued that nothing should be determined until the war was over.

The Albanian partisans liberated the whole of Albania proper by the end of November 1944, without the assistance of a foreign army. The Yugoslav partisan forces were aided in the liberation of Yugoslav territory by the Soviet Red Army. Albanian partisans from both Kosovo and Albania proper took part in the liberation of the Kosovo. However, in the winter of 1944–5 there was a major uprising in the Kosovo, which appears to have been a *nationalist* movement against the reimposition of 'Yugoslav' (seen as Serbian) rule. This uprising was crushed with heavy loss of life.

Enver Hoxha claims that during his discussions with Tito in 1946 Tito said that 'Kosova and the other regions inhabited by Albanians belong to Albania and we shall return them to you, but not now because the great-Serb reaction would not actually accept such a thing.' The Yugoslavs deny that Tito said this.

The trouble is that in the period between the Liberation of Albania at the end of 1944 and Tito's break with Moscow in June 1948, Belgrade had designs on Albania. The obvious solution, therefore, was for Albania to 'annex' the Kosovo, within the context of Albania itself becoming part of a Balkan federation, presumably dominated by Yugoslavia. This, of course, was not to be.

3. Yugoslavia now admits that the takeover of the Kosovo in winter 1944–5 was carried out with considerable harshness. The official Yugoslav position is that until 1966, when Ranković, the chief of the secret police, was removed, things were pretty bad, but improved thereafter.

The position of Tirana is that Yugoslavia failed to carry out its wartime commitments – in particular to allow the population of the Kosovo to express their wishes about the status of the territory. In fact, the Kosovo (under the name of the Kosmet, or Kosovo and Metohija) was made part of Serbia without the local population having any say. There is considerable ground for Tirana's claim that the Yugoslav central government chose to appease Serbian nationalism by denying the Kosovo the right to self-determination as a republic within the Yugoslav federation, let alone the right of secession.

In late March to early April 1981 major riots occurred in the Kosovo, with many deaths. A curfew and a state of emergency were imposed (for longer than in Poland). Some of those involved called for closer ties to Albania. But there is no evidence to support the thesis that the revolt was either a pro-Tirana secessionist movement or a right-wing 'pro-capitalist' one. Most of those taking part were young, many of them from the new university in the capital, Priština. In 1981 unemployment in the Kosovo stood at 27.5 per cent – and this was after very high emigration. The standard of living in the Kosovo, which is the most densely populated part of Yugoslavia, was one quarter the national average and falling, relative to the rest of Yugoslavia. Relations between the ethnic Albanians and the Slavs (mainly Serbs) are bad.

Leaving aside the question of what commitments were made, not made, or retracted during the years of the war and immediately afterwards while relations between Yugoslavia and Albania seemed good, Tirana is on good grounds in saying that Belgrade is discriminating against the ethnic Albanians in denying them the right to form a republic. (Equally, Belgrade's reasons for doing so are clear.) It is also manifest that the Kosovo is the poorest part of Yugoslavia (but it always has been).

The Kosovo represents two quite different things for the two states. For Belgrade, it is a backward region, populated mainly by an unwelcome national minority, bordering on a state (Albania) with which relations are frosty and difficult. For Tirana, the Kosovo is not only the historical centre of Albanian nationalism and resistance to the Turks, but also where some 1.7 million ethnic Albanians live – one-third of all Albanians in the world.

Appendix II. The Corfu Channel Incidents and Albania's gold[1]

Relations between Albania and Britain have been frozen since the end of 1946 as a result of two linked issues – events in the Corfu Channel during 1946, and possession of some £50 million worth of gold.

What is often referred to as 'the Corfu Channel Incident' was in fact three incidents. The first occurred on 15 May 1946, when Albanian shore batteries fired at or near British ships in the Channel. The second, and key, incident occurred on 22 October when two British warships struck mines in the Channel, with the loss of forty-four lives. The third took place on 12–13 November when British warships conducted mine-sweeping operations in the Channel.

Leaving aside the question of whether or not the Corfu Channel is a waterway through which other states have 'right of passage' for their warships (there is no actual *need* to pass through it since the channel between Corfu and Italy is much wider), and the exact status of Albania's right to exclude foreign ships in the interests of its own security, the basic issue boils down to: did Albania lay the mines which the two British warships hit in October. And, if it did not, did it know about them, or was it in any sense responsible?

It is generally agreed that Albania could not have laid the mines. It did not have the equipment, or the personnel. This is acknowledged in private by senior figures in the British Foreign Office. Must Albania have known they were there – and if so, could it have done anything about them? This is more problematic.

After the October incident, Britain took the case first to the UN Security Council and then to the International Court at the Hague. The court ultimately found (by eleven votes to five) that Albania was responsible because it must have known about the mines. However, re-examination of the evidence shows that this decision is not well founded. Britain's key witness, a Yugoslav defector, subsequently disappeared without trace. Core elements in the British case were mutually contradictory. It was never demonstrated that Albania must have known about the mines. Suspicion is fuelled by the fact that the British government, which has opened the papers on the May incident, has put an unusually long embargo (fifty years) on the documents relating to the October tragedy. Equally little examined until recently is what the British warships were doing there anyway. Anglo-Albanian relations were at a very low ebb (as were Anglo-Yugoslav relations). Britain was considering establishing diplomatic relations with Albania; the Admiralty signalled that the Attlee government first 'wish to know whether the Albanian government have learned to behave themselves' and suggested some warships put this to the test. The precise degree of testing is not clear: at a minimum, the British were challenging what Albania saw as its legitimate security concerns.

The bulk of informed opinion now considers it most likely that the mines were laid by Yugoslavia – but no one wants to say so. The case started before the break between Tito and the Communist bloc, but the International Court delivered its judgment *after* the break. The West does not want to rock the boat with Yugoslavia. Albania does not want to acknowledge that it did not have sovereignty over its territorial waters. The Yugoslavs have no interest in acknowledging responsibility. The official Albanian position is that Britain laid the mines.

The International Court awarded Britain £843,947 in compensation. While negotiations were under way with Albania, Britain impounded a much larger sum in gold (7100 kilos) which had originally been looted from Albania by the Axis powers and then seized from them by the Allies. Albania refuses to pay any compensation, on the grounds that it was not responsible. Britain refuses to return the gold, now worth about £50m. Title to the gold, which would seem to belong unequivocally to Albania, is legally complicated by the fact that the postwar Tripartite Commission (USA–UK–France) first allotted the gold to Albania, in 1948, and then annulled this decision two years later.

Notes

INTRODUCTION

1 – Quotes from Peter R. Prifti, *Socialist Albania Since 1944: Domestic and Foreign Developments* (Cambridge, MIT Press, 1978), p. 9; *ACKR*, p. 177; *TK*, p. 434.

2 – He did give occasional interviews, but not to representatives of the Western media; the last known interview, with the head of the Franco-Albanian Friendship Association, in December 1984, is published in *Le Monde*, 13 April 1985.

3 – Some reports say Hoxha visited Paris in secret for medical treatment; I have not been able to confirm these rumours, though they are plausible.

4 – Apart from the six volumes of memoirs and diaries, extracts from which are included below, Hoxha also published *Reflections on the Middle East 1958 –1983: Extracts from the Political Diary* (Tirana, 1984); *Laying the Foundations of the New Albania* (Tirana, 1984); *Childhood Years: Memoirs* (in Albanian); and *Among Plain People* (in Albanian).

5 – This is based on one of the most reliable sources on Albania: William E. Griffith, *Albania and the Sino-Soviet Rift* (Cambridge, MIT Press, 1963), p. 47; cf. ibid., p. 24: 'It seems quite probable . . . that Tito also tried to eliminate Hoxha.'

6 – *TT*, p. 73 (see text p. 31).

7 – Prifti, cit., p. 33; biography based on sometimes conflicting information in: Jean Bertolino, *Albanie: La sentinelle de Staline* (Paris, Seuil, 1979), pp. 72ff; *Yearbook on International Communist Affairs* (Hoover Institution); Ramadan Marmullaku, *Albania and the Albanians* (London, C. Hurst, 1975), pp. 66ff; Branko Lazitch, *Les Partis Communistes d'Europe* (Paris, Les Iles D'Or, 1956), pp. 68–9; the only reference to his earlier life in the volumes extracted here is the phrase 'when I was a student in Paris' (in *AAT*, pp. 332–3).

8 – *RC*, I, p. 466.

9 – *TK*, pp. 351ff.

10 – Vladimir Dedijer, *Tito Speaks: His Self Portrait and Struggle With Stalin* (London, Weidenfeld & Nicolson, 1953), p. 313.

11 – I am grateful to SOE officers for giving me their frank views on Hoxha. One British officer said Hoxha bore a striking physical resemblance to Orson Welles; another said that he found him 'rather wet . . . a bit like a seedy student'.

12 – Prifti, pp. 33–4. Probably the most brilliant analysis of the specificity of Hoxha and of his regime is that by Arshi Pipa, 'The Political Culture of Hoxha's Albania', in Tariq Ali, ed., *The Stalinist Legacy: Its Impact on Twentieth-Century World Politics* (Penguin, 1984); this is also an excellent source on the recurrent purges which have marked the regime.

13 – See, especially, *EIU*, pp. 227ff.

14 – In the pamphlet, *On the Liberation of Women in Albania* (Toronto, Norman Bethune Institute, 1976), pp. 15–16; the last phrase appears in Prifti as "leads to Nazism in politics, and to sadism in sex' (p. 105).

15 – *TK*, p. 236; *RC*, II, p. 148.

16 – *Khrushchev Remembers* (Penguin, 1977), vol. I, p. 508. (Henceforth *KR*.)

17 – *TK*, p. 199.

18 – *RC*, II, p. 529.

19 – *TT*, p. 629.

20 – *KR*, II, p. 316.

21 – Cited in Griffith, p. 71; cf. Mikoyan's speech at the 22nd Congress of the Soviet Communist Party, October 1961.

22 – Michael Kaser, 'A New Statistical Abstract from Albania', *Soviet Studies*, vol. 34, no. 1 (January 1982), pp. 123–5, for assessment of some fairly recent figures. Other useful sources on the economy include: Prifti, cit., ch. 4; René Dumont, *Finis les lendemains qui chantent . . . : Albanie, Pologne, Nicaragua* (Paris, Seuil, 1983), part I; Adi Schnytzer, 'The Socialist People's Republic of Albania', in Peter Wiles, ed., *The New Communist Third World* (New York, St Martin's Press, 1982); Wolfgang Russ, *Der Entwicklungsweg Albaniens: Ein Beitrag zum Konzept autozentrierter Entwicklung* (Meisenheim, A. Haim, 1979) for interesting analysis of *auto-centré* development; excellent material on Soviet–Albanian economic relations in Griffith, cit., and in Robert Owen Freedman, *Economic Warfare in the Communist Bloc* (New York, Praeger, 1971); I am particularly grateful to Berrit Backer for allowing me to consult her outstanding paper, 'Coping with the "Imperialist-Revisionist" Blockade – Albania in the East–West Context' (MS, 1982), and for much invaluable background.

23 – Dumont, p. 17.

24 – Schnytzer, p. 305; the same source estimated aid at about 3 per cent of GNP until 1975.

25 – Hoxha, *SW*, II, pp. 775; 775–6. Interestingly, his interlocutors, whose views are not recorded, came from a predominantly Muslim country.

26 – 'On Some Aspects . . . of Albanian Women', cit., p. 21; slightly different text in *SW*, IV. For excellent information on the position of women in Albania, see Prifti, ch. 5; cf. Maurice T. Maschino and Fadela M'rabet, 'L'Albanie ou la fierté nationale', *Le Monde Diplomatique*, November 1980, esp. p. 39; for two very good more critical views on the real position, see Dumont, pp. 69ff; and Bertolino, cit. H. W. Tilman, a very fair and rather pro-Partisan member of the British mission during the war, noted that women did all the heavy work in the partisan areas and the men conspicuously refused to help, in *When Men and Mountains Meet* (Cambridge University Press, 1946) p. 116.

27 – See Prifti, ch. 7, and Marmullaku, pp. 75–8, for good surveys.

28 – A decree dated 23 September 1975 said: 'Citizens who have inappropriate names and offensive surnames from a political, ideological, and moral viewpoint are obliged to change them' (Prifti, p. 164); curiously there is no sign that this occurred, at least among those with Muslim names.

29 – *SW*, II, 445; for Hoxha's later ruminations on the history of Islam, see 'The

events which are taking place in the Moslem countries must be seen in the light of dialectical and historical materialism' (1980) in *RME*, pp. 355ff.

30 – *RME*, p. 22 (= 1965); attacks on the Vatican (*RC*, II, p. 41), China (ibid., p. 20) and Carrillo (*EIU*, pp. 239–40). Dumont states fairly that in 1981 it was hard to see signs of religious practice in Albania; but he also shrewdly observes that 'the religion best adapted to clandestinity is Islam' (p. 61).

31 – *RC*, II, p. 520. *International Herald Tribune*, 2 August, 1985.

32 – According to Prof. Paul Milliez, President of the Franco-Albanian Friendship Association (*Le Monde*, 13 April 1985).

33 – I am grateful to Berrit Backer and her paper cited in note 22 for many valuable observations on this theme.

34 – *RC*, I, p. 232.

I WORLD WAR II AND ITS AFTERMATH

1 – *AAT*, pp. 14–15. Hoxha does not exaggerate the extent of British indifference. In July 1941, the influential official Pierson (later Sir Pierson) Dixon wrote: 'We have never supported the cause of Albanian independence and are even less disposed to do so now that the prospects of stimulating Albanian resistance to the Italians are so much less real than they were before the collapse of the Balkans.' (FO 371/29715.) Apart from its indifference to Albania's right to exist, Dixon's remarks show a patronising inability to understand the situation. Resistance was just about to increase greatly – and not because it was 'stimulated' from the outside.

2 – See Sir Andrew Ryan, *The Last of the Dragomans* (London, G. Bles, 1951), esp. ch. 14, for (uncritical) observations.

3 – Information on this important episode is scanty. Useful background and research (with some errors) in Elisabeth Barker, *British Policy in South-East Europe in the Second World War* (London, Macmillan, 1976), ch. 5. Julian Amery, *Sons of the Eagle: A Study in Guerilla War* (London, Macmillan, 1948), ch. 2. This interesting, if overwritten, book unfortunately remains a much used source for many later accounts, even though it is a very poor authority on most of the key issues; Amery was never with the Albanian partisans. For Tirana's views, see Hoxha, *AAT*, 20ff; and Arben Puto, *From the Annals of British Diplomacy: The Anti-Albanian Plans of Great Britain During the Second World War According to Foreign Office Documents of 1939–1944* (Tirana, the '8 Nëntori' Publishing House, 1981), part I. For the postwar involvement of British agents, Nicholas Bethell, *The Great Betrayal: The untold story of Kim Philby's biggest coup* (London, Hodder & Stoughton, 1984).

4 – The founding of the Albanian Communist Party is a subject of unresolved dispute. The official Albanian position is in *History of the Party of Labour of Albania* (Tirana, 2nd edn, '8 Nëntori' Publishing House, 1982), ch. 1 [henceforth *PLA*]. The Yugoslav version is given by Vladimir Dedijer, *Il Sangue Tradito: Relazioni Jugoslavo–Albanesi 1938–1949* (Varese, Editoriale Periodici Italiani, 1949) [*Blood Betrayed: Yugoslav–Albanian Relations 1938–1949*: Italian translation of *Jugoslovensko–Albanski Odnosi* (Belgrade, Borba, 1949)]. Useful back-

ground in William E. Griffith, *Albania and the Sino-Soviet Rift* (Cambridge, Mass., MIT Press, 1963), pp. 9ff; see also Sarah Whittall, 'The Origins of the Albanian Communist Party', *Mashriq* – Proceedings of the Eastern Mediterranean Seminar, University of Manchester, 1979–82; Bernhard Tönnes, *Sonderfall Albanien* (Munich, Oldenbourg, 1980), part II, ch. 5; Bertolino, with an excellent 'Postface' by Eric Vigne, 'Le guru et son avatar: Stalinisme et fait national en Albanie'. Peter R. Prifti, *Socialist Albania since 1944: Domestic and Foreign Developments* (Cambridge, Mass., MIT Press, 1978), is an extremely good source on all matters. See also the valuable text by Stephen Peters, a member of the American Military Mission in Tirana, 'Ingredients of the Communist Takeover in Albania,' in Thomas T. Hammond, ed., *The Anatomy of Communist Takeovers* (New Haven and London, Yale University Press, 1975).

For the founding of the LNC and the ANLA (below), see especially Prifti, cit., chs. 2 and 3. For wartime developments, cf. Enver Hoxha, *Selected Works* (in English) Tirana, '8 Nëntori' Publishing House, 1974), vol. I [henceforth: Hoxha, *SW*]; and *Laying the Foundations of the New Albania* (Tirana, '8 Nëntori', 1984); and *Problems of the Anti-Fascist National Liberation War of the Albanian People and the Socialist Construction in the PSR [People's Socialist Republic] of Albania* (Tirana, '8 Nëntori' PH, 1983), and *Précis d'histoire de la lutte antifasciste de libération nationale du peuple albanais 1939–1944* (Paris, Nouveau Bureau d'Edition, 1975).

5 – Moving and irrefutable testimony to the popularity of the Partisans can be found in H. W. Tilman, *When Men and Mountains Meet* (Cambridge University Press, 1946), e.g.: '[the LNC] embraced all classes, all political opinions, all religions, and a good three-quarters of the people of south Albania' (p. 108); cf. ibid., pp. 114, 153. Cf. the report from Lt. Col. Wheeler cited below (note 21). Popular support for the Partisans in northern Albania and the Kosovo was confirmed to me by several British liaison officers.

6 – Stevan K. Pavlowitch, 'Dedijer as a Historian of the Yugoslav Civil War', *Survey*, vol. 28, no. 3 (autumn 1984), p. 104 (a review article on the second volume of Dedijer's *Further Contributions Towards a Biography of Josip Broz Tito* (Rijeka, Liburnija, 1982)).

7 – On Mukje, see Prifti, cit., pp. 17–18; cf. Ramadan Marmullaku, *Albania and the Albanians* (London, C. Hurst, 1975), pp. 50–51; the official Tirana version is in *PLA*, and Hoxha, *SW*, I, and Hoxha, *AAT*, pp. 237–8.

8 – Interesting observations on German policy in the memoirs of the chief special political envoy for the Balkans, Hermann Neubacher, *Sonderauftrag Südost 1940–1945: Bericht eines fliegenden Diplomaten* (Göttingen, Musterschmidt Verlag, 1952, 2nd edn).

9 – For the controversy, see refs. in note 4; Griffith, pp. 9ff, refers to later observations by Dušan Mugoša.

10 – Milovan Djilas, *Conversations with Stalin* (London, Hart-Davis, 1962), p. 131, and Djilas's later reflections in *Rise and Fall* (London, Macmillan, 1985). *Rise and Fall* contains much new information on Yugoslav-Albanian relations during and immediately after the war; in it Djilas describes his visit to Albania in

May 1945 and provides sharp portraits of Xoxe, Hoxha, Spiru and others. He also reveals hitherto unknown details of his conversations with Stalin and of the role Yugoslav-Albanian relations played in Belgrade's break with Stalin. Djilas also confirms the substance of many of Hoxha's accusations against Yugoslav policy vis-à-vis Albania.

11 – Prifti, cit., pp. 197–8.

12 – The 1st National Conference of the ACP was held at Labinot, near Elbasan, in central Albania, 17–22 March 1943.

13 – This episode is described in extract below, pp. 157–159.

14 – CPY: Communist Party of Yugoslavia; NLA: National Liberation Army. The national question to which Tempo refers was particularly complex in the Balkans (not least because Stalin and the Comintern regarded Yugoslavia as an artificial creation); the Italians had given Kosovo to Albania; the Germans had given Macedonia to Bulgaria, so that during the war Albania had a common border with Bulgaria.

15 – Hoxha's note. Full reference: Svetozar Vukmanović Tempo, *Revolucija Koja Teče: Memoari* [*The Revolution Which Flows* [on]: *Memoirs*] Vol. 1 (Belgrade, Komunist, 1971); also in German as *Mein Weg mit Tito: Ein Revolutionär erinnert sich* (Munich, 1972). Hoxha has cut from the quote – without indicating that he is doing so – the words that Xoxe went 'in the name of the leadership of the Albanian CP'.

16 – PRO: FO 371/29715, November 1941; Tönnes, p. 433.

17 – Barker, 'British Policy . . .', cit., p. 174; it is useful to read Barker together with Puto.

18 – *AAT*, p. 72; Fanny Hasluck held the rank of Lt. Col. in SOE; apart from trying to teach bored SOE recruits basic Albanian by getting them to recite nursery rhymes, she distinguished herself by her fervid and unrealistic support for the Balli Kombëtar. As late as 9 January 1944, when the LNC was clearly the major force in the land, she wrote: 'The Albanian Civil War is ending . . . Soon most of the country will go BALKOM. Already the only important leaders left to the LNC are Myslim PEZA and Baba FAJE and, in a minor degree, Xhelal NDREU. The defection of at least the first two looms ahead. We must consequently, reckon with the BALKOM for our war effort.' (Fortnightly Appreciation, PRO: FO 371/43549.) A note in the file records: 'the head of the Albanian Section warns me that the compiler – . . . Mrs Hasluck . . . – is considerably prejudiced in favour of the Nationalist "Balkom" . . .' It may be added that this report came just before a major memorandum from 'Billy' McLean which concluded that 'Our policy should be to back the Partisans with all possible material aid as they are the only military force worth backing in the country.' (FO 371/43549.)

19 – Hoxha reproduces the text of Davies's recommendation in *AAT*. pp. 137–8 (PRO: FO 371/37145): see this volume, pp. 375–6; cf. Puto, pp. 151ff, for background; Barker, p. 179. As an example of rewriting (or censoring) history, even Hoxha would be hard pushed to beat Davies's achievement: in his autobiography, *Illyrian Venture: The Story of the British Military Mission to Enemy-Occupied Albania 1943–1944* (London, The Bodley Head, 1952), Davies

omits all mention of his recommendation and heaps criticism and abuse on the Partisans.

20 – Davies's account of the ambush in *Illyrian Venture*, cit., ch. 8. Hoxha's version in *AAT*, pp. 144ff. Hoxha's allegation that the Davies group may have been betrayed to the Germans by a captured British officer was regarded as plausible by one SOE officer I interviewed. For the second McLean mission (April–October 1944), see Amery, *Sons of the Eagle*; David Smiley, *Albanian Assignment* (London, Chatto & Windus, 1984).

21 – Wheeler's recommendation in PRO: FO 371/43551; cf. Puto, pp. 186–8, which alters Wheeler's text. In this report, Wheeler stressed that his decision was taken on military grounds, but he added: 'from what I have seen of the L.N.C. they are perfectly capable of running Albania, and to the satisfaction of the populace. The L.N.C. Party is extremely well organized and, considering the lack of communication in the country, well controlled.' Cf. Tilman, cit. The proof of Balli Kombëtar collaboration with the Nazis comes from the fact that it was a Balli–Nazi group which ambushed Davies in January 1944 and from the fact that the German political emissary Neubacher confirms Balli collusion (*Sonderauftrag*, cit., p. 108). A delirious 'Manifesto' put out by the Balli near the end of the civil war denounces the British and McLean's mission in harsh terms for giving an 'important moral and material contribution . . . to Bolshevism'. It says that when McLean and Smiley first arrived, 'Albanian public opinion believed that they were agents of the Third International in disguise.' An indignant note passing on the manifesto within SOE dismisses it as wildly inaccurate, and a scribbled annotation makes the important point that 'Actually we have had more BLOs with the Nationalists & Zogists than with FNC [= LNC]' (Boxshall to Laskey, 5 October 1944, FO 371/43554).

22 – FO 371/43551.

23 – For Tilman, see refs. in note 5; reports from Major Richard Riddell and Capt. Reginald Hibbert, confirmed in interviews. See also the interesting review of the Bethell and Smiley books by Hibbert in *International Affairs*, vol. 61, no. 2 (spring 1985).

24 – The first official OSS mission did not arrive until May 1944. It was headed by a very ineffectual figure, Tom Stefan, whom Hoxha treats with some disdain. There were individual US agents operating in Albania by winter 1943–4 (FO 371/43549).

25 – Hoxha was particularly incensed by the fact that Capt. David Smiley blew up the key bridge over the Shkumbini River, the Haxhi Beqari bridge, in July 1943 (Davies, *Illyrian Venture*, pp. 117–18; Hoxha, *AAT*, pp. 108–9; Smiley, *Albanian Assignment*, pp. 78–80). Smiley's action made sense in short-term military terms, but Hoxha's objection made more sense: by blowing up the bridge, the British effectively blocked the Partisans from moving into the northern part of Albania until after spring 1944, during which time the British tried to build up anti-Partisan forces in the north. It should also be said that the new roads built by the Italians were both a novelty and a considerable asset for Albania which the Partisans could reasonably ask not be destroyed by outsiders.

26 – Information from a BLO who witnessed the German officer (a major) arrive at Hoxha's HQ – and leave alive: the only case witnessed during the war.

27 – *TT*, p. 61 ('borrowed' by Tempo); *TK*, p. 11.

28 – *AAT*, p. 239.

29 – E.g. *TK*, pp. 387–9, and *TT*, p. 612, re meeting with Mikoyan in Moscow in February 1960: cf. text below, pp. 221–222.

30 – *AAT*, pp. 75–6.

31 – *AAT*, p. 34.

32 – *AAT*, p. 61. McLean confirmed the inaccuracy of part of Hoxha's account by assuring me that he (McLean) did not like chocolate (interview, London, 27 June 1984).

33 – *AAT*, pp. 85–92 (with cuts); cf. Davies, *Illyrian Venture*, pp. 76ff.

34 – Lt. Col. Arthur Nicholls, who was severely wounded in the January 1944 ambush and died shortly thereafter from gangrene and other complications. He was awarded a posthumous George Cross.

35 – In fact, Davies (known as 'Trotsky' – which caused considerable consternation to Hoxha) was only 43 at the time, but looked much older.

36 – Davies met the Balli leaders on 8 November 1943; see Barker, p. 178; Davies, *Illyrian Venture*, pp. 87ff. That Hoxha was not entirely wrong about government influence on the BBC is shown by many items in the archives: see, for example, a note by D. Howard, dated 17 November 1944: 'I think we might get BBC to pay slightly more attention to Hoxha, but we must warn them not to overdo it.' (FO 371/43564.)

37 – It has not been possible to compile a comprehensive estimate of British aid to the LNC. One official report (PRO: FO 371/43549) describes it as 'puny'. Tilman, cit., p. 132, says there were about three or four planeloads per month arriving in his area in September–October 1943.

38 – Haxhi Lleshi (born 1913 near Dibër/Dibra in a *bajraktar* family) was Chairman of the Presidium (head of state) from 1955 until 1982. Much information on events in Peshkopia in Peter Kemp, *No Colours or Crest* (London, Cassell, 1958). In fact, as the PRO files show, Major Riddell was under few illusions about the relative value of the LNC and the other forces in his area; he was the only BLO to place SOE agents under Albanian command – in this case under the command of Mehmet Shehu.

39 – Frederik Nosi, who had attended the American school in Tirana, was a nephew of the leading right-wing politician, Lef Nosi. After the war Frederik Nosi became a leading judge, prominent in trials of opponents of Hoxha.

40 – Davies, *Illyrian Venture*, p. 88.

41 – Although Hoxha seems to have had a general distaste for dogs, his dislike in this case seems well founded. Davies's own description of his bulldog (named after the SOE HQ, Biza) makes him sound a menace: 'He . . . seized Albs [sic] by their baggy trousers, and generally grinned and made a thorough nuisance of himself.' (*Illyrian Venture*, p. 73). The 'beautiful collar' Hoxha mentions was engraved with a Union Jack and had been specially parachuted in from Cairo. Albania had no tradition of pampering animals.

42 – Fan Noli, a bishop in the Orthodox church, had been head of a short-lived radical government in June–December 1924, which formed a brief democratic interlude between Zog's first and second periods in power.

43 – Edith Durham, among whose works *High Albania* (1909) was reissued by Virago, 1985. The passage above refers to Fanny Hasluck.

44 – There is a time jump in Hoxha's narrative; the SOE agents named did not get to Northern Albania until April 1944 (though the basic point is fair). Julian Amery became Minister of Aviation (1962–4). McLean became Conservative MP for Inverness, 1954–64.

45 – Baba Faja was a priest of the Bektashi sect, a branch of Sunni Islam and the least strict of all Muslim groups. The Bektashi were in effect a diluted form of Islam used by the Turks to win slack converts on the fringes of the Ottoman empire. The Bektashi accounted for about 25 per cent of the Muslim population of Albania. Baba Faja was powerless in the LNC (and a heavy drinker), but important as window-dressing vis-à-vis Islam. He was reportedly shot dead by the head of his monastery after Liberation.

46 – Babë Myslim, usually known as Myslim Peza (and from Peza), was a leading outlaw under Zog; he was an excellent fighter, with a powerful reputation in his area, and considered a major asset to the LNC. For a vivid description, see Kemp, *No Colours or Crest*, pp. 132–4.

47 – Apparently Major George Seymour.

48 – Gogo Nushi was one of Hoxha's closest colleagues and a full member of the Politbureau from 1948 until his natural death.

Shule was the nom de guerre of Kristo Themelko, later a member of the Politbureau and Chief of the Political Directorate of the Armed Forces, purged for pro-Yugoslav tendencies after the 1948 break.

49 – Pp. 99ff.

50 – On Mukje cf. Hoxha, *SW*, I, pp. 161ff. Accounts in Griffith and Prifti. In fact there were three LNC delegates, Dishnica, Gjinishi and Abas Kupi, though Hoxha rarely mentions the latter, as he left the LNC immediately afterwards. Interestingly Dishnica (who was a medical doctor), although severely criticised in public for his role at Mukje, and associated with two men subsequently vilified by Hoxha, was made Minister of Health in the early post-Liberation government.

51 – Anastas Lula (or Lulo), pseudonym 'Qorri' (below), and Sadik Premte, pseudonym 'Xhepi', had both been members of a group called *Të Rinjte* (Youth) which had originally broken away from the 'Korçe' group of Communists headed by Hoxha. In principle, this would seem to be enough to damn them; but in fact Hoxha's closest ally until his (natural) death, Hysni Kapo, was also a member of the Të Rinjte group (Griffith, *Albania and the Sino-Soviet Rift*, p. 13).

52 – This conference was held clandestinely in Tirana, in early April 1942 (*PLA*, pp. 83ff; Hoxha, *SW*, I, pp. 3ff).

53 – March–April 1941.

54 – Stojnić stayed on as Yugoslav ambassador to Tirana until October 1945. Djilas confirms the substance of Hoxha's accusations against Stojnić in *Rise and Fall* (pp. 112–113).

55 – Ramadan Çitaku was one of the main Partisan leaders and a member of the Politbureau until November 1944 when he was expelled under alleged Yugoslav pressure.

56 – Pandi Kristo was co-opted onto the Politbureau at the same time as Sejfulla Malëshova; he had been a member of the same group, *Puna* (Work), in Korçë with Hoxha before the formation of the ACP. He was put on trial in 1949 together with Xoxe and sentenced to 20 years' imprisonment for pro-Yugoslav tendencies.

57 – Some of Ranković's remarks on Xoxe (and Hoxha) to Stalin are recorded in Vladimir Dedijer, *Tito Speaks: His Self Portrait and Struggle with Stalin* (London, Weidenfeld & Nicolson, 1953), p. 281.

58 – Odriçan: September–October 1944; Berat: October–November 1944. The warmth of Hoxha's relationship with Spiru emerges from letters published in Hoxha, *SW*, I; e.g.; 'I miss you a lot, my old comrade in bad times', 'Do you ever spare a thought for us poor fellows here, surrounded and bored to death?' (pp. 267, 261). The latter was written while Hoxha and the Shtab were surrounded in early 1944; the first quote after they had broken out of the encirclement in March 1944.

59 – See refs. in note 21; cf. Barker, p. 180.

60 – *AAT*, 301ff; see esp. p. 303, where Hoxha writes that even after he spoke angrily to Palmer, 'Palmer always maintained his typical English aplomb, took notes, thought carefully before he spoke and replied to me tactfully and diplomatically.' There are major inaccuracies in Hoxha's accounts of conversations with Alan Palmer and his liaison officer, Capt. Marcus Lyon, e.g. that in *AAT*, pp. 285ff. (Interviews, 9 and 10 April 1984.)

61 – Barker, p. 183; similar sentiments were shared, especially about Amery, by many of Palmer's colleagues in SOE in Albania.

62 – *PLA*, p. 174; Stefanaq Pollo and Arben Puto, *The History of Albania: from its origins to the present day* (London, Routledge, 1981), pp. 241–2; Barker, p. 183, scales down the Albanian claims. Material losses, especially villages burned down, were very high.

63 – Cited from Dedijer by Pavlowitch, cit., p. 104.

64 – *AAT*, pp. 334ff.

65 – The LRDG operations are descibed in David Lloyd Owen, *Providence Their Guide: A Personal Account of the Long Range Desert Group 1940–1945* (London, Harrap, 1980), ch. 17. The Saranda operation is described in Marmullaku, p. 55. I am most grateful to Alan Palmer for his help in elucidating Hoxha's account of these events. Lloyd Owen, pp. 197–8, describes difficult relations between the LNC and the British at the time of the liberation of Tirana.

66 – For the 1943 plans, see F. W. D. Deakin, 'The Myth of an Allied Landing in the Balkans During the Second World War', in Phyllis Auty and Richard Clogg, eds., *British Policy Towards Wartime Resistance in Yugoslavia and Greece* (London, Macmillan, 1974), pp. 104–7; but it was not just a 'myth'. For the Yugoslav Partisan negotiations with the Nazis, see Pavlowitch, cit., pp. 101ff; cf. Oskar Gruenwald, 'Yugoslav Literature of Disclosure', *Survey*, vol. 28, no. 3 (autumn 1984); Edvard Kardelj, *Reminiscences: The Struggle for Recognition and*

Independence: The New Yugoslavia 1944–1957 (London, Blond & Briggs, 1982), p. 65, on Stalin's concern about a Western landing in Yugoslavia (which did actually take place between October 1944 and January 1945 in the Dubrovnik area).

67 – On the Spile landing, FO 371/43551 (document dated 5 August 1944), and Lloyd Owen, cit. For the Saranda episode, FO 371/43572 (the implication being that it was kept secret even from the Foreign Office).

68 – This and the information immediately below are from FO 371/43554.

69 – FO 371/43554, with only slightly qualified enthusiasm from the Foreign Office, mainly as regards the availability of troops for an occupation.

70 – One of the most ludicrous and least commented-on aspects of the 1949 invasion is that the British chose to land their mercenaries at a place called 'Seaview' which had been SOE's main landing site during the war (vividly described by both Alexander Glen in *Footholds Against a Whirlwind* (London, Hutchinson, 1975) and Anthony Quayle in his novel *Eight Hours from England* (London, Heinemann, 1945). Apart from those names in the text, another key figure resurfacing from the wartime adventures was Lord George Jellicoe, who had been active in the SBS. Oakley Hill returned to Albania after Liberation with the UN Relief and Rehabilitation Administration (UNRRA) (*AAT*, pp. 367–8); Hoxha accuses him of later stirring up the émigrés (*AAT*, p. 429). Smiley's account of his role in the 1949 invasion is at the end of his *Albanian Assignment*. Bethell, *The Great Betrayal*, is both disappointing and inaccurate: in particular, it fails completely to suggest that there was any popular base to the Hoxha regime; it also fails to show how the Albanian security forces could continue their run of successes against the invaders long after Philby had ceased involvement with the operation. The Western military missions left Albania in January 1945; the civilian missions withdrew in November 1946.

71 – *TT*, p. 630; some sources suggest that Zog's son, Leka, was involved in this attempt; cf. the section on Shehu below.

72 – Squadron Leader Tony Neel, RAF, who had operated in northern Albania, in the Shkodra (Scutari) area, where the majority of Catholics were; cf. Bethell, p. 16.

73 – Apparently Col. Wilfred Stirling, former commander of Zog's gendarmerie and later head of the Istanbul office of 'Section D' of British intelligence in the early 1940s. (Not to be confused with David Stirling of the SAS.)

74 – Philby's account of his role is in Kim Philby, *My Silent War* (London, Panther, ed., 1973), pp. 141ff; Bruce Page, David Leitch and Phillip Knightley, *Philby: The Spy Who Betrayed a Generation* (London, Sphere, 1982), ch. 13.

75 – Presumably Peter Kemp, former SOE agent in Albania; named by Bethell as involved in later attempts at subversion (*Great Betrayal*, pp. 101–2, 128–9).

76 – See Appendix II.

2 FROM LIBERATION TO THE BREAK WITH YUGOSLAVIA

1 – See Marmullaku, p. 56; Pollo and Puto, pp. 246ff.

2 – See passage cited by Marmullaku, p. 70; this section was cut out from later published versions of Hoxha's text. But the extent to which the Western govern-

ments actually thought Hoxha might be pro-Western, or at least 'non-aligned' – right up to the end of the war – has also been understated. On 5 October 1944, a senior British official wrote: 'The danger that the F.N.C. [LNC] . . . might turn towards Tito and possibly towards Moscow cannot be discounted altogether.' (FO 371/43554.) Even more startling is the American OSS's attitude as the civil war was ending. The British embassy in Washington cabled the Foreign Office on 5 December 1944: 'O.S.S. have recently been trying to persuade State Department to adopt a more encouraging attitude towards Hoxha on the ground that besides being independent of the political fight in Albania at present, he is neither a Communist nor a fellow traveller and is sincerely anxious to establish a westward orientation for Albania.' (FO 371/43554.)

3 – See *AAT*, 351ff, 381ff, for Hoxha's version of conversations with the head of the British mission in Tirana, Brig. D. E. P. Hodgson.

4 – Pollo and Puto, pp. 254ff; Marmullaku, p. 69.

5 – See Milovan Djilas, 'Tito and Stalin', *Survey*, vol. 28, no. 3 (1984), p. 81.

6 – For Tito's relationship with luxury, see especially Milovan Djilas, *Tito: The Story from Inside* (London, Weidenfeld & Nicolson, 1981), pp. 92ff, 109–10.

7 – See Appendix I.

8 – Djilas: 'the persistent attempt . . . to . . . subjugate [Albania] to Yugoslavia' (*Tito*, p. 35); cf. Djilas, 'Tito and Stalin', p. 81: 'The offer of Albania to Yugoslavia was Stalin's trap, but it was one constructed out of actual attitudes and the undoubted pretensions of the Yugoslav leaders . . . with regard to Albania, as well as out of our ambitions which were certainly not idealistic but inspired by a lust for power.' Cf. Djilas, *Conversations with Stalin*, pp. 121–3; 129–30.

9 – For the Yugoslav position, see Dedijer, *Sangue Tradito*, ch. 5; Marmullaku, pp. 93–4, for an overall assessment; Griffith, p. 15.

10 – Cf. Hoxha's account of Politbureau meetings (*TT*, p. 266).

Both during the years of the war and in this period [early 1946] we held the meetings of the Bureau at night. Mostly we met in my home, isolated one of the rooms which I used for work, and frequently continued the discussion till early morning. The occasions were by no means rare . . . when the debate took the form of a quarrel and voices were raised so high that not only the people of my household, but also the odd passer-by in the street could hear them. (At that time the street in front of the house where I lived and still live was not closed and anybody, good or bad, could walk past freely.)

11 – Moša Pijade (1890–1957), translated Marx's *Das Kapital* in prison before Second World War; leading figure in Partisan movement, organised uprising in Montenegro 1941; member of Politbureau after war; painter and journalist.

12 – Boris Kidrič (1912–53), Slovene, member of CC of YCP from 1940, member of Politbureau from 1948; leading economics expert.

13 – On the complex events regarding the Balkan Federation, see especially Fernando Claudin, *The Communist Movement: from Comintern to Cominform*

(Penguin, 1975), ch. 6, esp. pp. 465, 489–90; Djilas, *Conversations*; Joyce and Gabriel Kolko, *The Limits of Power: The World and United States Foreign Policy, 1945–1954* (New York, Harper & Row, 1972), pp. 408–9; the Kolkos note that during the war Britain backed Tito's plans in the hope of producing a counter-weight to Stalin's projects.

14 – The Peace Conference was held in August 1946; this was Hoxha's one and only appearance in public in the West after the war; text of his speech in *SW*, I, pp. 593ff. It was on this occasion that he made such a strong impression on Molotov and others.

15 – Tito's dog, killed in a German raid in June 1943 when he threw himself across Tito's body, saving his life.

16 – Sreten (Crni) Žujović (1899–1976), veteran Yugoslav Communist who had lived in the USSR before the war; commander of the General Staff for Serbia in Second World War; Lieutenant-General. In 1948 supported Cominform critique of Tito. Far from being 'liquidated', as Hoxha claims (a word which should mean killed), he was even readmitted to the Party later in life.

Andrija Hebrang (1899–1948), prewar Croatian Communist imprisoned and capitulated to captors' pressure, exchanged for Fascist prisoners late 1942. Became minister in postwar government. In 1948 sided with Stalin and Cominform; arrested, reportedly committed suicide in prison.

17 – It is doubtful that Tito actually said this, as things were not going well on this front between Yugoslavia and the USSR; cf. Djilas, 'Tito and Stalin', pp. 76–9; for background on Yugoslav–Soviet economic relations in this period, see Freedman, cit.

18 – In *WS*, pp. 14–15; 15; 34–5; 41.

19 – *WS*, p. 101.

20 – *WS*, p. 79; Dedijer, *Tito Speaks*, p. 312.

21 – Even as a trap: cf. note 8 above.

22 – 16 July 1947; note that this was Hoxha's third day there (*WS*, p. 55), indicating that Stalin was in no great hurry to see him.

23 – Griffith, p. 19; cf. ibid, p. 18, and re Yugoslav economic pressure.

24 – *Conversations*, pp. 121ff, pp. 129ff (especially p. 131).

25 – Hoxha probably was very close to Spiru, as the wartime letters cited in note 58 to ch. 1 above would indicate. But suicide is generally frowned upon in the Communist bloc (cf. Xoxe's remarks about Spiru's suicide). Equally, for Hoxha corpses are useful since they can be used for reinterpretation from the grave.

26 – Xoxe had been flinging accusations at Spiru (*TT*, pp. 379ff) – in particular that he was anti-Yugoslav and 'an agent of imperialism'.

27 – Spiru; the reference is to the reversal of policies and personnel accomplished at the Berat plenum in November 1944.

28 – Tuk Jakova was a member of the Politbureau expelled in 1951; in 1955, he, together with former Politbureau member Bedri Spahiu, was publicly condemned as being involved in a pro-Yugoslav plot (the timing coincided with Khrushchev's rapprochement with Tito). See Griffith, p. 22, p. 24; Hoxha, *SW*, II, pp. 429ff, for the 1955 indictment.

Milan Gorkić was Secretary General of the Yugoslav CP between 1932 and 1937, when he was liquidated by Stalin. In 1968 Tito told Phyllis Auty that Gorkić had not been a spy – though he had done a lot of harm to the Party. (Phyllis Auty, *Tito: A Biography*, (Penguin, 1974), p. 149).

29 – Djilas, *Conversations with Stalin*; Dedijer, *Tito Speaks*, pp. 280–81, 312–13; Kardelj, *Reminiscences*.

30 – Djilas, *Conversations*, pp. 155–6; 162; Kardelj, cit., p. 107; Dedijer, *Tito Speaks*, pp. 324, 328–9 (where Dedijer says that Stalin used Hoxha as 'his main stooge in the Albanian government, to plant the request').

31 – During the Second World War, Britain had tended to back the Greek claim to this territory. As the Foreign Office documents show, top British officials claimed that Greece's claim was (slightly) stronger; but they also argued for giving southern Albania to Greece as a 'reward' (see FO 371/29715). In November 1944 the Greek government put in a request to the Americans that Albania be treated as an 'enemy' state and that Greece be allowed to occupy the whole southern *half* of Albania (FO 371/43554). This attitude prevailed during the late 1940s.

32 – Kardelj, *Reminiscences*, p. 107.

33 – Stalin told the Yugoslavs in February 1948 that the Greek revolution had to be abandoned (Djilas, *Conversations*, pp. 164–5). Cf. Claudin, *The Communist Movement*, ch. 7.

34 – Beqir Balluku, see Biographical notes; Kristo Themelko, see above, ch. 1, note 48.

3 WITH STALIN

1 – Claudin, cit., is the fundamental source on all this.

2 – Dedijer, as reported by Pavlowitch, *Survey*, cit., p. 100.

3 – Freedman, *Economic Warfare*, cit., ch. 2; Griffith, cit; Dedijer, *Tito Speaks*, pp. 311–12.

4 – Dmitry Chuvakhin, Soviet envoy to Albania; cf. *WS*, pp. 95, 202.

5 – See Biographical notes for Dej. Ana Pauker (1893–1960), leading Romanian Communist who had been imprisoned in Romania and had lived for a long time in USSR; returned to Romania 1944 with units formed from Romanian prisoners of war; General Secretary of the Romanian CP 1944; Foreign Minister 1947–52; purged in Stalin's last wave of anti-semitism.

6 – Ion Antonescu, fascist dictator of Romania during Second World War; used title 'Conducator' ('Leader') now taken over by Ceauşescu.

7 – On the Balkan Federation, see Claudin, cit., ch. 7; the *Pravda* reply to Dimitrov mentioned immediately below was on 29 January 1948; for Stalin's brutal treatment of Dimitrov on this occasion, see Djilas, *Conversations*, pp. 156ff; Kardelj, cit., pp. 103ff.

8 – Paul Morand, *Bucarest* (Paris, 1935).

9 – This is a reference back to Dej's complacent description of his own behaviour (see *TT*, p. 522).

10 – Djilas, *Conversations*, pp. 164–5; Dedijer, *Tito Speaks*, p. 331; Kardelj, *Reminiscences*, pp. 107–8.

11 – Hoxha's claims are unconfirmed from outside sources, which date the Anglo-US attempts to later that same year. But it is quite possible that attempts on this scale were already being made.

12 – If this is what Stalin really said, it was a tragic misreading of the situation. In fact the Greek revolutionary forces had been doing very well until late 1948, but after the Tito–Stalin break Stalin forced the ouster of the most capable Greek military leader, Markos (Vafiades), and by the end of 1948 the royalists were already in a strong position: see Claudin, cit., pp. 512–4; Kolko & Kolko, cit.; Lawrence Wittner, *American Intervention in Greece 1943–1949* (New York, Columbia University Press, 1982), for the effectiveness of the US role.

Konstantinos Tsaldaris was the Greek prime minister.

13 – For religion, see Prifti, ch. 8; further discussion below between Stalin and Hoxha.

14 – Edgar O'Ballance, *The Greek Civil War 1944–1949* (London, Faber & Faber, 1966), p. 200; cf. p. 201.

15 – Nikos Zakhariades, Greek Communist; imprisoned by Nazis. Replaced Markos after Tito–Stalin break. Disastrous leader, presided over collapse of Greek Revolution; distinguished self by attacks on Tito. Dismissed 1956. Cf. Claudin.

16 – i.e. executed. Catholics accounted for about 10 per cent of the population, mainly in the far north; they collaborated en masse with the Italians and, to a lesser extent, with the Germans.

17 – Partsalides, Dimitrios (Mitsos); Prime Minister in the Provisional Government of Democratic Greece; at Varkiza (see note 19 below); denounced by Zakhariades, October 1950; reinstated in Politbureau February 1956 after denunciation of Zakhariades.

18 – This figure is from O'Ballance, p. 202; cf. Claudin, pp. 512–4.

19 – Varkiza: village outside Athens where agreement was signed in February 1945 in attempt to end civil war; Left made major concessions, especially commitment to surrender all arms within two weeks, without securing role in government or adequate protection against reprisals. Varkiza was disastrous for the Left. Hoxha claims that 'Mukje would have been the Albanian Varkiza.' (*AAT*, p. 238.)

20 – Zakhariades' version of events surrounding his return is confirmed by independent sources. Perhaps the Kremlin leaders were used to accusations that fraternal colleagues were British spies, and took them in their stride. Djilas records an episode when Kardelj told Molotov that a senior Yugoslav Partisan, Vladimir Velebit, was under suspicion as a British spy. To which Molotov nonchalantly replied: 'Aha, so Velebit is an English spy.' ('Tito and Stalin', p. 79.)

4 BATTLING KHRUSHCHEV

1 – *KR*, vol. II, p. 316; vol. I, p. 508. In an important article analysing the section of Khrushchev's memoirs relating to the Korean War, John Merrill has shown that there are very serious discrepancies between what Khrushchev said on the tapes and what the published version claims he said (*Journal of Korean Studies* (Seattle) vol. 3 (1981), pp. 181ff).

2 – *TK*, pp. 183–4.

3 – *WS*, pp. 33–4.

4 – *TK*, p. 389.

5 – *WS*, p. 31. However, it should be said that Harrison Salisbury considers there are good grounds for thinking that Stalin may indeed have been murdered by poisoning. (*A Journey for Our Times* (New York, Harper & Row, 1983).)

6 – *TK*, pp. 149–50. Georgi Dimitrov became famous as the defiant defendant in the Reichstag trial at the beginning of the Nazi period. In 1935 he was appointed Secretary General of the Comintern. After the war he became premier and head of the Bulgarian Communist Party. He died in Moscow on 3 June 1949. Kliment Gottwald, Czech Communist leader; premier 1946–8; President from 1948 until his death; de facto Secretary General of CP from late 1951 on. Became ill after Stalin's funeral; flown home and died in Prague. Boleslav Bierut (1892–1956), veteran Polish Communist closely tied to USSR; Secretary General of Polish CP after (first) fall of Gomulka in 1948 and then of Polish United Workers' Party; premier 1952–4. Died in Moscow, 12 March 1956. Elsewhere, Hoxha adds the American CP leader William Z. Foster to the list.

7 – *TK*, p. 294; Wanda Wassilewska, Polish writer, close friend of Khrushchev, who lived war years in USSR.

8 – *TK*, p. 285; for Nagy, see Biographical notes.

9 – Freedman, *Economic Warfare in the Communist Bloc*, ch. 3, is a very good survey; see also Griffith, *Albania and the Sino-Soviet Rift*, chs. 3 and 4, for excellent background and useful documents; for a comprehensive analysis of Albania's economic development strategy, see Russ, cit.

10 – Elsewhere Hoxha refers to the different versions of how Beria died. He adds one small revelation:

Later, when a general, who I believe was called Sergatskov, came to Tirana as Soviet military adviser he also told us something about the trial of Beria. He told us that he had been called as a witness to declare in court that Beria had allegedly behaved arrogantly towards him. On this occasion Sergatskov told our comrades in confidence: «Beria defended himself very strongly in the court, accepted none of the accusations and refuted them all.»

(*TK*, p. 31); cf. *KR*, I, pp. 344ff.

11 – Kliment E. Voroshilov, Soviet Marshal; incompetent, but lucky; in and occasionally out of favour with Stalin and Khrushchev as military leader and political figurehead. President of the Soviet Union 1953–60; later denounced as participant in 'Anti-Party Group' in mid-1950s. Died 1969 aged 89.

12 – Edward Ochab: succeeded Bierut as Polish Party leader on death of latter in March 1956.

13 – Jozef Cyrankiewicz, Polish premier 1947–52 and 1954–71; escaped from Auschwitz, recaptured and reincarcerated in Mauthausen.

14 – Lake Ohrid lies between Albania and Yugoslavia on the eastern border of

Albania; Lake Shkodra lies between the two countries on Albania's northern border. Tempo's references to 'the Macedonians' presumably refers to the regional government of Macedonia.

15 – Full text in *KR*, I, Appendix 4; cf. ibid., pp. 366ff, for Khrushchev's own account.

16 – On Comecon, see Michael Kaser, *Comecon: Integration Problems of the Planned Economies* (London, OUP, 1967, 2nd edn); cf. Freedman, cit.

17 – Walter Ulbricht, Communist deputy to Reichstag 1928–33; war in exile in USSR; First Secretary of CC of Socialist Unity Party in East Germany 1954. Antonin Novotny, born 1909, Czech Communist leader; in prison 1941–5. First Secretary of CC of CP from September 1953 until ousted in 1968 upheavals.

18 – Erno Gerö, born 1898, Hungarian Communist leader; long-time official of Comintern, especially in Spain (unsavoury role); war in USSR; Minister of Interior, July 1953; replaced Rákosi (see Biographical notes) as First Secretary of CP, June 1956; ousted in autumn Hungarian uprising.

19 – Two pages later Hoxha calls Zhivkov 'the prototype of political mediocrity' (*TK*, p. 154).

20 – Vulko Chervenkov, veteran Bulgarian Communist; long-time official in Comintern; General Secretary of Bulgarian CP 1950–54; premier 1950.

21 – Viliam Široky, born 1902, Slovak Communist leader; Foreign Minister of Czechoslovakia 1948; premier from March 1953; heavily involved in purges.

Jaromir Dolansky, born 1895, Czech Communist, wartime underground leader; member of Politbureau and vice-premier postwar.

22 – 'Bureaucratic functionaries of Czarist Russia' (Hoxha's note).

23 – Alexei A. Yepishev, long-time head of the Political Directorate of the Armed Forces, removed July 1985.

24 – F. R. Kozlov, member of Soviet Politbureau; considered likely successor to Khrushchev; died suddenly 1965. Involved (with Brezhnev) in discussions with Liri Belishova (q.v.) in 1960. In a later passage (*TK*, pp. 350ff) Hoxha contradicts himself and says he attended a spontaneous, unannounced meeting at a factory in Leningrad in 1957 where the workers, he claims, enthusiastically backed his position.

25 – Konstantin Rokossovsky (born near Warsaw), Soviet Marshal, who became Polish Minister of Defence. I. S. Konev, Marshal; Commander-in-Chief of the Warsaw Pact. Nina Khrushcheva (mentioned immediately below) was Nikita Khrushchev's wife.

26 – Wilhelm Pieck, veteran German Communist; arrested with Rosa Luxemburg and Karl Liebknecht 1919; head of Balkan section of Comintern, late 1930s; first President of East Germany, 1949.

27 – Yumzhagin Tsedenbal, long-time head of Mongolian CP; ousted 1984.

28 – Kim Il Sung, born 1912, Korean Communist leader, guerrilla in northeast China in late 1930s; de facto head of DPRK (North Korea) from 1945–6 as Secretary General of Workers' (Communist) Party and, later, President.

29 – This Plenum took place in August 1956. What happened is obscure and it is not clear that Hoxha accurately remembers or records Kim's remarks. The two

chief figures criticising Kim Il Sung were Pak Chang-ok and Choe Chang-ik, members of the Central Committee; they did not apparently flee to China; but four others did, including the Minister of Commerce, Yun Kong-hum. On their return they were purged and disappeared.

30 – The April 1956 Tirana Conference was a key event; criticism of Hoxha in the wake of Khrushchev's denunciation of Stalin reached a peak and Hoxha was on the verge of being pushed out. See Griffith, cit., pp. 24–6; *PLA* and Hoxha, *SW*, II, for official material.

31 – Boris Nikolaevich Ponomaryov, born 1905, head of the International Department of the CPSU; there is independent evidence to support Hoxha's account of Ponomaryov's views on Kim Il Sung.

32 – Peng Dehuai (Peng Teh-huai), Chinese Defence Minister purged after openly criticising Mao and Great Leap Forward in 1959; met Khrushchev in Tirana, May 1959 (see below). Mikoyan and Peng visited North Korea *before* the Chinese Congress opened, apparently to try to save their friends from Kim Il Sung.

33 – Liu Shaoqi (Liu Shao-chi), born 1898, Chinese Communist and head of state until Cultural Revolution; 'persecuted to death' 1969.

34 – Li Lisan, dominant figure in Chinese CP before Mao, ousted in wake of disastrous military adventures in 1930. Backed by Comintern against Mao. Minister of Labour in post-Liberation government. Member of Central Committee.

35 – Lu Dingyi (Lu Ting-yi), born 1906, head of Propaganda Department of CCP; key figure in '100 Flowers' movement.

36 – Traicho Kostov, Bulgarian Communist; head of clandestine party; arrested June 1949 and hanged. Anton Yugov, born 1904, former Minister of the Interior and vice premier of Bulgarian government.

37 – Presumably Koča Popović, Yugoslav Foreign Minister. Edvard Kardelj (1910–79) was no. 2 in the Yugoslav regime and long-time Foreign Minister.

38 – Emil Bodnaras, Romanian Communist of Ukrainian origin, former officer in royalist army; after war, head of secret police; December 1947, Minister of Defence and vice-premier.

39 – The famous interview by the Italian Communist leader Palmiro Togliatti first appeared as '9 Domande sullo Stalinismo', *Nuovi Argomenti*, no. 20 (June 1956).

40 – Rákosi was ousted in July 1956.

41 – For Khrushchev's account, see KR, I, pp. 449–50.

42 – Krylov: Soviet ambassador in Tirana.

43 – Yekaterina A. Furtseva, Minister of Culture in the Soviet government from 1960; close associate of Khrushchev; only woman in prominent position in CPSU in recent times.

44 – P. N. Pospyelov, editor of *Pravda* 1940–49; leading ideologist and close associate of Mikhail Suslov (q.v.); according to Khrushchev, in charge of the commission which produced the evidence for the 1956 'Secret Speech'. Attended both the 3rd (1956) and 4th (1961) Congresses of the PLA.

45 – Konrad Adenauer, postwar Chancellor of West Germany. Nobusuke Kishi, premier of Japan 1957–60.

46 – Dwight D. Eisenhower, President of the USA 1952–60. John Foster Dulles, Eisenhower's Secretary of State.

47 – *Scînteia*: the Romanian Party daily.

48 – Liri Gega, see Biographical notes. General Dali Ndreu was her husband. Both were allegedly captured trying to flee to Yugoslavia. On this episode, see Griffith, cit., pp. 24, 235; Prifti, p. 102; on this and the other purges, see the excellent piece by Pipa, cit.

49 – Panajot Plaku, Major-General and former deputy Minister of Defence; studied at the Soviet Military Academy 1948–50; fled to Yugoslavia in May 1957. See Prifti, p. 205; Griffith, pp. 24, 80, 110, 137, on this episode.

50 – Veljko Mićunović, former Yugoslav partisan, with extensive experience in the Ministry of the Interior and the Foreign Ministry; in charge of Yugoslav relations with Albania. Tito's first ambassador to Moscow after restoration of ties with Khrushchev (March 1956–October 1958) and again in late 1960s. Author of excellent *Moscow Diary* (London, Chatto & Windus, 1980), which has accounts of two meetings with Hoxha, pp. 229ff: the first, on 15 April 1957, at a reception given by the Albanians; the second, on 17 April, at a dinner given by the Soviet leadership for the Albanians. Hoxha appears to ignore the first meeting. Mićunović's account does confirm that he was standing apart (near the door, in case he had to walk out); he also reports Hoxha's accusations against the Yugoslav chargé in Tirana, Arso Milatović, and the remarks of King Paul of Greece about partitioning Albania, but says that this suggestion was firmly rebuffed.

51 – Hoxha has an account of this episode, reportedly based on what was told him by Dmitri Polyansky, then a member of the Soviet Politbureau (and later ambassador to Japan). The main point of interest in the Hoxha–Polyansky version is that when the members of the Central Committee reached the Kremlin to try to overturn the Politbureau decision to oust Khrushchev, it was Voroshilov (q.v.) who met them and tried to block their entry (*TK*, 186–7).

Georgi K. Zhukov: Soviet Marshal; outstanding military commander against Japanese in 1939 fighting and against Germans at Stalingrad and Leningrad. Defence Minister from 1955 until ouster in late 1957. Mićunović (*Moscow Diary*, pp. 307ff) records fascinating conversations with Khrushchev in which the latter, in effect, says he had to fire Zhukov because Zhukov had saved him (Khrushchev) from the 'Anti-Party Group'.

52 – A. I. Kirichenko, former close associate of Khrushchev and right-hand man 1957–60; dismissed 1960, reasons unknown. Otto Grotewohl, born 1894, German Socialist leader who presided over merger of Socialist and Communist parties after the war; first premier of GDR, 1949.

53 – Kardelj has a description of this same occasion in his *Reminiscences*, pp. 139–43, which tallies quite closely with that of Hoxha; cf. John Gittings, ed., *Survey of the Sino-Soviet Dispute* (London, OUP, 1968) ch. 7 (pp. 73ff), for elucidation of Mao's remarks. There is independent confirmation that Gomulka was opposed to proclaiming the Soviet Union as the head of the bloc.

54 – Hoxha's criticism of Rákosi is in *TK*, pp. 260–61; of Lin Biao, *RC*, I, p. 463.

55 – Jacques Duclos, born 1896, French Communist; worked in Comintern security apparatus.

56 – Panmunjom: village in Korea where peace talks took place 1951–3 between Communist side (China, North Korea) and UN forces headed by USA. It is not clear quite what Mao means by 'we' as regards Vietnam – whether China held secret negotiations with the French, or if 'we' refers to the Communist camp – or (less likely) to Sino-French negotiations *over* Indochina at Geneva in 1954.

57 – Elsewhere Hoxha describes an occasion in April 1957 when his anti-Yugoslav remarks and those of Shehu were censored by his Soviet hosts while he was at the opera with Frol Kozlov, in spite of the valiant efforts of Ramiz Alia (*TK*, pp. 351–3).

58 – Rodion Y. Malinovsky, close associate of Khrushchev during Second World War; succeeded Zhukov (q.v.) as Minister of Defence, 1957.

59 – Curiously, there is no account of the visit in Khrushchev's memoirs; Freedman, *Economic Warfare*, and Griffith for the economic issues.

60 – Griffith, p. 134; as Griffith suggests, Khrushchev must have been making a last effort to prevent a break with Albania – and, if possible, China. Peng's memoirs, *Memoirs of a Chinese Marshal* (Beijing, Foreign Languages Press, 1984), have no reference to the meeting with Khrushchev.

61 – *TT*, p. 612.

62 – *TT*, pp. 611–12.

63 – *KR*, I, p. 507; *KR*, II, 315–16. Khrushchev did not know, or did not remember, that it was Kosygin who visited Shehu in hospital.

64 – Brezhnev and Kozlov also met Liri Belishova in Moscow about the same time, but it is not clear if it was together with Nushi.

65 – On the Belishova case, see Griffith, pp. 48–9; Pipa, p. 444. Belishova was the widow of Nako Spiru, who committed suicide in 1947; *KR*, I, p. 507; *KR*, II, p. 316; *ACKR*, pp. 13ff; Koço Tashko had been Chairman of the Central Auditing Commission; cf. *ACKR*, pp. 55ff; on the Bucharest meeting of June 1960, see Griffith, pp. 41–5.

66 – *ACKR* is made up of extracts from vol. 19 of Hoxha's *Works* in Albanian, covering the period June–December 1960; it was published in 1976 by Gamma Publishing Co. in New York. A slightly fuller version was published in French as *La grande divergence 1960* (Paris, Nouveau Bureau d'Edition, 1976). *ACKR* was subsequently withdrawn, presumably because of its friendly references to Mehmet Shehu. Cf. Griffith, ch. 3.

67 – Ranković's speech was on 4 July 1960; cf. *ACKR*, pp. 24ff.

68 – See Griffith, p. 40, re Khrushchev's meeting with Sophokles Venizelos, the Greek politician, in early June 1960; Venizelos' published account of the meeting makes no reference to proposals for partition or territorial changes.

69 – The Albanian delegation was made up of Hysni Kapo and Ramiz Alia; cf. *ACKR*, pp. 128ff.

70 – On the Moscow Conference, apart from Griffith, *KR* and *ACKR*, see Donald S. Zagoria, *The Sino-Soviet Conflict 1956–61* (New York, Atheneum, 1967);

David Floyd, *Mao Against Khrushchev: A Short History of the Sino-Soviet Conflict* (London, Pall Mall Press, 1964).

71 – This story is rewritten in *TT*, pp. 614–15.

72 – Aleksandr Nikolaevich Shelepin, born 1918, head of the Komsomol (Communist Youth), 1952–8; head of KGB, December 1958 to October 1961; power later declined.

73 – A purported verbatim text of this meeting (8 November) is in *ACKR*, pp. 159–60. Though the text cannot be checked, it is not implausible.

74 – Maurice Thorez, born 1900, head of French CP; mediocre figure. Had been in Albania 'on holiday' in summer 1960, apparently to mediate dispute (Hoxha could communicate directly with him in French).

75 – Purported extracts from this conversation are in *ACKR*, pp. 161ff (10 November).

76 – 12 November; text in *ACKR*, pp. 171ff.

77 – Hoxha's speech of 16 November is in *SW*, II, pp. 794ff, and *ACKR*, pp. 178ff.

78 – Dolores Ibarruri ('La Pasionaria'), veteran Spanish Communist and leader in the Civil War, from 1943 Secretary General of Spanish CP; after decades of exile, returned to Spain after death of Franco. Ali Yata, head of Moroccan CP. Khalid Baghdash (or Bakdash), born 1910, Syrian Communist (of Kurd origin), head of Syrian CP; most prominent Arab Communist of his time.

79 – 29 November: anniversary of Liberation; cf. *ACKR*, pp. 233ff.

80 – This is the view of Griffith ('When, as seems probable, the Soviets countered with an unsuccessful *coup d'état* to overthrow Hoxha . . .'; p. 49).

81 – Marshal A. A. Grechko, Commander in Chief of the Warsaw Pact and later Soviet Minister of Defence. Key figure in 1968 invasion of Czechoslovakia.

82 – Text: *ACKR*, pp. 161ff. On the Vlora base, see Griffith.

83 – See Griffith, p. 81; the Russians withdrew their submarines at the end of May; eight Soviet submarines arrived at Gibraltar on 1 June.

84 – Josif Shikin arrived in Tirana on 19 January 1961. As Griffith points out, he was an important figure; from 1945 to 1949 he had been the head of the Main Political Administration of the Red Army (Griffith, p. 64).

85 – Rudolf Barák, member of the Czech Politbureau, purged shortly after this; see Griffith, pp. 74–6, on his role at the Albanian Congress; the Congress was held from 13 to 20 February 1961 (see Griffith, pp. 68ff).

86 – For Pospyelov's account, delivered at the 22nd Congress of the CPSU in October 1961, see Griffith, pp. 76–7.

87 – This is one of the murkiest of all the obscure affairs in postwar Albania. Rear Admiral Teme Sejko was the head of the Albanian Navy and thus, given the role of naval affairs and the base at Vlora/Sazan, probably the key military figure in Albanian–Soviet relations. Sejko had trained in Moscow 1947–9 and again in 1956–8. He was tried along with Tahir Demi, formerly Albania's representative to Comecon, and others. Sejko and Demi were shot and the plot denounced as a joint Yugoslav–Greek–US 6th-Fleet scheme. It is possible that Sejko was involved in a Soviet plot, which Hoxha chose to displace onto his Western foes. In his rewritten

account in *TT*, pp. 615–17, Hoxha suggests that there was a Western plot (in which Sejko may or may not have been involved) which the Russians then decided to manipulate to intimidate Albania. On the affair, see Griffith, pp. 47–8, 80–81.

5 DECODING CHINA

1 – *RC*, I, p. 232; entry dated 20 August 1966, titled 'What is Going on in China?'.

2 – See this volume, pp. 179–185.

3 – See, for example, *RC*, I, p. 3 (foreword, dated May 1979) and *RC*, I, p. 522. At certain points (e.g. pp. 586, 596, of *RC*, I) the tenses indicate some rewriting.

4 – For the fall of Balluku, see especially Prifti, pp. 212ff; for Këllezi, ibid., pp. 84ff; cf. Pipa, pp. 445–7. In a curious entry dated 24 July 1970, Hoxha records apparently false information being fed to Albania by a Romanian source about an alleged Yugoslav military commitment to Romania; Hoxha regards the claim as false, but suggests that the Chinese probably believed it (*RC*, I, p. 504).

5 – *RC*, II, p. 749.

6 – *RC*, II, p. 271; in this same entry (titled 'This Situation is Neither Normal Nor Revolutionary'), Hoxha has a pungent summing up: 'It seems that the opposing currents have captured the leading posts and one side has control of the microphones and the press, while the other side has the economy and the rifle. The former seems nervous, the latter calm, of course, because it has the rifle.'

7 – *RC*, I, p. 7; this claim conflicts with the version published by Albania, at the time of the break with China, of Hoxha's remarks to Chou En-lai during the latter's visit to Tirana in March 1965. See Enver Hoxha, *Conversation with Chou En-lai* (Tirana, '8 Nëntori' Publishing House, 1977), p. 32; this 'conversation', as published, is composed entirely of a monologue by Hoxha.

8 – *RC*, I. p. 603; see this volume, p. 286.

9 – *TK*, p. 437; this is not the picture given by Griffith, pp. 50ff.

10 – Hoxha seems particularly incensed about Mao's relationship with Edgar Snow (*RC*, I, pp. 563–4; *RC*, II, pp. 491–7); he attributes sinister designs to Snow, and is especially irate over the fact that Mao talked to Snow about his bowel movements.

11 – See Prifti, pp. 80–82; Pipa, p. 447.

12 – 'The Theory and Practice of the Revolution', editorial in *Zeri i Popullit* (Tirana), 7 July 1977; condensed version in *Journal of Contemporary Asia*, vol. 7, no. 4, 1977; China did not immediately respond to this text in public, but Peking's views can be seen from Huang Hua's remarks of 30 July 1977 in Huang Hua, 'Problems with Indochina, Albania, and Yugoslavia', in King C. Chen, ed., *China and the Three Worlds: A Foreign Policy Reader* (White Plains, NY, M. E. Sharpe, Inc., 1979), pp. 274ff. On 7 July 1978 China terminated its aid agreements with Albania. Albania's public response came in a *Letter* of the CC of the PLA and the Government of Albania to the CC of the CCP and the Government of China, dated 29 July 1978 (Tirana, '8 Nëntori', 1978).

13 – *RC*, II, pp. 269–70, 24 August 1976.

14 – See Prifti, ch. 7, for an excellent résumé.

15 – Cited by Paul Lendvai, 'Traveller in Albania', *Encounter*, May 1985, p. 64;

I have not been able to consult Lendvai's book *Das einsame Albanien* (Zurich, Edition Interfrom, 1985).

16 – Born 1901; Chinese Foreign Minister; former Marshal.

17 – *TK*, p. 322; see this volume, p. 215.

18 – Hoxha is apparently referring to remarks made by Mao to a delegation of the Japan Socialist Party; these were published in the conservative Japanese journal *Sekai Shūhō*, 11 August 1964; extracts are in Franz Schurmann and Orville Schell, eds., *Communist China* (China Readings 3, Penguin, 1968), pp. 368–70. The Chinese never published Mao's remarks, nor confirmed or denied the Japanese version.

19 – Hoxha is referring to remarks made by Chou to a group of ambassadors from Communist countries communicating China's views on the fall of Khrushchev and its aftermath (Khrushchev had been ousted on 14 October 1964).

20 – Malinovsky: see note 58 to section 4.

21 – This must be Ho Lung (He Long): born 1896; key figure in earliest Communist military actions against Kuomintang, vice-premier and member of Politbureau; starved to death in prison, June 1969.

22 – Kosygin also visited Pyongyang on this trip.

23 – This is the first entry after the start of the Cultural Revolution. Hoxha's observations on the cult of Mao are shrewd and, on the whole, fair. One of the most illuminating statements by and about Mao was made by Mao himself to an Albanian military delegation on 31 August 1967. See David Milton, Nancy Milton and Franz Schurmann, eds., *People's China* (China Readings 4, Penguin, 1977), esp. p. 263.

24 – Chou visited Tirana in June 1966. Peng Chen (Peng Zhen), born 1902, Mayor of Peking; one of the first leading officials to be denounced in 1966 at start of Cultural Revolution, imprisoned, later rehabilitated; key figure in preparing trial of 'Gang of Four' and revision of legal system; member of Politbureau.

25 – Big character posters.

26 – In August 1968 the Soviet Union and most of its Warsaw Pact allies invaded Czechoslovakia. Albania withdrew de jure from the Warsaw Pact. The invasion caused alarm in China, Yugoslavia and Romania (where it was used by Ceauşescu to boost his credentials on the basis of nationalism): it is highly likely that various political and military alliances were floated at the time, but firm confirmation is unavailable.

27 – Ho Chi Minh, the Vietnamese revolutionary leader, died on 2 September 1969, aged 79.

28 – Rita is Rita Marko (male), born 1920; member of the Albanian Politbureau since 1956.

29 – Kang Sheng, born 1899; long-time head of secret police. Disgraced after death in 1975; ashes removed and desecrated.

30 – On 2 March 1969 Soviet and Chinese troops clashed on the Ussuri River with deaths on both sides.

31 – Li headed the Chinese delegation to the celebration of the 25th anniversary of Albania's Liberation in November 1969.

32 – After reporting the Chinese accusations against Chen Po-ta (Chen Boda), Hoxha notes that he had also been formerly praised by Mao and other Chinese leaders.

33 – China's surprise invitation to the American ping-pong team, then in Japan, came in March 1971.

34 – Official talks between the USA and Vietnam opened in May 1968.

35 –Henry Kissinger, National Security Adviser to US President Richard Nixon, visited Peking 9–11 July 1971.

36 – Norodom Sihanouk, Cambodian leader until ousted in coup, 1970; formal head of coalition, in exile in China 1970–75.

37 – Kim had been a junior soldier under Chinese command in the Northeastern Anti-Japanese United Army in northeast China in the 1930s.

38 – China recovered its seat in the United Nations, on a resolution moved by Albania and other states, on 25 October 1971. Nesti is Nesti Nase, Albanian Foreign Minister.

39 – Dung Biwu [Tung Pi-wu], born 1886, veteran Chinese Communist; vice-President and, after removal of Liu Shao-chi (Liu Shaoqi), acting President.

40 – Hoxha begins writing about the Lin Piao (Lin Biao) affair from 10 November 1971 (*RC*, I, pp. 612ff). According to the (later) official Chinese version, Lin died on 12 September 1971 in a plane crash in Mongolia. For the official Chinese statement of 28 July 1972, see Milton et al., *People's China*, pp. 375–6. The best text I know on the question is by the Italian psychoanalyst, Elvio Fachinelli, 'Dov'è Lin Piao?' [Where is Lin Piao?], in Fachinelli, *Il bambino dalle uova d'oro* (Milan, Feltrinelli, 1974).

41 – Wu Fa-hsien (Wu Faxian): Member of Politbureau; commander of Air Force; tried and sentenced January 1981 with 'Gang of Four' and others.

42 – Yeh Chun (Ye Qun) had been made a member of the Politbureau of the 9th Central Committee at the height of Lin's power, in 1969, when Lin was written into the constitution as Mao's successor.

43 – The same could, of course, be said about Hoxha's fairy tales about the role of his no. 2, Mehmet Shehu, in *TT*.

44 – Hoxha is quite right to ask, 'Who is Lin?' No one seems to have known. However, it should be recalled that when Edgar Snow visited Yenan (Yanan), Lin figured prominently and in some ways emerges from Snow's *Red Star Over China* as one of the most, if not *the* most important person after Mao.

45 – American writer and supporter of radical causes. Born Nebraska 1885, died Peking 1970, where she is buried in the Revolutionary Martyrs' Cemetery. Although Strong had her blind spots, Hoxha's comparison is rather unfair.

46 – US President Richard Nixon visited China 21–28 February 1972.

47 – Chiang Ching (Jiang Qing), Mao's fourth wife; former Shanghai actress; member of Politbureau; arrested immediately after death of Mao in 1976, tried and sentenced to death (suspended) January 1981. For a revealing account, see Roxane Witke, *Comrade Chiang Ch'ing* (London, Weidenfeld & Nicolson, 1977).

48 – In a section of this entry not included here Hoxha records that the Albanians

decided to send their Minister of Agriculture to 'enliven' relations with Peking which seemed to have become cool since Nixon's visit to China. What Hoxha seems to be unable to grasp, in spite of his beady eye in such matters, is that the Chinese were quite capable of perpetuating the *ritual* of warm friendship even when relations were in fact cool, at least on their part.

49 – The Korean War lasted from June 1950 to July 1953. The 'Korean army' Hoxha mentions is the Korean People's Army usually known (inaccurately) in the West as the 'North Korean Army'; it liberated most of southern Korea in summer 1950, reaching almost as far as Pusan, in southeast Korea. The Chinese intervened in the war in strength after US General Douglas MacArthur led Western and South Korean troops under the UN flag to the Chinese border on the Yalu River and threatened China.

50 – The ambassador of the South Vietnamese provisional revolutionary government, the PRG.

51 – The Ussuri fighting took place in early March 1969. See this volume, p. 277

52 – In a long meditative piece titled 'Where Has China Been and Where Is It Going?' dated 1 April 1976 (*RC*, II, pp. 229ff), Hoxha, after surveying China's history, refers to discussions with Li Hsien-nien (Li Xiannian) and China's foreign policy during the Cultural Revolution: 'In the international arena the policy of China was a rigid, sectarian, megalomaniacal and xenophobic policy of isolation to the point of, so to say, undeclared "yellow racism"' (*RC*, II, p. 242).

53 – At the beginning of this entry, Hoxha quotes remarks made by Chou at the official Chinese banquet for Zaire's President Mobutu Sese Seko (*RC*, II, p. 5). Mobutu visited China earlier in January 1973.

54 – Patrice Lumumba, leader of the Congolese National Movement in the then Belgian Congo. First premier of the Congo (now Zaire). Murdered January 1961.

55 – Durrës is the main town on the Albanian coast and the port for Tirana and the central hinterland.

56 – Nguyen Van Thieu, South Vietnamese general, President of pro-US regime based in Saigon (now Ho Chi Minh City); resigned and fled 21 April 1975.

57 – Yao Wen-yuan (Yao Wenyuan), Shanghai official who played leading role in launching Cultural Revolution, one of the 'Gang of Four', received the lightest sentence of the four – 20 years' imprisonment.

58 – Behar Shtylla: long-time Foreign Minister.

59 – On this agreement, see Prifti, pp. 82ff; it was a five-year pact (1976–80) covering the period of the forthcoming Albanian Five-Year Plan.

60 – Balluku and Këllezi: see Biographical notes.

Petrit Dume, general; Chief-of-Staff of Albania's armed forces; candidate member of the Politbureau; in China 26 November to 27 December 1973; purged with Balluku, July 1974, presumed executed.

Hito Çako, chief of the Political Directorate of the Army; purged July 1974.

Koço Theodhosi, Minister of Industry and Mining, member of Politbureau; purged May 1975 with Këllezi.

Curiously, Hoxha does not mention the important figure of Kiço Ngjela,

Minister of Trade, purged along with Këllezi. On these purges, see Prifti, cit., and Pipa.

61 – An unusually frank admission from Enver! Hoxha also seems to shift his ground noticeably as to which foreign power was the main backer.

62 – Tachai (Dazhai) commune, in Shansi (Shanxi) Province, was lauded during the Cultural Revolution as a model for Chinese agriculture. The claims made for Tachai were later denounced as fraudulent and its vaunted leader, Chen Yung-kuei (Chen Yonggui), who had been made a member of the Politbureau, exposed.

63 – In English as *Albania Challenges Khrushchev Revisionism* (New York, Gamma Publishing Co., 1976); this volume contains *extracts* from vol. 19. There is interesting material on the break with the USSR in the novel by Albania's foremost writer, Ismail Kadare, *The Great Winter*.

64 – Mao died on 9 September 1976. Chou had died in January 1976. The 'Gang of Four' were arrested in October 1976, one month after Mao died.

65 – Chang Chun-chiao (Zhang Chunqiao), Shanghai political leader, member of Politbureau; member of 'Gang of Four'; sentenced to death (suspended) January 1981.

66 – This is in many ways an emblematic passage: Hoxha makes a valid point in criticising the sexist abuse heaped on Chiang Ching. But the fact that this abuse is sexist does not prove that those deploying it are 'agents of imperialism'! The valid question – How could Chiang Ching have reached both the position of Mao's wife and top posts in the Party and state? – is not answered by vilifying those who use degenerate vocabulary against her.

67 – The 8th Congress was held in September 1956. The *Renmin Ribao* is the Party daily.

68 – A good point; in 1981 the CCP produced a booklet-length document which partly fills the gap: *Resolution on Certain Questions in the History of Our Party since the Founding of the People's Republic of China*, issued 27 June 1981.

69 – For Hoxha's coolness to Hua and the post-Mao leadership, see Prifti, pp. 250ff. Prifti cites a particularly arm's-length telegram from Hoxha to Hua congratulating him on his 'arrival' as Chairman (pp. 250–51). Volume V of Mao's selected works was produced in April 1977, but it remains hard to evaluate its authenticity.

70 – Keng Piao (Geng Biao), former Chinese ambassador in Tirana; key figure during Cultural Revolution; close to Chinese military and for short period Minister of Defence after death of Mao. Hoxha elsewhere describes in detail Geng Biao's scorn for the tiny 'pro-Chinese' parties dotted around the world, often a handful of people supported by Chinese money (he fails to reflect adequately on Albania's role in some of these operations); cf. Hoxha, *I & R*, pp. 441–4, where he references Geng's remarks to a conversation with Albanians in Peking, 16 April 1973.

71 – Tito embarked on his visit to the USSR, the DPRK (North Korea) and China in August 1977, returning to Yugoslavia in early September. Tito waited for Mao to die before he would set foot in China.

72 – Hoxha is right about Kim Il Sung's personality cult, undoubtedly the most

extreme in the world. Hoxha has frequent sallies against Kim. In 1965 he wrote;
'Pronounced conceit has overwhelmed some Korean leaders and they are practis-
ing a kind of «Monroe doctrine», i.e., self-isolation in regard to the struggle in
defence of Marxism-Leninism.' (*RC*, I, p. 215; 13 March 1965); in 1975, he
commented thus on Kim's attempts at self-promotion: 'Kim Il Sung is a pseudo-
Marxist. He has begun to make «*la tournée des grands-ducs*» [The Grand Dukes'
tour] in Europe and Africa, like Tito and Ceausescu . . . [and he is] a 'vacillating,
revisionist megalomaniac' (*RC*, II, p. 148, 21 August 1975). Reflecting on the
phenomenon of the cult shortly after Mao's death, Hoxha has a strange paragraph
referring to himself – half evasive, half not:

We have condemned the cult of the individual and condemn it to this day
about anybody at all. On this question we follow the view of Marx, and
for this reason amongst us, in our leadership, there is Marxist-Leninist
unity, affection, sincerity, Marxist-Leninist respect towards comrades
. . . Amongst us there is no *idolâtrie*. Above all we speak about the Party,
while we speak about Enver only as much as the interests of the Party and
country require, and when from the base and the masses there has been
some excess in this direction, the Central Committee, the leadership of
the Party and I personally, as much as I can and to the extent that they
have listened to me about it, have always taken and always will take
measures to proceed on the right course (*RC*, II, pp. 419–20, 8 January
1977).

73 – *Juche*: roughly 'self-reliance'.

74 – In an entry dated 15 August 1977 ('Articles With Stale "Theorizing"', *RC*, II,
pp. 578ff), Hoxha pours scorn on the Chinese riposte to the Albanian text –
"Chairman Mao's Theory of the Differentiation of the Three Worlds is a Major
Contribution to Marxism-Leninism" (later in *Peking Review*, no. 45, 4
November 1977). In a sense, history may be said to have vindicated Hoxha, since
the Chinese later tacitly abandoned the so-called 'Three Worlds Theory'.

75 – The Congress (held in August 1977) marked the first systematic attempt to
overcome the catastrophe of the Cultural Revolution (Deng Xiaoping had been
rehabilitated in late July). Once again, Hoxha is not entirely wrong about some
things, like the inadequacy of Hua Kuo-feng (Hua Guofeng), but he fixates on a
nonessential remark by Yeh Chien-ying (Ye Jianying) and exaggerates it in an
irrelevant direction.

76 – The main square in Peking.

77 – A few days later, Hoxha added: 'The Chinese and the Koreans brought out
the people like a mob of sheep which bleated and gambolled' (*RC*, II, p. 636, 8
September 1977).

78 – It is not clear to whom the phrase 'the new Khrushchev of China' refers –
either Hua or Deng. The Amur is the river between China and the USSR on China's
northeast border; the Yangtze is the main river in central China.

79 – Bucharest: June 1960; the Moscow Meeting was in November 1960 (see
above, pp. 227–239). Peng Chen: note 24 above.

80 – Earlier, Hoxha names the Soviet ambassador to China, P. F. Yudin, as the person responsible for 'editing' Mao's published writings (*RC*, II, p. 232, 1 April 1976). In his memoirs, Khrushchev states that Mao wrote to Stalin to ask him 'to recommend a Soviet Marxist philosopher who might come to China to edit Mao's works. Mao wanted an educated man to help put his works into proper shape and to catch any mistakes in Marxist philosophy before Mao's writings were published.' (*KR*, I, p. 497.) Yudin had earlier been ambassador to Yugoslavia and editor of the Cominform newspaper.

81 – In 1965 at least 500,000 people and more probably about 1 million were massacred in a right-wing counterrevolution. D. N. Aidit was the exceptionally able chairman of the Indonesian Communist Party, the PKI. General Suharto, a leading figure in the massacre, is currently President of Indonesia.

82 – Another case of Hoxha's dogmatic blinkers. He refuses to recognise that the situation, while still most unsatisfactory and often arbitrary, was far better than under Mao.

83 – Georges Marchais, head of the French Communist Party; Enrico Berlinguer, (late) head of the Italian CP; Santiago Carrillo, then head of the Spanish CP.

84 – Chinese sage (?372–?289 BC), second only to Confucius.

6 MEHMET SHEHU AND HIS STRANGE END

1 – For Shehu's biography, see: Lazitch, pp. 67–8; Prifti, p. 34; *Yearbook on International Communist Affairs*, 1966, pp. 711–12.

2 – *KR*, I, p. 507; the incident involving the Italians is in Kemp, *No Colours or Crest*, p. 95. Shehu also spoke several foreign languages, including English, well. An article in the American magazine *Collier's* (15 September 1951), after claiming that Shehu was known in Tirana as 'the Butcher' and liked roaming the streets of the capital in disguise, described him as 'a tall and spare Hollywood version of a Balkan assassin' (p. 54).

3 – This is the version Hoxha gives in *TT*; on 1 March 1985, however, just before Hoxha died, the Party daily, *Zeri i Popullit*, stated that Shehu had been 'liquidated' – a term widely but not necessarily used to mean killed; an official in the Albanian embassy in Vienna explicitly denied that Shehu had been executed.

4 – Interesting background on the American school in Joan Fultz Kontos, *Red Cross, Black Eagle: A Biography of Albania's American School* (Boulder, Co., East European Monographs, 1981). Harry T. Fultz, who, Hoxha claims, was the key US agent, had been head of the American school before the war and returned to Albania in May 1945, allegedly on an intelligence mission. Larry Post, also mentioned below (presumably an Albanian of Greek origin – his original name was Llazar Papapostoli) is identified by Hoxha as 'political adviser to the American mission' after the war (*AAT*, pp. 404ff). That the OSS were active in Albania after Liberation is very likely, as emerges from a telegram from the British embassy in Washington to the Foreign Office, dated 5 December 1944 (immediately after the Liberation of Tirana), which says that the State Department felt it might be useful to have some kind of US office in Tirana soon but that the official, Cannon, 'did not seem to have worked out any precise idea as to the kind of

"office" which the United States Government might establish in Tirana, but he thought it might send an O.S.S. Mission . . .' (FO 371/43554).

To have fought in the Spanish Civil War was held against many important militants purged in Eastern Europe after the war – e.g. Rájk in Hungary.

5 – Hoxha later quotes a letter from Shehu to Mugoša in which Shehu calls Mugoša 'our teacher' and calls the Albanian Communists 'brigands' and a 'hotch-potch of bitter vegetables' (*TT*, p. 603).

6 – Griffith, usually well informed, says it was the *Queen Mary* (p. 60). A search of the passenger lists for all sailings of both ships in the month of September 1960 failed to turn up any of the names – but presumably none of them would show up anyway.

7 – FO 371/43554; the quote by Major Smith (below) about Shehu is from FO 371/43551 (13 July 1944).

8 – Succession disputes certainly occur, but are often hard to evaluate (as in China, for example). Hoxha quotes the senior CIA official urging Shehu into action in 1972, when Shehu was not yet sixty, with the remark 'You are getting old'. But, of course, by 1981 Hoxha, who was older than Shehu, was indeed nearing his end and there must have been considerable manoeuvring, and perhaps discussion, about the succession.

9 – According to Hoxha, Shehu had enlisted as a Soviet agent on the orders of Fultz in the immediate postwar period (*TT*, p. 601). In the years 1945–6 Shehu was sent to study at the Red Army Higher Academy in the USSR.

10 – This refers to the period immediately after the break with Moscow in 1960–61; Albania then was very much on its own in Europe, and in a loose form of alliance with China.

11 – The time lag between 1968 and 1972 (like many other things) is unexplained.

12 – Mehmet Shehu's nephew and then Minister of the Interior.

13 – Another unexplained element – hardly like Enver not to get his word in! Of course, he had plenty to live down himself – not least his ringing endorsement of Shehu to Stalin (*WS*, p. 96).

14 – Pipa notes that the original Albanian version ends with the expression: 'He was buried like a dog' – a piece of repulsive gloating, which, as Pipa points out, echoes a phrase attributed by Hoxha to Xoxe on the death of Nako Spiru ('The Political Culture of Hoxha's Albania', pp. 458, 464).

15 – Not so ridiculous at all, as this was standard Balkan behaviour, too. If Hoxha actually thought people were going to believe his version of events he was as out of touch, or as dismissively manipulative, as Mao in the case of his fairy tale about Lin Piao.

16 – Succeeded Shehu (Mehmet) as Minister of the Interior, 1954–70; then Minister of Defence; usually reported to be a nephew of Mehmet Shehu.

17 – The invasion, which was confirmed by émigré sources, including Zog's son Leka, took place at the end of September 1982. Hoxha is correct in claiming that it was immediately crushed.

HOXHA'S NOTES
Note to p. 47

In regard to this he wrote to his centre on December 17, 1943 as follows:

«1. Now recommend a change. Situation developed recently so much imperative now denounce Regency Council collectively and by name. Also BALKOM and ZOGISTS.

2. All are cooperating with Germans, who are exploiting them with arms in large quantities, setting them to guard main roads, police towns and lead patrols thus freeing German troops.

3. All recent actions fought by LNC have met mixed German Balkom bodies well armed German-trained. Battles PEZA and DIBRA areas, especially latter, have ample proof closest collaboration.

4. BALKOM and ABAS KUPI both promised me fight Germans actively, but not one action have they fought this past month, although there have been many chances for them to resist the Germans . . .

5. Both the BALKOM and ZOGISTS now publish expensive ambitious newspapers obviously German set-up. In eight editions there has not been one anti-German reference. Both parties boasting ALLIES will cooperate with them after Germans go quoting as evidence Britain's failure to name the Regency Council or any political party [in Albania]. Example: — BBC Director's speech to ALBANIA on 28th November.

6. I would have preferred to explain personally when I come out, but I may be delayed, and am unlikely to reach you before mid-January at the earliest.

7. I consider the ALLIES' attitude should be made public forthwith, showing Quislings, traitors and non-resisters to Germans will receive appropriate punitive treatment from the allies in due course . . . Therefore, I recommend an open declaration for the LNC.» *Telegram No. 3 to SOE in Cairo to be passed on to London, FO 371/37145-3741. PRO.* Taken from the photocopy of the original in the *AIH*, Tirana.

Note to p. 58

On August 1–2, 1943, the 2nd meeting of representative of the Balli Kombëtar and the National Liberation General Council was held in the village of Mukje. There Ymer Dishnica and Mustafa Gjinishi, failing to adhere to the instructions which they had been given, fell into the positions of reaction. They capitulated to the Balli Kombëtar, treating it as an antifascist organisation, and agreed to share the leadership of the National Liberation War and the political power with the representatives of this traitor organisation and accepted the proposal of the Ballists to create a so-called «committee for the salvation of Albania» with equal numbers of representatives, which would have meant the liquidation of the National Liberation General Council and violation of the interests of the people and the Homeland. On the initiative of Comrade Enver Hoxha, the CC of the CPA, and the National Liberation General Council rejected the Mukje Agreement as a dangerous and unprincipled compromise.

Note to p. 331

That Mehmet Shehu was a secret agent of the Americans and served them, is also borne out, among others, by a letter dated February 6, 1944 which the CIA agent Larry Post (who later was sent by the American secret service to Albania) wrote to another secret agent of the Americans Hasan Reci, «I repeated many times to them that we wanted **facts, facts,** and **facts** about every situation and everything,» stressed Larry Post in this letter and continued: «Transmit to Mjekrra – Mehmet Shehu – my warmest greetings. Is it possible for him to send me a report on his situation and activity?! You do not write whether you have contacted him . . . ! P.S. Mjekrra may read this letter, too.» (*From the original copy of the letter in* CAP.)

Note to p. 331

From its assessments of the situation in Albania [at] the end of 1944, the British secret service envisaged the eventual organisation of an opposition to the new state of people's democracy which was created. They included Mehmet Shehu among the main elements of this opposition. This is borne out by a document dated November 10, 1944, the photocopy of which has been taken from the archives of the Foreign Office, London, and which, among other things, says about Mehmet Shehu, «. . . he is a communist, but his personal ambition exceeds his loyalty to the Party». (*FO 371/43554 PRO.*) Whereas in another document dated February 10, 1945, the section of the British Intelligence Service for Albania (*Force No. 399*) describes Mehmet Shehu «to be the only man with sufficient following to prove dangerous to Hoxha, should they disagree» (read: over the programme of the British Mehmet Shehu brought with him on his return to Albania in 1942, which was found in his safe after his suicide). *WO-204.*

APPENDIX I. THE KOSOVO QUESTION

1 Among the most useful recent texts are: Mark Baskin, 'Crisis in Kosovo', *Problems of Communism*, March–April 1983 (cf. Viktor Meier, 'Yugoslavia's National Question', ibid.); Elez Biberaj, 'The Conflict in Kosovo', *Survey* vol. 28, no. 3, autumn 1984; Michèle Lee, 'Kosovo Between Yugoslavia and Albania', *New Left Review*, no. 140, 1983; some useful background in Prifti, ch. 11, and Marmullaku, ch. 10 (but unsound on later period); Alain Ducellier, 'Les Albanais et le Kosovo', *Le Monde*, 2 June 1982, gives an informed pro-Tirana view.

For the various positions adopted during the war, see Lee; for the 1944–5 events, Biberaj, p. 41, and Pavlowitch, cit. For Tirana's claims about Tito's 1946 commitment, see Hoxha, *TT*, p. 285; and the editorial in *Zeri i Popullit*, 17 May 1981, in English in *Communist Affairs: Documents and Analysis*, vol. 1, no. 1 (Sevenoaks, Butterworth, January 1982), esp. p. 313.

APPENDIX II. THE CORFU CHANNEL INCIDENTS AND ALBANIA'S GOLD

1 There is a succinct and fair summing up in Marmullaku, p. 116; cf. ibid., p. 128. The Albanian case and examination of the evidence is well presented in a pamphlet put out by the Albanian Society, *Miscarriage of Justice: The Corfu Channel Case* (Ilford, UK, n.d. [?1983]). The British position is expounded at length in Leslie Gardiner, *The Eagle Spreads His Claws: A History of the Corfu Channel Dispute and of Albania's Relations with the West, 1945–1965* (London, W. Blackwood, 1966). International Court of Justice, *The Corfu Channel Case* (the Hague, ICJ, 1949–50) contains a mountain of evidence on both sides. The Albanian case at the Hague was defended by the distinguished French lawyer Pierre Cot. Interesting observations on the missing links in Michael Davie, 'Gun-boat diplomacy that lost lives – but won gold', *Observer*, 21 April 1985.

Biographical notes

Albanians

Alia, Ramiz (born 1925) Hoxha's successor as Party leader, 1985; President of Albania since 1982. Joined Communist Party 1943 and fought in the war; studied in Leningrad in 1950s.

Balluku, Beqir Long-time Defence Minister, purged (and apparently executed) 1974.

Belishova, Liri Partisan leader (woman); member of Politbureau at age 22. Executed at time of break wtih Russia for alleged pro-Soviet activities. Wife of Spiru (q.v.).

Çarçani, Adil Prime Minister since fall of Shehu in 1981.

Gega, Liri Leading partisan, member of Politbureau, executed 1956 (shot while pregnant).

Gjinishi, Mustafa Partisan leader; killed in ambush, apparently by Germans, 1944; Hoxha accused of ties to British.

Kapo, Hysni Long-time member of Politbureau; apparently Hoxha's closest friend in regime; died 1979.

Këllezi, Abdyl Politbureau member; chairman of the Planning Commission; purged and apparently executed 1975.

Kryeziu family Wealthy tribal conservative family in northeast Albania/Yugoslav border area; closely linked to British.

Kupi, Abas/Abaz Officer in army of King Zog (q.v.); founded Legaliteti (q.v.) September 1943; main British candidate for power; illiterate.

Nushi, Gogo Politbureau member; natural death.

Peza, Myslim Prewar outlaw (from area of Peza); became leading Partisan.

Shehu, Mehmet Spanish Civil War veteran who became leading partisan commander. Postwar Minister of Interior; premier from 1954 until mysterious death in December 1981; denounced by Hoxha as multiple agent.

Shtylla, Behar Foreign Minister; ambassador to China.

Spiru, Nako   Wartime leader; in charge of trade relations with Yugoslavia until reported suicide in 1947; later denounced as traitor. Husband of Belishova (q.v.).

Xoxe, Koçi   Second figure in Party after Hoxha; Minister of Interior until purged in 1948 as pro-Tito; executed 1949.

Zog, Ahmed/Ahmet   Muslim tribal leader from north; proclaimed himself king 1928; exiled from 1939; died 1961.

Non-Albanians

Andropov, Yuri Vladimirovich (1914–1984) Secretary of Central Committee of CPSU, deeply involved in discussions leading to break with Albania, 1960–61; formerly ambassador to Hungary during 1956 uprising; later head of KGB; President and head of Party 1982–4.

Beria, Lavrenti Pavlovich (1899–1953) Chief of secret police under Stalin 1938–53; executed.

Bulganin, Nikolai Aleksandrovich (1895–1975) Soviet Marshal; member of Politbureau 1948; premier 1955–8.

Ceauşescu, Nicolae (born 1918) Romanian President; since 1965 head of Party; runs nepotistic regime with wife, sons.

Davies, Brigadier E. F. ('Trotsky') Second head of British mission to Albanian partisans October 1943–January 1944 (captured by Germans).

Dej, Gheorghe Gheorghiu- (1901–64) Romanian Communist leader; head of Party in postwar period.

Deng Xiaoping/Teng Hsiao-ping (born 1904) Chinese political leader; member of Politbureau and General Secretary of CC under Mao; purged in Cultural Revolution (1966) but rehabilitated 1973; ousted again in early 1976 after death of Chou; rehabilitated again July 1977; thereafter pre-eminent figure in regime.

Gomulka, Wladyslaw (1905–1982) Wartime and early postwar Polish Communist leader; purged; reinstated 1956 as main figure in regime.

Kádár, János (born 1912) Hungarian Communist leader purged under Stalin, returned to power after 1956 uprising.

Li Xiannian/Li Hsien-nien (born 1909) Chinese Communist leader; veteran of Long March; long-time aide to Chou En-Lai, dealing with economy. State President.

McLean, Lt. Col. Neil ('Billy') (born 1918) Head of first British mission to Albania April–October 1943; head of later mission to Northern conservative clans April–October 1944. Eton and Sandhurst; Scots Greys. Conservative MP for Inverness 1954–64.

Malenkov, Georgi Maximilianovich (born 1902) Stopgap successor to Stalin 1953; replaced as head of Party by Khrushchev in 1953 and as premier in February 1955 by Bulganin (q.v.).

Molotov, Vyacheslav Mikhailovich (born 1890) Long-time Soviet Foreign Minister; premier 1930–41; purged as 'anti-Party' element 1957; ambassador to Mongolia. Reinstated in CPSU 1984.

Mugoša, Dušan Yugoslav CP emissary to Albanian Partisans.

Nagy, Imre (1896–1958) Hungarian politician; premier at time of 1956 uprising; executed in Romania by Russians after promise of safe conduct.

Popović, Miladin Wartime Yugoslav emissary to Albanian Partisans; assassinated in Kosovo 1945.

Rájk, Lászlo (1909–49) Veteran Hungarian Communist; fought in Spain; Foreign Minister; hanged 1949; rehabilitated 1956 and reburied.

Rákosi, Mátyás (1892–1971) Hungarian Communist leader postwar; ousted in 1956 upheavals; Stalinist.

Ranković, Aleksandar (1909–1982) Yugoslav Communist; Partisan leader; Minister of Interior; ousted July 1966.

Stojnić, Col. Velimir (born 1916) Yugoslav emissary to Albania, August 1944 to late 1945.

Suslov, Mikhail Andreyevich (1902–1982) Soviet political leader; chief ideologist of regime.

Tempo, Svetozar Vukmanović (born 1912) Yugoslav Communist leader; wartime emissary for Balkan affairs; later trade-union leader.

Vyshinsky, Andrei Yanyuarevich (1883–1954) Chief Prosecutor at Moscow Trials; Deputy Foreign Minister of USSR.

Zakhariades, Nikos   (born 1903) Greek Communist leader; imprisoned in Dachau 1941–5; replaced Markos Vafiades as head of Greek Communists after defeat in civil war 1949; ousted 1956.

Zhukov, Georgi K.   (1896–1974) Soviet Marshal; Minister of Defence 1955–7; key role in saving Khrushchev 1957; ousted while in Albania.

Index

Abyssinia 58
Adenauer, Konrad 202
Agitation and Propaganda Commission 77
Agolli, Zeqi 57
Agriculture 12; collectivization of 127
Aidit, Dipa Nusantara 321
Albania; agriculture 12; aid from China 254, 303; base for Yugoslav troops 107; break with USSR 80, 155, 239–47; centralised planning 15; colony of Italy 22; communications with Communist world 61–62; defence 98–9; economy 11–13, 146; economic aid from Czechoslovakia 170; economy after break with Yugoslavia 115–16; economic and military aid from USSR 149–51; education 87; ethnic origins of population 97; exports 12; foreign policy 125; foreign trade 12; fruit growing 219–20; GNP 12; guerrilla warfare in 78; industry 12–13, 87; invasion of 1939 21–2; language 129; liberation of 1944 24; natural resources 12; occupation by Germany 64; oil 21, 146, 221; People's Republic proclaimed 87; plan to turn into 7th Republic of Yugoslavia 63, 121; population 11; pressure from USSR for reconciliation with Yugoslavia 154–9; reactionary forces 100; relations with Yugoslavia 24–5, 106–112, 115; requests extradition of war criminals 81; self-sufficiency in food 12–13; Soviet pressure on 224–7; standard of living 11; state control of industry and mining 87; suppression of human rights under Zog 40; territorial dispute with Greece 31; 'Third World' country 16; war casualties 78; Yugoslav Defence Alliance proposed 275

Albanian Communist Party (ACP) 22, 33; early achievements 78; role of Yugoslavs in 24–5
Albanian Democratic Front 87
Alia, Ramiz 14, 177, 183, 227; as Hoxha's successor 5
Althusser, Louis 7
American Technical School in Tirana 327
Amery, Julian 6, 22, 47, 78, 80, 81, 83
Amur River 319
Andreyev, Soviet official 241–2
Andropov, Yuri 143, 186–7, 193–5, 226, 227, 234, 236, 240, 244–5
The Anglo-American Threat (Hoxha) 16, 17, 33
Anglo-Iranian Oil (formerly Anglo-Persian Oil) 21
Anti-Fascist Council of National Liberation 87
Antonescu, Ion 117
Antonov, Aleksey Innokentyevich 174, 242
Aquinas, St. Thomas 7
Archaeology 220
Atheist state, Albania first in world 130
Athens 81, 107
Attila 190
Austerlitz 173
Austria 193, 227, 239
Axis Forces, war casualties 78

Baghdash, Khalid 238
Balkan Federation 27, 92, 115, 122, 155, 342; Yugoslavia's aspirations for 25
Balkans 27, 28, 37, 108, 110, 305, 307, 330–1
Balli Kombëtar 4, 23, 24, 30, 35, 38, 39, 42, 49, 63–5, 78, 81, 87; agreement with LNC 54; collaboration with Nazis 32

Balluku, Beqir 252, 254, 307, 309, 332
Barák, Rudolf 244, 245
Bari 79, 239, 329
Basques, theory Albanians descended from 97
Bata, István 189
BBC 40, 48, 58, 60, 376; broadcast messages for British Intelligence agents 57
Beaverbrook, Lord 48
Begeja 42
Beijing see Peking
Bektashi 2
Belgium 16
Belgrade 89, 93, 106, 116, 182, 185, 186, 201, 319, 343
Belgrade University, Albanian students at 92
Belishova, Liri 223–25; execution of 10
Ben Bella, Ahmed 15
Berat 75–6, 105
Berat Congress 87
Beria, Lavrenti Pavlovich 139, 143, 147, 148–51, 152–3, 157–8, 208, 331
Berlinguer, Enrico 322
Biçaku, Aziz 51
Bierut, Boleslaw 145, 154, 167
Biza 41, 43, 59
Black Sea 130
Bled 94
Blomberg, General 83
Bodnaras, Emil 186, 306
Bolshevik Party 121, 136
Bolshevik Revolution 214
Bolshoi Ballet 191
Bosnia-Herzegovina 25
Bosporus 220
Brezhnev, Leonid 143, 145, 197–200, 223, 246, 263
Brioni 195
Britain 132, 328, 333, 346; aim to establish regime sympathetic to 33; as 'pseudo-allies' 35; blamed for invasion by Italy 21; declines to return war criminals 81; interference in Albanian affairs 88; intelligence operations in Albania

41; mission in Albania 56; port facilities in Albania 129; possible occupation of Albania 78; supplies weapons to Albania 40–1; wants bases in Albania 125; weapon supply 78
British Empire 38, 44, 46
British Intelligence 31, 328–9, 331
Bucharest 116–18, 123–4, 185–6, 224, 226, 236, 260, 319
Budapest 130, 186, 188, 191, 196, 228
Buddhism 323
Bugging devices 236–7
Bukharinites 120
Bulganin, Nikolai Aleksandrovich 139, 147, 148, 149–51, 166, 188
Bulgaria 27, 30, 115, 137, 168–9, 171–2, 187, 210, 226
Butrint 220
Byron, Lord 6, 44, 45
Byzantium 318

Cairo 31, 37, 38
Çako, Hito 304, 309
Cambodia 286, 298
Çamëria Region 22
Capitalism 214
Çarçani, Adil 303, 305
Carnarvon, Earl of 173
Carrillo, Santiago 15, 300, 322
Carter, Howard 173
Carter, President Jimmy 314
Castro, Fidel 231–3, 251, 273, 274
Catholic Church 14, 129, 132–3
Caucasus 155
Ceauşescu, Nicolae 284, 285, 300, 305–6
Central Committee of the Youth 77
Central Intelligence Agency (CIA) 81, 299, 332–3, 336
Chamberlain, Neville 21
Chang Chun-chiao (Zhang Chunqiao) 310
Chen Boda (Chen Po-ta) 10, 283
Chen Yi 255–6, 273
Chervenkov, Vulko 168
Chiang Ching (Jiang Qing) 291–2, 311
Chiatura (Soviet Ship) 155

'Childe Harold' 44
China 234, 240, 251–323, 328; aid to
   Albania 254, 303; alliance with 4;
   cuts off aid 12; economy 185;
   equipment from 12; foreign aid
   from 12–13; foreign policy 271–3;
   Hoxha visits 175–86
China Sea 284
Chinese Embassy, Tirana 9
Chou En-Lai (Zhou Enlai) 179, 183,
   203, 254, 256, 259–64, 269,
   275–8, 280, 282, 285, 288, 291–7,
   299, 301–5, 310–11, 317
Chrome 12
Chuikov, Marshal 233
Churchill, Randolph 328
Churchill, Winston S. 6, 33, 37, 88,
   130, 133
Chuvakhin, Dmitry 117, 119, 123,
   126
Çitaku, Ramadan 71
Civil War 1944 4
Clausewitz, Karl von 38
Coal 12; Polish 164–5
Coldstream Guards 43
Colonialism 22, 38, 44, 46, 157, 214
COMECON See Council for Mutual
   Economic Assistance
COMINFORM 88, 106
COMINTERN 187
Communist movement, Hoxha
   working as clandestine leader 3
Communist Party of Burma 272
Communist Party of China 176, 183,
   222–3, 235, 244, 263, 271, 287,
   296, 308, 310–12, 317–18
Communist Party of the Philippines
   320–1
Communist Party of the Soviet Union
   138–9, 156–7, 170–1, 192, 196,
   265; Twentieth Congress (1956)
   161–3
Communist Party of Yugoslavia 63,
   69, 74–5
Conference of Communist Parties
   1960 1
Confucius 299, 322
Congress of Anti-Fascist Women 76
Conservative Party 47
Constantine, Emperor 318

Constituent Assembly 87
Co-operatives, establishment of 127
Corfu Channel 79, 83, 88, 139, 345–6
Council for Mutual Economic
   Assistance (COMECON) 4, 163–7,
   189, 217
Crimea 196, 229
Csepel 188
Cuba 262, 292
Cult of personality, Hoxha's remarks
   on 8, 253, 266–7, 314, 316, 371–2
Cultural Revolution 8, 266–70,
   280–2, 321
Cyrankiewicz, Jozef 154, 163, 166
Czechoslovakia 5, 21, 167–9, 172–3,
   187, 200, 244, 245, 332; economic
   aid to Albania 170
Czechoslovak Communist Party 174

Danube River Commission 116
David Copperfield 44
Davies, E. F. ('Trotsky') 6, 32, 36–8,
   42–3, 45, 47, 49, 50, 52, 55, 77
De Beauvoir, Simone 7
Dedinje 92
Dedijer, Vladimir 107, 115
Dej See Gheorghiu-Dej, Gheorghe
Democracy 46; Hoxha's approach to
   9
Deng Xiaoping (Teng Hsiao-ping)
   179, 183, 227, 235, 255, 260, 319
Dibra 41, 49, 375
Dimitrov, Georgi (George) 7, 115,
   122, 145, 168
Dine, Fiqri 41
Dishnica, Ymer 54, 65
Dizdarević, Nijaz 62, 65, 69, 71, 74,
   158
Djilas, Milovan 69, 89, 101, 107, 157
Doftana 117
Dolansky, Jaromir 170
Dragot Bridge 68
Duclos, Jacques 215
Dukat 241
Dulles, John Foster 203
Dume, Petrit 304, 309
Dumont, René 11
Dung Biwu See Tung Pi-Wu
Duras, Marguerite 7
Durazzo See Durrës

Durham, Edith 46
Durrës 79, 80, 99, 155, 300

Ecclesiastes 7
Economic success 12–13
Eden, Anthony 33, 48, 78
Educational reforms 87
Egyptology 6, 173–4
Eisenhower, Dwight 203
Elbasan 31, 49, 50
Elections 87
Elegy of Marienbad (Goethe) 174
Elleinstein, Jean 7
Engels, Friedrich 263
Esztergom 190
Ethiopia 58
Eurocommunism 322
Exports 12

Far East 321
Farkas Mikály, member of Hungarian
    Political Bureau 189
Federal German Republic 306
Federalism 25, 27
Feminism 7, 13–14
Fier 281
First National Conference 26
First Resolution 133
First Shock Brigade 4, 24, 327
Firyubin, N. 242–3
Fitzgerald, Edward 44
Foreign aid 12
Foreign Office (UK) 46, 345
France 16, 216, 225, 327, 328;
    maintains relations with Albania 88
Frashëri, Mehdi 60
Frashëri, Mithat 42
Free Albania Committee 81
Freud, Sigmund 7
From the Annals of British Diplomacy
    (Puto) 33–4, 330
Fruit growing 219–20
Fultz, Harry T 328
Furtseva, Yekaterina A. 198

Gagarinov, Soviet emissary 105
'Gang of Four' 255
Garaudy, Roger 7
Gas 12

Gega, Liri 65, 71, 75, 201, 204–5,
    329; execution of 10
Geng Biao See Keng Piao
Geraldina, Queen 31
German Democratic Republic 167,
    174–5
Germany: co-ordinated offensive
    December 1943 52; occupation by
    64; troops in Albania 1943–4 24;
    withdrawal from Greece through
    Albania 61
Gerö, Ernö 164–5, 177, 187, 189,
    192, 196, 200–201
Gheorghiu-Dej, Gheorghe 116–18,
    120, 123–4, 163–5, 169, 185–6,
    238
Gibraltar 220
Gjinishi, Mustafa 22, 40, 43, 45,
    47–8, 54–61, 65
Gjirokastra, birthplace of Hoxha 2,
    68, 117, 320
Glenconner, Lord 31
Goethe, Johann Wolfgang von 6, 174
Gomulka, Wladyslaw 163, 167, 215,
    226, 238
Gostivari, Ali 70
Gostivari, Xhem 41
Gottwald, Kliment 145, 167
Grain supply 225
Grammos 135
Gramsci, Antonio 24
Grechko, Marshal A. A. 241
Greece 22, 27, 72–3, 107, 128,
    134–9, 148, 328, 333; civil war 115,
    125, 128; preparation for attack on
    Albania 108, 112; refugees in
    Albania 131, 136–37; territorial
    dispute with Albania 31
Greek Communist Party 125, 131,
    135, 171
Greek Democratic Army (GDA) 130,
    135, 136, 171
Greek Orthodox Church 14, 129, 133
Griffith, William E. 101
Grimm Brothers 119
Grotewohl, Otto 209
Guerrilla warfare in Albania 78
GUM Store (Moscow) 171

The Hague 345

Hailé Selassié I 58
Halveti Sect 327
Hani i Hotit 68
Hanoi 275, 286, 294
Hare, Alan 50, 80
Hasluck, Fanny 31
Hazbiu, Kadri 336
Hebrang, Andrija 94
Hegedüs, András 193
Helmës 62, 69
He Long See Ho Lung
Henderson, member of American
    military mission 81
Herbert, Col. 81
Hibbert, Reginald 33
Hill, E. H. 317
Himara 78
Hitler, Adolf 21, 133, 165–6
Ho Chi Minh 16, 275
Hodgson, D. E. P. 32
Ho Lung 264
Hopkins, Harry 6
Hoxha, Enver: applies double
    standards 8; admiration of Stalin
    96; admired by de Gaulle 15;
    approach to democracy 9; attempt
    to maintain good relations with
    West 87; birth 2; brutality 10–11;
    character 5–7; clandestine
    Communist leader 3; death sentence
    on 1941 3; denunciation of
    Khrushchev 227; education 2–3;
    elected head of provisional
    government 1944 87; first
    meeting with Stalin 96–101; first
    post-Stalin visit to Moscow 1953
    147–54; head of Communist Party
    87; interest in Egyptology 6, 173–4;
    linguistic capabilities 6; literary
    knowledge 6; note keeping 28;
    psychoanalysis – dislike of 7; reads
    Western press 6; religious
    background 14–15; relations with
    Shehu 327–37; removal of enemies
    10; running tobacco kiosk 3; seeks
    economic and military aid from
    USSR 149–51; self-criticism 2;
    surrealism – dislike of 7; suspected
    of being 'dangerous liberal' 24;
    suspicion as central theme of

    memoirs 9–10; teaching in Tirana
    3; thoughts on love 14; visits China
    1956 175–86; years in power 3
Hoxha, Nexhmije (Mrs. Enver
    Hoxha) 157–8, 173, 210, 229
Hsinhua (New China News Agency)
    269, 274, 285
Hua Kuo-feng (Hua Guofeng)
    313–15, 317–19
Hungarian Workers' Party 189, 196
Hungary 146, 227–8; economy 188;
    Uprising 1956 186–201
Hydroelectricity 12

Ibarruri, Dolores ('La Pasionaria') 238
'If', (Rudyard Kipling) 51
Illyrian Venture (Davies) 50
Imperialism 22, 38, 44, 46, 157, 214
Indochina 298
Industrial raw materials 12
Intelligence Service, British 31, 328–9,
    331
Interior, Ministers of as foreign agents
    10
Internal Affairs, Ministry of 127
International Court of Justice at the
    Hague 345
International Herald Tribune 6
Iran 145
Iron Guard (Romania) 117
Islam 2, 13–15, 23, 129, 130, 133
Italian Communist Party 23, 327, 333
Italy 14, 126, 128, 148, 202, 227,
    239, 253; capitulation of 64;
    colonial treatment of Albania 22;
    invasion by 1939 21; surrender
    1943 4
Ivanov, Maj., Soviet Head of Mission
    62, 69, 244

'James Bond' 288, 330
Jakova, Tuk 106
Jerome, Jerome K. 6, 44
Jiang Qing See Chiang Ching
Joint companies 95
Jovanović, Blažo 25, 121

Kádár, János 146, 163, 164, 188–9,
    193–6, 200

Kafka, Franz 7
Kakavia 68
Kang Sheng 7, 276, 278, 279, 293
Kapo, Hysni 152, 223, 227, 231, 237
Kardelj, Edvard 69, 97, 107, 185,
    203, 208, 210–11
Kasatonov, Admiral 243
Kautsky, Karl 7
Këlcyra, Ali 47
Këlcyra Gorge 68
Këllezi, Abdyl 252, 304, 307, 309,
    332
Kemp, Peter 83
Keng Piao (Geng Biao) 313
KGB 225, 299, 331
Khayyam, Omar 44
Khrushchev, Nikita Sergeyevich 1, 2,
    5, 83, 91, 96, 124, 143–7, 153–4,
    155, 159–62, 164–7, 170, 175,
    177, 181, 184, 188–9, 195, 197,
    198, 200, 208–15, 217–18, 220,
    222, 226, 234, 242–4, 246, 253,
    255–8, 260, 263, 319, 322, 327;
    becomes First Secretary 1954 152;
    denunciation of Stalin 159–62;
    seeks to improve relations with
    Yugoslavia 201–8; visits Albania
    217–21
Kidrić, Boris 91, 101
Kiev 172, 228
Kirichenko, A. I. 209–10
Kim Il Sung 7, 9, 177, 179, 251, 286,
    314–16
Kipling, Rudyard 44, 51
Kishi, Nobusuke 202
Kislovodsk 155
Kissinger, Henry 285, 291, 297
Konev, I. S. 174, 233
Kopecký, Václav 170
Koran 15
Korça 22–3, 52, 101, 110
Korça-Erseka Zone 108
Korça Group 72
Korea, North 175–7, 197, 265–6,
    286, 294, 298, 314–16, 319
Korean Workers' Party 97
Kosovo (Kosova) 22, 24, 30, 88, 92,
    121, 330, 334, 341–3
Kostov, Traicho 185
Kosygin, Aleksei N. 222–4, 227, 232,
    254, 263, 264, 266, 275–7, 279,
    280
Kotovsky (Soviet ship) 155
Kozlov, Frol 172, 226, 228–9, 231,
    232, 236
Kremlin 135, 232, 236
Kristo, Pandi 72, 76, 106
Kruja 45
Kryeziu family 22, 54
Krylov, Soviet Ambassador to Tirana
    195–7, 205
Ksamil 220
Kucaka 28
Kupi, Abas 22, 32, 40, 45, 47, 49, 54,
    59; sets up pro-Zog movement 24
Kuprešanin, Milan, Yugoslav general
    108–9

Labinot 60
Lake Ohrid 159
Lake Shkodra 159
Laos 298
Laptiev, Soviet official 171
Latin America 273
Lavdar 73
Lavrentyev, Soviet Ambassador to
    Yugoslavia 93
League of Communists of Yugoslavia
    211
League of Prizren 342
Legaliteti 4, 24, 78, 81, 87
Lenin, V. I. 148, 177, 229, 238,
    263, 272
Leningrad 172, 221
Leninskie Gori 221
Levichkin, Soviet Ambassador to
    Albania 331
Lesakov, Soviet official 170
Li Hsien-nien (Li Xiannian) 244, 254,
    260, 281–2, 305
Lin Piao (Lin Biao) 214, 254, 268,
    280, 286–9, 293–8, 307, 330
Liu Shao-chi (Liu Shaoqi) 179, 183,
    234, 307
Li Xiannian See Li Hsien-nien
Lleshi, Haxhi 14, 41, 329
Li Lisan 182
London 37, 38, 56, 57, 81
Long Range Desert Group (LRDG) 78
Love, Hoxha's thoughts on 14

Lu Dingyi (Lu Ting-yi) 183
Lukács, György 7
Lula, Anastas 57
Lumumba, Patrice 299
Lushnja 66
Lu Ting-yi *See* Lu Dingyi
Lux, Tito's dog 94, 95
Lyon, Marcus 77

Macedonia 25, 26, 27, 30, 159
Machine tool industry 12
Maclean, Fitzroy 32
Macmillan, Harold 83, 237
Malenkov, Georgi Maximilianovich
    130, 134, 139, 143, 147, 148,
    149–51, 152–4, 188, 195, 200
'Malessori, Lulo' – pseudonym of
    Hoxha 3
Malëshova, Sejfulla 72, 76
Mali 273
Malile, Reiz 255
Malinovsky, Rodion Y. 217, 220, 263
Mao Tse-Tung (Mao Zedong) 8, 9,
    144, 175–6, 180–84, 214, 216–17,
    222, 252–5, 257–8, 263–4,
    268–71, 280, 283, 286, 288,
    294–7, 305, 307, 310, 312–14,
    318–20, 321–3; cult of 266–7
Marchais, Georges 322
Marcos, Ferdinand 320–321
Marienbad 174
Marko, Rita 276, 278–9
Martanesh 49
Marx, Karl 263, 266, 272
Marxism-Leninism 7, 120, 143–4,
    163, 176, 184, 213–14, 216, 222,
    234, 235, 253, 259, 266–7, 308–9,
    312, 321–2
Mat 41, 49
Maxentius 318
McLean, Lt.-Col. Neil ('Billy') 32, 47,
    78, 80–1, 83;
    Hoxha's dislike of 35
Mediterranean 220
Meeting of Communist Parties,
    Moscow 1957 214–17
Mehmet-Fatih, Sultan 45
Mencius 322
Mesopotamia 37
Metternich, Clement von 173

Michael, King of Romania 117
Mićunović, Veljko 201, 204, 206, 207
Mikoyan, Anastas 26, 91, 143–4,146,
    148–9, 155, 158, 175, 179, 187–9,
    195, 209, 210, 221, 236, 242, 263
Mindszenty, Cardinal Jozsef 190
Mobutu, General 298–9
Molotov, Vyacheslav Mikhailovich 5,
    6, 134–5, 138–9, 143, 147, 148,
    155, 157, 187–9, 197, 200, 208
Le Monde 6
Mongolia 175–7, 297–8
Montenegro 25
Montgomery, Field Marshal Bernard
    Law 48
Montpellier University, Hoxha studies
    law at 2
Morand, Paul 123
Moscow 22, 72, 88, 123, 125, 130,
    155–6, 160, 170, 188, 312,
    218–19, 221, 226, 230, 238, 246,
    252, 263; Hoxha's first visit 1947
    97–101
Moscow Meeting November 1960
    175, 253, 257–8, 278, 319, 327
Moscow Trials 1936–8 116
Moshatov, Soviet official 170
Mugoša, Dušan 25, 66, 75, 328–9
Mukje (Mukaj) Agreement 1943
    23–4, 54, 64–5
Mulleti, Qazim 56
Munich 81
Munich Agreement 21
Münnich, Ferenc 187, 193
Mussolini, Benito 21
Mustafa, Xhevdet 336
Myslim, Babë *See* Peza, Myslim

Nagy, Imre 96, 146, 187, 190, 192–5,
    200
Naples Military Academy 327
Napoleon 263
Nashi, Lipe 304
National Liberation Army (Yugoslav)
    27
National Liberation Front (LNC) 3, 23,
    46–8, 64, 87; agreement with Balli
    Kombëtar 54
National Liberation Partisan Army
    120

National Liberation War 98, 133
Natural resources 12
Ndreu, Dali 201, 204–5, 329
Neel, Tony 81
Negovan 73
Nicholls, Col. Arthur 36, 43, 45, 47, 50, 59
Nickel 12
Nietzsche, Friedrich 7
Nixon, Richard Milhous 254, 278, 288–92, 294, 296, 301–2
Nixon, Pat (Mrs Richard Nixon) 290
Noli, Fan 44
Normandy landings 79
North Epirus 135, 226
Nosi, Frederik 42, 51
Novotny, Antonin 163, 170, 174
Nushi, Gogo 49, 162, 223

Oakley Hill, Col. Dayrell 22, 40, 59, 80, 82
Ochab, Edward 154, 163–7
Odessa 155, 172, 197
Odriçan 67, 70, 75, 76
Office of Strategic Services (oss) 33
Ohri, Irfan 56
Ohrid, Lake 159
Oil 12, 21, 146, 218, 221, 284
Okshtun 51
'On Some Aspects of the Problem of the Albanian Woman' (Hoxha) 7
Orenja 43
Osum River 76
Ottoman Empire 2, 14, 45, 168

Palestine 35, 37
Palmer, Alan 33, 77–8
Panmunjom 216
Paris 123
Paris Peace Conference 1946 1, 94
Partsalides, Mitsos 134–6, 138
Party of Labour of Albania 97, 99, 146, 151, 233–5, 237, 246, 247, 273, 334
Pauker, Ana 117
Peking 179, 217, 223, 254, 260, 262, 274, 283, 288, 289, 292, 296, 307, 318; University of 268, 314, 315
Peng Chen (Peng Zhen) 269, 319

Peng Teh-huai (Peng Dehuai) 179, 218
Philippines 320–21
Peoples' Republic, proclaimed January 1946 87
Peqin 66
Përmet 87
Peshkopia 41
'Petöfi' Club 190
Petrov, Soviet official 170
Petrovna, Nina (Mrs. Krushchev) 209
Peza Congress 1942 23
Peza, Myslim 49–50, 54–6, 375
Philby, Harold Adrian Russell ('Kim') 83
Pieck, Wilhelm 175
Pijade, Moša 91
'Ping-pong Diplomacy' 283–4
Plaku, Panajot 10, 206
Poland 167–8, 197, 342; coal 164–5
Polish United Workers' Party 154, 164
Political Bureau 71, 75, 76, 334, 336
Polyansky, Dmitry member of Soviet Politbureau 229–31
Ponomaryov, Boris Nikolaevich 178–9, 205, 226
Pope, the 130, 133
Popović, Koča 185, 203
Popović, Miladin 25, 30, 61–2, 65, 70, 71
Pospyelov, P. N. 198, 226, 236, 244–5
Potemkin Steps (Odessa) 172
Premte, Sadik 57
Priština 342
Pravda 122, 217
Psychoanalysis 7
Pula 197, 205
Punëmira 73
Punjab 272
Pusan 294
Puto, Arben 34, 77, 330
Pyongyang 177, 316

Qarrishta 51
'Qorri', pseudonym of Anastas Lula 57
Quebec Conference (August 1943) 37

Radio Free Europe 193
Rájk, Lászlo 200
Rákosi, Mátyás 5, 7, 130, 187–9, 192–3, 196, 200–1, 214
Ranković, Aleksandar 73, 127, 158, 177, 203, 208, 210–11, 226, 342
Ras Tafari 58
Reagan, Ronald 80
Red Army (Soviet) 69, 97, 187, 342
Red Guard (Chinese) 270
Reflections on China (Hoxha) 8, 16, 17, 218, 251, 252
Reflections on the Middle East 1958–1983 (Hoxha) 251
Regency Council 376
Religion 125, 129, 130; abolition of 14–15; legacy of 14–15
Renmin Ribao 311, 317
Revisionism 7, 216, 319–20
Riddell, Richard 33–4
Ritual, role of 8
Ritz Hotel (London) 21
Rokossovsky, Konstantin 174
Rome 81, 133, 318
Roosevelt, Franklin D 88, 130, 133
Royal Air Force, bombing Tirana 79
Romania 116–17, 123, 167–9, 187, 204, 260–2, 284–5, 305–6

Saburov, M. Z. 166
St John Chrysostom 7
Sanxhaktari, Fiqrete (Mrs. Mehmet Shehu) 223, 328, 332, 333, 335–6
Saranda 78–9, 219
Sartre, Jean-Paul 7
Sazan Island 80, 99
Sazan Narrows 243
Schiller, Friedrich von 173
Scotland 51
Scots Greys Regiment 35
Second Shock Brigade 50
Secret Intelligence Service 81
Sectarianism 65, 75
Sejko, Teme 246
Serbia 25, 27, 121, 342
Sergeyev, Deputy Chief of Supreme Staff of Soviet Army 242
Shakespeare, William 6, 44
Shehu, Feçor 334, 336
Shehu, Mehmet 1, 4, 14, 23, 24, 34,

65, 101, 125, 134, 135, 138, 152, 162, 176, 183, 207, 218, 221, 223, 224, 227, 229, 230, 237, 238, 308, 327–37
Shelepin, Aleksandr Nikolaevich 233
Shelley, Percy Bysshe 39, 44
Shëngjergj 42, 49, 50
Shkodër 87
Shkodra, Lake 159
Shikin, Josif 244
Shtab (LNC High Command) 50
Shtëpani, Ali 42
Shtylla, Behar 177, 302
Sihanouk, Norodom 286
Sino-Soviet Dispute 144, 221–22, 260
Široky, Viliam 170
SIS *See* Secret Intelligence Service
Skanderbeg, Gjergi Kastrioti 45, 174
Skëndo, Lumo 42, 47
Slovakia 174
Smiley, Col. David 32, 80, 83
Socialism, Hoxha and 5
SOE *See* Special Operations Executive
Soviet Embassy (Tirana) 9
Spain 328, 335; Civil War 23, 327
Spanish Communist Party 15
Special Boat Services (SBS) 78
Special Operations Executive (SOE) 31, 32, 329
Spile 78
Spiru, Nako 58, 65, 69, 71, 73–4, 76–7, 335; 'Careerist tendencies' 74; death of 101–6
Sremska Mitrovica 226
Stalin, Yosif Vissarionovich 1, 2, 7, 69, 72–3, 89, 97–101, 107, 112, 134, 135–7, 156, 159–61, 168–9, 181, 187, 204, 206, 208, 214–15, 257, 258, 263, 265, 272, 314, 327, 331, 334; attempt to stage a coup against Yugoslavia 115–16; criticizes Tito for wishing to annex Albania 122; death of 1953 143; denunciation of 159–62; fifth meeting with 1951 139; first meeting with 96–7; fourth meeting with 1950 134–9; Hoxha's adherence to 4; lack of knowledge of Albania 97; second meeting with

Stalin – *cont.*
1949 125–30; abandons Greek
  Communists 125; third meeting
  with 1949 130–34
State Planning Commission 252
State Security Service 125, 127
Stirling, Wilfred 82
Stojnić, Velimir 61–63, 66–74, 76,
  158
Strong, Anna Louise 290
Studa Flat 53–4
Submarine Base at Vlora 240–41
Suharto, General 321
Sukhumi 130, 134
Surrealists 7
Suslov, Mikhail 9, 143, 154–5, 156,
  158, 186, 191, 195, 197, 199–200,
  212–13, 226, 236
Swift, Jonathan 44
Szalai, Béla (Szallay) 190

Taborite Uprising 173
Tachai 307, 308
'Tafari', code name of Mustafa
  Gjinishi 57
Taiwan Straits 283
Tashko, Koço 244–5
Tass 245
Tempo *See* Vukmanović Tempo
Teng Hsiao-ping *See* Deng Xiaoping
Tepelena, Ali Pasha 45
Tërbuf Swamp 219
Theodhosi, Koço 304
'The Theory and Practice of the
  Revolution' 316–17
Thieu, Nguyen Van 301
Third Shock Brigade 49
Thorez, Maurice 236
Tien An Men 319
Tilman, H. W. 33
Tirana 49, 50, 54, 58, 70, 78, 79, 80,
  87, 88, 96, 100, 123, 125, 126, 178,
  182, 194, 204, 208, 211, 218, 219,
  221, 224–6, 236, 239, 240, 242,
  243, 251, 252, 257, 261, 270, 274,
  286, 327, 343; Hoxha teaching in 3
Tirana Conference (April 1956) 186
Tito, Josip Broz 4, 23, 25, 27, 48, 62,
  63, 66, 69–71, 89–96, 108, 109,
  122, 125, 127, 136–7, 146, 158,

177, 185–7, 195–8, 208–211, 213,
  243, 255, 259, 261, 275, 300,
  313–15, 318–19, 322, 327, 342;
  criticized by Stalin for seeking to
  annex Albania 122; luxurious life
  style 88
Todorović, Mijalko 94
Togliatti, Palmiro 190, 215–16
Toska, Haki 281–2
Tokyo 229
Toynbee, Arnold 31
Treaty of Friendship and Mutual Aid
  (with Yugoslavia) 1946 95, 108
Trieste 115
Troitsky, Soviet economic adviser 105
Trotskyites 119, 120, 144
Trotskyism 322
Tsaldaris, Konstantinos 128, 132
Tsedenbal, Yumzhagin 177
Tung Pi-wu (Dung Biwu) 286
Turkey 202
Tutankhamun 173
Tzara, Tristan 7

UBD 336
Uji i Fjohtë 220
Ukraine 174, 228
Ulbricht, Walter 163–4, 166–7, 175,
  209
United Nations 286, 327, 347
United States: declines to return war
  criminals 81; interference in
  Albanian affairs 88; plan to occupy
  Albania 1944 80
University of Belgrade, Albanian
  students at 92
University of Montpellier, Hoxha
  studies law at 2
USA 128–9, 132, 276–8, 283–4, 290,
  293–4, 297, 301, 306, 320, 332–3;
  selling grain to USSR 161; war
  involvement 33
USSR 88, 125–6, 134, 154, 301,
  319–20; Albania's break with 1961
  80, 155; alliance with until 1960 4;
  buying grain from USA 161;
  communications with blocked by
  Yugoslavia 62; equipment from 12;
  foreign aid from 12; no mission in
  Albania 55; pressures Albania for

reconciliation with Yugoslavia
154–9; seeking naval base in
Albania 220–21

Varkiza 136–7
Vatican, 14, 15, 132–4
Venizelos, Sophokles 226
Vidali, Vittorio 115
Vienna 188
Vietnam 216, 273, 285, 286, 292–5,
298; War 251
Vitsi 135
Vjosa Gorge 68
Vlora 75, 99, 147, 218, 220, 240–43
Volga River 319
Voltaire 36
Voroshilov, Kliment E 153–43, 160
Voroshilov Military Academy 233
Vukmanović Tempo, Milica 30
Vukmanović Tempo, Svetozar 6, 25,
26–31, 66–7, 72–3, 121, 155,
158–9
Vyshinsky, Andrei 116, 118–20,
121–2

Wallenstein, Battle of 173
Warsaw 226, 283
Warsaw Pact (Warsaw Treaty) 4, 200,
241–3, 246, 332
Wassilewska, Wanda 145
Weapons, supplied by British 40–41
Wheeler, T. N. S. 32; recommends
recognition of LNC 77
White Palace (Belgrade) 90, 92
With Stalin (Hoxha) 125
Women 7; at war 13; emancipation of
13–14; oppression of by religion
14–15
World War II 17, 21

'Xhepi', pseudonym of Sadik Premte
57
Xhuglini, Nexhmije See Hoxha,
Nexhmije (Mrs. Enver Hoxha)
Xoxe, Koçi 9, 22–3, 27, 29, 30, 62,
65, 71–3, 76, 101–2, 104–6,
111–13, 122, 155, 158, 208,
212–13, 327, 336

Yalta 130, 132

Yalu River 294
Yangtzee River 319
Yao Wen-yuan (Yao Wenyuan) 302
Yata, Ali 238
Ye Jianying See Yeh Chien-ying
Ye Qun See Yeh Chun
Yeh Chien-ying (Ye Jianying) 318–19
Yeh Chun (Ye Qun) 228
Yepishev, Alexei A 172
Youth Congress 87
Youth Organization 73
Yu Chang 302–3
Yugoslav–Albanian Economic
Agreements 106
Yugoslav Communist Party 119;
relations with Albanian Communists
23–4
Yugoslav National Liberation Army
120
Yugoslavia 22, 48, 54, 59, 97, 125,
128, 148, 156, 158, 159, 180,
201–8, 217, 226, 253, 254, 302–3,
315, 328, 332–4, 342–4; border
security 111; defence alliance with
Albania proposed 275; economic
aid to Albania 89; foreign aid from
12; Hoxha visits 1946 88; meddling
in Albania's affairs 25; monopoly
over Albania's communications
61–2; negotiations with Germany
1943 79; plan to turn Albania into
7th Republic of 63; pressures for
alliance with right-wing groups 61;
raids into Albania 115; troops
stationed in Albania 107; USSR
pressure for reconciliation with
Albania 154–9; violation of
aviation regulations 100; wish to
annex Albania 2, 89, 112
Yugov, Anton 185, 238

Zachariades, Nikos 131, 134–6,
138–9
Zagreb 336
Zakharov, Marshal 233
Zarechie 229, 236
Zhang Chunqiao See Chang
Chun-Chiao
Zhivkov, Todor 163, 210, 326, 328
Zhukov, Marshal Georgi K. 208–10

Zhou Enlai *See* Chou En Lai
Zionism 167
Žižka 173
Zlatić, Savo 102, 106

Zog, Ahmed 3, 21, 31, 35, 45, 60, 83,
   88; currency reserves looted by 11;
   internal policy of 40
Žujović, Sreten (Crni) 94